Jan Goodwin is Executive Editor of *Ladies' Home Journal* magazine. British-born and educated in England and Switzerland, she has a Fleet Street Newspaper background, including experience as an investigative reporter and as a foreign correspondent in Israel and Greece. She has been a radio news reporter for the BBC. As a journalist, she visited forty-three countries and has covered wars in Israel, El Salvador, Cambodia and Afghanistan. She recently received the Newswoman of the Year award for her article on Afghanistan which appeared in *Ladies' Home Journal*.

Jan Goodwin lives in New York City.

JAN GOODWIN

Caught in the Crossfire

A woman journalist's breathtaking
experiences in war-torn Afghanistan

Futura

A Futura Book

First published in the USA in 1987 by
E. P. Dutton, a Division of NAL Penguin Inc., New York

First published in Great Britain in 1987 by
Macdonald & Co (Publishers) Ltd
London & Sydney

This edition published in 1988 by
Futura Publications, a Division of
Macdonald & Co (Publishers) Ltd
London & Sydney

ISBN 0 7088 3672 0

Reproduced, printed and bound in Great Britain by
Hazell Watson & Viney Limited
Member of BPCC plc
Aylesbury Bucks

Futura Publications
A Division of
Macdonald & Co (Publishers) Ltd
Greater London House
Hampstead Road
London NW1 7QX
A member of Maxwell Pergamon Publishing Corporation plc

Dedicated to:

Wakil, Hamid, and Tor,
  who love Afghanistan
  and lost the freedom to live there;

Mirbad Khan, and so many Afghans,
  who loved life
  and lost theirs.

Grant us grace fearlessly to contend against evil,
and to make no peace with oppression. . . .

BOOK OF COMMON PRAYER
KORAN

Contents

CONTENTS

□ X □

CONTENTS

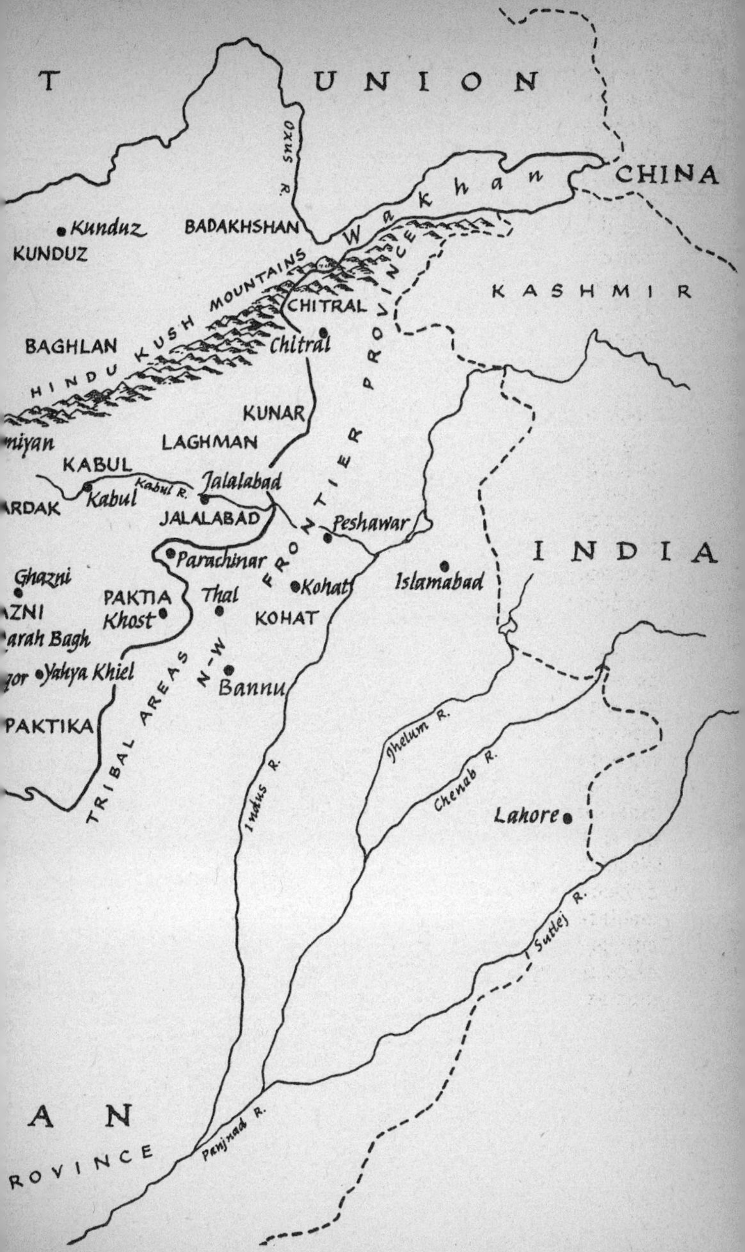
T
UNION
Oxus R.
Wakhan
CHINA
Kunduz
KUNDUZ
BADAKHSHAN
KASHMIR
HINDU KUSH MOUNTAINS
CHITRAL
Chitral
BAGHLAN
N-W FRONTIER PROVINCE
KUNAR
niyan
LAGHMAN
KABUL
Kabul R.
Jalalabad
Kabul
RDAK
JALALABAD
Peshawar
INDIA
Parachinar
Ghazni
Kohat
Islamabad
PAKTIA
Thal
ZNI
Khost
KOHAT
arah Bagh
gor
Yahya Khiel
Bannu
TRIBAL AREAS
PAKTIKA
Jhelum R.
Chenab R.
Indus R.
Lahore
Sutlej R.
AN
Panjnad R.
ROVINCE

Acknowledgments

A book of this nature could not be written without the help of a number of people for whom it would be life-threatening or career-threatening to mention by name. But although they must remain nameless, their assistance was invaluable. Numbered among them are diplomats and politicians, academics and bureaucrats in Washington, D.C.; London; Kabul; and Peshawar. They also include the Soviets in Moscow, Ashkhabad, and Tashkent who risked imprisonment by granting interviews to me, and John, a superb and sensitive interpreter, whose excellent contacts in the Soviet Union enabled me to reach them.

I also received a great deal of support and assistance from people who need not remain anonymous: Christine Sutherland, in London, who became for a while my alter ego and labored tirelessly on my behalf; Bill Spiegelberger, my Russian-language translator, who waded through five years of Soviet media coverage on the Afghan war and was never too busy to meet yet another tight deadline; political scientist and human rights specialist Barnett Rubin, who opened his files to me and who was always there when I needed advice; and David Isby, a Soviet weapons and military expert who shared his knowledge with me. Additionally, there are the many Afghanistan support, human rights, and relief organizations, both here and in Europe, who helped in my research and in locating myriad Afghan scholars and authorities, and there are also my fellow journalists who briefed me on what to expect in Afghanistan.

Beyond the professional assistance I have had the personal support system without which few writers can function: Myrna Blyth, the editor-in-chief of *Ladies' Home Journal*, who gave me the time to undertake this project; Doreen Rose, a preeminent sounding board who reined in my excesses and straightened out my convolutions; and Sherry Suib Cohen and Beth Weinhouse, who read every draft. Drora Kass, Sam McGarrity, David Nimmons, Rachel Rossow, and Ken Silverman worried about me while I reported on the war and worried with me as I wrote about it. And, of course, there were my agent, Connie Clausen, who believed in me and doesn't believe in writer's block, and my editor, Joyce Engelson, who believed wholeheartedly in the project.

Finally, there are the Afghans who trusted me enough to share their pain and to relive it for this book, and the NIFA *Mujahideen* who risked their lives to keep mine safe while we traveled through Afghanistan together.

Introduction

I first went to Afghanistan in July 1984 on a short assignment for *Ladies' Home Journal*. I returned again exactly one year later. Many people have found it hard to understand why I risked making that second, much longer trip behind Soviet lines when it was not something my job required of me, when I was a woman's magazine editor, not a combat reporter. For me, there is only one response to that question. When you have spent time, as I have, with Afghan women and men whose bodies and spirits have been destroyed by torture, when you have seen, as I have, so many young Afghan children who have lost their legs, arms, or eyes to mines disguised as toys, when you have stood rooted with fear, as I have, while wave and wave of jet bombers reduce to dust the Afghan village you have been visiting, there can be no forgetting.

Having been witness to the systematic decimation of a nation,

I knew it was a story that had to be told. With *Caught in the Crossfire*, I also wanted to show that although Afghans may live on the other side of the globe and speak a different language, there is a universality that doesn't change. Their love of life, freedom, and their country; their feelings of fear, grief, and despair are all emotions we understand. And it is the human side of war that this book is about. I feel, also, that as a woman, I was able to see a different side of guerrillas from the one that is normally shown to male journalists—with me the freedom fighters could allow themselves to be vulnerable. And I in turn came to respect and care for these men.

On my second trip I spent three months traveling with the freedom fighters through ten of Afghanistan's twenty-eight provinces. It was a tough journey physically, and an even more arduous one emotionally; there were times when I questioned my sanity in going and times when I was damned scared. But at the end, I could return home; half the population of Afghanistan can no longer do that. *Afghanistan* has been used as a newsroom euphemism for "too far away." It is my hope that this book will make such an assumption impossible.

□

A technical note: During my time in Afghanistan and also in the Soviet Union I used interpreters, when necessary. But since it is cumbersome to refer constantly to such interpretation, I have omitted mention of it in all but the opening chapters. All spellings of Afghan names are transliterations, and I have followed the styles of the sources used.

CAUGHT

IN THE

CROSSFIRE

Witness to War

I woke with an ominous feeling, a tightness in my stomach that became worse as the sun climbed. As our small party left the simple mud house village, the valley flattened out below us. The steep slopes of the snowcapped mountains lined with pines and spruces swept up on either side. I tried to lose myself in the beauty of the landscape and almost succeeded, finding it hard to believe that such a tranquil scene had been the site of so much devastation. Hamid, a twenty-year-old Afghan Resistance fighter, pulled me back to the present. "This is ideal weather for the helicopter gunships," he said unemotionally. The Soviet HIND MI-24 helicopter is one of the most lethal war machines in existence. It carries 128 rockets, four napalm or high-explosive bombs, and laser-sighted cannons that can fire one thousand rounds per minute; it is capable of annihilating a village like the one we had just left in seconds. It is these helicopters that the

West is so keen to examine that an American magazine is offering a one million dollar reward for the first one to be flown intact to the United States (they expect it to come from Nicaragua).

"The Russians don't like to fly in bad weather," explained Hamid. "If they come, they normally start around nine." I looked at my watch; it was 8:15 A.M.

We continued to walk past untended fields, hedgerows of hawthorne, and apricot and almond trees with Tor, Hamid's sidekick, pointing out the bomb damage. Bomb craters, twenty feet deep or more, pockmarked our route. Adobe houses were reduced to mounds of dust, with only the occasional domestic flotsam signaling that here a home had stood—a piece of quilt flapping in the breeze; an overturned cupboard, its doors torn off in the blast; an infant's cradle still swinging from a ceiling beam above which there was now only open sky. "Here the Kremlin is king," said Tor.

I stumbled repeatedly in the ruts of the dried mud track as my eyes constantly scanned a sky almost as deeply blue as the lapis lazuli mined in this country. This was only my second day inside Afghanistan, and already I was asking myself what I was doing here. Superstitiously, thoughts of the will I had had drawn up before leaving kept flashing into my mind. A friend in New York, whom I had asked to witness the document, had blanched when I made my request. "Aren't you planning on coming back?" she asked. "Every adult should have a will," I had replied offhandedly. Now I found myself wondering whether I had pushed my luck too far. The feeling I had woken up with wouldn't go away. Why was I so nervous? I asked myself. This wasn't the first war I had covered; I had come under fire in the Middle East and Cambodia and had reported on both sides of the war in El Salvador. But this was the first time the odds had been so disparate: I was traveling with a Resistance made up mostly of poorly armed peasants, many with guns that dated back to the turn of the century, who were pitched against a superpower armed with the most sophisticated weapons on earth, including chemical and biological agents.

At ten, the peace was still pervasive. The valley floor was now bare of ground cover. Gone were the trees and the shrubs. The terrain we were covering resembled a massive dried-up riverbed, just rocks, boulders, pebbles. Here and there were a few scrawny plants, perhaps two feet high at the most, and certainly nothing under which to conceal oneself from low-flying helicopters in a sudden air attack. I remembered mocking the journalist who told me before I left, "Make sure you take a *patou,* the woolen shawl the *Mujahideen* all wear—they're useful for hiding under so you blend in with the rocks when the helicopters come in low." "Surely you jest," I scoffed at the time. Now that suggestion didn't seem so farcical. In fact, an earth-colored *patou,* which I didn't have, would have been the best kind of camouflage in this region.

"Please be quick," Hamid pleaded, tension creeping into his voice for the first time. "We are very close to a Russian garrison." Shortly afterward, Tor dropped back to me. "Now we must walk in single line. Try to put your feet where I put my feet," he said matter-of-factly, as he led the way. "This area is heavily mined by the Soviets." Seconds later, the full meaning of what he had said sank in. Nineteen-year-old Tor was acting as a human mine-sweeper for me.

That a boy who was still young enough to bear the marks of teenage acne on his face and who had met me for the first time only twenty-four hours previously was willing to do this, stunned me. But I soon learned that in Afghanistan, where only the enemy has mine detectors, such a potentially sacrificial act is common, particularly around Soviet bases that are ringed with mines—a most effective method of announcing unexpected and unwelcome visitors. Yet Tor had seemed like any other kid his age the day before when we were first introduced. "What if she can't keep up?" he had asked as we stood in the sparsely furnished room in Pakistan, about one hundred miles from where we were now. He wasn't very pleased to see that he was expected to escort a female, particularly one who was forty, old enough to be his mother. His words fell like a gauntlet at my feet.

I could understand his reservations—I had asked myself the same thing before leaving. After all, back in New York, I'd been known to take a cab ten blocks on a rough day. And as executive editor of *Ladies' Home Journal* magazine, on a normal working day I was more likely to be fielding phone calls from Buckingham Palace on a cover story on Princess Diana, negotiating an exclusive interview with Katharine Hepburn, or guiding an investigative reporter through a libel minefield than picking my way through a real minefield laid by Soviet troops. My elegant thirty-sixth-floor office, with its panoramic view of Manhattan, was a predictable setting for what is often described as a "glamour job." And much of the time, the job was glamorous: expense account lunches, invitations to celebrity parties, first nights at the theater, private movie screenings. "But I knew there were two sides to you," a friend said, "when you turned down a dinner invitation to Le Cirque to celebrate your fortieth birthday and chose to go skydiving for the first time instead." Anyone who had known me longer, however, was aware of my news reporting days in London, where I was born. Then, in addition to war, I had covered riots, crime, terrorism, catastrophes, along with the usual news events and political happenings. As my career advanced, I had given up writing for editing and had relocated to New York, but the reporter in me was still very much alive. When the *Journal* wanted a story about Mother Teresa, instead of doing a straight interview, I thought I'd understand her better if I worked alongside her in the slums of Calcutta for a week. Similarly, my journey into Afghanistan had not been my original assignment for the magazine.

Like the average American, Afghanistan had not been foremost in my mind in 1984. Five years before, I had registered President Carter's outrage over the invasion as I read the morning newspapers, but the story was soon knocked off the front page by the escalating Iranian hostage crisis. Americans were much more emotional when the United States decided to boycott the Moscow Olympics because of the Soviet invasion of Afghanistan.

In those early months, too, my own reaction was more personal than global. From the time I had learned to read at the age of four, my favorite books had been atlases. Flopped on my stomach in front of the sitting-room fire, I would pore over them for hours planning the travels I knew I would one day take. Always my attention came back to the region where the Himalayas, the Karakorams, and the Hindu Kush Mountains met, a region the Afghans call *Bam-i-Dunya*, the Roof of the World. Raised on Kipling and tales of intrepid female explorers of the Victorian era, I knew Afghanistan was a country I would visit. At eighteen, when a group of friends decided to take time off between high school and college, they invited me to join them on one of those overland treks to India through Iran and Afghanistan that so many kids made in the sixties. I longed to go but in those days didn't quite have the courage, a decision I regretted the moment my friends' minibus left. Seventeen years later, when I read Carter's denunciation of Moscow's action, I remembered saying, "Now I guess I'll never see Afghanistan."

In 1979, I was more concerned with what was going on in Cambodia—reports that Pol Pot's genocidal policies had decimated his country's population by 30 percent had just reached the Western media. In early 1980, I had been asked to join the National Cambodia Crisis Committee, which was run by Rosalynn Carter from the White House. It was in helping to raise $70 million to stave off a famine in Cambodia that I would eventually find myself in Afghanistan. Actress Liv Ullmann, another committee member, had introduced me to a young Austrian schoolteacher, who had impressed her greatly as an example of how one person can make a difference. He was Peter Rainer, who had organized the entire school system for the Cambodians in Thai refugee camps. Peter and I had fund-raised together at the time and had then lost touch when he returned to Switzerland, where he taught. Then in March 1984, on a dismally gray afternoon when I was frantically editing late-arriving copy, I looked up and found Peter standing in my office grinning at me. He was in New York to meet with Bob De Vecchi, the executive director of the International Rescue Committee, an international relief agency, before going to Pakistan for them to research setting up a similar school system for the Afghan refugees. "They are the largest group of refugees in the world," he told me. "Fifty percent of the world's refugees are Afghan." "Are you sure?" I asked him as my deadline copy languished on my desk. He nodded. "That's one hell of a story," I responded. "Why on earth aren't we reading about it?" He shrugged. "Perhaps because Americans don't feel guilty about Afghanistan the way they do about the Cambodian part of the world," he theorized. My mind began to race, the reporter in me coming alive again. For some time, too, the old RAF saying "You can only fly a desk for so long" had been flashing across my mind like an internal neon light. "Peter, if my editor-in-chief and IRC agree, how would you like to give me a tour of your refugee camps?" I asked. Peter grinned. Three months later, I flew to Pakistan to do a story for the *Journal* on what life was like for Afghan women refugees.

Two weeks in those camps, however, convinced me my article

would be incomplete if I limited my research to Pakistan. In the dozens of interviews I conducted, I would hear recounted over and over again stories of the atrocities from which these people had fled, atrocities that recalled Pol Pot's Cambodia. The Afghan refugees told of entire villages wiped out in massacres, children set afire in front of parents who wouldn't or couldn't divulge information about the guerrillas, pregnant women eviscerated. And as a journalist who had covered several wars, I had never seen so many child amputees as I saw among the Afghans. The children had been maimed and frequently blinded because they had picked up the small antipersonnel mines, many disguised as brightly colored toys, that had been scattered by the thousands over their country. My own observations and the refugee reports were sickening, but the latter were too consistent to be discounted. Yet if these accounts were true, why had there been so little coverage of this war in the West, I would ask myself again. It was then that I had decided that I wanted to see for myself what was happening behind the curtain of silence the Soviets had managed to draw around Afghanistan.

It was Hamid's uncle, Wakil Akberzai, who enabled me to do that. Wakil, a large, gentle man who brings to mind a benign Henry VIII with a touch of amiable lion, is an official with the National Islamic Front of Afghanistan (NIFA), one of the seven major freedom fighter parties based in Peshawar, Pakistan, close to the Afghan border. Before leaving the United States, I had contacted the Committee for a Free Afghanistan in Washington, D.C., who had given me letters of introduction to two Resistance groups, NIFA being one of them. After a brief interview three days before, Wakil had agreed to arrange a short trip inside for me. "It won't be easy. Any trip to Afghanistan is tough, physically and mentally," he warned, as he handed me a shopping list that included a *kameez partouk*, baggy Afghan pajamas suit, and a *lungi*, turban. Looking at me, a five-foot, four-inch redhead with very fair skin, he conceded that even wearing these native clothes I probably wouldn't much resemble the bearded guerrillas, but at least, at quick glance, I would blend in with the crowd and not be immediately recognized as a woman. In this Muslim society, women rarely travel with men other than their husbands or immediate family, and any female journeying with freedom fighters would immediately telegraph something extraordinary such as the presence of a foreigner. And in a war zone, chameleons survive longer.

The Sunday after our first meeting, Wakil telephoned me at my hotel. "Be ready at seven o'clock tonight," he said tersely and hung up without another word. Telephones are monitored in Peshawar, and I'd already been warned to be circumspect when using them.

Like all time-conscious Americans, I was ready exactly at seven, but Wakil didn't appear. I packed and repacked my gear: sleeping bag, water bottle, one change of clothes, notebooks, the waterproof bag of film, camera, first-aid kit complete with painkillers and enough blister supplies to salve an army, dehydrated camping food—I had been warned there was a food shortage in many parts of Afghanistan—and a compass I'd sheepishly packed just in case I needed to find my own way back. I tried on my backpack and took it off again: was it too heavy, was it sitting properly on my back, could I really carry thirty pounds up mountains and for the sixteen hours a day I'd been warned these men travel? And my boots: were they too loose at the heels, the best way to lacerate one's feet, or was it just my imagination? The next two hours lasted a week. Just as I was wondering whether the group had changed their minds about taking me, a discreet knock at my hotel door shortly after nine set my nerves tingling.

"Come quickly." Wakil gestured me into a darkened jeep. The jeep's lights stayed off until we had left the hotel's grounds. When you're dealing in guerrilla warfare, even a hotel waiter or room boy is a potential informer. Ten minutes later we arrived at a two-story house on the outskirts of town. I was shown into a large room with many carpets on the floor but with other furnishings limited to cotton mattresses that lined the four walls, a *charpoy* —the wood and woven rush cots so common in that part of the world—and a television.

Wakil explained that there would be a permanent group of five men assigned to me throughout the trip. "These men are your bodyguards. Your life depends on them. Do exactly what they tell you, when they tell you." I wasn't about to argue, but had I been so inclined, Wakil's manner would have stopped me. Only twenty-nine, he looked ten years older and exuded the authority of a man twice his age, certainly one whose decisions were always respected and acted on. Educated in India, where he had earned an

M.B.A., Wakil spoke fluent English with British overtones, and his conversation was peppered with "jolly good" and "jolly chap."

Two of the five men were Wakil's nephews, Hamid and Fareed, age twenty-one. Tor, who was soon to act as a human minesweeper for me, had joined the Resistance shortly after Hamid, and they had been as close as brothers ever since. Wakil certainly treated them that way, and Tor responded to him as he would to his own father. Serious, bearded young men they had all become *Mujahideen*, warriors in a holy war, while still in school. The other two members of our party would join us in the morning. Once inside Afghanistan, we would pick up additional men, those who knew the various regions we were passing through, the positions of enemy troops, and the areas that had been mined. Without modern communication such as radios or phone sets, Afghan freedom fighters rely on this kind of local intelligence more than is necessary in most wars today.

"Change into your Afghan clothes, and then get some rest." Wakil pointed to his *charpoy*.

"We leave at 3:00 A.M., and you won't have time to do more than put on your boots."

I lay in the darkened room listening to each man's breathing become deeper and sonorous. Too tense to sleep, I finally had only the biting mosquitoes for company. The *charpoy* felt as hard as the rocks I knew I'd be sleeping on the following night.

I finally dozed off but was groggy and grumpy when shaken awake in what seemed like the deep of the night.

Wakil was right; I didn't have time even to brush my teeth before we were piling into a curtained van parked outside the door. The rest of our party were already seated inside the vehicle: diminutive, gray-haired commander Salaiman Zai, who would head up this trip, and a slim, quiet young man, Jan Akbar, made shyer by a pronounced and uncorrected harelip.

The trip to the border was to be a circuitous nine-hour drive through the North-West Frontier Province—a region made fabled by Rudyard Kipling, who used it as a setting for many of his short stories. The Tribal Area between Peshawar and Afghanistan has been off-limits to foreigners since the time of the British Raj, when this territory was a part of it. In those days, it was to safeguard His Majesty's subjects from the sanguinary and plundering Pathans who roamed both sides of the border. Today it is meant to protect foreigners from wandering into the drug dealer clashes that occur so often in this part of the Golden Crescent, where opium or hashish is frequently the crop of choice, and where heroin-producing factories are frequently the only guarantee of regular work.

To make sure the Tribal Area remains off-limits, the Pakistani government has a series of checkposts along all roads to the border, some more enthusiastically operated than others, hence the circuitousness of our trip. Journalists caught going through the checkpoints risk arrest, but it's the only way into Afghanistan unless one wants to add another day or two of overland trekking to an already strenuous journey.

Before we passed through each checkpost, I was told to drape the loose end of my turban across my face and feign sleep. My arms folded across my chest obscured the fact that this particular freedom fighter had breasts. As we traveled, Hamid, Tor, and Fareed began to reminisce about their schooldays. Hamid, whose English was as fluent as his uncle's except that it had a Victorian formality as if he had learned it from Jane Austen novels, translated for the other two. A tall, aristocratic young man, he had patrician features, an aquiline nose, high cheekbones, and a generous, well-shaped mouth, which gave him an undeserved air of hauteur. His long, expressive fingers suggested the hands of an artist, not a soldier. In talking with him, it soon became apparent that Hamid was both disciplined and devout. An enthusiastic scholar, he had wanted to go to law school but knew his chances were slim now.

Tor spoke six languages; although English wasn't one of them, he was such an accomplished mimic that didn't prevent him from communicating when Hamid wasn't around. Six inches shorter than Hamid, he had the sinewy, rock-hard build of the high school boxing champ he'd been. A gifted student who had planned on being a doctor, Tor had been graduated from high school three years ahead of schedule. Since joining the Resistance, he had taken a one-year medical course with the Union of Afghan Mujahideen Doctors in Peshawar and had been functioning as a medic behind enemy lines for two years. Fareed's most noticeable feature was his long curly hair worn in a large Afro-type style of which he was inordinately proud. Like all the freedom fighters, Fareed traveled light, carrying nothing more than his gun and the clothes on his back. But his breast pocket contained a small hand mirror and comb, which he used frequently. In Kabul, Afghanistan's capital, he'd been a science major and also a basketball coach.

All three boys had been graduated from high school without receiving their diplomas; after the invasion, Soviet-run schools in the capital refused to issue them to students unless they were members of the Communist party. "That's when I became a *Mujahid*," Tor explained. "I knew they wouldn't let me go to college unless I joined the party, and the only other choice was conscription into the army, and I wasn't going to fight my own people."

Jan Akbar was less forthcoming. But gradually he began to talk about himself. Now age twenty, he had been a gardener before the war. In 1981, four of his five brothers had been killed in a bombing attack. His father had died of a massive heart attack later that same day when he received the news. "I joined the *Jihad* [holy war] a week after I buried them all," Jan told me.

As we talked, all four men were methodically loading the magazines of their captured AK-47s, Soviet Kalashnikov machine guns, and fitting them into the pockets of the ammunition belts they wore around their chests, three magazines and four hand grenades per belt.

Suddenly we arrived in Teri Mangal, a small border town of brightly painted one- and two-story buildings and camel train camps for the thriving lumber industry in the area. We parked at the border end of the town. Stretching stiffly at the end of the drive, I found myself staring up at a wall of a mountain we had to climb. The granite face rose above us, the top obscured by cloud. Zigzagging steeply up it was the narrow goatlike track that we would follow, which clung so precipitously to the mountain face that there was often only eighteen inches of trail between us and sheer drops of hundreds of feet or more.

The moment the vehicle stopped, the guerrillas took off at what seemed like a sprint. Once again, the concern was local informers. The faster one left Teri Mangal, the less chance of a tip-off. Determined to keep up, I followed. Several hundred yards up the steep scree-covered incline, I was gasping. Pausing briefly to allow me to catch my breath and for Tor to relieve me of my pack, they would maintain the same pace for the next six hours. As we walked, a thick talcum powder–like dust sometimes as deep as several inches swirled up around us, making it difficult to walk, see, and inhale. Halfway, a fierce rainstorm something akin to a cloudburst turned the surface into a quagmire. Now as I battled my way up, I feared losing my grip in the thick mud and plunging over one of the many precipices. Despite expensive Italian hiking boots, I was having trouble maintaining my traction, but the freedom fighters didn't have the same problem, although they only wore *chaplis*, the traditional Afghan sandals. Hamid was wearing cheap Pakistani-made sneakers without socks.

We continued to climb, and the gradient didn't once level out. By now I was red-faced and wheezing, cursing those three ninety-minute sessions a week spent at a very strenuous gym for the last three months. Despite the hyperbole of health club advertising copy, I was convinced I couldn't have felt worse if I'd been a sloth all year.

Near the summit, the sheet rain reduced visibility to a few feet. The *Mujahideen* took shelter under a dwarf oak. They laughed uproariously as I slipped and slithered to where they sat, finally falling flat on my face at their feet.

"She's not a good goat," chuckled Fareed, as he gave me a helping hand. "No, and nor is she a good donkey," added Tor, gesturing to the backpack he'd gallantly carried for me. I was too exhausted even to smile. We sat there drenched. The mountain rain, combined with the altitude, had made the temperature plummet. We had left Peshawar on a steamy July day, when 120 degrees Fahrenheit is the norm, and now, despite the exertion, I was shivering. I thought of the women refugees I had met in the Pakistani camps who had traveled for days over topography like this, many with small infants in their arms. And I remembered twenty-three-year-old Kabalee, who was blind, who told me her biggest fear was not the landmines or the Soviet MIGs but crossing the the mountain passes carrying her five-month-old son. "Every time I lost my footing, I was afraid of dropping my baby over the edge," she said.

I admired the fortitude and sheer guts of women like Kabalee, but it didn't make me feel less miserable in my discomfort.

I was concerned, too, although I didn't want to admit it, that if our journey were to remain this arduous, I would have trouble keeping up with the men.

□

"Let's move." The commander's voice, gravelly from his heavy smoking, cut into my self-pitying reverie. "And no talking. There are lookout posts at the top, and voices carry up here." We trudged through the thickening gloom, with the silence disturbed only once as Tor fell heavily on the loose rocks. Was he hurt? He laughed as he scrambled to his feet. "I am brave *Mujahid*," he said. I saw him flinch as he put his weight on his ankle, but he continued, uncomplainingly, at the same pace as before.

Seventeen hours after leaving Peshawar, and eight hours after we began hiking, we stopped in a small village, Sargal, in Paktia, an alpine border province. We would spend the night in a two-story adobe house, one of a handful that hadn't been hit in the bombing. Many of the villagers had already left; they could no longer live with the constant fear. Our host, Raheem Jan, proudly showed us the dugout bomb shelter he had built for his family under his apricot trees, as his twelve-year-old son shinnied up one to gather the fruit his father wanted to offer us. On the way back to the house, he pointed out the camel sitting in the basement, as if it were a Porsche parked in the garage. As we sat cross-legged on the carpeted floor of the whitewashed room, with its two-foot-thick walls, drinking the proffered green tea and *nan*, the flat, unleavened Afghan bread, Raheem Jan told us that the bombing had been very heavy that day five kilometers farther down the valley, and that he'd seen more refugees leaving.

A little while later, dinner was served by Raheem's son Abdul. His wife and her sisters who prepared it stayed in the women's quarters out of sight of these male visitors. I suddenly realized I hadn't seen a woman's face all day: the few we'd passed had been wearing *chadoris*, the full-length veils with eye grills that make women resemble small, mobile tents. Normally, as a woman, I, too, would not have been permitted to sit and eat with the men, but since I was dressed as the *Mujahideen* and was traveling with them, the village elders who had joined us for dinner seemed prepared to overlook that fact. But they didn't forget I am female, either. Calloused hands selected for me the tastiest pieces of chicken, killed especially in our honor, from the communal dish of meat and rice.

And having accepted me into their circle, they also assumed I would sleep in the same room as the men. Once again, I was given the sole *charpoy*. But that was as far as catering to my gender went. They watched in fascination as I prepared for bed. When I removed my turban, revealing my red hair, I received the kind of attention that a skilled striptease artist would get elsewhere. And I realized I was the floor show when I started to take out my contact lenses. One elderly man moved out of his darkened corner to get a better view. *"Feranghi,"* he nodded, as if that explained everything he'd just seen. And maybe it did; *feranghi*, "foreigner," is often used synonymously here for "bizarre." But turban, boots, and lenses were as far as the undressing went; guerrillas sleep fully clothed and so would I.

That night I had no trouble sleeping; the forced march was a guarantee of that. And as I drifted into sleep, I was aware of a sense of well-being, which is odd in a war zone, but I put it down to endorphin-produced euphoria from the exercise. The feeling had fled by morning and was replaced by the foreboding I couldn't explain.

When we left, our host sent three local men to accompany us. All villagers, they were farmers during the day and freedom fighters at night. They would travel with us as guides and extra guns until we left their region.

Three hours after Hamid's first warning about helicopter gunships, we heard sporadic firing from the far end of the valley. "Gunships," said the commander, but we couldn't see them and the sound didn't get any closer. We paused for a noontime break at a site where fifteen or so burned-out Soviet tanks paid silent tribute to the skills of these poorly armed guerrillas. This effectiveness has forced the Soviets more and more to take to the air, and attacks such as these have caused them to pound the local villages with carpet bombing so ferocious it seems as if they are trying to level the mountains of this nation.

Lunch consisted of water from the bag I was carrying and a shared handful of American gorp, the high-energy mixture of dried fruits and nuts favored by hikers. Afghan freedom fighters rarely carry food or water. Before we moved on, I stepped behind the shell of the tank we'd been resting against in a quest for privacy to relieve myself, something that wasn't easy to find in the terrain through which we'd been traveling. In doing so, I almost stumbled over the bodies of two badly burned and very recently dead Russian soldiers. A swarm of buzzing flies crawled over them. Too shocked to move, I stood staring at the dead men. As I did, I wondered whether their families had yet been informed that they weren't coming home. And I couldn't help thinking that the average Soviet conscript was very much like the average American GI in Vietnam—fighting a war he didn't understand, in a country he knew little about.

Someone had started digging the two soldiers a grave but hadn't progressed very far when he had obviously been forced to leave. Now scavenging animals in the area would dispose of the remains. Tor looked at the bodies and addressed me in Dari. Hamid translated his remarks for me, "These men are *kafir*, unbelievers. They don't need a proper burial if they don't believe in God. It is just that the animals eat them."

We continued our tour of the battle-scarred valley, heading east toward the Pakistani border, and away from the bombing. As we walked past a harvest-ready corn field, I was startled when a yelling and grinning man leaped in front of us. "He's lonely," one of the *Mujahideen* explained. "He wants us to have tea with him over there at his post." "Over there" was a solitary Dashaka, a captured Soviet antiaircraft gun set up in the middle of the field. The only such weapon for miles around, his post was a suicide mission. Unless he was lucky to find a lone MIG or helicopter gunship, the Soviet pilots would locate him as soon as he opened fire and blow him out of the field. And anyway, his 12.7 mm Dashaka, without armor-piercing shells, was useless against either aircraft unless it came in very low and he had a very lucky strike. The Soviet HIND-24 gunships are so well armored that they are only vulnerable at the tail or when shot at from above. But none of this, which the man who introduced himself as Rahim must have known, affected his playful mood as he danced around us, trying to convince us to accept his hospitality. As I was the *Mujahideen*'s guest, the decision was left to me; although I would have loved something warm to drink, I declined. An open-air tea party soon lost its charm when Soviet gunships were tearing up the countryside only a few kilometers away. And Rahim didn't look the type who would be content to play possum if a jet or a helicopter flew over us just because he was entertaining a foreigner in his gun trench. I would soon learn that many Afghans feel the way Rahim does: no matter how outranked they may be by superior firepower—and they invariably are—they often let loose a volley of bullets at an enemy too high or too far away to even register it. Sometimes this reminded me of a nervous bird trying to draw a carnivore away from its young; other times it was pure bravado.

But bravado, or just plain foolhardiness, was something I would witness more than once inside Afghanistan. Minutes later, Tor was to demonstrate to me that while he had been fighting in this war since he was fifteen and the experience had prematurely matured him in many ways, he could still be an injudicious boy. We were now on a narrow, flinty footpath that was winding upward toward the forested mountain slopes. Picking our way over the rubbled remains of a destroyed stone house, we found two unexploded five-hundred-pound bombs sitting outside what had once been the front door of the building. With the Soviet markings looking as fresh as the day they'd left the factory, I pondered why the five-foot-long monsters hadn't exploded, and how long they'd been there: But for Tor, the five-hundred-pounders were nothing more than a chance for target practice. I turned around from studying the markings to find Tor leveling his Kalashnikov at the nose of one of the bombs.

"Tor! Don't!" I shouted in the English I knew he didn't speak at the same time I started running backward away from him. He grinned. "It's hokey, no afraid, I your bodyguard," he replied in the pidgin he was quick to pick up.

Still aiming at the nose, he flipped the safety switch on his machine gun to automatic fire. "Are you insane? You're going to kill us all," I screamed at him as I kept running and wondering how much space I needed to put between the bomb and me, and how big a crater the damned thing would make if it went up. I was aware that the others were also backing away from Tor, although I was the only one yelling at him. Whether it was the rising hysteria in my voice or the sudden realization that what he was doing might not be such a good idea, Tor suddenly tired of his game. With his Kalashnikov swinging from his hand, he jogged over to me. Patting me on the back, he repeated, "It's hokey, no afraid, I your bodyguard." I glowered at him before exploding in a good imitation of any bomb, "Bodyguards can't do their jobs unless there are bodies left intact to guard." Grabbing Hamid by the arm, I insisted he translate while I told Tor what a stupid thing he'd done. He did, and Tor continued to smile.

"If it didn't explode when it was dropped from a jet, why should it explode now?"

"Because they often do explode later," I countered, "particularly when a magazine of a machine gun is emptied into one."

"Not this kind," said Tor; "look, I'll show you." He pointed his gun again and then ducked as I threw a pebble at his head when I realized that this time he was joking.

As we continued our journey, I realized that much of that valley floor was dotted with unexploded five-hundred-pounders, which didn't say a lot for quality control in the Soviet Union's munition factories but did bear mute witness to the volume of bombing that had taken place here. I had also been told before leaving that Afghan pilots frequently dropped their bombs with the safety catches on. This ruse is a major reason—along with frequent air defections—that the Soviets now consider the small Afghan air force a traitorous hindrance rather than a help to their own pilots.

□

Shortly after this experience, we arrived at a small hamlet of about ten houses. It was hard to be more precise, as only one was left intact, and even that, a three-story building, had had one side sheared off in a blast. Entering the village, we passed wing segments of a MIG 21 decorating the top of a woodpile; they had obviously been carried back as trophies from where the plane had hit the ground. As I went to examine them, the commander cautioned me to be careful about what I touched or picked up as we traveled. "The Russians have boobytrapped all sorts of things, even pieces of wood like the kind you just stepped on." I froze. "Oh" was all I could muster, glancing down.

We were invited inside the three-story house for our first meal of the day: *nan*, already hardened since its early morning baking, which was made more palatable by a delicious homemade butter, a rare treat that our party promptly dispatched, and soothing green tea. The room in which we sat had a brightly painted and ornately carved ceiling and walls that were further decorated with travel posters of Switzerland. There were two armchairs and a sofa onto which I gratefully flopped, only to have every spring in it hit me in the rear with such force I wished I'd sat on the floor with the rest of our party. To the side of me were what I took to be two carved wooden window shutters. Pulling them open to see the view, I found myself staring into a closet full of hand grenades. Nobody but me registered surprise. Our host, Ghafoor, didn't mind my curiosity and went on to tell me that there was an unexploded five-hundred-pound bomb in the basement of his home, in which he and his family were still living. It had landed there during the bombing attack that had wiped out most of his community a few days before.

Had he thought of moving out? "No, if God wills it to explode, it will, and if he doesn't, it will be safe to live here."

There it was, that simple acceptance of fate that is such a part of Islam. This was the first time I would see it in action, but it would not be the last. But although Muslims accept God's will unquestioningly, the Afghans did not see the Soviet invasion of their country as part of Allah's divine plan. The Koran instructs them to wage war against "infidels" who threaten their religion, and it is this tenet that is the basis for *Jihad*.

It was 3:00 P.M. by the time we moved on. We continued up the mountain track, and soon the valley disappeared from view as we were enveloped by forest. The climb became steeper, but my lungs were not complaining as much as they had the day before. The exercise felt good. A few more days of this pace and terrain and I would achieve a level of conditioning I hadn't had since high school. Lost in reveries of my youth, I was brought up with a start by a foul odor. The pungent, acrid smell hit my nostrils as we rounded a rocky incline and found ourselves entering a vast blackened and charred clearing. The giant pines had been reduced to charcoal stubs that crumbled at our feet as we walked past them. As if on one command, our entire party fell silent. The smell, the deadness, the strange stillness were eerie, macabre. I tried to push down the rising feeling of anxiety and longed for the sunlight of the valley.

The clearing stretched for thousands of yards. What had caused such extensive destruction? Napalm was my first thought, but where was the accompanying gasoline smell? White phosphorus? Possibly. The odor was strange, slightly sulfuric, but perhaps that had more to do with the destroyed vegetation. My biggest concern was that this devastation had been wrought by one of the chemical agents I knew the Soviets had been using in Afghanistan, one that had a half-life we didn't know about. In my research before leaving, I had come across accounts of something referred to as "liquid fire," a tarlike substance that is dropped from planes and lies on the ground in globules or coats vegetation until something touches it, when it bursts into flames. Some reports on liquid fire suggested that it may have an active half-life. We picked our way warily through the devastated area. Fear of the unknown made me check the soles of my boots several times to see whether they had been affected. They hadn't.

None of the *Mujahideen* knew any more about what had happened than I did. For them it was just another "fire bomb" that had been used to destroy their forests, something the Soviets were increasingly doing, in the same way the United States defoliated Vietnam's jungle so the enemy couldn't hide in it.

For me, this place was the stuff of nightmares. I couldn't wait to leave the clearing, and the thirty minutes we took to cross it stayed with me for days.

It was getting dark as we came out onto a cliff top, which didn't help to banish my mood. We passed home-going woodcutters who told us the fire bombs had been dropped two weeks before, and the mountain had burned for several days.

Shortly after, we came across a tethered camel, then another. They were tied up to trees flanking a skillfully camouflaged pickup truck, whose bright orange color could scarcely be detected under the leaf-covered branches adorning it. Behind it were several tents with the lettering in English: DONATED BY SAUDI ARABIA. We had arrived at our lodging for the night. The owner of the largest tent, Niab Khan, a short, fierce-looking but friendly man, came out to greet us. Like all Afghans, he loved company. We were ushered inside and shown to large cushions arranged on the Kilim carpeted floor. Almost immediately, two small boys came in carrying large silver teakettles containing black and green tea. We were obviously expected, and Niab confirmed that his children had watched our progress up the mountain. Tea served, the boys began to energetically massage the legs of the freedom fighters closest to them. As a woman, this was one luxury I would not be offered. A pity, my muscles probably ached a lot more than the men's. Every *Mujahideen* on the trip with me seemed to have a body made of steel. And as if reading my thoughts, Fareed, with no hint of the strenuous day, began to do push-ups, the one-finger, one-leg variety. Tor joined him briefly, then stopped to examine the ankle he had twisted in yesterday's climb. His foot was badly swollen, and his Afghan sandals gave no support in the kind of hiking we'd been doing all day. He must have been in pain, but he wasn't about to admit it. Nor had he lagged behind once during the day, and he'd insisted on carrying my pack throughout. I offered him an elastic bandage from my first-aid kit, and he expertly applied it.

By now, the twenty by ten foot tent had filled up with men who were camped nearby. The women of this settlement were housed in smaller tents farther down the slope, where they could continue to live in *purdah*, behind the curtain, even as refugees. Here, they cooked the meals that the small boys carried up to us. As we sipped our tea, Niab told us why his people had left their homes.

"Most of us are from Bargawai at the far end of the valley. Twenty days ago, our villages were attacked. People were bombed out of their homes . . . two or three were lost in every house. About a quarter of the people in my village were killed.

"The planes bombed us for two days. When it was over more than six hundred people were forced to leave, like us, because their homes had been totally destroyed.

"We came here to hide in the forest. And the *Mujahideen* gave us our tents. We will stay here until the snow comes; then we will go to Pakistan. We have no choice. We love our country, but the Russians don't want us to live in it."

As Niab talked, I became aware that an elderly man dressed all in white had begun to weep. With his white hair, deeply lined face, sunken eyes, and grief he looked about eighty years old. I learned later that Nawab was in his late fifties. He began to mutter; then his quiet tears turned to heavy sobbing.

"Yesterday all his family members were martyred in the bombing near here," explained Hamid. "His wife, brothers, sisters, his children, and his grandchildren were killed. He keeps asking why he, an old man, survived, when everyone else in his family died.

"He has lost everything; everything he owned has been destroyed. He has nothing left. It is very sad. But this has happened to so many families in Afghanistan."

Hamid lapsed into brooding silence broken only by the heaving sobs of Nawab, who would continue to cry on and off throughout the night and ask his same tragic question over and over again until he finally fell asleep from exhaustion just before dawn.

□

It was Christmas Day 1979 when the Soviets invaded Afghanistan, a land whose name is often translated as "Land of the Free." As much of the world celebrated a day of peace on earth, the Soviets rolled their tanks over the Texas-sized country just as they had over another neighbor, Czechoslovakia, eleven years before. And the same Soviet general who planned and commanded the Czech invasion, Ivan Pavlovsky, was deployed to mastermind the takeover of Afghanistan. But unlike Czechoslovakia, the Russians didn't control the country in days; nor did world headlines scream their outrage. At the beginning, few people knew. Even fewer seemed to care.

What began that December day has been dubbed a "War Without Law," a war of systematic genocide. Of the preinvasion population of 15 million people, only half that number now remain. Five million Afghans have been forced to flee as refugees; this is the equivalent of 76 million Americans being confined to camps in Mexico or Canada. Of the refugees, 3.5 million are sheltered by Pakistan; they are the largest single group of refugees in the world, equaling the population of Israel or New Zealand; a further 1.5 million are in Iran. Afghanistan also has an estimated 2 million more internal refugees: it is not uncommon to find families who have been bombed out of as many as six homes. Many of these internal refugees have made their way to the capital, doubling Kabul's population.

The death toll in Afghanistan increased substantially in 1985, when the Soviets escalated the war dramatically at the very time when negotiated settlement talks were being conducted in Geneva. Although exact figures are impossible to determine, it is estimated that since 1979, between 1 and 2 million Afghans have died in blanket bombings and mass executions, of war-induced disease or malnutrition, or in chemical weapon attacks—the cheapest form of mass destruction known to man. Tens of thousands have simply disappeared in prisons that are little more than houses of torture. "It is as if Afghanistan is a laboratory for the Soviet military to learn their trade," says former Afghan Supreme Court judge Omar Babrakzai, who is now a commander in the Resistance. "Every single weapon in the Soviets' arsenal, with the exception of the nuclear bomb, has been unleashed on us." And indeed it has, but why? Why has the Soviet Union mired itself in Afghanistan, a war it has now been fighting considerably longer than it fought against Germany in World War II?

The Kremlin, of course, rarely explains itself. Reasons put forth by Western analysts vary, depending on the favorite theory or theories of the pundit espousing them. They include simple Soviet expansionism: the USSR waited until the United States was distracted in Iran with the hostage crisis before it flexed its colonializing muscles and began again its inexorable bid to rule the world. Other experts say Russia was alarmed at the Islamic resurgence: the invasion was Moscow's attempt to fend off what might happen in the Muslim Soviet Central Asian states if the unrest in neighboring Afghanistan were to spill over the border. "The Soviet Union was concerned that the rise of Islamic revolutionary movements on the Afghan side of the border would present an internal security problem on their side of the border," says Professor Barnett Rubin, a political scientist at Yale University. This Soviet fear is exacerbated by the fact that the rapidly growing Soviet Muslim population, which is now estimated to total 60 million, making it the fifth largest Muslim population in the world, is expected to be in the majority in Russia in the next twenty to thirty years.

Afghanistan historians prefer to see the invasion as another attempt by Russia to acquire a warm-water port—something the czarist empire had wanted for two hundred years. The Soviet Union, which suffers from some of the worst weather in the world —indeed, half of the country is permanently underlain by permafrost—has all of its ocean ports iced over in the winter. With the borders of the Soviet Union extended to southern Afghanistan, all that would separate Russia from the warm-water bay of Gwadar, which is deep enough to handle modern aircraft carriers or all but the largest oil tankers, is the unstable region of Baluchistan. And the Baluchistan province often gives the impression it would like to secede from Pakistan, emulating Bangladesh. Indeed, the Baluch separatist movements have received considerable support from Moscow, and several have their headquarters in Communist-held Kabul. Even without acquiring a warm-water port, Soviet bases already built in southern Afghanistan put Russia 350 miles —an easy air strike reach—from the Straits of Hormuz. And it is through the Straits, a narrow channel between Iran and Oman that could be easily closed, that much of the free world's oil passes. Says Milan Hauner of the Foreign Policy Research Institute in Philadelphia, "A Sovietized Afghanistan could be, and very likely would be, transformed from a historical buffer zone to a stepping stone for destabilization and continued Soviet expansion in a region vital to Western security interests."

Another cause of the invasion, say mining and geology experts, is Afghanistan's natural resources, as yet mostly untapped. With a topography frequently described as consisting of rocks, dust, and desert, Afghanistan more than compensates for what it lacks by the richness of what is under the surface: emeralds, rubies, diamonds, gold, silver, lapis lazuli, copper—which the Soviets believe to be the largest deposit in the world—and iron ore, estimated by French geologists who conducted exploratory tests to be the third largest deposit in the world. Afghanistan is also fuel-rich: natural gas, the nation's major export item; oil; uranium; and coal. Afghanistan's geological makeup is the same as that in which the oil and gas bonanza of the Middle East accumulated, points out John Shroder, professor of geology at the University of Nebraska, who was also a Fulbright lecturer at Kabul University before the Soviet invasion. "Basic imperialism is always motivated by a desire for resources of one kind or another," says Shroder, "and the Soviet invasion seems a clear case of the classic phenomenon. The concept of 'resources wars' has begun to emerge as a major topic of interest in Washington and elsewhere." And Ajab Khan Taniwal, who was the Afghan Ministry of Mining's director for exploration and drilling until 1980, told me, "From Soviet studies I saw, Afghanistan's oil resources are estimated to be equal to Iraq's, which rank fifth in the world in oil deposits. And bear in mind also that every cubic meter of natural gas that Afghanistan produces is already piped into the Soviet Union, and the meters gauging how much is extracted are all on the Russian side of the border."

The last of the "big five" reasons for the Soviet Union entering Afghanistan is that Moscow wanted to prevent the slipping away of a client state, with whom it shares a thirteen-hundred-mile-long border. Always cognizant of having the world's largest country on its northern rim, Afghanistan was the first nation to recognize the newly formed Soviet Union. Three years later, in 1920, the Bolsheviks signed their first friendship treaty with Afghanistan. And relations between the two countries continued to stay cordial, but not close. Afghanistan was the only country bordering the Soviet Union that did not have a Communist movement; it finally acquired one, the People's Democratic Party of Afghanistan (PDPA), in 1965, although in its early years, it was an underground movement. All other neighboring countries had Communist parties that either predated the October Revolution or were founded within six years of it.

After World War II, Afghanistan, like other Central Asian countries, looked to the West for development aid. The United States began a modest Afghan aid program, but the Eisenhower administration refused military assistance because it was not impressed with Afghanistan's strategic importance. Embroiled in a border dispute with Pakistan at the time, the Afghan government then turned to the Soviet Union for military aid. Khrushchev was happy to comply. It was then that Afghan military officers began to train in the Soviet Union. Other aid quickly followed, but it wasn't always beneficial. Says Abdul Wardak, who until the invasion was president of administration in the Ministry of Interior: "There were no spare parts for the military equipment Afghanistan received from the Soviet Union, so the country had to buy new trucks and aircraft, incurring further debts to the Soviets and straining the Afghan economy. The irrigation project built near the Khyber Pass cost three times what it should have and was also a burden on the Afghan economy. Oranges, lemons, and olive oil were produced—and exported to the Soviet Union. Afghanistan was forced to import its oranges from Pakistan. For another irrigation program, the Soviets diverted the course of the Amu

Darya River [known as the Nile of Central Asia], which divides the two countries. And in doing so, they claimed thousands of Afghan acres as Soviet soil. The Soviet-built Shindand Air Base near the Iranian border and close to the Middle East oil fields was built with a far greater capacity than Afghanistan could ever use."

"Never trust a Russian with a rope; he'll throw you one end of it, and use the other end to tie you up," goes one Afghan saying. Perhaps Prime Minister Mohammad Daoud had it in mind when he started to dissociate himself from the Soviets and look elsewhere for economic assistance. That decision cost him his life. In a 1978 coup, Daoud and most of his family were killed, as were cabinet members and numerous generals and military officers. It was in this uprising that Afghanistan's tiny Communist party, which then numbered no more than five thousand, came to power, led by Noor Mohammad Taraki. Seventeen months later, in September 1979, he was killed and his deputy prime minister, Hafizullah Amin, a brutal Marxist idealogue, became president. During this period, seven hundred Soviet advisers arrived and moved into government offices and educational institutions. But Taraki and Amin's regimes were so repressive—thousands were jailed, tortured, and executed under both leaders—that the Afghan Resistance was born, and the country began to plunge toward civil war. Finally, the Kremlin saw Amin as an intransigent obstacle to a broadening of the regime's political base. Three months after he came to power, the Soviets acted to remove him.

□

In the evening of December 24, many residents in the Afghan capital, Kabul, were watching a Pakistani film called *Country* on television. Shortly after 9:00 P.M., their screens went black. Radios fell silent about the same time. Sporadic gunfire broke out in the city.

"When the movie went off, and we heard the shooting, I went up on the roof to see what was happening," recalled Tor, who was fifteen years old at the time. "As I stood up there trying to see what was going on, we heard the first of the planes go over. The roar of the planes soon became constant. There were so many, it made it difficult to sleep. In my family, we were all still awake at 4:00 A.M. My father said it was probably another coup."

The massive airlift into Bagram Airport just outside Kabul signaled the arrival of the 103rd and 104th Soviet Airborne Divisions. At the same time, at Kabul's International Airport, the 105th Guards Airborne Division were arriving in three hundred military transport planes. Throughout the night, planes continued to land at three-minute intervals. Four motorized divisions crossed the Soviet/Afghanistan border and began racing toward the cities of Mazar-i-Sharif and Kunduz, before continuing on to Kabul. The military airlift would continue for three days.

At the beginning of the invasion, the eighty-thousand-strong Afghan army was rendered all but impotent in a simple but ingenious manner—with guile. Two divisions of tanks were disarmed when Soviet advisers told Afghan officers to "winterize" the vehicles—batteries were to be removed for maintenance purposes and ammunition removed for inventory. Other units were informed they were about to receive new weapons from the Soviet Union and were required to return their old ones beforehand. Some units were ordered to exchange live ammunition for blanks for upcoming training operations. But the prize for sheer audacity should probably go to the Soviet official who was responsible for inviting Afghan officers in Kabul to a reception to be given by their Russian counterparts and then locking them in. So skillfully was the invasion planned that Soviet troops reportedly suffered more casualties in road accidents as they raced toward Kabul than they did in combat.

Of the Afghan troops who were not disarmed, many went over to the Resistance, taking their weapons with them, thus beginning a defection pattern that has been the bane of the Kremlin ever since. In what is now called a "revolving door" army, recruits defect faster than they can be conscripted. The Afghan army today numbers approximately thirty thousand.

On December 27, three days after the invasion began, President Amin was murdered in the presidential palace. He became the third Afghan president to be killed in twenty months. Amin died shortly after he reportedly had rejected a Soviet request to resign or to make a formal request to the Soviet Union to intervene in Afghanistan. The following day, Babrak Karmal, Moscow's choice, was installed in Amin's place. Karmal had last been seen in Czechoslovakia in 1978. In a surprise announcement over Kabul Radio, later discovered to have been made on a prerecorded tape, he declared an end to "the bloody apparatus of Hafizullah Amin and his minions, these agents of American imperialism." At the same time, he requested the Soviet Union to "render urgently political, moral, military and economic assistance." But when he broadcast that appeal, a request the Soviets have always cited as the reason for their presence on Afghan soil, Karmal wasn't even in Afghanistan; he was in Tashkent in Soviet Central Asia.

"Radio Kabul told us the Russians had come to help us because the Chinese and Americans had invaded our country and were killing our people, our children," recalled Tor. "I asked my father why the Americans had come to our country. He told me it wasn't true. But he never went to work again." At that time, Tor's father was director of transportation at the American Embassy, a job he had held for over seventeen years. He fled the city almost immediately afterward. His five colleagues were less prudent and continued to work. "They were all arrested, paraded on television and denounced. Then they were executed, even my father's assistant.

"Everything began to change. A few days after the Russians came, a man visited my school and told us, 'Today the revolution became successful. The bandits are dead. Your country is like a flower; we will make it grow. We will build super-schools and universities. We will have schools for the rich and the poor. We will give you a good education because you are the future of the country.' Then they said there would be a new organization in the school that we could join that would help our country. I went home and told my father what had happened and said that I wanted to join the organization. He told me he would cut my throat if I joined, that it was the Communist party. But fifteen boys in my class did become members." Sovietization of Afghanistan was under way.

Afghan students did not remain that docile, however, for long. Three months after the invasion, on a sunny spring day, thousands of high school and college students began marching through the center of Kabul chanting, "Russians out of Afghanistan"; "Down with communism, Down with Karmal"; and *Allah o Akbar* (God is great). As their numbers started to swell to what would eventually be more than thirty thousand, they were joined by elementary schoolchildren, some as young as seven. They hadn't been marching long, when around 1:00 P.M. the tanks began to roll toward them. Soviet and Afghan forces flanked the youngsters. Then without warning, the troops began shooting straight into the crowd. The tanks kept moving forward. "It was scary," said Tor. "Everybody was screaming, pushing and running, trying to get away from the tanks, which didn't stop. A girl near me who was shouting 'Freedom, Freedom, We Want Freedom,' was shot in the head and back. Friends tried to stop the bleeding with a girl's veil, but before they could the soldiers started to fire again. She was hit several more times in the back and died instantly. She was sixteen."

Dozens of other students died, too; they were either machine-gunned down or crushed beneath the tracks of the tanks. More than two thousand students were arrested, many of whom were taken to Pul-i-Charki prison, which had recently become known throughout the country for the skill of its torturers and for the "disappearances" of its inmates.

The blood stayed on the streets of Kabul for days afterward. This massacre, the first after the invasion, was a portent of what was to come.

Today, the war in Afghanistan has been labeled genocide. In a world that vowed "Never again" after the holocaust of World War II, in a world that screamed its outrage after Lieutenant Calley slaughtered 347 civilians and their children in Vietnam's My Lai, why were they being silent now?

□

This was the question that began to gnaw at me when I left Afghanistan after that first brief four-day trip, and it would continue to do so as I researched further for my *Journal* article. Then a few weeks after my return to the States, I learned that the house in which I had stayed that first night inside Afghanistan had been blown out of the ground; the boy who had picked apricots for me and the rest of his family were dead. A little while later, I was informed that the freedom fighter group Hamid and

Tor were with was encircled by Soviet forces, pinned down in the same province we had visited together, and expected to run out of ammunition at any time.

They survived that experience, but would their luck continue to hold? The death rate for the *Mujahideen* is one in five. And a freedom fighter's chance of survival once injured is also one in five, almost twice as bad as it was for soldiers fighting in the American Civil War. These pitiful survival rates are due to a paucity of doctors in Afghanistan—many were executed or fled at the start of the war—and to the fact that it can take several weeks for an injured fighter to reach hospitals in Pakistan, by which time loss of blood or gross infection may have already taken its toll.

And as women have always done about war, I questioned why young men who should have been exploring life for the first time were daily being forced to confront death.

Two months after I returned, a French television journalist, Jacques Abouchar, was captured by the Soviets inside Afghanistan. Taken to Kabul and tried, he was sentenced to eighteen years' imprisonment but released forty days later after an outcry in France and a protest by the French Communist party. On his release, the Soviet ambassador to Pakistan, Vitaly Smirnov, told journalists in Islamabad: "I warn you, and through you, all of your journalist colleagues: stop trying to penetrate Afghanistan with the so-called guerrillas. From now on, the bandits and the so-called journalists accompanying them will be killed. Our units in Afghanistan will help the Afghan forces [to do it]." It was obvious from that statement that Moscow was determined to make impregnable the curtain of silence around Afghanistan.

If Afghanistan were closed to the world's press, there would be no public accounting of this war. A perversity in me didn't see why it should be that easy. My decision to return for a longer trip met with the disapproval of colleagues and friends alike; some went so far as to question my sanity. Arguments ranged from "Isn't it time you settled down?" and "Isn't New York exciting enough for you?" to a former Vietnam war correspondent telling me, "You may be covering the right side of this war, but from your survival point of view, you'd be better off flying in the helicopters, not traveling on foot over Afghanistan's terrain with the Soviets looking for you." But the more they tried to dissuade me, the more determined I found myself becoming. I kept thinking of the family whose house I had stayed in that first night in Afghanistan, and how they had been slaughtered, and of white-haired, bewildered Nawab, who couldn't understand why he lived when his entire family was wiped out. And I kept remembering meeting eight-year-old Abdul in the Red Cross Hospital. He'd lost both his legs up to the hips. "But they won't stop me walking. Look, I can walk on my hands," he'd boasted to me when I went to visit him six weeks after he'd kicked a small, four-inch "butterfly" mine.

I knew that I would have to go back. It would take me a year to do so.

2

Peshawar: Moles, Mujahideen, and Marijauna

A journey into Afghanistan begins in Peshawar, a city thirty miles west of the legendary Khyber Pass, the former gateway to Kabul. Landing at Peshawar airport, one receives the impression that it is Pakistan that is at war, not neighboring Afghanistan. The airport is cordoned with very substantial looking antiaircraft guns, and many of the country's F-16 fighter jets—courtesy of Uncle Sam's $3.2 billion aid package over the last five years—are clearly visible. The hardware in evidence in Peshawar must be the envy of every Afghan freedom fighter headquartered there, particularly the Stinger missiles, which had recently arrived in Pakistan; the *Mujahideen* were yearning for them but the United States was refusing to give them.

Waiting for one's luggage in the air-conditioned baggage area, an observant arrival soon becomes aware that foreigners are closely scrutinized, not from cultural curiosity but for official reasons. Lists of foreign nationals arriving in Peshawar and lists of those checking into the city's three main "tourist" hotels, Dean's, Green's, and the newly named Pearl, once the Hotel Intercontinental, are forwarded daily to the Joint Intelligence Branch. Welcome to Peshawar, a city that could have been invented by Ian Fleming for one of his James Bond books. And while 007 never did come through town, Francis Gary Powers put it on the modern espionage map when his ill-fated U2 spy plane mission took off from here in 1960 and was downed by the Soviet Union. Since the Afghan/Soviet war, however, Powers's use of the airport facilities is small potatoes in the surveillance business. In Peshawar, which challenges East Berlin for the title of world spy capital, it is said that everyone is KGB; KHAD, the Soviet-trained Afghan equivalent; CIA; or Pakistani Special Branch. Those who aren't are journalists, arms dealers, the occasional would-be mercenary, smugglers, and drug dealers. All of them have business with or interest in the *Mujahideen*, who are the reason, of course, for Peshawar being a town of intrigue. Set against a summer backdrop of swirling dust, heat, and humidity of Hadean proportions, and a winter one of biting winds and freezing temperatures, the various intelligence services vie with one another to keep track of *Mujahideen* movement, no simple task as the Afghan guerrillas move back and forth across the closed border, past numerous Pakistani checkpoints, with as much ease as they did when their nation was mostly nomadic. The proliferation of so many intelligence-gathering groups frequently gives the town a sense of farce—everyone is suspect, phone bugging is downright amateurish, and every taxi driver seems to know the location of the guerrilla headquarters. At least, they did on my first trip to Pakistan.

□

I remembered taking a cab from the airport to Dean's Hotel on that previous occasion in 1984 and being greeted with, "You American? You journalist? I know *Mujahideen* offices." I smiled a limp smile, made limper by the 120 degree heat that had nearly knocked me over as I left the air-conditioned airport. Obviously, cover stories here weren't going to hold up long. If I had asked for Green's Hotel he would have concluded, probably correctly, that I was a refugee relief worker or a member of a European medical organization such as the French-based *Médecins Sans Frontières,* Doctors Without Borders, who volunteer to spend six months inside Afghanistan treating the wounded. I remembered being warned before leaving the States that many of the taxi drivers were informers for anyone who was buying information.

The fifteen-minute drive to the hotel was the nadir of the thirty-five-hour trip from New York. Jet-lagged and exhausted, my senses were assailed by Peshawar. The cab's wide-open windows admitted the stench of traffic fumes made particularly pungent by the emissions of the motorized rickshaws, with their two-stroke engines, which buzzed in and out of the vehicles like angry bees on the swarm. Familiar throughout Asia, they originally must have been designed for the smaller oriental frame, because their open passenger cabs are so cramped that they require contortionist skills to climb in and out and are agonizingly uncomfortable rides for heftier Westerners. Nerves still jangled by the journey, the sound of Peshawar was even more overwhelming than its smell. Just as Italians often say that they cannot talk if you tie down their arms, so must it be impossible for Peshawar residents to drive if their vehicle horns give out. Cacophony seems too mild a word to describe the clamor of the city that first day. Whether in brilliantly painted trucks, crammed-to-the-roof buses, Mercedes, or motorbikes, everyone drove everywhere with the horn constantly blaring.

Driving through Defense Colony, it was apparent that it had been built by the British for its army garrisoned here. Its neat little bungalows and trimmed lawns suggested soldierly spruceness and were made even more orderly by the brilliant white paint on fences, on rocks bordering all paths, and on rings around the bases of all trees. And everywhere there were signs to military headquarters and units, and their concomitant clubs, and laundries. Even the men walking on the Colony's streets had the erect bearing of career officers.

Order is left behind, however, when leaving the Defense Colony. The bazaar surrounding Dean's and its near neighbor Green's is anything but orderly. Here street vendors and tourists, shop-front salesmen and residents all vociferously haggle for the best in bargains. Outside Green's Hotel, black market money changers and equally discreet drug pushers quietly approach foreigners. Peshawar is one of the world's heroin capitals, and U.S. drug enforcement agents estimate that half of the American supply of heroin passes through this city.

Dean's Hotel, considerably more conservative than its colorful surroundings, looks as if it were misplaced by the Defense Colony. Its bungalowed rooms were obviously built by the same architect, although the upkeep is less spiffy and its gardens less trimmed. "Stay in Dean's," advised Karen McKay, then executive director of the Committee for a Free Afghanistan in a briefing she had given me in Washington, D.C., before that first trip. "The bungalows make it easy for the *Mujahideen* to come and go unchecked without having to walk through a lobby or be observed by the front desk. All journalists stay there." And she was right. A glance through the reservations book confirmed it, as did my fellow guests. Dean's is a small hotel, yet it was home that week to Eddie Girardet of the *Christian Science Monitor;* a CBS-TV film crew; an Italian film crew; Ken Silverman, a freelance photographer on assignment for *Time* magazine; Sandy Gall, an award-winning documentary maker for Britain's ITV; and Peter Jouvenal, another British journalist. All of them were waiting for their *Mujahideen* contacts either to contact them or finalize details on trips over the border. Eddie, who was on his sixth Afghan assignment for the *Monitor,* had been waiting three weeks. An old hand at trips inside, he was good-humoredly patient, unusually so for a journalist, but then he was headed for the Panjshir Valley, an arduous three-week trek from the border, and he knew that advance warning of his arrival had to be conveyed by foot messenger before he could leave. Eddie stayed just as unruffled when his room was broken into on my third day there. He lost his passport and five thousand dollars in traveler's checks, and his cameras were smashed after the window of his room was shattered. "I think it was a warning; I've had them before," said Eddie calmly before going off to call his Boston office collect and arrange for new funds to be wired to him.

Eddie's trip to the Panjshir, where most of Afghanistan's emeralds can be found, was to report on the activities of Commander Ahmad Shah Massoud, the brilliant, then twenty-nine-year-old Resistance leader who had taught himself guerrilla warfare from books authored by such specialists as Che Guevara and Ho Chi Minh. Known as the "Lion of the Panjshir" and frequently compared to Tito, Massoud had had a high price placed on his head long ago by the Soviets, who would be willing to pay it whether he were delivered to them dead or alive. In fact, the Russians become so excited at the thought of a Panjshir without Massoud that they have announced his demise on radio and television on at least five occasions. Eddie's long-term relationship with the commander was probably the reason for his break-in. Just as a man is known by his friends, when a man has enemies, anyone in his orbit is likely to be caught up in the maelstrom. And the commander has many enemies, not all of them Russian. Massoud is a member of Jamiat, one of the fundamentalist groups of *Mujahideen*, which is composed mostly of two ethnic groups, Uzbeks and Tadjiks. His adversaries among the Resistance would almost certainly be members of Hezb-i-Islami, headed by thirty-seven-year-old Gulbuddin Hekmatayar. Consisting mostly of Pathans, the Hezb-i-Islami group has strong ties with the fundamentalist Muslim Brotherhood and, at that time, with Ayatollah Khomeini, a man Gulbuddin frequently sounded like when I met him.

Jamiat and Hezb-i-Islami have been engaged for most of the war in an internecine battle that is conducted both inside Afghanistan and in Pakistan. Each side blames the other, but the general consensus among the *Mujahideen* population is that Hezb-i-Islami are the provocateurs. Their leader, Gulbuddin Hekmatayer, stands accused of extraordinary treachery, although much of his notoriety may be earned on apocryphal deeds. When a colossal car bomb blew up outside his Peshawar office in the summer of 1984 exactly at the time Gulbuddin always arrived, destroying a house, damaging his office, killing seven, and severely injuring twelve passersby, including children, many ranking Afghans chose to believe that Hekmatayer planted it himself for self-aggrandizing reasons. He wanted to make himself seem more important, they insist; he knew nobody tries to assassinate the insignificant. They base their argument on the fact that on this particular morning, Gulbuddin had arrived an hour late—something he never did. "Gulbuddin is ruthless," they say. "He wants to be dictator of Afghanistan." Whether Gulbuddin is ruthless and, if so, to what degree, is hard to say, but the *Mujahideen* who are increasingly defecting from his party frequently do so because they claim they object to being ordered to kill commanders of other parties. Then there are the stories that Hezb-i-Islami has been infiltrated by the KGB. How can that be? says another, "He's pro-Communist." But one thing that is verifiable, by his own words, is Gulbuddin's megalomania.

In an interview with me, the slim, seemingly quiet-mannered man told me in all seriousness that the Soviets invaded Afghanistan only to destroy him and his party. And almost without missing a beat, he launched into a litany that left me waiting for his laughter or punchline: "The first man to fire a bullet at the Soviets was mine. The first Afghan to die in battle was mine. The first Russian tank destroyed, and the first captured, were by my men. The first helicopter shot down was by my men. The first Soviet captured alive was mine." Since Gulbuddin wasn't laughing, I bit my tongue so I wouldn't, but I wanted to. That his fanfaronade was blatantly false seemed not to bother him. But what is true about this much-talked-about man is that he is the only Afghan I met of whom *Mujahideen* from all seven parties admitted being afraid.

When I decided to try to arrange that initial trip to Afghanistan after two weeks of interviewing refugees, it was conversations with Eddie Girardet that made me choose to present my first letter of introduction to Jamiat. When I hailed the same cab I had taken from the airport, the driver proved that he did, indeed, know the *Mujahideen* offices, even though Jamiat's was located at the end of a circuitous and steamily sticky twenty-five-minute drive. He pulled up at a shabby two-story house with peeling, yellowed walls just long enough for me to climb out. Lounging about outside in an apparently casual manner were half a dozen young men whose lighter skins set them apart from their Pakistani neighbors, as did their heavy beards. If their appearance hadn't already done so, their careful examination of me confirmed that these men were Afghans, security guards, in fact, for Jamiat's headquarters-in-exile.

"Abdul Rahim?" I asked. They continued to stare. Maybe they hadn't understood my pronunciation of the name, or perhaps they were unaccustomed to a woman visiting the office. "Does anyone speak English?" I tried again.

"Engineer Rahim is in, but he is busy," replied a stocky youth I judged to be about nineteen. In Afghanistan, engineers are as esteemed as doctors, and Rahim's honorific was a sign of that respect. No one in the group moved; obviously they had no intention of disturbing him for my benefit. Shrugging, I walked past them into an alley bordering the house, which led to an open doorway. Only as I crossed the courtyard in search of any of the residents did the boy who had spoken catch up with me. "Upstairs, the Engineer is upstairs," he said sourly, leading the way into a small room with an old leather couch and two desks. Sitting at one of them was a slight, intelligent-looking young man, in his late twenties, wearing the ubiquitous full beard. Talking into the phone he motioned to me to sit. The room was stifling, hotter inside than the 120 degrees outside, and the leather of the couch made sweat trickle down my back. Someone brought me an ice-cold Pepsi. Never a drinker of sodas normally, I pounced on it like a dying man in the desert. The cloying sweetness of the first gulp confirmed my distaste, and I used the rest of the bottle like an ice cube to hold against my cheeks. By now, I was so hot that sweat was running down the sides of my bright red face.

A sodden lump melting into the floor was not the image I would have wished to present to a leading Resistance official I was trying to impress. And I cursed my English skin and genes that made my sangfroid anything but skin-deep.

Twenty minutes later, Rahim finished his phone call. It had taken so long because he had been forced to repeat himself over and over—Pakistan's antiquated phone system was built by the British and often seems as if it hasn't been serviced since they went home in 1947. He listened patiently as I explained that I wanted to visit Afghanistan to document the war damage, but I didn't want to be gone long, and I needed to arrange it quickly. As I finished talking, I realized I must have sounded like an impatient New Yorker ordering a package deal through a travel agent. He smiled, as if he were having the same thought. "These things take time to arrange," he said. "This is a war; unexpected things change plans all the time. Why don't you telephone me in about five days?"

I did. Rahim was out. Three days later, I still hadn't reached him. Two visits to his office were equally futile. I envied Eddie Girardet his patience and kept trying to remember that wars were hard to plot. On my third visit, I found the engineer in. This time he was conducting conversations on two phones. In between bellowing into them, he shook his head at me, and his face expressed the Afghan equivalent of "Tomorrow ... maybe," but his manner wasn't very convincing. It occurred to me that Jamiat were not thrilled by my request and may have even decided not to take me because I was a woman. I was aware that the Soviets, in an effort to discredit Commander Massoud among his own people, had spread rumors stating that the Resistance leader was not a good Muslim, that he had been sexually involved with two attractive female doctors with *Médecins Sans Frontières*. To protect his reputation, the devoutly religious Massoud had banned female medical volunteers from his Panjshir Valley region. Perhaps Jamiat had decided that despite the need for the *Mujahideen* to get their story published and the paucity of journalists willing to travel inside Afghanistan, women reporters could be similarly problematic.

Discouraged, I left. My time was running out; I was due to leave Pakistan in seven days. Now I wished I hadn't concentrated all my efforts on Jamiat. Returning to the hotel I telephoned NIFA. They agreed to see me that afternoon at four o'clock.

This time the taxi took me to a gracious-looking home in a prosperous suburb of the city. The house was indistinguishable from its neighbors until my taxi pulled into its driveway, and the vehicle was immediately surrounded by four turbaned men armed with Kalashnikov machine guns, bayonets fixed. Climbing out of the cab, I was glad I had an appointment. Glancing around, I realized there were concealed guard towers, all manned, in each of the four corners of the high wall surrounding the house. Behind the house, I would later learn, was what amounted to a small military camp of about forty freedom fighters. Obviously, this was not a place where unexpected visitors were welcome.

I was expecting to meet Pir Sayed Ahmad Gailani, the spiritual Sunni leader of nearly half of Afghanistan, whose family is revered as descending from the Prophet Mohammed. Head of the most Westernized of the seven parties, Gailani, an erudite man, is a liberal specialist on Islamic law and advocates secular democracy for a free Afghanistan. His followers can also be found in Pakistan, Saudi Arabia, and Iraq. Gailani is related by marriage to Afghanistan's deposed king, Zahir Shah, who was ousted by Mohammad Daoud in 1973, and who now lives in exile in Rome.

Since NIFA was the most Westernized of the Resistance

groups, I hoped they would respond to me differently from Jamiat and see me as a journalist first and a woman second.

"My father is unavailable," said the young man who greeted me. After all the strapping Afghans I had met until now, Hamed Gailani was a surprise in several ways. About my height of five feet, four inches, he was beardless, as fair-skinned as I, and he spoke impeccable Oxford English. Slightly overweight, his physical appearance made him look bookish, which he was, and a far cry from the muscle-hard *Mujahideen* surrounding him. "I hate guns," he said, referring to the greeting that I had just received, as he showed me into a large sparsely furnished reception room. And then as a weary afterthought, he added, "But then there are thousands of Afghans who feel as I do."

Twenty-nine-year-old Hamed, who has a B.A. in political science and economics from Kabul University, was taking a graduate degree in Islamic studies in Islamabad. It is his younger brother, Mohammad, who is the freedom fighter in the family. Hamed did not look like the kind of man from whom I could order a package tour of the war in Afghanistan. We began to talk about the recent report from the London School of Tropical Medicine on impending famine inside his country—the food-shortage being war-induced, and the effect it would have on the freedom fighters. "*Mujahideen* have eaten grass and leaves before. I am not worried about famine as far as their fighting is concerned. Shortage of food cannot change their desire for freedom.

"You know, if you were to put the facts of this war into a computer, it would say that we could not survive the might of the Russian army more than a few weeks, but we have; we continue to fight."

The door to the room opened, and a tall, heavyset man with a mane of black hair; a black, bushy beard; and high cheekbones that suggested Mongolian ancestry came quietly in and sat down opposite us without saying a word. Hamed didn't stop talking to introduce us. The newcomer was dressed in khaki-colored Afghan *kameez* pajamas with a black vest. Whether because of the somber color of his clothes or his silence, I found his presence intimidating, and the feeling interfered with my concentration during the interview. When it was over, both men stood up, Hamed to take his leave, and the heavyset man to introduce himself. "My name is Wakil Akberzai," he said, extending his hand. "I understand you want to go inside."

I agreed I did.

"For how long do you want to go, and when could you be ready to leave?"

I was surprised at his understanding of Western urgency.

"As soon as possible, and for no more than a week," I responded.

He chuckled. "Well, we'll see what we can do. We don't have satellite communication with our men in the field. We need time to get in touch with our commanders inside to let them know you are coming and find out where we should send you. We haven't lost any journalists yet, and we don't want to spoil our record.

"I'll call you at the hotel as soon as I get a response. In the meantime, you can go shopping for the clothes you'll need.

"And now, let me have a jeep take you back to your hotel."

Wakil's efficiency and thoughtfulness were a pleasant surprise. And it was mainly because of his logistical competence and incisiveness that I chose to approach NIFA again when I wanted to make my second trip inside Afghanistan. After several letters hand-carried back and forth between the United States and Pakistan, Pir Gailani agreed to my proposal and invited me to spend three months with his *Mujahideen* in the summer of 1985.

□

When I arrived at Peshawar airport the second time, the weather was even hotter than it had been the previous year. The day before I got there, the city had been hit by an earthquake that registered 6.5 on the Richter scale. Surprisingly, only three people had died. For the next week Peshawar would continue to have tremors, which panicked the more highly strung residents and played havoc with an already deficient phone system. As I stepped outside the arrivals' lounge I was greeted by a grinning Tor, Hamid, and Fareed, who swooped down on me and my baggage. Ushering me into a waiting van, Hamid and Fareed seemed unchanged. Fareed, peacock that he was, still couldn't climb into a vehicle without first glancing into the mirror and checking his hair. Only Tor was different. He was substantially thinner and seemingly less spirited than the last time I'd seen him. When I commented on his changed appearance, he explained that he'd been very sick earlier that year. He also explained it in English, something he hadn't been able to do the previous year. And although his grammar was nonexistent, and his sentence construction amusingly idiosyncratic, it was a delight to be able to converse directly with him.

As the four of us caught up on a year's worth of news, I didn't take note of the route we traveled and was surprised when we stopped outside a house I hadn't seen before. Until then, I had assumed that when I was in Peshawar, I would be housed in Wakil's dormitory. "Pir Gailani felt you would be more comfortable here," said Wakil, greeting me at the van door. The nine-foot-high metal gates clanged shut behind the vehicle. And as they did, I realized that this place, too, had a squad of six armed guards, only this time they would be guarding me. Once again, being friendly with freedom fighters meant sharing their enemies.

Leading me into the modern two-story house, Wakil began a guided tour. "Here is the kitchen; Abdul Hai here will cook your meals. Anything you need, ask him, but he doesn't speak a word of English, I'm afraid." Abdul Hai, a friendly-faced man of about forty, beamed at me. *"Salaam alaikum. Chator Hasti?"* Hello. How are you? So far, I was doing fine.

The room next to the kitchen was out of bounds, explained Wakil. "We use it for military briefings sometimes, and you'll also find commanders meeting here from time to time. When they do, you should stay upstairs and out of sight. The fewer people who know you are here, the better." The last room on the ground floor, bare except for two pallets, was for Hamid and Tor. "They'll sleep here while you're here," said Wakil. "This room is directly underneath yours." And although he didn't say so, it was implied they were also close at hand for my security. The house was beginning to feel more like a fortress than a rented family home.

My quarters were on the second floor. "I hope you'll be comfortable," said Wakil, waving me into a small but air-conditioned room. With its two narrow cots, sofa, matching armchairs, coffee table, and desk, the room was, in fact, considerably more comfortable than I'd been expecting. I had prepared myself for a cotton mattress on someone's floor. Here, I even had an attached bathroom with cold-water shower. Left alone to unpack, I found a cardboard box containing shampoo, conditioner, perfumed soap, a bag of hard candies, cookies, and a box of tissues—all luxuries in this part of the world, and a sort of guerrilla Welcome Wagon present. I guessed correctly that the thought had been Wakil's.

The remainder of the rooms on my floor were all closed off. But the whole second floor had a wide balcony skirting it, edged by a six-foot *purdah* wall, which enabled Pakistani women to enjoy the fresh air without being seen by men outside their families. This house would be my base while I was in Peshawar.

Unpacking, I was glad to see that my gift for NIFA, a set of walkie-talkies, had arrived intact. Because they were surprisingly heavy, I had nearly left them behind. But knowing how ill-equipped most *Mujahideen* groups are, I made room for them in my baggage at the last minute. I remembered that on that first trip, Resistance commanders would borrow my binoculars because they didn't have any of their own, and on one occasion when our party had split up, we had had no idea whether they were alive or dead for nearly a day. Then I had thought what a difference some kind of communication equipment, no matter how basic, would have made. Now, as I looked at my gift, it seemed pitifully small.

There was a knock at the door. Wakil had returned to make sure I had settled in. Ordering tea for both of us from Abdul Hai, he collapsed into an armchair, removing as he did so a gun belt I hadn't realized he was wearing under his *kameez* tunic. As he tossed it onto the table, the silver hammer and sickle on the buckle landed facing me. My face must have looked questioning.

"It was a Soviet officer's; so was the gun," he said. The heavy-looking revolver was an automatic 9 mm Makarov.

When he wasn't inside Afghanistan, Wakil had told me he functioned as a director general of refugee relief for NIFA and the seven *Mujahideen*-party unity.

"Are the refugees getting mean?" I asked. "Why the gun?"

"It is necessary, but not for the refugees." He looked tired. "There have been a number of incidents recently." Wakil went on to tell me that NIFA's chief of staff had been shot at three weeks before as he was driving home. The windscreen was shattered, but the bullet had missed him. "Then there were the bombs planted at the Shan hotel last week. The hotel is where a lot of unmarried *Mujahideen* stayed. Two bombs went off at 2:00 A.M. when everyone was asleep. Two freedom fighters died; twenty-two were injured. Obviously our presence here is making some people very unhappy."

Concerned about city security after incidents such as these, the Pakistani authorities had recently ordered all Afghan Resistance parties to move their offices outside Peshawar. They had also begun evicting single Afghan males from the city. The ordinance was a problem for the *Mujahideen* and their visitors alike. The Resistance parties claimed that they would find one office outside the city, start to settle in, only to be told the location wasn't suitable and they'd have to move again. "It amounts to harassment," said one official. "Every time we unpack, we have to pack again. It's hard to keep track of anything; our filing cabinets are constantly on the move." This time around, too, local taxi drivers weren't so savvy. Jamiat's new location, for example, was well outside the city in a large mud village with no street names. To counteract that problem, someone had painted on the side of their building in four-foot-high black letters MUJ. Although it wasn't neon lights, it probably wasn't very wise, either. And in the shakedown, NIFA had lost the large house where I had first visited them. Now Gailani's offices were accommodated in much smaller premises.

But sizes of offices and relocation problems were not on Wakil's mind. He'd just come back from a trip to the border, where he'd observed a stream of refugees leaving Afghanistan. "It was hot at the border, as hot as it's been here. I could feel the burning rocks through the soles of my sandals. But the children I watched leave were barefooted. They'd been walking for three days, climbing our Afghan mountains.

"They were just small kids. They reminded me of little chicks. They looked dazed.

"Looking at them, I found myself saying, 'God, You know better. What have You done?' " Wakil's voice broke, and he looked away.

"One mother was sick. She'd just given birth to a baby; it was premature because of the bombing terror. She was holding the baby, and she had two more children with her. But she could barely walk. She didn't know where she was going, what she was going to.

"I looked at her children, and I wanted to put their bare, bleeding feet in my pocket." Wakil struggled for the words to express himself. "I wanted to carry them back. But I just stood there.

"All I could see were women and children leaving. And young men going in. The first group to live, and the second to probably die. It was never the reverse.

"If this keeps up, the country's going to be empty," he said, despair in his voice.

□

Since the beginning of the war, refugees flooding into Pakistan have averaged 11,000 a week, with 80 percent of them settling in camps in the North-West Frontier Province. In some areas such as Parichinar, 125 kilometers east of Peshawar, they now outnumber the Pakistani inhabitants 300,000 to 270,000. Yet Pakistan, despite being the ninth most populous country in the world and one of the less developed, has continued to accept the Afghans. Part of the reason is that many of the refugees are Pathans, members of one of the largest ethnic tribes in the world. Numbering 12 million, the Pathans can be found on both sides of the Afghan/Pakistan border. They were divided in 1893, when the British, who were fond of gerrymandering to their Empire's advantage, placed the border where it is today, leaving the Afghans and the Pakistanis to dispute it ever since. So although Pakistan is being asked to absorb the largest number of refugees in history, there have not been the tragic incidents that have scarred the acceptance of Cambodian refugees into Thailand. Thailand, a country less economically handicapped than Pakistan, had always insisted they would only accept the refugees as a place of first refuge; the Cambodians were never to be settled there permanently. Even despite this assurance, and tens of thousands of the refugees being accepted into Western countries, the Thais have still panicked several times and marched Cambodians back across the border at gunpoint, frequently to their deaths. Pakistan has never done this, although there are reports that Afghan refugees in Iran have been subjected to the same treatment. In view of this, Pakistan's president, General Muhammad Zia-ul-Haq, may be the only military dictator to enter the annals of history labeled a humanitarian.

Another major reason for Zia's continuing acceptance of the Afghans is that it has brought his country $1.2 billion in international relief aid. Then, of course, there is economic pressure from the United States. Since the fall of Iran, Pakistan is the eastern pillar for U.S. defense of the strategic Persian Gulf region. President Zia has replaced the Shah of Iran as America's new best friend in this part of the world.

The day after the Afghan invasion, President Jimmy Carter telephoned Zia and offered to help Pakistan improve its military capability. Two months later, Washington suggested they would do so to the tune of $400 million. But Zia rejected the offer as "peanuts." For the next nine months, Zia exercised his negotiations skills. Finally, the newly installed Reagan administration came up with figures that Zia contended were worthy of "best friends." By the end of 1986, the United States will have poured $3.2 billion, half of it in military assistance, into Pakistan, making it the third highest recipient in the world of U.S. aid and enabling it to leapfrog over Turkey and Greece, who now rank fourth and fifth. The package included forty F-16 jet fighters as "a deterrent against the Soviets attacking the heart of Pakistan," explained one U.S. official.

The United States sees Pakistan as a frontline state resisting Soviet expansionism. And as the Soviets become more involved in Afghanistan, the United States becomes more involved in Pakistan. In the summer of 1986, President Reagan promised a further $4.2 billion over five years in aid to Zia's government.

And it is Pakistan, of course, that administers and distributes U.S. military aid to the *Mujahideen*. The largest covert military support operation run by the Central Intelligence Agency since Vietnam, it is also, ironically, the most publicized and perhaps the most mismanaged. For the first five years of the Afghan/Soviet war, Washington spent $600 million on military aid to the *Mujahideen*. This was a figure that was frequently leaked, but never officially confirmed. For the fiscal year of 1986, Congress "secretly" allocated $470 million, with, according to Washington sources, an additional $300 million supplementary allocation. And although the total figure of $1 billion to $1.3 billion looks pale next to Pakistan's $7.4 billion, it should translate into a sizable accumulation of arms for Afghanistan. It does not. In fact, if Washington's General Accounting Office were ever allowed to monitor the CIA's covert aid to Afghanistan, which of course, it will not be, it might well discover the grandest U.S. arms supply boondoggle of all time.

According to intelligence sources, a shipment of arms is supposed to be delivered every week to the Afghan freedom fighters, enough, they say, to supply nearly a quarter of a million men. The arms are purchased from China, Egypt, and Israel, the latter having a large stockpile of Soviet arms captured in the 1973 Yom Kippur War and in 1982 in Lebanon. Then they are shipped through circuitous routes meant to disguise direct links with the United States. The program begun in 1980 is reportedly run by several dozen Afghan expatriates, who are CIA-trained, operating through export companies, travel agencies, and other front companies. When the arms arrive at the port of Karachi, the crates marked SPECIAL are given priority handling and are not inspected by customs officials. Transferred to Pakistani military vehicles, they are transported to Peshawar.

Once in the city, the arms are stockpiled until Pakistan decides which of the seven *Mujahideen* parties are to receive a particular delivery. Then after a late night phone call, Resistance officials are summoned by a Pakistani brigadier for a midnight meeting at his large, comfortable home, which sits just behind the American Cultural Center and offices of the U.S. Information Agency in the elegant University Town district of the city. There the *Mujahideen* take delivery on paper of the weapons they so desperately need. Finally, produce trucks supposedly carrying rice or wheat and traveling only at night deliver the arms to the parties' munitions depots. Like the *Mujahideen* headquarters, the depots used to be in the city itself, but, concerned about a potential pyrotechnic disaster, the Pakistani government has forced them to move outside; most are within an hour's drive of Peshawar. Once in the hands of the Resistance, the weapons travel to the border in *Mujahideen* trucks. The final leg of the journey is made in jeeps and pickups in the few Afghan provinces that have accessible roads, or by donkey, mule, camel, or on foot in the majority that do not.

Somewhere between the authorizing of the money in Washington, however, and the delivery of arms to the freedom fighters inside Afghanistan, an estimated 70 percent disappears. And since the Pakistani government, like the CIA, denies that the pipeline exists, monitoring inside Pakistan is also impossible.

Obviously, a situation like this is ripe for corruption, and corruption exists. Just as in countries that receive food aid, large sacks of dried milk or rice clearly marked DONATED BY . . . can be found openly on sale in street markets, so can arms destined for the *Mujahideen* be found on the open market in Pakistan. And the largest such market in the North-West Frontier Province is Darra Adem Khiel, a thirty-minute drive from Peshawar. Because Darra is off-limits to foreigners, Pakistani doctors en route to nearby refugee camps obligingly smuggled me into the small town shortly after I arrived in Peshawar.

Of the 250 or so arms dealers in Darra, half that number are engaged in copying "any kind of weapon from anywhere in the world that you require." And that is not an empty boast. In this dusty, mazelike town, where the sound of gunfire is continuous as guns are tested and demonstrated for customers, it is possible to purchase light and heavy machine guns, mortars and rocket launchers, in addition to ordinary rifles, all of which have been skillfully copied. But it is the other stores where the CIA-funded arms end up. Wandering through the warren of streets, one can see Egyptian and Chinese weapons in profusion. Crates of ammunition from both countries are stacked on floors, as are tank and antipersonnel mines. SAM missiles are also available here from time to time. "We've had the occasional Howitzer, and we even had an armored personnel carrier here last year, but those are captured from the Russians, of course," I was told.

Darra's extraordinary bazaar came into being a hundred years ago when the British decided it was easier to allow the Pathans to make their own inferior weapons than it was to have them keep raiding British armories. Today, the arms that are not manufactured by the town's gunsmiths are either captured from the Soviets in Afghanistan or siphoned from the CIA pipeline. And, of course, anyone who is involved in the covert shipment of the arms, from the dock workers who unload the crates, to the truck drivers who transport them to Peshawar, to the Pakistani officials who oversee delivery, and to the Afghans in Peshawar responsible for getting the arms inside Afghanistan, is in a position to contribute to the pipeline's leaks. And black-marketed arms in Darra is big business. Among the frequent purchasers of the weapons originally destined for Afghanistan are the drug traffickers who need to protect their product from pillaging kindred souls. Last year, a Pakistani narcotics agent found that one drug trader had installed an antiaircraft gun on his roof. Even the Afghan regime's secret police, KHAD, have found it cheaper to purchase required arms in Darra than through regular channels.

But it isn't just the porous pipeline that is the despair of the grossly underarmed Afghan Resistance; the problems occur long before the pipe begins to leak. The snafu starts in the CIA's Directorate of Operations, which is responsible for purchasing the arms. Just as the Pentagon was found in 1982 to be purchasing regular hardware nuts for $2,000 each and and toilet seats for $640, the CIA is also apparently a sloppy shopper. Washington sources estimate that of the $342 million appropriated by Congress in the first four years to purchase weapons for the Afghan Resistance, only about $100 million worth actually entered the pipeline in the first place. And balancing the books on even a reduced amount was made substantially more complex when a clerical staffer at the CIA headquarters in Langley, Virginia, decided to save time and mixed the authorized funding for the Afghans with the unauthorized funding for the Nicaraguan contras. When the "Contragate" scandal burst on America's conscience last winter, it was revealed that profits from Iran arms sales, which were destined for the contras, were placed in the same CIA secret Swiss bank account with money intended for the Afghan freedom fighters. It was a bookkeeping blunder the Reagan administration would later describe as a "dumb" mistake. But, a major part of this cost discrepancy in funding the Afghan resistance is caused by favorable prices for arms dealers who are former CIA employees, a revolving-door conflict of interest that plagues many federal agencies. Beyond the apparent cronyism, however, there is also sheer incompetency. "The CIA has spent several million dollars of American taxpayers' money to buy SAM-7s for the Afghan Resistance," says Washington lobbyist Andrew Eiva, executive director of the Federation for American Afghan Action, "even though they learned in its last secret war —in Angola—that they proved totally useless against armored helicopters and jet fighters." But the CIA has known about the flaws in the SAM missiles for a lot longer than that: "In the 1973

Yom Kippur War, the Arab armies reported that of five thousand SAMs fired there were only four aircraft shot down, and twenty-eight damaged," says David Isby, an arms expert and author of the authoritative *Jane's Weapons and Tactics of the Soviet Army*.

Adds Eiva, "The CIA also has purchased a reported $20 million worth of 12.7 mm ammunition for the guerrillas' only effective antiair weapon, the Dashaka heavy machine gun. Unfortunately, 85 percent of the ammunition is non-armor-piercing, ineffective against armored gunships." The Federation for American Afghan Action has also documented that hundreds of $4,500 machine guns are rendered useless inside Afghanistan because "the CIA doesn't have a resupply officer brilliant enough to provide a supply of spare barrels." And weapons put into the pipeline with insufficient ammunition is another problem *Mujahideen* face. "Ammunition shortage for their key arms is the greatest debilitating factor for the Resistance fronts fighting in Afghanistan," says Eiva. "The RPG-7 Soviet rocket launcher, the world's best light antitank gun, is a valued guerrilla weapon. But the resupply for it averages one round a month, enough to conduct two or three ambushes a year. Dashakas are averaging six hundred rounds per month, an amount sufficient for a skirmish."

But no matter how few or how many arms are arriving in Pakistan for the Afghan Resistance, the Kremlin, not surprisingly, considers the amount excessive. And their warnings to Pakistan have been both verbal and violent. When President Zia attended Konstantin Chernenko's funeral in Moscow in March 1985, Gorbachev took the opportunity to issue a stern warning to him. "Aggressive actions" against Afghanistan, a Soviet ally, are being carried out from Pakistan's territory, reported *Tass* on the meeting. "It was stressed that this cannot but affect in the most negative way Soviet-Pakistani relations."

Three months later, Pakistan's minister of state for foreign affairs, Zain Noorani, told his country's National Assembly that Communist pilots, both Soviet and Afghan, had violated Pakistani territory 615 times since 1979. Since then, the bombing incursions have increased sharply; in the first six months of 1986 there were 619 violations, more than in the preceding six years combined. The Pakistani death toll from such incursions now numbers over three hundred, with twice that many injured. Refugee camps close to the border have also been shelled from Afghanistan. The latter is perceived as being a sign of Soviet anger over their allegation that refugee camps are often used as recruitment centers for the Resistance or as recuperation bases for war-weary *Mujahideen*. A map published by the Soviets identifying refugee camps they claim are *Mujahideen* military bases brought jeering laughter from Resistance officials when I showed it to them. "They've labeled virtually every refugee camp in Pakistan, and they've also invented quite a few more. If the bases they claim we have in Pakistan were translated into freedom fighters, we could not only drive the Soviets out of Kabul; we could also reach Moscow."

And the deadly game of checkmate continues—one month after Noorani's statement to the Pakistani National Assembly, the United States rushed one hundred Stingers to Pakistan. The portable antiaircraft missiles are designed to be fired on one shoulder. The shipment also included Sidewinder air-to-air missiles. "In response to repeated violations of Pakistan's airspace and territory by Communist aircraft operating from bases in Afghanistan," said Robert Smalley, a State Department official, "President Reagan has approved an expedited delivery to Pakistan of Sidewinder and Stinger missiles and technical assistance aimed at shoring up Pakistan's ability to detect and deal with these air threats." The U.S. ambassador to Pakistan, Deane Hinton, went further: "Pakistan is not alone at this time; nor will Pakistan be alone, if, God forbid, the situation were to worsen."

Not willing to gamble on direct U.S. assistance, Pakistan's military stays on the alert. "We know we can't rely on the U.S. to intervene directly if the situation does get worse," said one politician.

This Pakistani preparedness became apparent my second day in Peshawar when the muezzin's call summoning the faithful at 5:00 A.M. to the mosque 300 yards from the house was drowned out by the deafening roar of low-flying jet fighters over the city's rooftops, a sound that was to be an accompaniment to most days there.

Unable to sleep because of the din outside, I dressed and, glaze-eyed, made my way downstairs in search of Abdul Hai and, I hoped, some tea. I was met by Hamid and Tor, hair tousled and wet, as were their clothes, from "our ablutions" before prayer. The Koran's exhortation that Muslims wash arms, head, genitals, and feet before each of their five daily prayer sessions has always seemed impractical to me as Islam is invariably practiced in countries where water is anything but plentiful. "The Koran does say we may use dust to cleanse ourselves when water isn't available," said Hamid, ever eager to explain Islam to an interested party. But today there was ample water, and the bathroom looked as if the boys had been swimming in it.

Helping Abdul Hai lay the table for a breakfast of fried eggs and *nan*, I received another lesson as I began stacking the bread onto a plate. "Stop," said Tor; "the *nan* must all face upward. Otherwise, it is a sign of disrespect to God, who has given us this food." During the meal, Tor invited me to visit the Afghan hospital, Ebneseena-E-Balkhi, where he had done much of his paramedic training. "Not before she buys some Pakistani clothes," said Wakil, walking into the room and helping himself to tea. "Her hair this color makes her stand out less than last year, but the clothes will help even more." At Wakil's suggestion, I had dyed my hair and eyebrows a rather shocking—to me, at least—black before coming. Bright red hair never goes uncommented on in Asia, and even in Pakistan, NIFA wanted me to keep as low a profile as possible.

The *shalwar kameezes*, loose-fitting pants and long tunics, we purchased were similar to the baggy pajamas worn by the men except they were in feminine prints instead of the solid pastels they wore. We also stopped off at an Afghan tailor to have another of the men's outfits made up for me in light khaki, a color that blended in well with the rocks of Afghanistan. Wakil added a rough cotton turban and *patou* to my packages before he considered the shopping expedition complete.

As the temperature had now reached 110 degrees and it was still only 10.30 A.M., I decided to change into my new clothes, which were considerably cooler than my Western ones. Leaving the house for the second time that morning, we headed to Ebneseena hospital in NIFA's blue minivan. The sixty-bed hospital is housed in a small two-story building with the overflow in a large, stifling marquee outside. With a proprietary air, Tor began his tour with a flourish, which was supplemented by various doctors as we walked through their departments. "Dysentery, malaria, heatstroke, possible cerebral thrombosis," said Tor, reading the charts hanging on the ends of the metal beds so crowded together they almost touched. "Osteomylitis, typhoid fever . . ."

"Typhoid fever!" I interrupted. "Shouldn't this patient be isolated?"

"Possibly, but they don't have the space, and he probably isn't infectious anymore."

We changed wards and entered one filled with war wounded. A young man, who Tor told me was nineteen, grinned at me as I squeezed past his bed and then shot out his hand to clasp mine. He hung on tightly and alternatively giggled and grinned while I learned his medical history. He'd been a freedom fighter, fighting since he was sixteen, until a bullet in his brain had completely paralyzed his right side. A Norwegian relief agency had flown him to Oslo, but their leading neurosurgeons were unable to remove the bullet. It would be there permanently and so would the resulting brain damage, which had left him with the mental age of a toddler. Now he was back at Ebneseena, while his relatives, who had lost everything when they fled Afghanistan, decided what to do with a teenager labeled untreatable. Prone on his cot and seemingly weak, the boy gripped my hand with surprising strength. As I tried to move on, Tor had to force open the hand that was clamped around mine. The youth giggled as we said good-bye.

The next room housed four amputees, all mine wounds. One of the leading causes of injury in Afghanistan, they were identifiable without reading their medical charts—the sheets covering their beds were flat where the shape of one leg or two should have been. The room's only ambulatory occupant was a man built like a blacksmith. Said Mohammad Raza, deputy commander for the Harakat party, was from Kunduz Province. He was naked to the waist, and his chest and massive shoulders glistened with sweat. His right arm was encased from elbow to shoulder in a primitive leather and iron brace that looked as if it had been forged by the smithy he could have been. The arm had been shattered by machine gun fire three years ago, and another hospital in Peshawar had attempted to graft a bone from his leg to repair it, but the graft hadn't taken. Since then he had been a Dashaka gunner, using a weapon he said he could operate with one hand. But the continual excruciating pain had finally driven him back to Peshawar for further medical help. Ebneseena saw only one option at this stage, amputation, and Raza refused to agree. "With one arm people look at you differently in the *Jihad*; they treat you like an invalid and don't want you close to the enemy," said Raza. Distance from the enemy was something he wouldn't accept. Now age fifty-five, he had lost two of five sons to this war. "I want the Soviets to keep paying for the deaths of my sons."

He thrust the X-ray of his arm at me. There was a four-inch section of humerus bone missing. When I looked up, Raza was removing the brace, fumbling with the buckles with his left hand. Freeing his injured arm, he began to massage it; the iron struts of the brace had deeply indented the skin and must have added to his discomfort. Then, without warning, he suddenly swiveled the limb, and as though there were a universal joint installed halfway between his elbow and his shoulder, it turned a floppy 360 degrees. He laughed at my intake of breath, but his mouth quickly reshaped to a grimace as the pain shot through him. As he used his good arm to steady himself, a wave of nausea swept over me.

"I'm sorry, but I have to leave," I told Tor as I moved out into the corridor. Outside, I suddenly went cold and beads of sweat broke out on my forehead. I started to shake and the hallway went dark. Tor grabbed me before I slumped to the floor, and half-carried and half-dragged me to the waiting van.

"I think it was the heat," I said a few minutes later when the trembling had ceased. After all, in the course of my career, I had seen bodies more mangled than the ones that I had seen today. "No, I think you're nervous about the trip inside," replied Tor. "Well, anybody going into a war zone is going to be apprehensive," I told him. "But if I fainted every time I'd come under fire in Israel, I'd have died of fright a long time ago." And although I had been nervous driving in from El Salvador's airport to the capital along the same near-deserted route the American nuns had taken when they were kidnapped and then murdered, I had still traveled around the country in both government- and guerrilla-held territories.

Sitting in the hospital parking lot, I realized that those few hours at Ebneseena spent looking at other people's pain had made me see with clarity once again that war is deceiving. It's easy from behind the carapace of a reporter to see war as it is seen on film, dramatic but distanced. Even when one is in the turbulence of battle, adrenaline, excitement give it a dreamlike quality. It is only far removed from the battlefield that war is most real—in the hospital wards filled with shattered bodies, around a family dining table with its empty chair. War was stripped of its glamour again this morning.

Wrung out from the heat of the day, the visit to Ebneseena, and jet lag, I begged off from more touring and went back to my room to unwind.

A few hours later there was a tap at the door. "I've been asked to tell you Pir Gailani will receive you tonight," said a driver I hadn't seen before, "at 7.30 P.M." He made it a statement, not a request. I was left with a feeling that I had just received a royal command, and I was unclear whether I was meant to interview the Resistance leader, have dinner with him, or join him for the Muslim teetotaller equivalent of cocktails. At 7:20 P.M. a cream-colored jeep came to fetch me, and after a few minutes' drive, I learned it was dinner. In the reception room of NIFA's headquarters, which was also Gailani's home, a servant offered me a Pepsi or a Fanta. The room didn't give me many clues about my host. The carpet covering the terrazzo floor, the locally made sofa and armchairs conveyed nothing of the wealth this man had once enjoyed. The walls were decorated only with a calligraphic painting I guessed to be a quotation from the Koran and a large map of Afghanistan over the mantelpiece of a gas fire. Otherwise the room was bare. Only the bank of three phones gave a suggestion that matters of urgency took place here.

Five minutes after I arrived, Gailani and his youngest son, Mohammad, appeared. Pir Gailani looked just like his party's poster, which shows him wearing Western clothes, an anomaly among the other Afghan leaders. That night he was wearing Afghan dress, but his silver hair, pointed beard, and trim mustache were the same as on the bills I'd seen plastered around the neighborhood. He was an older version of his graduate student son, Hamed, and had the same hands and surprising fair skin. But there was a formality, an elegance of bearing that seemed to affect even the arch of his eyebrows, and a quiet but definite presence that set him apart and suggested a diplomat in a gracious milieu, not the arena of war. His youngest son, Mohammad, was his physical antithesis. Slim and dark, he had sculpted good looks that would make him a welcome addition at any society gathering. Instead, at twenty-six, he was NIFA's deputy chief of staff. Clean-shaven and initially shy, he looked at first meeting to be a boy soldier, a fact he may well be aware of as it is rumored that he has added two years to his actual age.

The other two dinner guests were Wakil and Brigadier Rahmatullah Safi, a career soldier in his fifties, whose military background reflects the modern history of Afghanistan. Trained in the Soviet Union in the fifties, he also spent time with U.S. special forces at Fort Bragg, North Carolina, and in Britain's Special Air Service and speaks excellent Russian and English. At the time of the Communist coup, he was chief of Special Forces of the Royal Afghan Army. Imprisoned in Pul-i-Charki prison for a year, he was tortured so severely he still won't discuss that period of his life. Today, he is military adviser to NIFA, and in charge of *Mujahideen* training.

Such a high-powered dinner party is a war reporter's delight. Here I was with a religious warlord, his deputy chief of staff, one of his most experienced commanders, and his logistics expert, but "No," said Gailani. "No interviews tonight, this evening is purely social." I silently gnashed my teeth. We made perfunctory conversation, and I began to feel I had shed my persona with my Western clothes. Somewhere between the kebabs and rice and dessert, Safi switched the conversation to Pushto (one of the two main languages spoken in Afghanistan, the other being Dari, a form of Farsi), and suddenly the discussion came to life. I played with my apple, feeling invisible in the way I imagine Muslim women have always felt in the company of their menfolk. Twenty minutes later, Wakil translated for me. "Safi is saying you're a woman; you'll be all alone with the *Mujahideen;* there'll be no other Westerner with you. . . . And also it's a hard trip . . . maybe we should reconsider." He looked at me questioningly. I willed myself to stay calm. Had I come all this way only to have them change their minds? Suddenly, I realized the purpose of the dinner—I was the one being interviewed.

Before I could respond, Mohammad began to regale me with tales about the American television team who had gone in shortly before. "Many of them turned back, one after the other. And those who did all told us before that they ran fifteen kilometers a day. Several of them went running every day in Peshawar. There was a woman with them; she cried from the physical hardship and asked to be sent back."

Wakil joined in, "If we take you, it will be to Khost, where there is a major offensive going on now. To get there we have to cross several mountains on foot. There are two—I'll be frank with you—I have grown to hate; they are bad."

I looked at him. "Hell, I don't know if I'm up to this trip," I said, aware that I was not as fit as I had been the previous year. My heavy workload at the magazine before leaving had scarcely permitted me time to sleep, let alone to visit a gym on a regular basis. Suddenly, every overweight pound felt like ten. "All I know is that what I may lack in physical strength, I make up for in determination," I said, wondering whether the project I had spent so much time planning was ending before it had begun.

Mohammad changed his tack. "You don't need to be in the frontline; you just want to see the country, no?"

"No." I hoped I said it patiently. "You can't write about war unless you see it."

They switched back to Pushto. I tried to guess from their faces how the discussion was going. I couldn't tell, but it seemed to me that Safi dominated the conversation, which wasn't a good sign. Fifteen minutes later they turned to English again. "Mohammad is in Peshawar to get fresh military supplies," said Wakil. "When he returns to Khost, you can go with him." The entire discussion had only lasted about an hour, but I felt drained. And I wondered who had had the deciding vote. "Pir Gailani," said Wakil later, although he didn't say what had changed their minds.

Next morning, Sunday, Wakil joined Hamid, Tor, and me for breakfast. "You are leaving tomorrow," he announced; "pack today, it's a 5 A.M. start." Khost, in Paktia Province, sits astride a major route to Kabul. It was also part of a main supply route for the *Mujahideen*, which the Soviets had been trying to close. The region had come under attack several weeks before, when the Soviets launched an all-out offensive, the largest since the war began, to clear Khost of *Mujahideen*. A reported fifteen thousand troops had been moved in, including the elite Spetsnaz commandoes, the one element of the Soviet army that the freedom fighters truly respect. The fighting had been so intense, NIFA's men were low on ammunition, which was why Mohammad had returned. Mohammad wasn't going with us, however, as the expected ammunition supply had not arrived. "It's happened a lot recently: material we were relying on didn't make it here." The CIA's pipeline was apparently leaking more profusely than before.

Halfway through the meal, Safi joined us. A loud, blustery man, his handlebar mustache jiggled as he laughed, which was often. Tearing a sheet of paper from my notebook, he began to hurriedly sketch a map of the route we would take the next day. He addressed Wakil: "You cross the first two mountains and then make your way to the *chaikhana* [teahouse]. Rest there until 5:00 P.M. Then take this route"—he stabbed the paper with his pen for emphasis, and I noticed he had the widest hands I had ever seen on a man. "Don't take the paved road; it's shorter, but it's heavily mined, and the Khost enemy artillery knows the road's location and angle—they shell it constantly. Your way is longer but safer. It's desert and rocks, a dried riverbed. There's nowhere to hide, so travel at night.

"Once you get close to our bases, the area is dangerous."

"Yes, and it's got my two enemy mountains, as well," said Wakil, trying to lighten the moment.

"Mountains are better," said Safi, all business. "There is water in the mountains and bushes to hide under if helicopters and planes come.

"The most important thing to remember is take the route overland, not the paved road."

Long after breakfast was finished, I sat at the table thinking about the following day. I realized that for the next three months beginning tomorrow, I would be solely in the company of men, and men, for the most part, who were not used to being in the company of women except those in their immediate family, and certainly not on the battlefield. Normally, as any soldier knows, friendships are forged very rapidly during war. But these were men who had never had women as friends. And although this was hardly the time for thoughts of sisterhood, I was a woman who had been born assuming I had equal rights with members of the opposite sex. Even when I was a child, no one had ever told me my world was circumscribed because I was a female. How would I respond if this all-male Muslim movement designated me a second-class citizen and decided I was not worthy of their acceptance on the basis of my gender alone? And if we got beyond that hurdle, how would they react to me? We would be living in such close proximity that privacy would be nonexistent. Would I inhibit them, would they avoid me, or would they resent me? From previous experiences I was aware how tensions can build when men come under fire. And I was aware, too, that several male journalists on protracted trips inside Afghanistan had fallen afoul of *Mujahideen* when tempers flared because of personalities that didn't mesh or clashes of culture. Sometimes fights had broken out because foreigners had unwittingly but repeatedly offended Afghan mores. One cameraman raised Muslim ire by stripping off to bathe in rivers in view of the *Mujahideen*, something none of the modest freedom fighters, who are instructed by the Koran not to expose themselves from waist to knee, would have done. A photographer had his cameras smashed when he tried to photograph Afghan women despite frequent warnings not to. As a woman, I was aware there were myriad ways I could offend; I only hoped my earlier homework would help me avoid the most offensive faux pas. But although I wanted to make sure I wouldn't tread on cultural toes, I knew there were edges to my personality that might get me into trouble. I remembered a conversation I had had before leaving the States. "You are going to drive a military commander crazy," a former veteran told me. "Traveling with the Resistance, you'll have to follow orders as if you were one of them or risk getting your head blown off. You're far too independent, endlessly curious, constantly challenging, all traits that make for a lousy foot soldier. I can see you following orders for a week, for a story, but for three months?"

Sitting there as the Peshawar sun climbed, making the room ovenlike, I was less concerned about whether I'd make a good foot soldier, than whether I'd be able to make it on foot for that period of time over Afghanistan's tough terrain. Afghanistan's high mountain passes had defeated much fitter people than I. I tried not to dwell on the physical problems. But my mind began to play one maddening note: "Out of the heat of Peshawar, into the heat of war."

3

A War on Two Fronts

Monday 4 A.M.: I fumbled in the dark for my traveling clock as its alarm insistently beeped. I had set it for an hour before we were due to leave on purpose. No morning owl, I was the type whose eyes didn't really open, and who clumsily bounced off furniture, before 8 A.M. The hour was meant to give me time to become compos mentis, to make one last equipment check when I was wide awake to spot whether anything vital was missing. Once inside Afghanistan, camera batteries, flashlight bulbs, contact lens solution—the vital detritus of twentieth-century existence—would be impossible to replace. Even in sizable villages, paper and pens were rarities since the war. If you didn't carry something in with you on your back, you did without. Despite the precautionary check, I was pretty certain that I had omitted nothing crucial. I had packed carefully the night before, finding that the mechanical task pacified the on-edge feeling that

most journalists experience the night before going on a dangerous assignment. I knew from past experiences that my most tense
moments would come in those countdown hours. Once you begin
organizing, running through the minutiae that makes up the
whole, that feeling, for me at least, disappears. There is a point
in the last-minute planning where one crosses an emotional line.
From that stage on, one is in a kind of twilight zone. In your
planning, you've chosen where you want to go, whom you want
to talk to, and whom you want to trust. You've made the best
choices you can to eliminate careless risks, and you've made them
with all your faculties. You know the points where you can back
out, until that last stage, when you can't because there is no place
to go. You hope that your preparations have been thorough
enough to carry you through, but from now on in, the outcome is
mostly outside your control. At that stage, all you can do is relax.
I remembered a conversation with New York photographer Ken
Silverman, a Central American veteran who has had a number of
his colleagues die under fire, in which we agreed we felt the same
way before such assignments. He told me, "Once you've done all
the advance detail work, you are in fate's hands. All you can do
is breathe deeply, and relax, and just make sure all of your senses
are operating. I know if I'm unlucky, I'm dead. But I can't allow
myself to think about that." Ken and I both knew that it is after
the assignment is over, when one does an action-replay and realizes how close some of the calls may have been, that the fear
really hits you.

Getting up early that morning also allowed me to take a long
shower and shampoo my hair. I knew I wouldn't get the chance
to do either again until we returned to Peshawar. I was toweling
dry my hair at 4:30 when there was a knock at the door. Opening
it, I found a grinning Tor and Hamid, both wearing ammunition
belts around their chests and toting folding commando-style AK-
47s. After a lifetime of rising before dawn to pray, they appeared
to have inner alarm clocks and never had trouble waking no matter what the hour. "Good morning, good morning, you're up; that
is good," they chorused. I groaned. Their cheerfulness was repel-
lent, and I told them so. Ignoring me, they inspected my male
attire and found me passable, if somewhat amusing. "But you
forgot the *lungi*," said Tor, sweeping the ten-foot-long turban off
the bed and wrapping it around my head. Since I had never seen

Tor wear anything on his head other than a *chador*—a yard-square piece of cotton—that he wore Arab-style like a *kaffiyeh*, his only practice must have been when he was bandaging head wounds. And he certainly wound the turban tight enough to stop any bleeding, and even the circulation to my brain. Hamid tied it again, pulling the turban low down over my eyes. "We want to leave as little of your face showing as possible," he said. "Then with this loose end, you cover your nose and mouth. It will keep out the dust, and hide the fact that you don't have a beard." "Yes, but she can't eat breakfast with it like that," said Tor.

I didn't want breakfast, I retorted, my stomach resisting the thought of Abdul Hai's greasy fried eggs at that time in the morning. Wakil was waiting for us in the dining room. "I'll just have tea," I said, sitting down. "No, you must eat, and eat a lot," insisted Wakil. "You don't know when you will get the chance again once you are inside."

That comment aside, the mood during breakfast was festive, Tor cracking jokes and Hamid and Tor teasing Wakil. As they bantered back and forth, it occurred to me that all three of them were behaving as if they were about to leave on vacation instead of enter a war zone. I said as much.

"You are surprised?" asked Tor. "You think we like living in Pakistan? You think we like being refugees?"

"For us, going to Afghanistan gives us pleasure, even if there is fighting," said Hamid. "We didn't want to leave. We'd go home tomorrow, if the Russians left."

"Is the van packed?" asked Wakil, changing the subject. The curtained minibus that was to take us to the border had been restyled for *Mujahideen* convenience. Stow areas had been installed under the seats, so that weapons, ammunition, and other questionable supplies such as journalists' backpacks could be hidden away. When the Pakistani military and militia manning the checkpoints to the border inspected these vehicles, as they frequently did, a foreigner might pass anything but close scrutiny, but a reporter's notebook or tape recorder left casually on a seat had flagged their presence on more than one occasion.

"Sit there," Wakil told me, pointing to the back seat of the van. "Unless the Pakistanis come right inside, it is unlikely that they'll spot you in the back.

"I can't come with you," he said, shaking my hand. "I would

like to, but I'm needed elsewhere." There was no further explanation. He hugged each boy, kissing them on both cheeks. "God be
with you. All of you," he said, as we climbed on board.

Poking his head inside the van, he added, "You'll be picking
up the commander, Abdul, who is leading this trip before you
leave the city. You will join other *Mujahideen* at the border." And
then as an afterthought, "Make sure you keep the curtains tightly
closed, particularly when you come to the checkpoints."

Fifteen minutes after leaving, we stopped at a large sand-
colored adobe house surrounded by a thick wall about ten feet
high. Abdul was waiting for us. Short and wiry, he greeted us
briefly and jumped into the front seat next to the driver. Hamid
stowed the commander's Kalashnikov and a supply of hand grenades under my seat. "Cover her feet," ordered Abdul in heavily
accented English as he glanced back into the van. "Her boots look
too new." Hamid threw a rough-woven, dirty blanket over my
legs. Its brillo pad texture scratched through the cotton of my
kameez.

It was now 6 A.M. and light. Even at that time, the temperature was beginning to rise; Peshawar was going to suffer through
another sweltering day. As we drove out of the city, a large fruit
and vegetable market was beginning to open, and the pungent
smell of rotting fruit mingled with the fumes of the delivery
trucks. We were heading south on the Kohat road, which would
take us through Bannu and onto Miramshah, the border town. A
journey of about 150 miles, it would take between seven and eight
hours, said Hamid, as the roads were so bad. Last year, this road
had been monitored by seven Pakistani checkpoints; now there
were sixteen such posts between Peshawar and Miramshah.
"Don't worry," said Tor when he saw my look of concern, "the
military are always sleeping, even during the day." I hoped he
was right.

We had left the city behind now. The single lane road, lined
with trees full of feathery yellow blossom, was still giving us a
relatively smooth ride. Tor had opened the windows and curtains
in the rear to give us some air. The vehicle was beginning to get
stuffy. "I close them before checkpoint," he said, as he did with
a start five minutes later. "Checkpoint," he hissed. I slumped in
my seat, arms folded across my chest. Hamid draped the turban
end over my face, completely covering it as if I were trying to

close out the light to sleep. He needn't have bothered. Two Pakistani militia, uniforms dapper, languorously waved us through without even stopping us. They weren't sleeping, but they weren't alert, either. Tor smiled. "No problem, checkpost," he said with a shrug. "They get much tougher as you get closer to the border," added Hamid, always the more cautious.

Soon what little green there had been in the parched countryside disappeared. The arid scenery became monotonous. Both boys settled down to doze. I envied them the ability to catnap at any time. We began to climb toward the Kohat Pass. Now the terrain was beginning to resemble that of Arizona. Rock outcroppings gave way to towering cliffs. The rich reds, oranges, and browns of the crag faces gave an impression of permanent sunset. It was in this area at the turn of the century that the Pathans had kidnapped the unmarried daughter of a ranking British officer and held her for ransom. Several weeks later, when her release had been negotiated, she refused to go home. The resulting scandal rocked the stuffy British community. Exactly why she chose to stay has been debated ever since. Pathans who tell a visitor the story insist their culture has always prized a woman's honor; she was merely bored with her very proper existence, they say. Whatever the reason, the British authorities made sure no other young lady would ever again be faced with such a choice. They decreed the entire region off-limits to foreigners, and it has stayed that way ever since. As an expatriate Brit, I was amused by the tale.

We had reached the top of the Kohat Pass. The checkpost on the summit had been signaled to me some distance back by a long line of traffic, mostly covered trucks, snaking up to its large memorial arch, which was built to commemorate British officers who had fallen in battle in the area. As we drove closer to the arch, I could clearly see the sign that read FOREIGNERS NOT PERMITTED IN THIS TERRITORY. "Don't worry," said Hamid after I nudged him awake in case I needed him to interpret for me. "This checkpost is mostly for the trucks. They are looking for smuggled goods—drugs, or fabrics, cigarettes from Kabul."

"From Kabul?"

"Yes, Kabul is like a free market; even now it is possible to buy many goods that you can't get in the rest of Afghanistan or even here in Pakistan. You should see the Russian soldiers when they arrive; they go crazy with buying. In Kabul they can find all sorts of things that are not available in the Soviet Union." I wondered how high the smuggling profits had to be to risk driving a truck on a regular basis through wartorn Afghanistan.

Finally, it was our turn. A Pakistani officer pulled us over, while four of his colleagues peered under the tarpaulin of the truck ahead of us. I held my breath as the man spoke to our driver and cursorily glanced inside the van. Then he waved us on. I exhaled loudly. Our driver, Ismaiel, who didn't speak English, waved back at us as if to confirm how easy it was to deceive the Pakistani authorities. Then, still exalted with our success, he floored the accelerator and began to race down the Pass, taking the hairpin bends as if he had been racing in the Indy 500 for years. The Kohat Pass, a tortured and twisted road with plunging ravines, was dotted with signs exhorting motorists not to overtake. Everyone ignored them, including Ismaiel. He also ignored the signs stating SPEED THRILLS BUT ALSO KILLS, but that may have been because they were in Urdu and English. I tried to give him the benefit of the doubt as I kept fingers and toes crossed that we would survive his driving. I had not expected to worry about my physical safety while still in Pakistan.

Shortly after, the commander stopped the van and joined us in the back. "His stomach is sick," explained Tor, as Abdul tried to stretch out on one of the free double seats. After Ismaiel's Grand Prix exhibition I wasn't surprised. And I remembered from the previous year how many of the Afghan freedom fighters, more used to traveling on foot than driving, had suffered from motion sickness. I commiserated with him, but he ignored me. "No problem; he brave *Mujahid*," said Tor dismissingly. By now the road surface had deteriorated considerably, and for long stretches disappeared altogether. The van bucked and skidded crazily every time we hit such a section but Ismaiel maintained the same speed. How many tires did the Resistance go through, I wondered, if all their vehicles were driven in this fashion over roads like these? The dust we churned up as we bounced across the pebbled surface poured through every chink in the van, leaving a thin film over everything, and sticking to the sweat that covered us.

The seven-hour drive was beginning to seem interminable. I tried to brace myself between the side of the van and the back seat, so that I wouldn't be dislodged every time we hit a pothole. My head had already smashed against the roof of the van twice in the last thirty minutes, and we still had four more hours to go. The position I finally achieved guarded against certain concussion but meant my left leg was constantly slammed against the side of the vehicle, and I knew the bruises would be colorful. If we had to go through any checkpoints on roads such as these, I questioned how I was supposed to feign sleep when I couldn't even guarantee staying on my seat. I longed for the drive to end, and if I felt like that, I wondered what the journey must be like for the severely wounded freedom fighters who have to travel this route before they receive any medical attention.

Now we were passing through salt flats. The salt glistened like snow in the unrelenting sun, and I was glad the van was curtained. "Forget your sunglasses," Wakil had told me before leaving. "The *Mujahideen* don't wear them, so you can't. They will immediately mark you as a Westerner." But that wasn't a ruling that only affected foreigners. Tor was one of the few Afghans I had seen wearing glasses. Myopic without them, he nevertheless left them behind when he went on operations inside Afghanistan. "How did he manage to see to shoot?" "I manage," he said, patting his machine gun. He knew that a burst of automatic fire from an AK-47 would cut down anything in a wide path and needed none of the marksmanship skills required by the Afghans using the outdated but deadly accurate British Enfield 303 sniper rifles. Tor had chosen to travel to Afghanistan shortsightedly after he had twice been dragged out of vans by the Pakistani authorities and accused of being a *feranghi*. Their error was understandable; with his neat little beard and glasses, he did appear more French or Hispanic than Afghan.

We passed through the salt flats, and just at their edge, we were met by a yellow pickup coming in the opposite direction. "Escort vehicle," said Hamid tersely. We stopped long enough for the commander to swap vehicles. As he climbed into the pickup, I saw there were four armed men sitting in the back. The pickup stayed in sight of us, but whenever we reached a checkpoint, it appeared to be traveling independently. Three checkpoints after the yellow pickup joined us, the Pakistani militia flagged us down. They waved us to the side of the road. Once again, I sprang into my now familiar dozing pose and covered my face. I heard the officer question Ismaiel, and his short, abrupt responses. Then the side door of the van slid open. Hamid and Tor moved forward as if to greet him, but also I imagined to block me from his view. They talked for two or three minutes. Then the door slid shut again, and Ismaiel started the engine. As we drove on, Tor and Hamid broke out in applause. "Okay, come out, come out," Tor called to me, pulling the turban off my face. We had passed the thirteenth checkpost. Three more to go. There was less distance between them now that we were closer to the border. In between checkpoints, we stopped briefly for Abdul to rejoin us in the van.

Tor handed me his Kalashnikov. "Hold it with your legs," he said, placing it between my knees. He thought the gun would be an authentic prop in my pose as a freedom fighter. But the AK-47 was much more hindrance than help as the van bucketed over the rutted track. I just didn't have enough hands to hold on, keep my turban in place, and grip the gun, which was too heavy to keep upright with only my legs. The sharp metal edges of the magazine dug into my flesh as we hit every bump. I kept thinking how much easier it must have been for male journalists, who could at least grow beards, and not have to worry about covering their faces with turbans at every stop.

My discomfort was suffered silently. Under the circumstances, I didn't think it wise to complain. After all, we hadn't even reached the border, and I didn't want to give the impression that I was another female who would end up crying to go home.

Hamid broke into my reverie. "This is Miramshah," he said. "On the right is the runway where the two helicopter gunships landed two weeks ago." The MI-24s, piloted by defecting Afghan pilots, had surprised the Pakistanis as they had come over to the other side with no prior contact or warning, a dangerous gamble in which they risked being shot down by Pakistani missiles or forced down by F-16s. The West was delighted; it would be the first time they would be able to inspect one of these gunships intact. The Soviets, however, were insisting that the pilots had been lost and were demanding both the return of the helicopters and of the pilots and crew. The Pakistanis were being diplomatically silent on the issue. But unofficially, the defecting Afghans had been hustled to the capital, Islamabad, for lengthy debriefings. The helicopters were still in Miramshah under strictest security. There was no sign of them from the airfield perimeter road on which we were traveling.

"One more checkpoint to go and then we are in Afghanistan,"

Hamid suddenly said, beaming. I was relieved. Even the thought of a forced march seemed more pleasurable than being buffeted around in this suspensionless mobile oven.

We stopped at the sixteenth and final checkpoint. The uniformed militia walked around the vehicle, peered through the windows, and waved us on. Hamid and Tor began applauding again; the commander joined in. "Now we are in Afghanistan," said Abdul. I felt my body relax, and I found it ironic that just as the Afghans looked forward to returning to their country even though it was at war, so, too, was I feeling less tension now that we were here than I had en route.

Less than five minutes later, we came to an abrupt halt. Outside I could hear shouting and yelling. Through a gap in the curtains, a crowd of about fifty turbaned men was visible. "Sleep; sleep," someone barked at me. I did as I was told. The voices continued, getting louder and angrier. No one in our vehicle moved. Someone began thumping on the front of the van. Then a man clambered up on the driver's side of the cab, bellowing the whole time at Abdul and Ismaiel. I heard the cab door open and realized Ismaiel had climbed down.

What the hell was going on? I had no idea, and obviously this wasn't the time to ask. My first assumption was that we had encountered a group of refugees leaving Afghanistan, and perhaps the van had clipped one of their animals or, worse, a child. But I certainly hadn't felt us hit anything.

Suddenly, the van began to rock, slightly at first, then more dramatically, as the crowd increased the tempo. Christ! I thought. They're going to turn us over. I partially sat up, the turban end falling away from my face as I did. Without moving, Tor said softly, "Sleep." I slumped in my seat again, but not before I had caught a glimpse of the faces staring in at us through the front windscreen. I twitched the turban back into place. As the motion of the van increased, the commander also got out. A roar went up as he did so. I began to feel afraid for his safety. The guns were all in the van, and in an angry crowd this size, they wouldn't have done much good as many of the mob were armed themselves. I remembered the reports of drivers being lynched by angry peasants after traffic accidents in remote areas of undeveloped countries.

For a brief moment I even entertained thoughts that this was a tribal kidnapping. But I dismissed that idea almost as soon as it came to me. It did happen on occasion in this region, but kidnappers, although inclined to violence, were unlikely to be frenzied like this horde.

Hamid and Tor also must have become concerned about Abdul and Ismaiel's safety. I felt them brush past me and heard them get out.

I was left alone in the van. My emotions were swinging almost as violently as the vehicle. On the one hand I was frightened, and the fear was compounded by being totally unable to understand what was going on. And on the other I felt like some bit player in a bad farce. All hell was breaking out around me, and my only role was to pretend to sleep through it. Anyone observing my performance must have thought I was deaf or comatose.

A window halfway down the van was prized open. Curiosity got the better of me. I looked up. Several men were jostling one another to look in. They stared at me, then laughed. I glared back, and then dropped my head.

The rocking and the shouting abruptly subsided. The side door opened, and the man who had first bellowed at Ismaiel got in. Walking up to me, he yanked the turban from my face. "Come," he glowered in English, before grabbing the machine gun. I didn't move.

Where the hell was Abdul, or Hamid and Tor for that matter?

In answer to the question I hadn't spoken aloud, the commander put his head round the door. "It's okay; come," he repeated. I did as he said.

The crowd's clamoring began again when I left the van. I recognized the word *feranghi* several times. It was obvious from his expression that the man who had ordered me to leave the van was expecting a foreigner, but that I was a female seemed a complete surprise.

I pushed my way to Abdul, who appeared very small in the crowd. "What's going on?" I demanded.

"Arrest," he said, "we are all arrested. These men are Pakistani militia; this is new checkpost." I was stunned. Of all the lurid explanations that had run through my mind, arrest wasn't one of them. Wasn't this Afghan territory? Did new checkposts sprout overnight like mushrooms? The answer to the first question was probably, but there were no neat fences demarcating any border.

And, yes, I later learned, checkposts came and went as the Pakistani authorities deemed them necessary. This one was brand-new.

The militia officer didn't speak English. Abdul translated, "They are taking us to Miramshah to be charged. Hamid and Tor will remain here." I looked at the boys for the first time, and they stared back at me sadly and suddenly very young. They were under armed guard in a red open truck. There was no sign of our yellow escort vehicle.

Someone prodded me in the back. Another man grabbed my arm. He nodded in the direction of a green pickup. Our arresting officer got into the driver's seat and gestured for me to go around to the passenger's side. Abdul squeezed in beside me. As the driver started the engine, three plain-clothes militia, armed with 303 rifles and the AK-47 I'd been holding, climbed into the back. Almost immediately, Abdul and the driver, a thin, tall man with coarse features, began to harangue each other. The commander's tirade seemed to have a pattern to it. His outbursts would last a minute or two; then he would drop his voice, reach across me to grab the driver's arm, and begin cajoling. The driver violently shook off Abdul's arm, and the harangue would begin again. I sat in between them, ignored and totally uncomprehending. Their arms flashed back and forth across my face so violently I began to think the exchange would end in my nose being broken.

The wrangling continued for thirty minutes as we drove back in the direction we had come but along a different route. We passed tents of newly arrived refugees, and here and there a few horses and donkeys optimistically searching out somewhere to graze. Abdul suddenly broke off to snarl in English, "They are corrupt, they all want money." He went on to explain that he was trying to bribe the driver to let us go. "If the price is right, they always agree. But this one is being difficult. He says he can't take money, but his boss does. We must speak to his boss because if this man agrees on a price, he says he will be accused of taking more than his share. So we are going to see his boss in Miramshah."

My head was splitting from tension and the commotion, my bladder was bursting, we hadn't had a pit stop for more than five hours, and I was angry—angry at being caught so close to my goal, and angry that months of planning had come to an abrupt halt before the project had really begun.

Forty-five minutes later we reached Miramshah bazaar. We turned down a narrow lane and began a tour of the labyrinthine streets of the market. "Now what are we doing?" I asked Abdul.

"Looking for the driver's boss."

We stopped outside an open-fronted shoe store that seemed to be on its lunch break. The driver disappeared inside. Ten minutes later he reappeared, shaking his head. "He isn't here; we must continue to look for him," Abdul translated. We continued the tour of the bazaar without success. "Maybe he's back at the barracks," said the driver, heading in that direction. We parked outside a large fortlike military base, Idak Gate, while the driver went inside. "He says we are to stay here, and he will bring his boss out to speak to us," Abdul explained.

The driver returned with three gold-braided army officers. Looking sheepish he explained that his boss wasn't there but that the political officer in charge of the entire region was, and he'd been informed I had been arrested at the border and was on my way here. We were ordered inside the barracks.

Abdul and I were ushered into the office of Mr. Rahmatullah, the political *Niab Tehsildar* (administrator) of Ghulam Khan Tehsil, according to the sign above his door. Mr. Rahmatullah was seated at a small desk covered with a dark green cloth; the papers on it flapped gently as the ceiling fan whipped them each time it rotated. He scratched away at the one in front of him with a nib pen, which he dipped frequently into an ink well. He was a handsome man with light green eyes and fair hair who was obviously a Pathan and would have looked at home on either side of the border. His windowless office was lit by a single bare bulb no stronger than forty watts. Around the edge of the room, about twenty turbaned men waited in the dim light, occasionally spitting into a corner spittoon.

Abdul and I were left standing in front of him. He addressed the commander first in Pushto. Then Rahmatullah spoke to two men standing in the door, before switching to near-fluent English. "We are putting him in custody," he told me. Abdul was led away. I felt very lonely once he had left. "Sit down." The political officer pointed to the chair nearest his desk, which lacked most of its woven reed seat. I perched on the edge, not wishing to add a touch of slapstick to the proceedings by falling through it. I was already feeling very foolish sitting there dressed as a man.

"Name?" I told him.

"Father's name?" I watched him write "Daughter of Charles Goodwin" at the top of the form.

"Nationality?"

"American."

"Ah, America the superpower."

"Under the circumstances, I think Pakistan is the superpower, don't you?"

He smiled.

"Come with me," he said, interrogation completed. I followed him outside to a car parked nearby. We drove to a block at the far edge of the barracks. "It is time for my lunch; will you join me?" he asked, ushering me inside. A servant came in, spread a cloth on the floor, and laid out several dishes. I declined, asking only for a toilet and tea, in that order.

"Why don't you take off that turban," he suggested when I reentered the room. "It's probably very hot." Before he could begin eating, the telephone rang. He talked briefly and hung up. "That was our local Intelligence," he said. "They'd heard I had a foreigner and wanted your name. Intelligence will inform Special Branch in Peshawar. I am sorry, but matters are now out of my hands." He didn't say so, but I got the impression any negotiations for my release had just been curtailed. If Mr. Rahmatullah had been open to bribes, he no longer was. He continued to eat lunch.

"You will stay here for a day or two; then we will return you to Peshawar," said Rahmatullah. "After that, who knows?

"Now, where to put you is a problem." I assumed he meant that since his barracks jail was for men only, he didn't know what to do with a female prisoner. "Maybe you had better stay with my cook's family . . . no, he's too dirty. Perhaps we'd better put you in the Circuit House."

When I saw the Circuit House, once used for visiting judges, I realized there were advantages to being a female journalist. The low stone building was set behind a high *purdah* wall. The small lawn was surrounded on three sides with narrow flower beds of dahlias, night blooming jasmine, hollyhocks, and a rosebush with a solitary perfect red rose. Only the clanging shut of the large metal gates was a reminder of why I was there. The house staff came out to stare, but they scuttled back inside after my armed escort shouted at them. I was shown to a room at the end of the house. A guard gestured me to go inside and banged the door shut behind me. The room contained two metal single beds. The window was painted over and locked. But there was an attached bathroom with a real bath, although the place was filthy and the water intermittent.

I sat down on the bed and wondered what happened next and when. It was only 3:00 P.M., and the rest of the day looked as if it were going to be very long. Patience had never been a virtue of mine. I had always loathed waiting, and my doctor, dentist, even my hairdresser were selected on the basis of how prompt or tardy they were. And I also abhorred not knowing, being kept in the dark on something. Now it looked as if I were about to get a crash course on how to handle both. I paced the room, fourteen steps long, twelve wide. Five minutes later I stopped. The monotony of pacing would drive me crazier sooner than just staring at the wall. I chose to sit, and as I did several flies settled on me. About to flap them away, I stopped myself. Hell, this was company, and it appeared to be as good as it would get. All I knew about flies was their annoyance factor. Now I started to watch them as keenly as an entomologist: their flight patterns, their interaction with one another. They even seemed to have a hierarchical system. An hour passed quickly, and I found myself even seeing a certain beauty in the flies. I laughed wryly. Always rather squeamish about insects, I wondered whether I would have felt so friendly if they had been cockroaches. Later in the bathroom, I found two small frogs bathing in a puddle caused by a leaky pipe under the sink. Hell, this was better than television. I settled down on the floor to observe their activities. Then I heard the door to the room open. I walked out of the bathroom, and I found a man I hadn't seen before.

"Why did you break the law?" he demanded, glowering at me. "Why did you come here? Who are you?"

"Who are you?" I repeated back to him, cutting into his stream of questions.

His voice rose. "It is a very bad thing what you have done. You can go to prison for three years." And then, as quickly as he had come, he left, slamming the door shut behind him.

I sat there, staring at the door, unnerved by his visit. I was aware that journalists occasionally had been arrested trying to reach Afghanistan. But to my knowledge, all had been released after a reprimand. I was beginning to wonder whether the Pakistanis were playing by different rules with me.

An hour later, Rahmatullah paid me a visit. He seemed aware of my previous visitor and apologized. "You are my guest, not prisoner," he said. "You are confined, not arrested." On another occasion, I might have been amused at his definitions. The day was beginning to take on an Alice in Wonderland feel.

"Tomorrow I will take your statement. For now, I have brought me something to read." He handed me two books, one about Bayazid Anseri, who, the title told me, was the sixteenth-century founder of Pushto prose and script. The other was titled *What Islam Gave to Humanity.* His selection was no more esoteric than my other activities that afternoon. I took them gratefully.

At 9:30 P.M. the mournful sound of a bugle playing *Taps* at the barracks reached me. Shortly afterward, exhausted, I climbed into bed. At 11:00 P.M., Rahmatullah returned. "I have come to visit you," he said. His arrival made me uneasy. Muslim men don't normally sit alone with women, and they certainly don't visit them at 11:00 P.M. I suddenly realized how vulnerable a lone woman was in this situation. I sat primly on the bed opposite him. Before he could say anything, I began to interview him on his wife. She's not educated, he replied, while informing me he had a Master's degree. "Uneducated women are good," he said; "they don't demand many things." He asked me whether I had a husband and then said, "Is it true that women are allowed to have friends in America?" It was clear what he meant by friends. I didn't like the turn of the conversation, but I was determined to keep talking, so I switched the subject to politics. I asked him his opinion of Soviet policy in the region. He looked embarrassed and didn't reply. I related mine to fill the silence. I longed to ask him to leave, but I wasn't sure what would happen if I offended him. Half an hour later, he excused himself and left. I decided he was harmless, just lonely. But I was relieved to see him go. I slept badly that night.

I kept wondering whether I would have any more unexpected visitors, and what had happened to my Afghan companions.

I was awake and up at 4:00 A.M. Shortly after nine, Rahmatullah arrived. "This is your statement; please sign."

"I haven't given one, and the document is in Urdu," I told him.

"Please sign," he repeated, handing me the paper. I signed the form, but under my name I added that since I could not understand the document's contents, I did not know what I had signed. "I will tell you," he said.

"But I still can't read it," I responded. Rahmatullah sighed. "I will translate it into English and return."

Two hours later the political officer still hadn't returned, but two armed guards arrived and beckoned me to follow them. Outside the Circuit House gates, a horse and cart were waiting. Except for the bright red pompons on the horse's bridle, the cart looked exactly like the drawings of tumbrels on their way to the guillotine in my school history books. The men signaled me to climb into the back. As I did, I heard Tor's voice calling my name. Parked across from the cart was the yellow pickup. In the back were Hamid, Tor, and Abdul. I was delighted to see them. They informed me they were released. "I told you they are all corrupt," yelled Abdul in English as the guards looked on uncomprehendingly. "It cost one thousand rupees. They wouldn't take money for you because you're a foreigner. But don't worry; we'll sort it out in Peshawar."

The horse started moving off. The freedom fighters drove away in the opposite direction. My cart headed for the barracks. Once again, I was shown into Rahmatullah's office, told to sit, and then ignored. For the remainder of the morning, he received what appeared to be petitioners, many of whom kissed his hand on arriving. He listened to their complaints and requests and made his pronouncements. Then without warning, he handed me a ten-line statement in English, which said that the Khassadars at Spin Khiwara, past Zhawar, had arrested me and that I was prosecuted in the court of the Political *Niab*, but it didn't say with what I was charged. This time, he didn't ask me to sign it.

"When I have a vehicle, you will leave," he said, turning back to his work. I continued to sit. Three hours later, a short, fat man in a green *shalwar kameez* arrived. He stood staring at me and smirking, his sense of self-importance bigger than he was. "This man is taking you to Peshawar," said Rahmatullah. I disliked the newcomer on sight.

Outside in the steaming heat a Datsun pickup was parked. In the back were six guards armed with rifles, with cartridge bandoliers slung across their chests. One man had a large horn-handled dagger hanging from his waist. In addition to the guards, there was a driver, and the leader of the group. An armed escort of eight men seemed a little excessive for one unarmed female journalist, but since none of them spoke English, I couldn't ask why.

The man in green pushed past me to get into the driver's cab and then gestured for me to get in last. I did, trying to shrink away from the searing heat of the metal door and also from him. We began the long drive back in 120 degrees. The heat and the dust were miserable, but for me the drive was made worse by my companion. A heavy user of *naswar*, the green chewing snuff popular in this part of the world, he spat loudly and energetically past my face and out the window every few minutes. I began to cringe every time he cleared his throat. As if he were aware of how offensive I found his behavior, he suddenly spat straight at the dashboard. I gagged as the bright green gobbets of spittle ran slowly down the front of the van. The driver didn't seem to notice. I hugged the door of the van, my hatred for the man rising with every mile. My animosity reached its peak when two hours later he stopped the van, locked me in it, and organized a swimming party in a nearby river for himself and the rest of the escort. Parked in the sun, the vehicle began to feel like one of the metal boxes the Japanese left World War II concentration camp victims to roast in. But at least my hostility distracted me from my discomfort.

Arriving at Peshawar's Special Branch was a relief after the journey there. But that feeling soon vanished when I was shown into a small room beyond which I could see cells. The room appeared to be sleeping quarters for the prison guards, two of whom were sprawled on wooden *charpoys*. I asked one of them for a glass of water. Without rising, he dunked a filthy cracked cup into an even dirtier bucket of water and handed it to me. As hot, tired, and thirsty as I was, I couldn't bring myself to drink it. My short tormentor sat down on one of the *charpoys* and almost immediately proceeded to spit into a corner of the room. Suddenly I creamed at him, "Stop it; stop it!" He looked at me blankly, not understanding what I had said. But I understood I was losing control. Thirty-eight hours after my arrest, I felt close to tears for the first time. Whether it was the sight of the prison cells, the tension, or the lack of food and drink, I didn't know, but I realized my nerves were raw. And I was frightened. How long would I be kept here? And how long would it be before there was anyone who spoke more than two words of English so that I could find out? I decided I needed some help. I wanted to telephone I said, dialing a phone in the air. "I want to speak to the American Embassy," I enunciated slowly and clearly. The guards looked at me. "I am an American; I want to telephone the American Embassy."

"No," said the older one finally. It was my turn to look at him. "No," he repeated before turning back to his conversation.

"Oh, shit," I thought. "Now what?" I answered my own question. This was a military dictatorship, a repressive regime; why did I expect prisoners to have rights? I was aware that Amnesty International often castigated Pakistan for its treatment of prisoners: torture, shackling, incarceration without trial. Why was I bitching over being deprived of the right to telephone? I played out the conversation with myself, trying to forget movies like *Missing*, and finally decided it was unlikely the Pakistani authorities were going to get too rough with an American journalist. My fear gave way to anger. It would help me get through the waiting game.

The hours passed slowly. My jailers sprang to their feet when an officer arrived. "My name is Sultan Mehmood; I am deputy supervisor of police, Joint Intelligence Service," he said. His full beard and mustache made him look Edwardian. "Your passport, please."

I explained that I had been separated from my passport along with the rest of my belongings when I was arrested. "I imagine you have impounded the vehicle I was traveling in." He confirmed that they had.

"What happens now?" I asked, explaining that I still hadn't been charged.

Mehmood held out a form for me to read. It was written in English, but all I could see was "remanded to custody for fifteen days." My stomach contracted. "The next step is your interrogation. But it's too late tonight, and tomorrow is Independence Day;

we'll have to do it on Thursday. So you have two choices: you can come back on Thursday, or you can stay in my lockup. Have you seen my lockup? Come with me." He led the way to a large holding cell containing three prisoners. One man looked European and had the emaciated build of a heroin junkie. "He's our Russian. We caught him as he was crossing the border. I think he is a spy. He's been here three weeks, but we can't interrogate him until our interpreter is free to come from Islamabad.

"So what is your choice? Do you want to come back for your interrogation or stay here with our Russian?" This turn of events left me blinking. One minute I was being told I was remanded to custody for fifteen days, the next I was free to leave as long as I returned, or I could share a cell with a possible Russian spy. I thanked him for his hospitality and headed for the door. "Of course, to make sure you return, we will keep your passport. And you are not permitted to leave the city."

Assuming my activities would now be closely monitored, I checked into Green's Hotel rather than return to the *Mujahideen* house and contacted Wakil from there. "I'll have a vehicle pick you up; meet them outside, but keep the room for several days," he advised. Back at NIFA headquarters, Wakil was enraged. In an effort to locate my whereabouts, he had gone to the Special Branch office. "They told me NIFA was being fined Rps. 5,000 [$333] for trying to take a foreign journalist into Afghanistan, and they said if it happens again it would be Rps. 30,000 [$2,000]. This is the first time they have fined anyone. I told them it would happen again, that I will continue to do it until my country is free. I asked the Pakistani authorities why they were forcing us to fight a war on two fronts—the Soviets and theirs. Pakistan supposedly supports our cause. They are assisting the Soviets when they stop journalists from reporting on the atrocities in Afghanistan."

Two days later I returned for my interrogation. It started like a complete resume but soon took on that same Alice in Wonderland air with which my arrest had been marked. "Elementary school, high school, college, every address you've ever lived at, Father's name." Once again, I saw myself described as the "Daughter of Charles Goodwin." Mehmood questioned me about my father's professional history for fifteen minutes. I was starting to feel that as a woman I had little validity alone. I was also having trouble remembering some of the details of my father's career. "Excuse me, but my father wasn't arrested; I was," I interrupted him.

He returned the questioning to me. "Name all the countries you have visited."

"All forty-five of them?" I began the long litany, but he got bored after the first fifteen.

"Enough," he said. "ID marks?" I don't have any.

"No scars or moles?" No.

"Show me your arms." I did; they are blemish-free.

"Not even a mole?" I shook my head.

He sighed and wrote "Nil."

"Were you trained in subversion or sabotage before you came here?"

I laughed. "Give me a break; I work for *Ladies' Home Journal.* I came to document why the refugees are leaving Afghanistan."

"Ah, that was your problem; you were traveling with a refugee. That was where you went wrong. You should have gone with one of the *Mujahideen* groups. They will disguise you. Next time you will be wiser. Yes, man learns by his mistakes. But it is true; Pakistan has many refugees."

"Yes, it is actually quite remarkable that Pakistan has taken so many."

"We only do it because the U.S. makes us do it. We are their puppets."

"President Zia wouldn't like to hear you say that."

"I was trained by the U.S. even in interrogation. I am the only person in the entire North-West Frontier Province to have been taught how to interrogate by the United States."

I couldn't resist it. "Did they train you in torture, too?"

"No, not torture, interrogation. Let me show you my certificate." Mehmood fumbled around in a desk drawer. "Look, here it is," he said, proudly handing me the certificate, which read, "Special Training Group U.S. Government. Special Group Course in Interrogation 20/4/84–21/5/84 completed by Sultan Mehmood." It was signed by a David W. Harris. Mehmood dug out the training manual that went with the course. I idly flicked through the different chapters on the seven psychological profiles of prisoners and how to interrogate them, which ones to intimidate, which ones to coax.

"Was I fierce with you on Tuesday night?" he asked. "Sufficiently fierce?"

"Yes," I responded, "you were quite fierce." Now it suddenly seemed we were friends. But, of course, we were not.

"Your passport is being given to my superior, Mr. Mohammad Saeed Khan, the deputy chief of police. You must come back to see him tomorrow." And I did, to sit waiting all morning before being told, "Your case is being handled by Qazi Shams Udin, superintendent of police, Special Branch; come back and see him tomorrow."

The next day I was referred to the inspector general of police, who was as high as one could go in the North-West Frontier Province. He had told me he would see me at 10:00 A.M. He arrived at 2:30 P.M. On the wall behind his desk was a large criminal statistics chart, which might have explained why he was late. In his province, murder was up, heroin use was up, *zina* was up. *Zina*, loosely translated as "adultery," is sex outside marriage whether the perpetrators have spouses or are single. The sexual revolution had obviously arrived in Pakistan. But here instead of herpes, they risked a public flogging.

"Your case is being handled in Islamabad by the home secretary. Come back tomorrow." I was on a Pakistani merry-go-round, and nobody seemed to know when I was getting off. The limbo state I found myself in was like being on probation and having to report to a probation officer every day. No doubt, this schedule was designed to keep me out of trouble.

In the course of the week, I was constantly told, "You should have applied for permission to go through the Tribal Areas."

"But Pakistan doesn't give permission to foreigners to go there."

And in typical Mad Hatter logic, "Unfortunately, that is true."

I was also told that Special Branch had just been ordered by Islamabad to "get tough" with any foreigners caught going inside Afghanistan. "We've been told they don't want any 'problems' before the negotiated settlement talks on Afghanistan with the Soviets in Geneva." Later, a high-ranking Pakistan diplomat would tell me, "The U.S. has been putting pressure on us. They don't want U.S. journalists or doctors inside Afghanistan."

I was aware of the State Department ban on American doctors' entering Afghanistan to aid the war wounded. Dr. Robert Simon, professor of emergency medicine at UCLA, had founded the International Medical Corps in 1984 to establish clinics inside Afghanistan to be staffed by volunteer American doctors and nurses. IMC was to operate in a similar fashion to the very successful French group *Médecins Sans Frontières*. But then in 1985 a grant of $675,000 from the State Department to enable him to start an advanced emergency surgical medic program for Afghans in Pakistan was made contingent on his agreeing in writing that no more American medical personnel would travel inside Afghanistan. If that agreement were violated, Simon was told, he would have to repay the money.

The State Department's ambivalence on U.S. support for the Afghan war was well known in Washington and opposed by numerous officials in other agencies, as well as by a growing number of politicians, one of whom told me, "Washington has four governments where Afghanistan is concerned: the State Department, CIA, Department of Defense, and the Executive Branch, all of whom are pulling in different directions on the issue. The last two want to support the Afghan Resistance, but CIA and State seem to spend much of their time trying to hamper such efforts."

"Career diplomats at State don't want to rock any boats that will get in the way of their ambitions. They feel that the Soviets will behave themselves as long as we don't offend them. And yet history proves otherwise," said a senior Pentagon official. This attitude has been apparent for several decades, during which the State Department chose not to recognize the strategic importance of Afghanistan. Today, many Washington insiders see the agency as having sacrificed Afghanistan to its Soviet neighbor. Adds Professor Leon Poullada, political scientist at Northern Arizona University and formerly an Afghan affairs specialist for the State Department, "One would think that American diplomacy would recognize instantly the need to strengthen the Afghan resistance in every way—but once again American support for the Afghans is timorous, rhetorical, and vacillating. American policy toward Afghanistan remains paralyzed by appeasement: the belief that if the U.S. does nothing to 'provoke' the Soviets, they will ultimately see the error of their ways and quietly fade away from their commanding position in the Middle East and South Asia, leaving the region peaceful and secure and firmly in the American camp. It is the great illusion of our time."

It was this attitude of appeasement that made me choose not to go to the U.S. Embassy for assistance, the normal route for an American journalist to take when falling afoul of a foreign government. Even though I was beginning to sense my arrest was going to end in more than a verbal reprimand, I was convinced that American authorities would only tell me I shouldn't have attempted to enter Afghanistan.

Having come to that conclusion, and also being wholeheartedly sick of spending half of each day in various offices of Pakistan's Special Branch waiting for the axe to fall, I finally ran out of patience. I was going back to Afghanistan. I had come here to report on the war, and since Afghanistan's closed borders didn't have passport controls, my impounded passport wouldn't be missed. "But this time no arrests, please," I said to the *Mujahideen*. *"Inshallah"* was their response. I could only hope God was willing. I knew the Pakistani authorities would show their teeth if I were caught twice in one week. They weren't going to be very pleased, either, when I dropped out of sight.

Red Skies, Scorched Earth

The black flags of NIFA were visible before the tents of the base camp came into view. The ambulance creaked and groaned as it rose and dipped over the badly rutted track caused by a recent flash flood. Several times in the last ten miles we had been forced to turn back in search of an alternate route because of severe erosion. The ambulance had obviously made one too many runs over terrain like this: its suspension was shot, and the fumes it belched had been wafting through the vehicle ever since Peshawar. "What I wouldn't give for a four-wheel drive ambulance," said Wakil. "Even a healthy man is made sick in this one; a wounded freedom fighter doesn't stand a chance."

We had left Peshawar nine hours before. This time Wakil was with us to assess the military situation in Khost. His presence eased my tension slightly as we approached each Pakistani check-post, but my aching back muscles told me that I'd been holding myself rigid with apprehension since we'd left the city. Because of my earlier arrest, Wakil had taken the precaution of deviating from the normal route to the Khost region. But what we made up for in security, we paid for in discomfort. All of us were relieved to reach the relative comfort of the NIFA camp. Eighteen kilometers inside Afghanistan, the rear base functioned as a rest and relaxation center, as well as a supply depot.

The camp was virtually empty when we arrived. The day before, the commander had sent five hundred men twenty kilometers farther in to meet thirty thousand advancing Soviet troops. Part of the guerrillas' Eastern Division Front, they would swell the number of *Mujahideen* there to eight thousand. "You arrived at the right time," the commander told Wakil. "But you should have let me know you were coming."

Forty-year-old Commander Fatah Khan was a friendly, good-looking man of medium height, who wore his straight black hair and short mustache in a fashionable style. He had a reputation for sartorial elegance even in the heat of battle, and he was also something of a folk hero among the Afghans. A graduate of Kabul's military academy, he had been chief of artillery at Khost until the invasion. His claim of knowing "every nook and cranny" of the Khost region was an accurate one. The Soviets had trained him in the use of BM 13 ground-to-ground rockets, and today, he was a rocket specialist.

In 1979, when the Soviets arrived, he brought his entire battalion of 830 men over to NIFA. His package deal included a large supply of ammunition, nine mortars, nine Dashakas, twelve RPG-7s, and several light machine guns, plus the eighteen vehicles they traveled in. Not surprisingly, the Soviets were not very pleased to see them go—ninety of his men died in the defection battle. Now he was planning a three-base attack the following day.

Fatah Khan showed us to an outdoor carpeted area surrounded by large overstuffed pillows. After we had been served tea, he ordered the ambulance driver to take the vehicle several kilometers farther on to where it was needed. "In the last two weeks, fifteen of my men have been injured and two have been martyred," said the commander; "one of the men killed, a fine officer, was decapitated."

Khan pulled out a briefcase, fitted out as a traveling office, and started putting the finishing touches to his battle plan sketches. Wakil went to check on the supplies stored in a tent at the edge of the base. Next to large sacks of rice, tea, and sugar and cans of cooking oil were stacked ammunition boxes, many of them empty. Standing next to them were two Chinese-made MBRLs, multibarrel rocket launchers. "New weapons?" I asked.

"New!" exclaimed Wakil. "We've had them six months, but they've never been used. We've never received any ammunition for them. And every time you fire one of these, you're using twelve rockets." Fatah Khan joined us. "I've had two small deliveries of ammunition in the last month; each one lasts about three days. Then we have to retreat and spend the rest of our time sitting with our hands under our chins, waiting.

"I've got eight bases of twenty-four hundred men in this area. With these numbers, in some locations I could keep up a twenty-four-hour show. As it is, too many times we are nothing but mosquitoes, an irritant to the Soviets. Right now, I'm very low on AK-47 and 303 ammo, and there are only fifteen 107 mm ground-to-ground missiles left. I've got enough for tomorrow's operation as long as nothing goes wrong. If we had the food and the ammunition, we could recruit fifteen thousand men in this area. For every ten men who want to fight, I've got one gun."

But what the base lacked in supplies, it made up for in creature comforts, at least of the kind in the field. There were piles of cotton mattresses and thick quilts, even a number of *charpoys*. The excellent cuisine was courtesy of the women in a nearby village, who also washed the laundry of the guerrillas. And when I'd gone in search of the open-air latrine area, I was just about to duck behind a rock when a freedom fighter came running after me, shouting at the top of his voice. I assumed he was going to tell me this spot was out of bounds to women, but no, he was waving at me a roll of bright pink toilet paper. Even the weather was kind, about forty degrees cooler than Peshawar, with a gentle breeze wafting up the valley.

"This place is a deluxe hotel," I told Fatah Khan. "Enjoy it," he said. "Tomorrow will be hard; then you will suffer." He said it with a grin, but I knew he wasn't joking. As he spoke, the distant boom of Soviet shelling began. "They keep it up all night, when they are advancing," explained the commander. Addressing Wakil, he brought him up to date on the Soviet offensive. A thousand or more paratroops, the elite rapid strike forces, had just landed northwest of Khost. Wakil turned to me: "If you hadn't been arrested last week, that's exactly where you would have been right now. You should consider yourself lucky." I did; I knew that paratroops on the ground meant a hell of a lot of helicopter gunships overhead.

At 9:15 P.M. someone turned on the radio for the BBC news in Farsi. Wakil kept up a running translation. "The Soviet Union has cut its oil export by one-third, a drastic decrease. Thirty thousand Soviet troops are advancing in Paktia Province (where we were sitting) in an effort to seal off the border. The town of Parachinar, ten miles inside Pakistan, has been bombed by Communist forces, killing eleven. Pakistan's deputy foreign minister announced that Pakistan's patience has ended. "Now is the time to defend ourselves. We will retaliate," he said.

"They must be scared about thirty thousand Soviet forces' being so close," said Wakil. Yeah, so am I, I told myself.

We turned in early that night. "We have an early start in the morning," Wakil said. "And unless one of the jeeps makes it back, we're going to be walking all the way."

I awoke at five o'clock to see in the dim morning light the twenty-odd men left in the base, moving mattresses out of the way so they could pray. There was a chill in the air, and a heavy dew had left my bedding sopping wet. I was pleased I'd remembered to stash my cameras in my backpack. Prayers over, Tor began preparing hand grenades for the day's battle. I got up to keep him company as he screwed the pins into the grenade bases. He seemed distant, and I couldn't tell whether it was because he missed Hamid, who had been sick and couldn't come with us, or whether he was always like this before going on an operation. As we sat in less than companionable silence, I picked up a grenade pin and started fiddling with it. Wakil's voice cut across the sleeping area. "Put that down," he said curtly. "Don't play with it. Those pins have a fuse; they can take off a hand." Minutes later, a bright red jeep and two Toyota pickups arrived. "Lousy color for a war zone," I said pointing at the jeep. "It's just been given to us and we haven't had the chance to paint it," the commander said. "But we'll pour some diesel over it, and then the dust will stick to it as we drive. You'll see; the jeep will be as good as camouflaged." Great, I thought, we have a choice of enemy aircraft using us for target practice or bursting into flames when a forgetful *Mujahideen* lights a cigarette, to say nothing of the nauseating stench that would get worse as the sun rose.

Fatah Khan joined Wakil and me and three officers in the jeep; the remaining *Mujahideen* including Tor rode in the pickups. As Tor waved good-bye, he theatrically yelled something at me in Persian. Wakil translated it, "I'm an Afghan soldier, and my poem is victory." We pulled out at 6:00 A.M. In the jeep, Fatah Khan acknowledged Wakil's higher rank and offered to let him take over command of that night's operation. Wakil declined. "Why interfere with a good commander?" he said. We were heading fifteen kilometers due west, a journey that would take a jolting three hours and would leave us ten kilometers from the bases we were to attack later that day.

We drove through a large spread-out village, whose flat-roofed mud houses brought to mind a biblical scene. Camels kneeled in the dust on their calloused knees. Women baking bread on outdoor cooking fires or fetching water covered their faces as we passed. And the regular clop, clop of the water-operated flour mill was as comforting as a heartbeat. But the dragonflies flitting across our path reminded me of miniature helicopters, making me realize I was more uneasy than I was admitting.

Leaving behind the village, the scenery became monochromatic. The parched land, the rocks and distant outcroppings all were the color of dust. Three and a half hours later, we pulled into the new base, which was temporary home to a couple of hundred men. The camp consisted of a few tents, but mostly of hastily erected flysheets. With no groundcover except for the occasional cactus or scrub palm, the only protection was blending in with the rocks or "prayer," as Padagul, a twenty-eight-year-old champion wrestler, complete with cauliflowered ear, told me. But just in case prayer needed a little assistance, the base was relocated every second or third day.

Five minutes after arriving, a spotter plane flew lazily by. "Here we go," said Wakil. "Something heavier will follow." A few minutes later, four MIGs screamed overhead, proving him right. "They'll be back; get down," he yelled in English, as the *Mujahideen* scattered. I followed Padagul's lead to a small overhang. Almost immediately, the jets roared back the other way, but they hadn't seen us. The *Mujahideen* jeered and returned to unloading and sorting ammunition, much of it dated 1949. The fact that it was Egyptian signified that it was probably United States–supplied. Hadn't anyone ever told the CIA that the maximum shelf life of most of this stuff was around thirty years, even under the best of storage conditions? "Is it still good?" I asked, kicking the date on an ammunition box. "Only God knows," replied the commander. "We don't find out until tonight."

"Get some rest," I was told. "We aren't moving out until three. Find some shade; it's going to get a lot hotter here by midday." I returned to my rock ledge and dozed. When I woke several hours later, I learned the commander had been moving out the *Mujahideen* in twenty-man parties. Larger groups are easily spotted from the air, as many fleeing refugees had learned to their cost. The slow-moving refugee caravans are easy targets and are frequently strafed by low-flying fighter planes and helicopters. As I traveled through Afghanistan, I became accustomed to the sight of bloated corpses of donkeys or camels that had died after being raked with machine gun fire from the air. Nearby invariably would be the stone-covered burial mounds of the Afghan graves.

We left at 3:00 P.M. We were to regroup for a final briefing at a dried-up riverbed two kilometers away where some 150 men were waiting for the commander to arrive. They were resting in a man-made recessed shelter carved out of a cliff, their weapons stacked in neat piles around them like so many sheaves of wheat. The commander brought out his battle plans. "We begin at seven o'clock. It will be getting dark then; there will be less casualties." The three Communist bases were close to one another. He planned to attack all of them but would direct his main force at the biggest, Ali Shier. Tor volunteered for the front-line assault and the commander agreed, but Wakil vetoed him. Tor was to stay with me as an interpreter, and I would be with the missile operators. As always, Tor obeyed without comment, although I could see he was angry. But I was relieved, since all three Communist bases were ringed with mines. Earlier I had asked the commander how his men crossed the minefields. "We cross them. If we are martyred, it is God's will. We have no mine detectors." How many casualties did he take this way? "Casualties? This is war. That belongs to God."

Now Fatah Khan was giving a similar speech to his *Mujahideen.* "In the name of God, in the command of Gailani . . ."—he repeated the evening's plans, and then he added—"If we have injured, he is injured. If he dies, he is martyred. It is the choice of God. We don't stop fighting.

"For the injured we have ambulance. For the martyred, be proud of it." He synchronized watches with those who had them and then added, "If you capture Babrak Karmal or Soviet troops, bring them to me. But if you capture militia, just bring me his head." The militia are local men, Fatah Khan explained. "When they capture *Mujahideen*, they torture; they are very cruel."

The men began moving out in groups of two and three. "We have to cross a flat valley," said Wakil. "The enemy forces have several tanks pointing straight up it. They have a clear view for miles, and they frequently shell it. We want them to think these men are just local villagers."

As the first batches left, a string of donkeys arrived to carry the heavy weapons. "*Mujahideen* helicopters," quipped Padagul. Four 107 mm rockets is all the average donkey can carry. The mortars would be broken down; whatever the animals couldn't take, the *Mujahideen* would. Helping with the mortars was a heavily wrinkled and nearly toothless old man. "That's Melaband; he's seventy, our oldest freedom fighter," said the commander. Fatah Khan looked at my face. "Why are you surprised?" he asked. "Here in Afghanistan we say even the rocks are freedom fighters. Young men, old men, they all want their country to be free." He called over the white-haired freedom fighter to introduce us, and this time it was Melaband who was surprised. He hadn't realized I was a woman, he said, until he was told I was a female journalist. Men within earshot mocked him. "If you can't tell that, then you can't find your way out of here," said one. "The *Mujahideen* live with the rocks and the mountains; we forget what women look like," he retorted good-humoredly. "And anyway, women don't go to *Jihad*. American women must be crazy." I was inclined to agree with him. By now the temperature registered one hundred degrees on my small camping thermometer, and the sun was blinding as it reflected off the rocks. My feet were uncomfortably hot in the thick hiking socks, and my boots felt as if they weighed a ton. The last thing I wanted to do right at that moment was witness war, particularly one I had to walk to. Just then I began to feel the first twinges of menstrual cramps. Great timing, I thought: just when I needed all my physical strength, I was going to feel enervated for the next couple of days.

It was our turn to leave. Our party consisted of Wakil, Tor, Padagul, me, and Fatah Khan, who was carrying a megaphone. For fifteen minutes we followed the dried riverbed. Then we began to cut across open country. The ground was deeply fissured as if tectonic plates were engaged in a desperate tug-of-war. At each crevasse, we slithered down the freshly loosened soil on one side and flayingly scrambled up the other, kicking dust in the face of the person behind. Little of the region's topography was flat as it was here, but the badly striated terrain required almost as much energy to cross as climbing Afghanistan's mountains.

We reached the valley plain. Here the only ridges visible were the dried mud of the tank tracks, which crisscrossed the valley like blade marks on a skating rink. "Now we have to be fast," said the commander. "The tank troops can clearly see us once we start to cross. If they get suspicious, they will either start firing or move the tanks out to investigate." The men picked up speed, until it seemed they were almost jogging. I tried to keep up but couldn't. The heat was proving too much for me. Embarrassed, I tried to make a joke of it. "I was born in England," I said breathlessly. "Anything over seventy degrees there is called a killer heat wave. We never get the chance to go on forced marches in one-hundred-degree heat." The men were sympathetic, but they didn't change their pace. "It's important that you keep up," said Wakil quietly. "This is not a good place to be." One by one the men relieved me of what I was carrying. Padagul took my water canteen, Fatah Khan my cameras, adding my equipment to their already heavy machine gun and ammunition loads. My pack had gone with the donkeys. The sun was blazing directly into our faces. I had taken off my turban because it was too warm, a mistake on two counts. The sweat ran down my hair and into my eyes, causing them to burn, and without my head covered I had no protection from the sun. I noticed the backs of all our *kameezes* were salt-encrusted from perspiration. The heat had also made my feet swell. They felt tight against my boots, and I could feel the blisters forming.

I was beginning to feel a little lightheaded. "I need to stop," I told Wakil when he dropped back to egg me on. "You can't." He was obviously disappointed at my lack of stamina so early on. How, I wondered, did you tell a guerrilla leader it's the first day of your period, and you'll be fine tomorrow?

Wakil pointed to a series of small mountains that seemed miles away. "That is where we are going. Once we get close, you can stop." We moved on, and I trudged miserably behind them, head down, trying to think of one step at a time. Could this valley only be a few kilometers wide?

The sun had shifted in the sky, and as we drew close to the mountains we found shade for the first time that day. An old lady in a faded maroon dress hailed us. She was making buttermilk; would we like some? Buttermilk was Tor's favorite refreshment; he reminded me of a puppy as he darted across her land. I was too drained to drink. The woman, whose thinning hair was hennaed bright orange, was too old to be veiled. She looked to be in her eighties but was probably twenty or more years younger. The physical hardships of daily life and constant childbearing age rural women rapidly in Afghanistan. As we left, she said, "If a woman can come here from America, Afghanistan can drive out the Soviets."

The remainder of the hike was all uphill, but at least it was cooler now. We were heading for one mountain ridge to set up the 107 mm rockets; a nearby peak would hold our mortars. Three kilometers ahead, near the top of yet another peak, the red flag of the Ali Shier base was visible through the dusty haze. So was the road to Kabul, which passed in front of the fort.

The last quarter mile of our trek was almost perpendicular. As the gradient suddenly steepened, the donkeys were unloaded. "They can't go any farther; it's too difficult for them," Fatah Khan said. I started following the men carrying the missiles up the near vertical cliff. The rocks had jagged edges, as painful as coral. They grazed my hands as I groped for handholds, and also my shins as I tried to keep upright. My pathetic mountaineering attempts brought good-humored mocking from the freedom fighters as they passed me. Then one of them, a towering man wearing a bright green *kameez*, grabbed my hand and pulled me to the top. About six foot seven, with curly black hair and beard, he was an Afghan version of the Jolly Green Giant. I flopped on the top waiting to regain my breath and for the muscles in my legs to stop feeling like Jell-O after the effort.

The commander was already setting up the missiles. Lacking their firing tubes, as missile deliveries to the *Mujahideen* invariably did, the rockets were rested on suitably level rocks. They would be discharged by a method that was as simple as it was effective, with nine-volt batteries and electrical wiring. The range of these rockets should have been nine kilometers, but with this method seven couldn't be guaranteed. Nor could their accuracy. But Fatah Khan's skill gave him the same edge the firing tubes would have given.

I started looking for somewhere comfortable to perch so that I could still see Ali Shier but also would have some shelter when they started firing back. Shrapnel and flying rock can be as deadly as a direct hit. I was almost dislodged when the first volley of rockets was fired without warning at six minutes to seven just a few yards from where I had positioned myself. So much for synchronization of watches. It was impossible to follow their trajectory in the twilight. They seemed to take forever to reach their destination, but it was only a matter of seconds before they exploded. Six plumes of smoke shot into the air but were soon overtaken by a wall of flame. The *Mujahideen* cheered and threw rocks over the cliff. "I think we hit either their fuel or ammo supply," said Wakil, patting the commander's shoulder. Three minutes later we discharged another salvo of three 107s. Before they could land, a Kalashnikov was fired from somewhere below us. It was the signal for the *Mujahideen* assault force to move. And move they did with as much whooping and screaming as any Hollywood version of an Indian attack. The thump of the mortars, rat-tat-tat of the Dashakas, and clip-clip-clip of the Kalashnikovs were a rhythmic counterpoint to the screams of the freedom fighters: "You have three minutes to live, you bastards. Still there is time to forget communism and find Islam. Die, you sons of Lenin." Stealth and surprise were of little value to an Afghan in battle.

The base stayed silent. Why weren't they firing back? "They will; they are probably still trying to locate us," said Wakil.

We fired our third and final round of rockets and were enveloped in a cloud of smoke, caused by the lack of the firing tubes, that hovered over us for ten minutes, pinpointing our position as thoroughly as any klieg lights. As if that were what they had been waiting for, the base began firing back. "When you see the flash as the tank guns fire, there are fifteen seconds before the shell reaches its destination. That's how long you have to duck," Wakil told me. The words were barely out of his mouth when he pushed me flat on my stomach. The whistle of the shells followed almost immediately. But they passed overhead and landed with a crump behind us. I squirmed as the razor-sharp edges of rocks cut through the thin cotton of my *shalwar kameez*. "Stay there," Wakil barked in my ear. The next broadside fell short and hit the front of the cliff, making the mountain under us shake. The *Mujahideen* scrambled to their feet. "They don't know where we are; they're firing back out of fear," said the commander.

The valley in front of us was alive with sound and fire. Tracer bullets and flares, theirs and ours, illuminated the sky. The sound of the *Mujahideen* screams were now much closer to the fort, surprising me with the speed with which they were covering the ground on foot in the dark. Twenty minutes into the attack, a dramatic electrical storm began. It seemed superfluous, as if some unseen stage manager were overdoing it with the special effects.

At 7:30 P.M. with the shells still flying over our heads or wide, the *Mujahideen* around me took time out for evening prayers. Bending their heads to the ground and convinced that God was on their side, they were unperturbed that at any moment the Communist forces could land a shell in their midst. While they were praying, I found myself staring out over the valley we had crossed. At first I thought I was imagining the flashing lights. But as I continued to stare, I realized I wasn't. I watched them for several minutes, red and then white, on and then off. It looked as if someone were signaling. That everybody wasn't a friend in the darkened valley we were to recross later on was something I didn't want to think about. I pointed out the lights to Wakil. "Yes, I see them," he said, his mouth tightening. He called Fatah Khan over. "I've got men down there in the village of Sabari; don't worry. If it's an informer, they'll find him; that's why they are there." Fatah Khan explained that on one of their last operations in this area, a government spy using red and green flashlights had signaled the location of the *Mujahideen* to the base. "In the villages around the bases, the government tries to bribe people to work for them. If we find an informer, we'll take him prisoner and burn down his house as a warning to the rest of the village. Then we make use of him. Either he works for us as a double agent or he dies."

We made our way to the top of the ridge again. Now the fighting was much closer to the fort, but the shells were still heading in our direction. Every few minutes, like puppets in a Punch and Judy show, we ducked down as a shell passed overhead and then popped back up again. Only Tor wasn't ducking, I noticed. I worked my way over to him. He was angry. "This is not fight here; this is foolish," he snapped. "The *Mujahideen* go to the front; I sit here. Look, all around us fighting. I should be there." He lapsed into sullen silence.

Shortly after this conversation, Fatah Khan let out a shout. Through his binoculars he'd spotted a convoy heading toward the base. Somebody snatched my binoculars from my hand. "It's a big one, tanks and jeeps." I could see their lights. "It's much too soon for them to be here as reinforcements. They must have been on their way already to resupply the base." The convoy kept moving, their lights brightly on, as if they didn't realize what they were driving into. Suddenly, the *Mujahideen* Dashaka operators spotted them and brought them under fire. Almost immediately, two jeeps burst into flames. Only then did the convoy lights go out. I waited for the convoy tanks to start responding, but they didn't. From our grandstand seats, I could only imagine the confusion among the newly arriving troops. Then in the light of the next few flares, we saw the convoy beginning to reverse. "Why? They far outnumber the freedom fighters," I asked. "You know that, but the Communists don't," Wakil told me. "They rarely attack at night unless they have air cover."

Had the convoy stayed they could probably have encircled the freedom fighters; then all they would have had to do was sit and wait for them to run out of ammunition. It would have taken about an hour.

At 9:00 P.M. the commander told us to pull out. "It's not going to last much longer," he said. "If the *Mujahideen* aren't inside the fort by now, they'll be forced to retreat. They'll have nothing left to fight with." If they made it into the base, they would have fresh supplies of ammunition. Either way, we wouldn't know until the following day, when the survivors would gradually rejoin us.

Going down the cliff in the dark was more terrifying to me than sitting on top ducking shells. Each step was a potential leg breaker or worse. This side of the mountain was now in total darkness. The storm had left a cloudy sky to obscure the moon. My night vision was lousy compared to the *Mujahideen's*, and within minutes I felt vertiginous, as if every step I was about to take were out into space. I moved at a snail's pace. Out of nowhere came Mirbad Khan, the green giant. Even with his leading me by the hand, I found myself bathed in sweat by the time we reached the bottom.

With the rockets spent, there were several free donkeys. I was offered one of them and took it gratefully until I climbed on its back. There were no saddle, stirrups, or bridle, and the bony ridge of the donkey's spine was almost as uncomfortable to sit on as the jagged rocks had been. We had a three-hour walk back to the base, which had been moved in our absence. At least the donkey was less likely to stumble in the dark, I thought, than I would be. But that soon proved to be a fallacy. The donkey lost its footing as often as I would have, finally tripping theatrically halfway home so that I went sailing over his head in an arc before landing flat on my back in front of him. The *Mujahideen* chuckled as they picked me up unhurt but winded. At least the tumble allowed feeling to return to my donkey-numb rear. We continued to walk with men joining us, appearing as silently as shadows until we were about sixty strong. They were the mortar operators, returning rear guard, and village security force.

We finally located the base at 1:00 A.M. Too tired to sleep, I was still awake when the first of the *Mujahideen* rose at 5:00 to pray. Almost immediately, and even before breakfast, we were told to get ready to move again. "Today the planes will come looking for us," said the commander. "This camp is too open; the other side of the mountain is safer." My body ached from yesterday's climb and the rocks we'd been sleeping on. My sleeping bag, although warm, was thin, and the smallest pebble could be felt through it. We got our gear together. Tor's feet, I noticed, were bloodied, as were those of several *Mujahideen.* The walk back in the dark in open sandals and without socks had taken its toll. We began hiking again, but this time only for forty-five minutes. We stopped at a small shelter made of loosely piled rocks, half built into a cliff. Its roof was palm fronds supported by two roughly hewn beams of wood. "This is our bomb-proof shelter," joked Wakil. We settled to wait for breakfast, green tea, hard candy, and two-inch-thick corn bread. We were just finishing the meal when there was a commotion outside the doorway of the shelter. Three men in khaki uniforms were pushed inside. All three were underweight, had the rough features of peasants, and had shaven military haircuts, which made their ears look large and protruding. One had an oozing eye infection. They were captured Karmal troops, and they looked frightened. They were given tea, and I noticed one man's hand shook as he held the cup. Asked their names, they stayed silent. "Eat this bread; it's special freedom fighter bread. It will give you guts to talk," said Padagul, offering them the remains of our breakfast. "And don't worry; we are all Afghan, all Muslim."

"Once you give them food, they will relax, when you don't punish them," said Wakil. The commander and Wakil began to interrogate them. The braver soul in the middle, Atta Mohammad, became their spokesman. He claimed they were nomads from Helmand, a desert province in the south, and had all been forcibly conscripted. "They all say that. We have to find out if they were, or if they volunteered," said Wakil. The prisoners said they had been at the fort for nine days and were used as laborers making bricks, explained Atta Mohammad. "When we weren't making bricks, we were locked up. When you attacked the base, it gave us a chance to escape." As he talked, the day's shelling began. It sounded as if it were several kilometers away. Wakil and the commander began playing good cop/bad cop with the prisoners, with Wakil being bad cop, a role that seemed out of character. He asked the man where the paths through the minefields around the bases were.

"We don't know."

"How did you work outside the base then?"

Atta Mohammad became flustered.

Wakil changed the subject. "That's a very nice watch you are wearing. Where did you buy it?"

"In Kabul."

"With what? When? Poor nomads who become forcibly conscripted don't have the money to buy such good watches. But recruits do; they get paid a lot more."

"We are not recruits." Atta Mohammad lapsed into his local dialect, visibly scared.

"Have you had any contact with *Mujahideen* before?" the commander asked.

"We didn't know what *Mujahideen* were," said the man with eye infection.

The *Mujahideen* laughed. "These men aren't nomads; they're donkeys," said one.

"Well, they're obviously not ready to talk yet," said Fatah Khan. "Give them some pickaxes; we need some more caves dug. They can do that until they want to talk. We can wait."

What would happen to the men? It depends, said Wakil. "We may send them to headquarters and let them decide, or they could be made to walk barefooted back to the fort." Why? I asked. "To show us the safe entrance to the fort through the mines."

"As human minesweepers?"

"Yes."

Wakil looked at my face and laughed. "Don't worry; they always talk."

With the prisoners came the first reports of what had happened at Ali Shier. Our rockets had apparently caused substantial damage to one end of the base, but the *Mujahideen* had been forced to retreat because of lack of ammunition before they could breach the walls of the fort. So far there were no reports on the casualties on the enemy side—that would take several days to filter in—and as yet there were only two known casualties on our side, both shrapnel leg wounds. Later we would learn that Ali Shier's fuel depot had been destroyed in the attack, sixteen Afghan army soldiers had died in the ensuing conflagration, three had defected, and nineteen had been captured. In addition to the *Mujahideen* with leg wounds, two freedom fighters died in the attack.

The rest of the day was passed in sitting around, talking and sleeping, and listening to the planes fly back and forth overhead. Few *Mujahideen* returned that day. "No, they may have to hide out and wait. After a *Mujahideen* operation, the military always carry out reprisal attacks. They tend to bomb anything that moves," said the commander. Mirbad Khan whiled away the hours fashioning a woven scrub palm fan for me so I could flap away the flies. As deft as he was large, he produced an intricate work of beauty. He grinned shyly when I praised his handiwork. (Eight months later, Mirbad Khan would be killed, his body slashed to ribbons by shrapnel, in an offensive in this same region that nearly claimed Wakil's life. "We were pinned down in a bombing attack," said Wakil. "By the time I reached Mirbad Khan, he was barely recognizable.")

The following day we pulled back to the rear base. Mohammad Gailani, NIFA's deputy chief of staff, was there to greet us, but he'd come empty-handed. "Still no new ammunition," he said. In three days' time, Eid Adha, a religious holiday as important as our Christmas, was coming up. "I may as well give the men home leave," said Fatah Khan. "It's pointless keeping them sitting here doing nothing."

Wakil decided to leave that same day. "I've seen all I need to here. I want to check out the situation in Zazi." I was pleased; it meant I'd get a chance to see again the alpine valley I had visited the previous year. We said good-bye to Fatah Khan and the others, even Tor, who was to return with Mohammad. Eight of us squeezed into the small Toyota jeep, along with weapons, my pack, and blankets, one of which was thrown over my head every time we went through a checkpoint. Although Zazi is only fifty miles to the north of where we were, the mountains and the Soviet troops forced us to return to Pakistan to reach it. We drove through Saddar and Parachinar, heading for Teri Mangal, the border town. Recent Soviet bomb damage in all three Pakistani towns was clearly visible from the road. En route, we passed a *Mujahideen* truck used to transport ammunition supplies for the Resistance pulled over at a checkpoint. We drove some distance beyond the post, and Amin, one of the local guerrilla officers traveling with us, told our jeep to stop and walked back to investigate. He was angry when he returned. "Same old story," he said heatedly. "They want a bribe to let it go. They stop these trucks on trumped-up reasons at least once a week. Then it takes us five or six days to get them back because we refuse to pay. The bribes are normally about one or two thousand rupees, but we don't pay them; otherwise we'd be paying out constantly." The confiscated truck, which Amin managed to get released, contained five cases each of Dashaka rounds and antitank mines and three cases of RPG-7 ammunition, a paltry amount but vital to the undersupplied guerrillas.

Near Teri Mangal, we stopped at a NIFA base to pick up more hand grenades, AK-47 ammunition, and five RPG-7s. The antitank rockets were passed to the back of the uncomfortably overcrowded jeep, where they smashed against us at every jolt.

"We may need them where we're going," said Wakil, while I wondered whether I would ever get used to traveling sitting on top of enough explosives to blow us all sky-high. "This lot should be fun to carry up the border mountain," I said, remembering the steep climb from last year. "We won't have to," replied Wakil. "This year we have a road; we can drive. The *Mujahideen* spent all winter building it." Although the result may have been a masterpiece of engineering, "road" was far too grandiose a description. The track that zigzagged above us would have challenged a mountain goat. Each incline looked as if it clung to the mountain at a sixty-degree angle. And as with last year, the ground was covered in several inches of fine, talcum powder–like dust. "Can a vehicle really get up that?" I asked. "No problem," replied Padagul, as our driver, twenty-one-year-old Omargul, moved the jeep slightly forward. A few minutes later, we ground to a halt. "Four-wheel drive isn't working properly," said Omargul. I wasn't surprised; I imagined the entire engine to be choked full with the fine dust. "We can't make it in two-wheel." "Sure we can," said Wakil. "We'll push it." And push it they did, forcing me to ride inside with the driver. Watching the sweat roll off them, I remembered the legendary tales about the strength of the Afghans—how one man would grab a loaded packhorse that had slipped off a mountain precipice and hold it by its tail until other *Mujahideen* could help it back on the track. The gradient they were pushing the jeep up was so steep that every time they paused for breath, they had to wedge large rocks under the rear wheels to prevent the vehicle from rolling back over the side of the mountain. Finally, the jeep coughed and began moving under its own steam, and we left the *Mujahideen* behind. As we rattled around at each corner, I quietly prayed that without our human brakes, we wouldn't plunge over the edge. Omargul, who didn't speak any English, grinned at me each time the jeep conquered yet one more hairpin bend. My face was too rigid with fear to respond. While climbing up this mountain was tough physically, it was a lot easier on the nerves than being inside the jeep. Finally, at a pine forest at the top, we stopped to wait for the others to catch up. I was so relieved that I bent over and kissed Omargul on the cheek. The look of shock on his face told me I was probably the first female other than his mother and sisters to kiss him, not a surprising situation in this land of arranged marriages, where grooms often only see their brides for the first time at the end of the marriage ceremony.

When the others caught up with us, we bounced our way over the route I remembered well from my previous visit, only this time there were burned-out armored personnel carriers and jeeps that hadn't been there before. We passed the rubble of the German-built school and the king's former summer house. There had been nothing left standing in this area last year, but the deep bomb craters that pitted the ground suggested that the Soviets had pounded this region again recently anyway. At a small *chaikhana*, with a few men lounging outside, the road forked, and instead of taking the one that led down into the valley, we took the mountain route. The road narrowed and steepened as we climbed, the jeep's wheels sinking into the soft earth. Wakil stopped the vehicle, and three of the *Mujahideen* got out to walk in front of us. "This soft surface is good for mines," he said. I would never get used to men acting as mine detectors, nor would I get used to their acceptance of doing it. It wasn't just mines buried in the soil that we were concerned about here. On well-traveled routes, "butterfly" bombs had also been dropped in the thousands. A small antipersonnel mine, the *butterfly bomb* gets its name from the sycamore fin at one end that causes it to flutter down to the ground. Camouflaged to blend in with the terrain, they are difficult to spot on the ground. They are designed to maim, not to kill, on the principle that it ties up more Afghans to carry someone whose leg has just been blown off than it would if its victim were killed outright. Invariably, it is the children, drawn by the mines' curious shape, who fall victim to these weapons.

Cheap to produce, the butterfly bombs were originally designed by the United States to drop over Vietnam, but they were shelved when it was realized they would make the jungles equally treacherous for our GIs. Since 1981, they had been banned by an international agreement, which the Soviets had signed, but they hadn't stopped dropping them. Although the butterflies were one of my biggest fears throughout my stay in Afghanistan, particularly in rocky areas, they were not the most invidious weapons. That title went to the toy bombs some twisted mind in a weapons lab had dreamed up. Brightly colored plastic dolls, birds, trucks, and pens were also scattered across the countryside by low-flying helicopters. I remembered standing at the foot of a hospital bed in the Afghan Surgical Hospital in Peshawar, with ten-year-old Jahan Zeb Khan, who had just been blinded and had his right hand blown off. His legs were also badly burned, and he kept twisting in pain. "Daddy, it was a pretty green plastic parrot. Why did it blow up when I touched it?" he asked his father, who was crying tears his son would never see.

The Soviets have vehemently denied producing toy bombs; then ironically they produced them recently at a televised press conference in Kabul, where they claimed they were manufactured by the Afghan Resistance.

The *Mujahideen* walking in front of our jeep yelled at us to stop. The charred remains of a tractor-trailer, used to transport people and goods in the mountains, was blocking the road. "Helicopter with a napalm bomb," said Wakil, surveying the large burned-out area around it. I remembered Fatah Khan's warning that the helicopter gunships shoot at anything that moves in a reprisal. While I was photographing the wreckage, six freedom fighters, one on horseback, came down the mountain. "Don't go any farther; the local people say the road has been mined," they said. We turned the jeep around.

□

We heard the bombing long before we would see the jets. The MIGs screamed the length of the valley, and then at the far end we would hear the hollow crump as the five-hundred-pounders landed. Since the burned-out tractor-trailer, Wakil had been at the wheel of the jeep. "I like to drive," he said and then added with a grin, "I also like to be in control if things turn nasty." The vehicle slowly wound its way down the valley side, and as it did, I realized the view of Zazi from a distance was deceiving. From afar, the valley looked picturesque with its green terraces and fruit trees. Close up, however, it was a different picture, worse than last year. The fields and terraces were turning to weed; the apricot and almond trees were untended. Many more of the villages were abandoned; they looked as if they had been victim to simultaneous earthquakes and tornadoes, so thoroughly were they reduced to rubble. Just outside one of these empty villages, a local commander, Rahim Jhan, who was dressed all in black, and one of his freedom fighters joined us. Our guides for the duration of our stay, they clung to the outside of the vehicle because the jeep was too crowded to take them on board.

We were heading toward the village of Sargal, about halfway down the valley, where I had stayed the previous year. I wanted to see how Sargal had fared. We reached the outskirts of the village, and Wakil parked the jeep under a clump of trees so it wouldn't be visible from the air. A boy of about twelve came to greet us. I recognized his face from before but had never known his name. "Karnaiel," he said in Pushto introducing himself and extending his hand. "The planes have been bombing since six this morning." As he spoke, four MIGs shrieked overhead in our direction then veered south to drop six bombs over the village of Sarai, about two kilometers away. We watched as the plumes of smoke rose slowly into the sky. "That's where my house is," said the commander quietly. "The forces have been moving forward for three days. They want to close the border. And they're flattening everything in their path to make sure there isn't any resistance." Many people in the area had moved their families up into the mountains; others remained, still unable to accept that their valley was a free-fire zone, and that being a civilian was no protection. "I think it is better if you stay here, outside the village, until we see where those planes are heading next," said Rahim Jhan, who then dispatched Karnaiel to fetch us tea. We remained standing under the almond trees. A few minutes later, the MIGs returned and dropped two five-hundred-pounders and several incendiary bombs on Sharief Kelai, the village opposite us about three kilometers away. Dashakas and a Zigovak chattered back in response from the top of the peak above the village. "We have a *Mujahideen* camp up there," said the commander. Obviously, the MIG pilots figured out the same thing. Four planes, the sun glinting off their metal, screamed in for the kill. As if someone had stopped a film, they seemed to hover momentarily over the camp as they released their incendiary bombs. We saw them fall, one, two, three, four. Then the mountaintop burst into flame. "Bastards, Communist bastards," snarled Rahim Jhan.

The planes headed west to the end of the valley, to be replaced by others. I guessed from their distinctive shape that they were SU-25s, "Frogfoot" fighters. They howled down the valley and hit Sarai again. The ground underneath us reverberated. Women holding infants in their arms, one of them heavily pregnant, ran from Sargal past us to the fields. "They feel safer there than in the village," Rahim Jhan said. Back and forth the planes swooped, like hawks certain of their prey. I tried to keep a running total of the bombs they dropped, but it was soon impossible. In between attacks, Karnaiel ran back to us, all apologies. "My mother is too frightened to make tea; give her some time," he said, embarrassed even now that Afghan hospitality had to be put on hold. I giggled. "Why are you scared; I'm not," bragged Karnaiel, who began picking almonds to prove it. "You are safe nowhere. The planes can get you anywhere."

The fighters circled and dived again, black streaks against the clear blue sky. This time they came low enough so we could see the pilots. I felt my bowels contract. We heard the explosions, and my ears rang as the ground shook. The goats in a nearby field bleated in fear. I watched the planes climb steeply after they had released their bombs. They had hit the other side of Sargal, probably no more than five hundred yards away: too close for comfort.

Two men came out of the village toward us. They began to yell. "You must leave; our children are here. If they see your jeep, they will bomb us. They know only the *Mujahideen* have jeeps." Their voices were drowned out by the roar of the returning planes. The trees around us vibrated, and in unison, we flattened ourselves in the ditch at the side of the road. But the jets passed overhead to drop incendiary bombs on the far side of the village again. A cloud of acrid smoke rose up.

The villagers stood up and continued to shout, "Our children are in those houses. You must leave." Wakil walked toward the closest one, speaking soothingly all the way. "You should get your children out; take them to the fields. We can't move the jeep right now; the planes will see it if we do. We've parked it under the trees to hide it."

The commander interrupted. "They are here to help you, for your defense. If they leave now and die, you are no better than the Soviets."

Wakil continued, "God has kept you safe for the last six years. Your duty is to dig cellars or bomb shelters to keep your women and children safe. But you can't escape from death, today or tomorrow; we can't know when it will come." I didn't find the end of his speech comforting—quite the reverse—but it seemed to calm down the villagers.

The bombing suddenly stopped. "Lunchtime," joked Wakil; "the Soviets are bureaucrats." In the lull, the commander directed us to move the jeep farther up the mountain, where we covered it with a blanket. Then he took us to a relative's house at the edge of the valley and perched on top of a small wooded ridge set into the mountainside. "You'll be safer here than in the middle of the valley," he said. Introductions weren't even completed before the jets returned. This time they were accompanied by helicopters. We heard the chopper blades before we could see them. Crump . . . crump . . . the bombing began again. It sounded close enough to be Sargal, but we couldn't see from where we were.

For the rest of the afternoon we sat in our host's apricot grove, as the valley was blanketed with bombs. The ground shook almost continually. And an old man with white hair began to pray. The family's dog trembled and whimpered pathetically. "I would like to capture one of these pilots and bring him here," said Omargul, "and show him what he has done. I'd like to ask him, do you have a child of your own, a mother of your own? What do you think of when you release those bombs?"

Unable to sit, I got up and walked around the back of the low wooden house. I found a small pool fed by an even smaller waterfall, which overlooked the terraces down to the valley. The pool was surrounded by the purple flowers of sage and clover. A gentle breeze was blowing, and the smell of wild peppermint wafted toward me. It was a place to believe in God, and it calmed me. Yet in the background, there was the constant noise of jets, and the thundering bombardment. Sitting there alone under the damson trees, I came to the conclusion that if I had to die inside Afghanistan, I wanted it to be with a direct hit of a five-hundred-pounder. There was a randomness about such a death. It frightened me less somehow than being chased by a helicopter or coming up against a tank.

"You know, you're strange," commented Wakil when I returned to the men. "Most journalists would be begging to leave; you just sit here." Sitting there looking at him, I wondered what preparation he'd had in life to make him any more comfortable than I in this holocaust. I remembered the story he'd told me one night in Peshawar. He'd been a research scholar at India's Mysore University, working on his Ph.D. in business administration, when the invasion took place. He'd been having dinner with friends in a restaurant that evening, when someone told them what had happened. "There was a hotel in town with a wire service machine in its lobby. We sat by it all night. But we didn't get any confirmation until the following day.

"I went back to my room. I needed to be alone. I was scared for my family. I had no way of finding out if they were safe. Three weeks later, I received a letter from mother. I was surprised it got through since the country was closed. I didn't hear from them again.

"At first I didn't know what to do. I hung around the campus but I couldn't concentrate on my studies. Weeks went by, then I started hearing reports about Resistance groups being set up in Peshawar. Finally, I decided that was where I had to go."

Saying good-bye to Mysore was difficult on two counts. "You know, I still miss college," he said. "I'd still like to finish my doctorate." The other reason is something he doesn't like to talk about. Wakil was engaged to be married to a fellow student. "I knew I couldn't get married if I was joining the Resistance. If I died, what would happen to my wife? I made a decision I wouldn't think of marriage until the war was over." Wakil was twenty-three. But that wasn't the only relationship he had severed. By joining the Resistance, he knew he would not be able to contact or visit his parents again. To do so could cause their deaths. "I haven't seen my parents for eight years. My father is a very special man; everyone who knows him, loves him. When he dies, something in me will die."

At 6:00 P.M., there was a break in the bombing. "Come on," said Wakil; "I want to check out the damage to the valley before they start up again." We scrambled hurriedly down to the jeep and drove back the way we had come until we met the road on the far side of the valley. Here the countryside had taken a pounding. Huge craters dotted our route, many of them still smoking. We passed a group of refugees leaving, with infants lashed onto the sides of camels. One family had a donkey with its foal tied to its back. It couldn't have been more than a few hours old, and its large brown eyes stared out at the world in terror.

We pulled into Sharief Keilai, the village below the *Mujahi-*

deen camp that had been consumed by fire earlier. The mountain-top was still burning. In the village, there wasn't a building left intact, and the rubble was covered with a thick layer of fresh dust. A man came out to meet us, and Wakil introduced me as an American journalist. "They killed my son; they killed my nephew," he said. "It is good you are here; you must write about what is happening. They are trying to empty the country of peo-ple; they only want the land." We followed him into a courtyard. The bodies of the two boys, age sixteen and twenty, were laid out, their faces uncovered and waxen yellow in the dimming light. Two veiled women sat nearby and cried. "We heard the planes and started running, but we didn't get very far when the rockets began. Metal from the shell hit my son, Jamal, in the back and came out the other side. He didn't say a word; he just sank to his knees and died. Agha Mohammad didn't die so quickly. The shrap-nel cut his leg off above the knee; he died from loss of blood. Look," he said, pointing to a large red stain in the dust; "that's where it happened."

The men grouped around the bodies of the two boys and Wakil led the villagers in prayer in a short funeral service. As we left, we passed the fly-covered corpses of cows almost torn apart by shrapnel.

By now it was too dark to continue, and shelling of BM 13s had taken over where the bombing had left off. We drove back slowly the way we'd come, with the jeep lights off. Wakil tore out the wires to the rear brake lights so they wouldn't glow red every time we braked. I didn't know how he could see to keep the vehicle on the track, but he did. Halfway home, they stopped the jeep and got out for evening prayers. As they chanted *Allah o Akbar*, God is Great, I willed them to hurry up.

At the house that night, we shared the family's meager meal and then spread our sleeping bags on the flat roof. There wasn't room for us to sleep inside. The roof gave us a ringside view of the mountain slopes that still continued to burn. We fell asleep to the sound of continual shelling. At dawn we were woken by a sudden heavy barrage of shells coming down the road on the far side of the valley. "Why are they doing that?" I asked. "There is obviously no traffic on it." "The Soviets know that when their forces are advancing, the *Mujahideen* mine the roads at night. This way the shells detonate the mines before the tanks drive over them," explained Wakil. "And since they are doing that, it means they are much closer than they were. I think we should get out of here. And if we leave now, we can be gone before the planes begin again at six."

We packed and made our way down to the jeep. At least the vehicle still seemed in one piece. I'd no sooner thought that than there was a loud whistling noise overhead, and the commander pushed me flat on my face and hit the ground next to me. There was an ear-splitting explosion as six shells landed about 150 yards ahead of us. We hugged the earth as a rain of pebbles came pelting down. Almost immediately after, another six landed 150 yards behind us. "Oh, shit," I said, pressing my face into the dust. The second series of explosions seemed louder than the first. I turned my head to locate Wakil; he was in a nearby gully. "They've seen us?" I half-asked, hoping he'd say no. "Doesn't really matter, we can't stay here." But neither did I want to climb into the jeep. "Oh why, God," I asked, "why do we have a bright red jeep?"

"If we can get the jeep down to the road, we'll be sheltered till the top of the valley, when we have to cross an exposed ridge," said Wakil.

White-knuckled driving was how I remember that return trip. I gripped the dashboard of the jeep so tightly that the blood drained from my fingers. And every yard we drove, I expected to be blown off the ground. Nobody spoke; I imagined the others were having similar thoughts. But we crossed the ridge safely. On the other side, in the shelter of an outcropping, they stopped the jeep to pray. I offered up a silent thank you of my own, then turned back and looked at the valley. "My God," I thought, "this is what nuclear winter will look like." Much of the stately forest had gone, the mountain sides bare, blackened, and charred, victim to napalm and incendiary bombs. And there wasn't a human or animal moving. The ghost of that valley seemed a microcosm for Afghanistan.

Twelve hours later we were back in Peshawar. The Red Cross Hospital was taking unprecedented numbers of war wounded from this offensive. They had tents and wall-to-wall beds on every spare inch of ground. Even casual visitors were pressed into donating badly needed blood. "We've never had anything like these numbers," director François Zen Ruffinen told me, before asking me my blood type. "Good, a universal donor, just what we need," he said, when I told him.

The following day I attended a VIP visit of seven U.S. congressmen, led by Peter Rodino, chairman of the House Judiciary Committee, and Colorado Democrat Pat Schroeder, to Kachaghari refugee camp on the outskirts of the city. Home to thirty-two thousand refugees, and called the "show camp" by the Afghans, its neat streets are lined with adobe houses, its school and hospital fully staffed. As I sat with Tor in the stifling tent waiting for them to arrive, I kept wishing the congressmen could see what I had seen in Zazi twenty-four hours before.

Suddenly, Tor was beckoned over to the far side of the crowded tent. He returned with a strange expression on his face. "That was Shams Udin from the Special Branch," he said. "He told me to tell you he'd been looking for you everywhere. You've been expelled."

5

The Two Faces of Kabul

Expelled! "In the interest and security of Pakistan . . . and in exercise of the powers conferred by Section 3 of the Foreigners Act, it is hereby ordered that Pamela Janette Goodwin shall not remain in Pakistan, and will quit Pakistan within seven days. . . . And it may please be ensured that the individual concerned does not go under ground in Pakistan." My first reaction was to laugh: even in their delivery of this news, the Pakistani government seemed to prefer dealing with a male, no matter that he was a young Afghan freedom fighter, rather than approach me directly. But when I looked at the document Shams Udin handed me in his office later that day, I was no longer laughing. The expulsion notice had been distributed to ten agencies, including the Ministry of Foreign Affairs, the director of Intelligence, the director of immigration and passport control, the inspector general of police, and the governor of the North-West

Frontier Province. "Isn't this a little heavy-handed for someone who has been declared 'white' by your own Intelligence people?" I asked. Shams Udin looked at me quizzically, and I explained that I had long ago learned to read upside down, and that I read that designation on my intelligence file. "Doesn't that mean I'm not a dangerous subversive?" He agreed that it did.

"It is not my fault. Please don't blame me for it; it is out of my hands," he said in a manner Uriah Heep would have admired. I assured him I didn't. He smiled; we shook hands, so utterly civilized with each other; and I left.

Under the circumstances, there was nothing else to do. I would leave as ordered, go to India, and attempt to return illegally in a couple of weeks. There was another reason I wanted to visit India, but it wasn't one I could share with the *Mujahideen*, at least, not without possibly destroying the trust between us. I wanted to go to Afghanistan's capital, Kabul, and the only way to get there was through Moscow or Delhi. Kabul was totally in Soviet hands, and very few journalists had visited the city since the invasion. The handful who had been granted visas had mostly been socialist. The *Mujahideen* had offered to smuggle me into Kabul, but they had pointed out that with the tight Soviet security in the city, all they would be able to do was take me to the outskirts and move me from one safe house to another at night. "You won't really see anything," they said. "To be honest, the limitations we'd have to place on such a visit wouldn't be worth the dangers involved for you. If you are caught with us, they would immediately label you as CIA. You'd get a show trial and after that a long-term prison sentence, if you were lucky."

Since I had had articles published in the States that were critical of the Soviet presence in Afghanistan, I was sure that I would not be granted a visa as an American journalist. Eddie Girardet, I knew, had been trying to get one for five years. His frequent requests were not even acknowledged. I had also explored the chances of getting a visa as a carpet or antique dealer but had abandoned that idea after learning that once I published anything, the Afghans who assisted me might well pay with their lives. It was then I decided to try my luck as a British-based journalist claiming to work for *Ladies' Home Journal*, London, a publication that doesn't exist. The actual U.K. equivalent, *Woman's Journal*, sounded close enough but would leave me room to maneuver if the Afghan Embassy in London contacted the magazine. In my application, I would use my first name, instead of the name Jan, under which I write, and my British passport, instead of my American. This way, I thought my application shouldn't send off any warning signals.

I decided to contact Dr. Anahita Ratebzad, a senior Afghan Politburo member. I knew that Ratebzad, in addition to being the sole female member of the Politburo, was also president of the World Peace and Solidarity movement and president of the Democratic Women's Organization of Afghanistan, all positions that gave her a lot of power. But there was another reason for her to wield tremendous influence—she was also reportedly the long-time mistress of the Afghan regime's then-president, Babrak Karmal. I was aware that she had been ignored by the foreign press and would probably be flattered by my request. If I could persuade her to grant me an interview, I was sure the visa would follow.

Unable to telephone Dr. Ratebzad from New York, I arranged for a friend to do so from London pretending to be me. To my amazement, Ratebzad said yes to the interview immediately, even though the call to her home was finally put through at 3:00 A.M. her time. She said she would try to arrange a visa, and that if it were granted, it would be through the Afghan embassy in Delhi, India. I silently groaned when I learned that, as it created yet another logistics problem. Once I was in Pakistan, I knew it probably would be impossible to telephone Afghanistan's Delhi embassy. Relations between Pakistan and India are frigid at best, not surprisingly after three wars in four decades. Calls to India are difficult to make and often tapped. The Pakistanis, also, would have suspected my motives had they known I was trying to visit Kabul. I had been relying on the same friend in London to call the Afghan Embassy in Delhi periodically to obtain an update on the visa situation. Her last conversation with an embassy official sounded encouraging.

Now since I was being forced to leave Pakistan, I would be able to visit Delhi in person. The day I left Peshawar, there were front page stories in the newspapers that no one but me seemed to find contradictory in any way: "President Zia to lift martial law" and "All mail to be censored for six months." Pakistan's Special Branch was to intercept all ingoing and outgoing mail of suspicious politicians, journalists, students, lawyers, and their associates. I told Wakil as I left that because of this new ruling, I obviously wouldn't be able to let him know in advance whether I was coming back. "If I make it back, you'll hear from me. Otherwise . . ." I thanked him for his help, not sure whether I would ever see him again.

Cosmopolitan Delhi with its tree-lined avenues, five-star hotels, air-conditioning, elegant restaurants, and stores was a delight after seedy Peshawar. Even the Afghan Embassy was housed in an opulent building set back on a wide boulevard. Presenting myself there the moment it opened, I asked to see Mr. Rahmatullah, an under secretary. I introduced myself and tried to sound convincing when I told him we had talked to each other a week ago when I called from London. Rahmatullah looked at me blankly. He didn't remember my name, nor did he know anything about my visa application, he said. Could he telex Dr. Ratebzad in Kabul? I asked. He could, but a response might take weeks, he explained, obviously used to telling visitors their visas hadn't, and probably wouldn't, come through. As he talked to me he was unpacking his briefcase. One of the papers he stacked on his desk was a short visa approval list. Much to Rahmatullah's surprise and mine, my name was on it. I was approved for a ten-day visit to Kabul.

The next stop was the Indian Airlines office, but here my luck suddenly evaporated. There were no seats for two weeks, they told me. I had been advised against taking Ariana, the Afghan national airline, whose planes before the war had been maintained by West German mechanics but were now infrequently serviced. But after a little fast talking about how Dr. Ratebzad was expecting me that week a place suddenly materialized on the plane leaving the following morning. I wasn't really surprised; India's pro-Moscow leanings also meant they were friendly with Afghanistan's Communist regime. I spent that evening in my hotel room cutting off MADE IN AMERICA labels on my clothes and peeling them off my toiletries, feeling more and more like Mata Hari every minute. I didn't really expect the KHAD secret police to be stationed in the hotel laundry for the sole reason of reading the labels on guests' underwear. But I also knew that since Kabul had very few foreign visitors, particularly journalists, I would probably have more attention paid to me than I would want. It was my

American passport that was the real problem. I knew no one in Delhi, and to leave it with the hotel authorities required more explanation than I was willing to give. In the end, I decided to open the lining of my pocketbook and sew the passport inside. Looking at my stitching afterward, I hoped it would pass even thorough custom and security checks. Now all I had to do was forget thirteen years of American colloquialisms in my speech and remember to answer to the name Pam, a name I'd elected to drop at the age of seven because it didn't suit my childhood image of myself.

Flight 451 to Kabul held forty-eight people, most of them Indian, one Russian, and one instantly recognizable U.S. Marine. About six foot, six inches, with a very fresh military crewcut, his origin was as obvious as if he'd been wrapped in the Stars and Stripes. One of three marines based at the U.S. Embassy in Kabul, his posting was about as enviable as being in Iran just before the hostage crisis. Most of the passenger section of the plane had been stripped down and was given over to large cloth-covered parcels from UNESCO, giving one an impression of traveling on the mail train. The two-hour flight went by quickly. Then, just before landing, there was a flurry of excitement. Looking out the window, I realized why. Two helicopters were dropping flares to mislead any heat-seeking missiles the *Mujahideen* might send up. A DC-10 with three hundred passengers on board had been hit by one when it was landing the year before. It managed to touch down safely, but that was only due to the superlative skill of the pilot. The irony of being shot down by freedom fighters, possibly even those I had been traveling with the previous week, didn't escape me. Only after the helicopters had ringed the airport with flares did our plane begin to lose height. We landed in a corkscrewing spiral that left the majority of passengers regretting any snacks they'd consumed and gave us only a brief glimpse of the jagged, barren mountains surrounding Kabul. We taxied past row after row of military planes and helicopters with the Soviet red star insignias on their tails.

The airport arrival lounge was still under reconstruction after being partially demolished eleven months before when a briefcase bomb planted by the Jamiat Resistance group exploded, killing twenty-seven and injuring dozens more. At passport control, I learned that any foreigner arriving without a diplomatic passport was unusual. That I was a journalist was greeted with frank surprise, but Anahita Ratebzad's name was open sesame here, too. Formalities completed, an airline official walked me to the only taxi waiting outside the terminal. During the drive in from the airport along Bibi Mehru Road, Kabul was considerably more Western and less exotic than I had expected of the city that is said to sit at the crossroads of the world. The shabby two- and three-story buildings and apartment houses that lined the streets were more reminiscent of Eastern European than Asian architecture. The large revolutionary and industrial posters and billboards echoed that sensation. Most of the trucks we passed were Russian-made, and the predominant color of the vehicles on the road, many of which were jeeps, was khaki. Military uniforms were everywhere, the Afghan soldiers with their sand-colored fatigues and pillbox caps, the Soviet conscripts in olive drab with floppy bush hats. The streets were crowded, not surprisingly since the population had jumped from 750,000 in 1979, to 2 million since the Soviet invasion. There is a desperate housing shortage in Kabul, where many internal refugee families find themselves living with relatives as many as fifteen to a three-square-yard room. Microrayon, the sprawling prefabricated apartment development whose design is depressingly similar to the cheaply constructed housing that blights Soviet cities, is doing nothing to alleviate the problem. Accommodation in Microrayon is limited to Russian advisers and their families and Afghan Communist party officials, a fact the *Mujahideen* take advantage of during their regular nighttime shelling attacks.

Kabul fashions, too, were as occidental as most of the city's architecture. A few women wore *chadoris*, the shapeless shroud-like veils, but most were in Western dress, not surprising, perhaps, in a city where women embraced the miniskirt with almost as much enthusiasm in the sixties as did their counterparts on London's Carnaby Street.

Reaching the northwest section of the city, we began to climb up the short, steep hill toward the American-built Hotel Inter-Continental, renamed the *Mailmah Pall*, guest place, now that it is government-owned. We passed the three military checkposts, one every two hundred yards, designed to keep outsiders out and to monitor the activities of guests. Inside the hotel, I felt as if I had wandered onto an unused backlot at Universal Studios. The scenery was all in place, but the players were missing. The dimly lit hotel lobby was deserted and apparently frozen in time with the WE ACCEPT AMERICAN EXPRESS signs still displayed. The Pan Am office was untouched, except for a thick layer of dust, since the day the airline recalled their staff. The gift shop, with its outdated books and magazines and fading postcards, had a bleak, abandoned air, as did the antique store, whose owner had fled to the West shortly after the invasion.

But despite its forlorn appearance, the two-hundred-room hotel was open for business, I learned fifteen minutes later, when a reception clerk finally appeared with apologies. I was the sole guest, and an unexpected one at that. "Things haven't been the same here since the tourists left," he said in an understatement more classically British than Afghan. But although communism may have brought many changes to the hotel, the prices were still distinctly capitalistic. A single room cost $77.50 per night, and television rental $10.00 a day, giving viewers a few hours nightly of such stultifying programs as *Inside Moscow's Metro System* or the latest on the local party conference. These prices seemed pure robber baron in a city where the average monthly salary was 3,000 afghanis, $25.00 per month. The room, however, was comfortable, if lacking in air-conditioning—"too expensive to turn on for one guest"—and room service, despite the hotel's claim of still maintaining a staff of 120.

Unpacked, I decided to let people know I had arrived. My first phone call was to the British Embassy to ask for a briefing that afternoon; my second to Dr. Ratebzad's office to let her know I was in town. When I picked up the phone the second time I learned that my presence had already been telegraphed and was being monitored—a recording of my first phone conversation was playing in the background as the operator made my call.

Although I expected surveillance, I hadn't expected such promptness, naïve perhaps in a city where Khedamat-e-Atla'at Dawlati (KHAD), Afghanistan's KGB-trained secret police said to number more than twenty thousand, has a budget bigger than that of the country's military, is directly financed by the Soviet Union, and whose aim, it boasts, is to have "a member in every family." Certainly its informer network was more widespread this year, both in the capital and outside it, than it had been the previous year according to Resistance sources. KHAD's rapidly growing size has also proved to be cumbersome. There have been a number of incidents in which people have been picked up, imprisoned, and tortured only to be released several months later because they were "mistakenly arrested" in the first place. In addition to the KHAD, every government agency, department, and learning institution is monitored by the more than four thousand Soviet advisers in the city.

It has become increasingly hard to move around Kabul freely. Roadblocks are frequent, with some areas of the city having checkposts every quarter of a mile. Women have been recruited into the militia for the sole purpose of having them check under women's *chadoris*, a garment much favored at the beginning of the war by *Mujahideen* trying to hide their movement about the city. Soviet-style internal passports also were recently introduced because of the rising number of urban guerrilla attacks. A *cordon sanitaire* has been established around the city in an effort to keep out the guerrillas and force them back beyond the range of their 107 mm rockets. Even diplomats find themselves restricted to a ten-kilometer radius of the city center.

"We are issued maps marked with a large red circle," said one. "Fortunately, the nine-hole golf course is just within it; otherwise recreation here would be limited to dinners with the ever-diminishing diplomatic corps. Nowadays, the Western countries party together, and the Indians dine with Russians. But even dinner parties are becoming dangerous. Not so long ago, during a rocket attack, the Japanese Embassy was hit; the dining room was carved up by 170 pieces of shrapnel. By some miracle, no one was in the room at the time. And because of the frequency of such attacks, many embassies have banned the families of foreign service officers. In addition to all this, our chancellories and residences are bugged. A posting to Kabul now is a far cry from what it was not so long ago."

At 10:30 A.M. I heard the first of the day's gunfire. The thud of shelling appeared to come from the other side of town; distant smoke plumes rose up through the haze of dust over the city. Shortly afterward came the responding chatter of heavy machine gun fire. A few minutes later, there was a knock at my door. Sohaila Sherzai, a young emissary from Dr. Ratebzad's office, had arrived. An earnest twenty-four-year-old, Sohaila would be my guide for the duration of my visit. An economics graduate of

Kabul University, Sohaila was obviously on the fast track in her career. She had joined the Women's Democratic Organization at thirteen and the Communist party at sixteen when membership in both was hazardous. At twenty-two she had been sent to the Soviet Union for further training, and then six weeks before we met, she had been one of two women to represent Afghanistan at the UN Decade for Women World Conference in Nairobi. "In Nairobi, two Norwegian delegates likened Afghanistan to Hitler's Germany. They also told us we didn't have freedom. I tried to explain that, of course, we have freedom, that here everything is for everyone, not just the elite," she said. Sohaila then launched into a ninety-minute discourse on the achievements of the revolution. "One of the benefits of the revolution is equality for women," she explained. "Before, women were exploited. Only a few were working. Now thousands of our young girls have gone to the Soviet Union and other socialist countries for higher education. They have many more opportunities." As Sohaila spoke, the distant but distinct thudding of shells continued. I asked her whether equal rights could be practiced when her country was being accused of violating human rights. "The problems in my country have been exaggerated. It is true we are the victims of an undeclared war by America, and by the counterrevolutionaries who kill our children and destroy our hospitals and schools. But bombing does not take place day and night as you read in your press. This is just foreign propaganda, BBC and Voice of America propaganda.

"I know this to be the case because I have traveled around the country to Kunar, Jalalabad, to Laghman, talking to women about the revolution, telling them what my life is like, telling them about the achievements of revolution. One of my memories of these trips is of Laghman Province, where I met many simple and illiterate women who told me they wanted to be educated. Now we have organized literacy and handicraft clubs for them."

I had memories of Laghman, too, but I chose not to share them with Sohaila at that first meeting. Six months prior to our conversation, Soviet armed forces had massacred fifteen hundred Afghans, mostly women and children, in the Qarghaie district of Laghman in northeastern Afghanistan. The killings, reprisals for *Mujahideen* attacks on local Communist bases, had taken place in a dozen villages suspected of aiding or supporting the freedom

fighters. I had met survivors of the Laghman massacre at a refugee camp in Pakistan. Six of them, all men who had each lost their
wives and every one of their children, and I shared a simple meal.
"It was early in the morning; we heard the tanks and helicopters,"
said Shakeer Jamagul, a twenty-nine-year-old farmer. "We
thought they had come to conscript the men. This had happened
before, so I hid in the storage cave at the back of our house. I
thought my wife and children would be safe. Seven Russians
came into my house armed with machine guns. I could see the
faces of the soldiers; they were too young to have beards. They
were laughing as they searched the house. Then, without saying
anything, they raised their guns and fired, shooting my wife and
four children. My youngest son was sixteen days old, my oldest
child seven years old. It happened before I realized what they
were doing. There was nothing I could do but pray. Before they
left, the soldiers took my wife's clothes and jewelry, our lanterns;
they even took soap and candy.

"When I came out, my children and wife were dead, shot
through the head. I found thirty-one bullets in my house."

The farmer's voice trailed off. He stared into space, the pain
still as acute as the day he had witnessed his family's slaughter.
"I left; I couldn't stay there. Outside I found our animals dead;
the soldiers killed our village's cows, goats, ducks. Everything
alive, they killed.

"Seventy-two people died in my village that day, all women
and children. It took us from early in the morning until after dark
to bury them.

"Why did the Russians do this? Why did they kill our babies,
and even our animals?"

Mohamad Fazeer, a thirty-one-year-old twelfth grade
teacher, had a similar story to tell. From a neighboring village of
Kali Raheem, his hands shook as he told me the names of his five
children, age six months to ten years.

"It was just after dawn when the Soviets arrived; there were
twenty helicopter gunships, and I counted two hundred tanks. We
thought they had come for the men, so we ran to the mountains.
Afterward, an old woman who survived told us what happened.
They rounded up the villagers and said 'If you believe in God,
where is your God now?' Then they shot them. They shot my wife

and daughters, but they burned my two sons alive. They were six and seven years old.

"I couldn't bury my family; my relatives did it. I left my village. I could never go back. At night I cannot sleep; the memories come. I am so lonely for my wife, my children. The Russians killed my soul that day."

The end of our meal was interrupted when our host's young son, thirteen-month-old Mir Nasrudin, wobbled into the room on fat little legs and launched himself into his adoring father's arms. As the child snuggled against his father's chest, the look of loss on each man's face told of their pain as clearly as their words.

Other reports from Laghman included children disfigured beyond recognition and a two-week-old baby hung from a tree and bayoneted while his parents were forced to watch. When the infant was dead, the parents were killed. In the village of Shah Mangal, a pregnant woman was asked, "What's in your stomach? A grenade? A mine?" Then the soldier stabbed her in the abdomen with his bayonet, killing the woman and her unborn child.

□

As Sohaila found, memories of Laghman are hard to forget. I also knew that with the restriction on information in Kabul, news of the Laghman massacre would never have reached Sohaila. I wasn't sure that was true of Mohammad Kamal, the twenty-seven-year-old staffer of the government owned Bakhtar Information Agency who arrived at my hotel room two hours later. Like Sohaila he was to be an official guide. Unlike her, he openly noted on a yellow legal pad everything I said and did. Diplomatic and Resistance sources told me he was certainly KHAD secret police. Almost from first meeting, Kamal and I would clash over his pompous officiousness. His company was like having a tireless sheepdog nipping at one's heels. His instructions were constant: "Do this; don't do that; you can't photograph that, photograph this."

Kamal had arrived in a Russian jeep. It would be my transport vehicle for the duration of my trip, something I quickly learned had a major disadvantage. Arriving anywhere in the jeep meant one was immediately assumed to be a Soviet, and the hostility of the average Afghan was clearly visible. I knew that a number of Russians had died when knives were quietly thrust into their backs as they shopped in Kabul's bazaars. The situation had become so bad that most of the markets were declared off-limits to Soviet personnel and their families. Several male diplomats told me that the Caucasians among them also had taken to growing beards so that they would not be mistaken for fair-skinned Russians, who were usually clean-shaven. Anytime I moved around the city on foot, I found myself speaking English very loudly until I had made it clear that I wasn't Soviet. It was always a relief to watch the enmity turn to friendliness the moment the Afghans realized that I wasn't Russian.

As we drove through Kabul that afternoon, I was surprised to see numerous billboards, depicting lurid crashes with corpses strewn across the street, advising motorists not to drink and drive. Muslims are forbidden alcohol, and such public exhortations would normally not be necessary; indeed, they would be considered offensive. Today, however, drunks—both Soviet and Afghan—on the streets are not uncommon. Kabul has a brand-new distillery, a first for Afghanistan, which produces vodka, brandy, and wine. And conscripts in the Afghan army complain they are pressured to drink alcohol as part of Moscow's anti-Islam campaign. The Soviet army, like Soviet society as a whole, has long been plagued with alcoholism. And anti-Russian feelings in the city soared in May 1985, when a tank driven by a drunken Soviet failed to stop at an intersection and mounted a bus, killing sixty passengers and crushing between the two vehicles the traffic policeman whose signal the driver had ignored.

That Kabul was a city at war was obvious that first day. Schools and public buildings had military guards outside, often supplemented with a tank or armored vehicle. A number of buildings were sandbagged. The Indian Embassy had all its windows taped against bomb blasts, and at the main post office even a stamp couldn't be purchased before one was physically searched. I thought of the Afghan Tourist Office on Fifth Avenue in New York, which had been open for business until a month before I left the States. What could they have told potential customers who might have wandered in—"See the bomb damage in downtown Kabul"?

The city's militaristic presence contrasted sharply with the red banners festooning the streets, which proclaimed in Dari WE WANT PEACE ALL OVER THE WORLD. I was reminded of George Orwell's *1984*, in which he predicted that peace will be war; freedom, slavery. An element of "Big Brother" was also lent to the old section of the city as the regime-run Radio Kabul transmitted political broadcasts from loudspeakers in the streets. And yet life went on. Kabul's stores were crammed full of consumer goods from around the world, far more than were available in stores in the Soviet Union, as Russian troops discovered to their delight. The city is a clearinghouse for goods traveling from India, Japan, and China to Western Europe and the Gulf States. Afghan custom duty and taxes are extremely low or nonexistent. On sale in Kabul's only department store were clothes from Hong Kong, New York, and Paris. There were Wrangler jeans, perfumes and cosmetics from West Germany, Sony televisions and radios, Seiko watches. And although Russians went home laden with such purchases, a particular favorite being the large "boom box" radios, many of the items on sale were beyond the budgets of most Soviets and Afghans alike. A color television costs two years' salary for the average Afghan worker; a small, waist-high refrigerator a year's earnings; and a Toyota economy car twenty-seven years' income.

But despite the apparent plenitude of goods, there were shortages. The price of gasoline, if it could be found, rose almost weekly. Food staples have increased considerably in price since the invasion. Prices have risen so steeply that the regime offers heavy food subsidies as an inducement to join the party. Meat, for example, cost three hundred afghanis per kilo at market price, almost half a week's salary. To government employees and party members, the subsidized price was two hundred afghanis. Wheat per seven kilos cost two hundred afghanis, the subsidized price was eighty afghanis. Similar discounts exist for clothing. "This is why almost forty percent of Kabul residents now work for the government," one Afghan official told me. "These people are radish Communists, red on the outside, white on the inside." Large sections of the city often go without water, and while I was there water tankers were servicing some neighborhoods. The water shortage was due to little snowfall in the past two years, plus the rapidly swelling population overtaxing the system. For this reason, too, there are frequent sewage problems, and hepatitis and cholera outbreaks are not uncommon. Much of Kabul is also blacked-out. The freedom fighters frequently blow up the electricity pylons, plunging the city into darkness so often that key government buildings, the Microrayon district, and the Soviet Embassy now have their own generators. The uncertain electricity supply has caused another shortage: the locally bottled Coca-Cola, a favorite with the Soviets, is hard to find these days because the factory is often without power.

My official tour of the city ended at 5:00 P.M. I was deposited back at the hotel and cautioned not to leave it that night. Kabul has a 10:00 P.M. till 4:00 A.M. "shoot on sight" curfew, but the city streets are normally deserted by 7:30 P.M. Taxis refuse to pick up passengers after 7:00 P.M. As my footsteps echoed through the empty hotel, I knew I was in for a lonely evening. I spent it watching the "son et lumière" show supplied by the *Mujahideen* from the balcony of my room. It began at 9:00 P.M. when the first rockets hit the far side of town. Soviet flares and searchlights came into play almost immediately. At the same time, tanks and armored personnel carriers began to clank through the streets to set up positions at important office buildings and intersections, which they manned nightly throughout the curfew. With the exception of these pyrotechnics, much of the city was in darkness; street lamps rarely work anymore. That evening, most of the shelling seemed to be directed at the airport. I was relieved, aware that a shell had landed two hundred yards from the hotel the night before I had arrived, although it was probably meant for a different location. Being hit by friendly fire, stray *Mujahideen* rockets, was one of the risks of being in Kabul. Having watched the freedom fighters fire the 107s without their firing tubes the previous week, I knew all too well how off-target the rockets could be even in experienced hands. It wasn't a very comforting thought.

Staring out over the city, aware of the silence of the hotel behind me, I found myself remembering fondly the Camino Real Hotel in El Salvador's capital, where the media always stayed and where after a day of covering war, there was the instant camaraderie of the press corps to help you forget it. No matter how awful the day in the field, in the Camino Real's restaurant or bar in the evening, the horrors and the difficulties retreated for a while, buried under gallows humor shared with colleagues who'd been through similar experiences. Rattling around in the empty Mailmah Pall Hotel, with only myself for company, it was easy to get jumpy. That first empty evening, I almost wished I didn't know the hotel was often targeted when Soviet or Eastern bloc advisers were staying there. And I hoped the current *Mujahideen* intelligence on the hotel's occupancy level was accurate.

The hottest spot in town during the regular *Mujahideen* shelling attacks, of course, is the Russian Embassy in the Karteseh district. It draws as much fire as the American Embassy did in Saigon. While I was in Kabul, the Soviet Embassy suffered several direct hits and a number of fatalities. The shelling that first night subsided by 11:00 P.M., no doubt when the freedom fighters ran out of rockets. But the Soviet flares continued until early morning.

The life of an urban guerrilla in Kabul is rarely a long one. Few commanders who were operating at the beginning of the war are still doing so. One who is, is twenty-six-year-old Abdul Haq, but he has been injured fourteen times in six years. "A guerrilla's life in Kabul is very short," he told me. "Yesterday, five good friends of mine died. In three years I've lost about eight hundred men. Always you wait for death. Often it is a chance of one second either way that decides whether you live or die. Yes, I'm afraid, afraid that I won't live long enough to get to know my eighteenmonth-old son. The boy doesn't see me often enough to recognize who I am. But fear is not enough to make us stop fighting the Soviets." Another survivor is thirty-five-year-old Dr. Shahrukh Gran, who is now the chief of staff of Kabul Province for NIFA with five thousand men under his command. Both Gran and Haq have a price on their heads. Until 1983 when the secret police raided his house, Gran lived a double life. During the day he was a surgical resident at Kabul's Jamhouriet Hospital; at night he organized shelling attacks from outside the city and hit and run strikes by his explosives teams inside Kabul. "God, we were so naïve when we began," recalled Gran, a short, clean-shaven man, with a serious, thoughtful demeanor, who spoke fluent English. "We were freedom fighters without weapons. All we had was propaganda, which we distributed through *shabnamah*, night letters. In the beginning, we knew nothing about explosives. Sometimes we nearly blew ourselves up. Later, friends in the West mailed me a few books on the fundamentals of demolition.

But it was difficult for me. I'd been taught to save lives, not to take them. For eighteen months I went through a personal hell trying to accept that I could be a killer." It was after Gran had treated two particular patients for the freedom fighters that he finally became convinced that what he was doing was necessary. One was a seventeen-year-old schoolgirl who had been arrested during the student demonstrations. "She had been tortured with electric shock treatment to her breasts, legs, and back. They had placed her on a block of ice to do it: this makes the pain much worse. They had also injected her joints with something, I imagine a chemical of some kind. This girl was permanently damaged, physically and emotionally. Her crime had been to demonstrate. She certainly wasn't important enough to have known anything worth this kind of torture.

"The second patient was a twenty-five-year-old man. He, too, had been tortured with electrodes. He'd been badly beaten, and they had pulled out all his nails. His toes and fingers were a mess. When I saw him, he couldn't concentrate; he couldn't sleep at night—he was too afraid. And he complained of pain throughout his entire body. All I could give him were antidepressants and vitamin B for his nerves. Like the girl, this man will probably never be normal again. When I saw these two patients, I realized that if we didn't kill, we would be killed. There was no other choice. It's like falling into a fast-flowing river: you want to get out, but you can't. You have to go where it takes you.

"In 1983, when the KHAD searched my house, I knew it was only a matter of days before I would be arrested. I gave up medicine, went underground, and became a full-time freedom fighter. I discovered you can save more lives fighting for your people than you can in treating them."

Gran explained that today it is difficult for the *Mujahideen* to operate in Kabul. "There are about four Soviet divisions totaling forty-four thousand men here, plus about four thousand Afghan troops. Then there are the thousands of KHAD, police, militia, and party members. The informers and infiltrators are paid very well: an employee of KHAD makes eight thousand afghanis a month, and they get special bonuses; there's a lot of incentive for them to do their job well. Of course, there's a lot of incentive for them not to get caught, too—we shoot them."

To move around the city now, Gran explained, requires a

military service ID, a regular ID and a workplace or party membership card. "Another problem is we have never been supplied with urban guerrilla equipment like remote detonators," he said. "On any operation in the city, the security forces can locate us within two minutes and seal off that region. Attacking the city from outside is just as difficult today. When we got mortars, the Soviets placed a three-kilometer security belt around the city; when we got rockets, which have a longer range, they built a ten-kilometer belt. They've destroyed all the villages around the city, and they've put antipersonnel mines everywhere.

"And as the city becomes more crowded with refugees, we are faced with a moral dilemma of bombing civilians. We try to hit military areas, but without the firing tubes, the rockets aren't always accurate. But I don't hesitate to bomb Microrayon. The Russians have to understand if our children can be killed, theirs can be, too."

☐

I was awakened at 5:00 A.M. by an aerial convoy of helicopter gunships that flew straight past my window, shattering the morning peace. I counted twenty. A little later, three smaller choppers began to circle, dropping flares to act as decoys for any *Mujahideen* rockets. And then at 5:30 the constant rumble of planes' taking off began. The windows to my room vibrated continuously with the sound. As the gunships and fighter planes flew into the sunrise, I wondered where they were heading. I thought of Hamid and Tor, of Wakil, and of the men I had met in Khost, and I uttered a silent prayer for their safety. It felt strange, too, looking out over this city and knowing that probably only a mile or so from where I was standing were the families of the three men I already felt I knew so well, families they hadn't been able to contact for years. But even if I had told Wakil and the two boys that I was going to be in Kabul, I knew they wouldn't have risked my contacting or visiting their parents. Looking out over Kabul, I was reminded of how Wakil, Hamid, and Tor loved this city. Here, they had been raised and educated and had made plans for their futures. Here, they learned abruptly and with finality that those aspirations wouldn't be.

Five hours later, Sohaila and Kamal arrived to pick me up. I asked them about the constant planes and helicopters overhead. "It looks as if something big is going on. Where are they going, to Khost?"

"It's military practice," said Kamal. "Why would they be going to Khost? The situation there is normal." I mentioned that *The Sunday Times* of London had just run an article with photographs on the current offensive in Khost, and that the BBC had described the offensive as the largest of the war.

"Imperialist propaganda! It just isn't true. People are going to work, schools are open, life in Paktia Province is normal. Recently, West German television showed a film they claimed was made in Paktia. It was perfectly clear to us that it had been made in Pakistan. We had elections in Khost two weeks ago. How could we do that if there were fighting going on? It's the same with these refugees we keep hearing about. The Afghans in Pakistan are not refugees; they are nomads, nomads who have always traveled back and forth between our two countries. They were trapped inside Pakistan when the Americans and Chinese began their undeclared war."

Kamal's brief diatribe left me speechless. Did he really believe it, or was it merely a case of saying it often enough and it becomes true? His polemic was repeated again that afternoon at the Central Council of the Women's Democratic Organization, by the president of Law Commission, Jamila Nahide. "The Afghans living in Pakistan and Iran want to come back to Afghanistan, but those governments won't let them. These people are nomads, members of the Kuchi tribe; they are not refugees."

"But we're talking about five million people; that's a lot of people to feed. Why would Pakistan and Iran want to?"

"Pakistan changes the figures all the time; they are not accurate."

"The figures are supplied by the United Nations High Commissioner for Refugees."

"And where does the UNHCR get these figures? Pakistan inflates them to get money. If there were one million, they would say there were seven million. Pakistan keeps half the money it gets, and it gives the other half to the counterrevolutionaries to wage war against Afghanistan. We want the Afghans living in

Pakistan and Iran to know that if they want to come back, we will give them a house and land."

That there was "no fighting," but Afghanistan was the victim of an undeclared war, that there were "no refugees," but the Afghan regime openly tries to woo them back shouldn't have surprised me. Minutes before this conversation, Jamila, a strikingly attractive thirty-five-year-old, who had the Italianate beauty of a younger Sophia Loren, and I had had another Kafkaesque exchange. I had asked whether the Women's Democratic Organization of Afghanistan was part of the Communist party. "Our party is not the Communist party; it is the People's Democratic Party of Afghanistan. We are here to solve problems of economy, to build a new future for our children, to create new schools, new hospitals. We are not Communist, we are not democrats; we are here to benefit the masses, the peasants. If this is communism, if it benefits the masses, it is very nice. If our enemies say this is the Communist party, we don't care."

There were other surprises that afternoon. Sitting around the twelve-foot-long table in the elegant conference room decorated with badges and decals from socialist women's associations from around the world, I was introduced to Marzia Jahish, the secretary of the Social Commission, who told me she had set up the programs to send Afghan children to the Soviet Union for up to ten to fifteen years. The massive Sovietization program, which recalled Lenin's maxim "He who has the youth has the future," began in 1980 but was not acknowledged until November 1984, when Radio Kabul announced that the children were being sent to Russia to be taught "Marxist-Leninist thinking, and an appreciation of the greatness of the Soviet state and the evils of imperialism." In those first four years, a total of fifty-three thousand Afghan youngsters from the age of seven on up were uprooted from their homes. Forty-seven thousand went to the Soviet Union, the remaining six thousand to Bulgaria, East Germany, and Cuba.

In the subsequent twelve months, ten thousand more were sent. "These children will be the leaders of the party when they return to Afghanistan," Marzia explained matter-of-factly. In her purple blouse with frills at the collar and cuffs, shoulder-length hair, and discreet pearl jewelry, Marzia looked like a kindergarten teacher. It was hard to reconcile the gentle-mannered woman with whom I was sharing tea and melon with the reports of children being separated from their parents at gunpoint and herded in floods of tears on board Soviet airliners. And yet a number of diplomatic sources I spoke to had witnessed such scenes at the city's international airport several times that summer. Such a program violates Article 49, Section III, of the Geneva Convention—"Individual or mass forcible transfers, as well as deportation of protected persons from occupied territory to the territory of the Occupying Power or to that of any other country, occupied or not, are prohibited, regardless of their motive"—which the Soviets signed in 1949. "I see no difference between this and the transportation across Europe of blond, blue-eyed Aryan children for the Nazi cause," a specialist in international law told me.

"How are the children selected?" I asked Marzia.

"We have different programs; some children we send for a month for a rest, a vacation; others go for six months to a year; and others for their entire education. We select the top students; we also choose the children of the poor, or those whose parents have been martyred in the war. We have programs to select children from orphanages, kindergartens, schools. The Soviet Union pays for everything: their transportation, their education, and their lodging. College students, in addition to free tuition, board, and lodging are also given a monthly stipend of ninety rubles." I remembered Tor telling me he had been offered such a chance. "We will send you to medical school in Moscow, all expenses paid," he was told. "But you must join the party first."

"This is a wonderful opportunity for our young," Marzia continued. "They are being given educations their parents could not afford. When they return, they give radio and television interviews; they all have very favorable impressions." This was certainly true of one youngster I was introduced to, eleven-year-old Kadija Zardad, who had just returned from a month's visit. Orphaned two years ago when her parents were killed in a bombing attack in the Panjshir Valley, she told me: "I went for a month's rest. It was very nice: we had sports; they took us to a circus. I would like to live there. Now I am learning Russian. They said I can go in two years' time. My sister went last year when she was six; she will stay in Turkestan for ten years."

I asked Marzia Jahish whether she were planning to send her own ten-year-old son. "He wants to go very badly. But I have told him, first we must send the children of the peasants and the martyred."

Later that week, I would meet the Afghan regime's first lady, Babrak Karmal's wife, Mahboba. We spoke at the Parwarish-gah-e Watan, a national group of orphanages of which she is president. Established for "orphans of the revolution," namely children of party members or soldiers killed in the war, a growing number of the young residents are children of the poor. Youngsters living in these centers receive a more intensive Soviet-style education than in the regular schools. I had just received a tour of the main orphanage, which has room for two thousand children, but housed only nine hundred. "Children are constantly arriving here; each day we receive about ten, but we don't have many here because we send them to Soviet countries for education. For the same reason, we don't permit the children in the orphanage to be adopted. It isn't necessary when the Soviet Union helps us.

"Because of the undeclared war in our country, we don't have enough teachers, or money for new schools, so it isn't easy to keep the children here."

"How do the children live in the Soviet Union?" I asked.

There was a long pause and then much discussion between Kamal, who was interpreting, and Mrs. Karmal. After several minutes' interchange, she replied, "An Afghan teacher accompanies every thirty-five students because of the language differences, and also to teach them the Koran. The children live in hostels in the Soviet Union. They don't become homesick because when our trade delegations go to the Soviet Union, they visit the children. I myself have done so. The Soviet Union is a peace-loving country; all our students have a nice life there."

I could think of at least one child who would disagree with Mrs. Karmal. I had met thirteen-year-old Naiem Jambourai in Peshawar. The son of a school principal and party member in Herat in western Afghanistan, he had been sent to the Soviet Union at the age of seven. "I had been going to school in Herat for four months," recalled Naiem, "when six men came to our classroom. They selected two of us; I was one of them. They told us they were sending us to Russia for special education. My father said that was good."

Naiem was taken to a Party Palace in Kandahar. "They told us we were going to Moscow and that we must study well and do a lot of physical exercise. You are going to be tomorrow's party people, they said." Along with two hundred other youngsters between ages seven and thirteen, Naiem was flown to Kabul, and then to Tashkent in Soviet Central Asia. "A lot of the boys were crying. They were scared; they thought they were being imprisoned. I didn't cry.

"When we arrived, we were taken by bus to what looked like a school. We were given new clothes, then shown where we would sleep. There were seven boys in my room."

Naiem, a slightly built youngster, had large hands and feet like a puppy whose body would eventually grow to match his extremities. The whole time he talked in a voice so low he was hard to hear, he fiddled with his fingers nervously. "In the morning, we were taken to see an officer; he told us we were in a military camp. He said we had to be prepared for the enemy, and they would show us how to fight. We were taught how to hold our breath, how to move quietly, how to crawl on our stomachs, zigzag run, and how to hide. I was the best of all the boys at this, they said.

"After a few days, they showed us how to use an AK-47, and they gave me a Tokarov pistol. They said it was to kill freedom fighters," Naiem laughed, embarrassed, then borrowed Wakil's revolver to demonstrate how well he could handle a gun. "They told us the *Mujahideen* were bandits, that they weren't human. After they taught us about guns, they started giving us half a glass of vodka in the morning and the night. I liked it; they said it would make us grow fat and give us energy."

Six months later, Naiem was sent back to Afghanistan to spy on the *Mujahideen* in the Kandahar region. "I was a good spy; it was easy. We were told to go to *Mujahideen* camps and tell the men our fathers had been freedom fighters before they were killed. The *Mujahideen* were very nice to me. They fed me, let me sleep there. Every two weeks, I reported back to the Russians what I had seen or heard. Once I was taken up in a helicopter that was bombing an area I had reported on. I knew that people died because of my reports. I thought it was a good thing." Finally Naiem was himself informed on. Running from the *Mujahideen*, he was shot in the hip. The boy was lucky. It was only a flesh wound, but he still carries the scar. Naiem spent a year inside Afghanistan living with the freedom fighters, and then was sent to Peshawar for "reeducation." A lonely, disturbed young man who is trusted by no one, he would like to meet his father again "so I can kill him for doing this to me." Naiem is illiterate, although shortly after I met him, a *Mujahideen* family hired a tutor for him.

But for Sovietization, it isn't necessary for the children to be sent to Russia. A rapidly growing program is already under way in Kabul's kindergartens, schools, and colleges. As I toured all three, I became used to seeing signs written in the Cyrillic alphabet with the much smaller equivalent in Dari underneath. With the younger children, even two- and three-year-olds, I was greeted with revolutionary songs. Ten-year-old boys wearing the red kerchiefs of the Young Pioneer movement saluted me Russian military style and then proudly showed me round their "Friendship Rooms," which were decorated with pictures of Marx and Lenin, and banners from youth organizations in Cuba and Eastern Europe. Most schools taught Russian, and graduation and subsequent college entrance were limited to youngsters who joined the Youth Organization of the Communist party. At the Zarghona High School for Girls, the largest in the city with a student enrollment of three thousand, I attended a monthly "Peace Lecture," which was mandatory for the students. This one was castigating the United States for its "Star Wars" program. It was given by seventeen-year-old Nelofer Pazera, who summed up by saying, "The people who don't want peace are those who dropped the bombs on Nagasaki and Hiroshima. They are the enemy of progress and democracy. Until now, the United States hasn't responded to the Soviet Union's desire for peace. The United States wants only to drink the blood of our young people. We can see the tears of the mothers, the orphans. We must unite in peace against imperialism." The end of her lecture was greeted with whistles and catcalls, which I found encouraging but perhaps misread, and nobody would explain to me. Later, I was told that Nelofer was a star pupil but hadn't always been that way. "In the beginning, we had trouble with her. Her family has relatives in America, and she was against our party. But in two years we were able to teach her the reality of our state and our revolution. Now we expect her to go to university and study science."

At university, students are required to attend courses in Marxist-Leninist political theory. Other classes include dialectical materialism, history of Russia, and history of the workers' movement. To make way for such courses, many Islamic classes were dropped. According to the official English-language newspaper, the *Kabul New Times*, 60 percent of the Kabul University faculty is from socialist countries. The article didn't say, of course, that the former faculty members had been imprisoned, executed, or forced into exile. Professor Hasan Kawun Kakar, Afghanistan's leading historian, for example, and a number of his colleagues were imprisoned in April 1982, after planning to found an organization to defend human rights and academic freedom at Kabul University. A former research associate at Harvard University, Kakar has spent much of his time in solitary confinement in the notorious Pul-i-Charki prison, where his health is said to be uncertain since he was severely tortured.

The majority of students at Kabul University today are female. Third- and fourth-year male students frequently flee the city to avoid being drafted. But being exempt because one is a student is no longer a guarantee against forcible conscription. Boys as young as fourteen have been press-ganged on the streets of Kabul to combat the massive desertions that occurred when the term of service was extended from three to four years in 1984. While in Kabul, I saw youths who looked as if they were junior high school students stopped by the military and asked for identification. On one occasion, one young boy was driven off in an army jeep. And I remembered Farouk, a freedom fighter I had met in Peshawar. He had been forcibly inducted into the Afghan army at the age of seventeen on his way home from school in Kabul. "I was grabbed on the main road. I told the soldiers I was a high school student and showed them my exemption card. They laughed and tore it up. I was thrown in the back of a truck with other boys. My family didn't know if I was alive or dead for a week. I was sent to Khost, where I wasn't even allowed to go to the toilet without being accompanied, in case I escaped."

And because the Afghan armed forces have become so depleted, it isn't unusual to find men who've been conscripted several times. Although the age of conscription is supposed to be eighteen to forty, I interviewed prisoners of war held by the *Mujahideen* who were as young as fifteen and as old as fifty-five; the latter, Sultan Mohammad from Takhar Province, had been forcibly conscripted three times. "I was never given the chance to go home and tell my family," he told me. "My mother, wife, and children were left with no means of support." Forced recruits receive two hundred afghanis a month; volunteers get between three thousand and six thousand afghanis.

This lack of concern about family members left uninformed was detailed by Farouk. "While I was in the army, they brought in a forced recruit who had been press-ganged while his wife was in the hospital giving birth to their third child. She needed blood, and he had been sent to get it when he was stopped by soldiers. He pleaded with them to let him go. He explained that he had also left his two children age two and three locked in at home alone because in the emergency, he hadn't had time to find anyone to watch over them. For eight days, he kept telling the authorities why he needed to go home, but they watched him constantly. Finally, he fled. When he got back to Kabul, he found his wife had died in childbirth, and his two children were dead from dehydration. The authorities caught up with him later and brought him back to the base; he was almost out of his mind."

With all the effort required to maintain an Afghan army, perhaps the most ineffectual and least cost-effective in existence, it doesn't seem worth Moscow's trouble. But it does have public relations value. Without the army, of course, Babrak Karmal would have found it difficult contending that his was not a Soviet "puppet" regime.

□

After two days of being fed the party line, I knew I needed to explore Kabul alone and meet some ordinary Afghans. Having been dropped back at the hotel, I waited until Sohaila and Kamal's jeep had left; then I strolled back down the hill, hoping to find a cab on the main street at the bottom. The Afghan soldiers at the third and last checkpost came out and shouted at me as I walked by. Without waiting to see whether they wanted me to stop, I hailed a passing taxi. But the driver didn't speak a word of English, and since he would be useless as an informal guide, I stopped him after we were out of sight of the hotel checkpoint. I was luckier with the second cab. The driver spoke fluent English; he was a graduate from the agricultural school of New Mexico's State University. He also had a brother who worked in banking in Berkeley, California. The driver refused to give me his name: "It wouldn't be safe for me to tell you; call me Abdullah," he said, before explaining he had been an official in the Ministry of Agriculture before the invasion.

"We had a nice house in Helmand Province, but we lost everything; the government took it," he said. "In the purges, my two brothers and two of my nephews were arrested; so was my wife's father. They were taken to Pul-i-Charki; we've never heard from any of them since. They are probably dead. I was told they were going to arrest me, too, but they didn't. I just lost my job. Then when our house was bombed a year ago, I moved my family to Kabul. I bought this old car and became a taxi driver."

"Wouldn't it be safer for you to leave Afghanistan?" I asked.

"I would like to go to Pakistan, but now it is difficult to leave. The journey is very arduous, my youngest child is only four months old, and I was recently told I have a heart condition. I am only forty-three, so I think it's caused by nerves, by the situation here. Then the security on the roads now is very strict, and it also costs between twenty thousand and forty thousand afghanis for a guide. I don't have that much money."

Concerned about whether he was all he seemed to be, I made only a vague offer to mail a letter for him to his brother in California or to friends he might have in Pakistan. "One letter isn't enough; you need continuous contact," he replied. I let it go at that and changed the subject. It was a warm evening, and I offered him a soft drink from a roadside stand. "I'm sorry; I can't. It would be dangerous for me to be seen talking with a foreigner on the street." I bought a solitary Fanta, while he sat in the taxi; then I purchased six lollipops, one for each of his children. He was pleased. "You know, I would like to take you to my home and introduce you to my wife and children, but I can't. In the past, we used to entertain a lot of foreigners, show them our culture, but now it wouldn't be safe to do that."

As we continued on our tour-cum-interview through the now darkened streets, he suddenly became angry. "Ninety percent of the ordinary people in Kabul prefer the *Mujahideen*. They don't want this government; they hate it," he said in an emotional outburst. "The only truth we get is when we listen to the BBC, when the government doesn't jam it. With all my education, look at me, driving this broken-down taxi when I can afford and can find gasoline. But that's true of a lot of things here. You can buy silk in this town if you have the money, but you can't find sugar."

At seven-thirty, with traffic considerably thinned out and the first of the evening's flares lighting the sky, "Abdullah" decided it was time to take me back to the hotel. I asked him how it felt living in a city where they were regularly shelled by the people they supported. "Obviously, the *Mujahideen* shells do kill innocent civilians," he replied. "But I don't think the majority of Afghans would want them to stop. I know I don't want them to."

When we returned to the hotel, after a two-and-a-half-hour drive, he refused to take any money. I thanked him and wished him luck. "It is good you are here to see what is happening. *Zamana Kharab Ast*—times are bad—" he said, driving off in a cloud of fumes.

Behind and Beyond the Veil

My third day in Kabul, I was again awakened with a start at dawn as the first of the planes began to fly over. But this time it quickly became apparent that this was no "military practice." By 5:30 the sky was so full of jets and gunships heading west that they looked like clouds of birds migrating for the winter. Sleep was impossible, and I went out onto the balcony to watch what was an intimidating display of Soviet aerial power. From the valley, wafting up with the smoke from an early morning cooking fire, came the strains of a flute played no doubt by a young goatherd I had seen the day before. The sound was appropriately melancholic. But the music was abruptly wiped out by the clattering of a line of helicopters that swung so close to the hotel, perhaps no more than a hundred yards from where I was standing, that I could clearly see the features of the pilots. Soon, the sound of Howitzers firing out of the city could be heard. Whatever was going on obviously wasn't far from Kabul.

As Kabul residents began their day, I wondered how they responded to the plane-filled sky that greeted them that morning. In a city where all news, print and electronic, is state-controlled, where information is strictly limited, did they still react, or were they after six years of war numb unless they were the target? And how did it feel for the parents of *Mujahideen* like Wakil or Tor who lived in the city and who had no way of knowing whether their sons were alive or dead, but must watch with dread as these machines of death flew off on their missions. Sohaila and Kamal's reactions were predictable: the aircraft were not on their agenda; therefore they would be ignored. Possibly Sohaila had trouble seeing them; her vision was obscured by the enormous arrangement of flowers she was holding. "We are going to put flowers on the tomb of the unknown soldier at Tappe Shohada, our martyrs' cemetery," she said, pointing to a peak on the far side of town, one of six that dissect Kabul. "Visitors should see how many of our young men we have lost in this undeclared war against our country."

Fifteen hundred feet above Kabul, the cemetery dominated the summit of the Tappe. Rows of graves stretched as far as the eye could see, each one marked by red and green flags flapping in the breeze like standards on a medieval battle field. "The red flags are for the Communist revolution; the green is the color of Islam," said Sohaila. Like Sohaila, the families of those buried there obviously saw nothing contradictory about these two beliefs. But then neither did their leader, Babrak Karmal. In an effort to win the hearts and the minds of his countrymen, staunch Communist Karmal also claimed he was a devout Muslim. Pious Muslims, however, were outraged when he forgot to remove his shoes on visits to mosques, and they also referred to his heavy whiskey consumption. But in rhetorical overkill, the president had even gone as far as describing the Soviet invasion as being God-given. On Radio Kabul he declared: "The date of December 27, 1979, represents the intervention of God Almighty. That the USSR is helping us is also an act of God."

Would he also describe the waves of MIGs and HIND helicopters roaring overhead that morning as another act of God? I mused. The aircraft were flying so low over the cemetery that the metal railings around the graves were vibrating. The noise was deafening, yet Sohaila and Kamal both commented on the peace of the cemetery. "It used to be the king's favorite picnic ground; it's easy to see why," said Sohaila, pointing to the spectacular view over the city. Unable to deny, as they could, that we were in the direct flight path of a major offensive, I finally pointed my camera at the sky and started taking photographs. Almost as suddenly, Kamal pushed the camera down, knocking it out of my hands; it swung from the strap around my neck as we glowered at each other. "This is a military exercise, and you cannot photograph military activity," he snapped. I waited for him to demand my film, but he went on to lecture me on how "every country forbids photography of such things." I corrected him. "That's one of the reasons the free world is so named," I said. Sohaila was clearly embarrassed. "Why don't we walk a little?" she said.

We began to stroll along the rows of graves. Most of the headstones were decorated with photographs of the soldiers buried there. The weather-faded color prints made the dead seem less anonymous than plain stone markers. I found myself stopping several times at particularly young faces or sympathetic ones. The photographs served as a reminder for me that both sides of this war had their grieving parents, widows, and orphans. Sohaila led me over to a grave where two women were sitting. The headstone was marked with the name Lt. Mohammad Rassoul; he had been twenty-one when he died two years previously, but in his photograph he looked like a playful eighteen. Despite the warm day, both women, Rassoul's mother and aunt, were wearing the traditional, heavily embroidered black and red velvet dresses and *tombons*, baggy pantaloons, of country women. The centers of their foreheads were marked with the decorative indigo tattoos they had received in their teens. Their heads were covered with black veils. Both women had lost sons in this war. Sohaila introduced me as a British journalist. Rassoul's mother turned on me. "This is the fault of the capitalist countries," she said angrily, pointing to her son's grave. "He was my oldest son; he was killed by the counterrevolutionaries near Kabul. Both our sons have poured their blood into this country. I raised him; he was a good son, and then the counterrevolutionaries came and killed him because he was a member of the PDPA. Then they burned our house." She began to cry, but her tears didn't dissipate her anger. "I'm a mother; I cry as a mother. My son was killed defending the revolution. It was an honor for him to die this way. If my other children die for the revolution, it is a good thing. But if I find the enemy of my son, the enemy of our people, I will take up a gun."

Sohaila had said something very similar to me at our first meeting. "I would like to go to the front and fight. If the counter-revolutionaries kill me, it will be a big honor. I don't want to die without a reason, but when I go in defense of our revolution, I am glad if they kill me, if it benefits our society. At the front, I am not afraid if it is in defense of our revolution." I asked her if she had seen any fighting or knew how to fire a gun. "No, not yet. But I have had friends who've been killed."

"Are there women fighting in the revolution?" I asked. "We have many; the WDOA has set up Women's Defense Groups all over the country. They are armed, taught how to use the weapons, and then they are responsible for defending their communities." She said she would arrange for me to meet such a group.

Driving back through town, it was obvious there was a great deal of troop movement on the ground, as well as in the air. We passed military trucks, tanks, and armored personnel carriers heading out of Kabul. The traffic was much heavier than I had seen it before, and we were forced to crawl past the Soviet military hospital. Originally called the "four hundred-bed hospital," it now held sixteen hundred. That the Soviets were also taking heavy losses because of the recent military escalation had become apparent several weeks before my arrival, when the hospital announced it would no longer treat diplomats and their families, because it didn't have enough room. If the line of ambulances snaking into the hospital grounds was any indication, that was not an exaggeration. The ambulances were backed up half a block from the hospital. Teams of conscripts could be seen through the open gates unloading them. But for Kamal, they were invisible; it was as if he were playing some weird DRA version of "the emperor has no clothes." He did it again a few minutes later, when our jeep caught up with a massive armed convoy heading past my hotel. Moving at the slow pace of the tanks, many of which were carrying missiles, the convoy quickly caused a large traffic buildup behind it. A few impatient taxis pulled out into oncoming traffic to pass it. Our driver began to do the same. But Kamal instructed him to drop back. I imagined he wanted to prevent me from seeing how large the convoy was. Or perhaps he really hoped that if we didn't pull alongside it, I wouldn't notice it. I burst out laughing. "You know, a convoy this big doesn't disappear just because you pretend it isn't there," I said. He didn't reply.

Later that day, I learned that a major offensive had been launched in Paghman, twenty kilometers west of the capital. The previous month, the *Mujahideen* had continuously rocketed the Khargha military base from this region. Now the army was trying to flush out the freedom fighters and ensure that civilian support of the Resistance came to an end. As we passed several cinemas showing propaganda military movies, I wondered whether such films convinced the Afghans who served in the DRA army that the devastation of places like Paghman was necessary. The posters of upcoming movies outside the Zenab Nindary Cinema in the Shah-renaw district were inexplicably in English, although a number of the films were made in Russia: *They Fought for Our Motherland, The Great Patriotic War, The Lad from Our Town,* and *Our Destiny* all glorified war. Sohaila recommended we see *Sabor the Soldier,* which had been made in Afghanistan, and offered to translate the dialogue for me. Sabor's storyline was simple and blatant. A chubby, rather lazy youth, Sabor had had grades too poor for him to enter college; therefore, he would be conscripted. But Sabor had been terrified of being drafted ever since he'd witnessed *Mujahideen* stop a bus and drag off everyone in army uniform. The unfortunates were all slaughtered on the spot in a vivid technicolor flashback. He also knew the *Mujahideen* were the enemy of the people because he had attended a wedding where most of the guests had been blown to pieces after several bombs were planted under their tables. The scene of ensuing mayhem in which dismembered limbs sailed across the screen went on for several long minutes.

Despite his fear, and his threats to go to Pakistan, Sabor was forcibly inducted. Through boot camp he was inept and cowardly. Finally, however, he vindicated himself when he rescued a friend and then singlehandedly wiped out several hundred counterrevolutionaries, all of whom were portrayed as evil fellows with effulgent beards. When the lights came up nearly two hours later, the cinema was crowded, mostly with young men, many of them in army uniform.

The *Mujahideen*-are-monsters propaganda wasn't limited to the movies. Posters depicting the nefarious deeds of the leaders of the seven *Mujahideen* parties were plastered all over the walls of public buildings, particularly schools and colleges. One that was common showed Sibghattula Mojadeddi, head of the moderate group Jabha-ye-Nijat Milli Afghanistan. The bespectacled professor of theology, who is recognized throughout the Muslim world as a respected Islamic scholar, was pictured with a large bloodied dagger between his teeth and wearing a prominent American dollar sign. Behind him a filmstrip showed drawings of him shooting mullahs in a mosque, stabbing a father as he walked his two young sons, and burning a school.

Such campaigns were obviously effective. Sohaila believed they were factual, as did the members of the Women's Defense Group I met the following day. We were in Golkana, a large adobe village a few miles outside Kabul, which had just recently received electricity. "This village is an example of the progressive life for all the workers in our country," said Kamal, as he and I trudged through the winding mud lanes thick with dust and leaped over ditches used as open sewers. Plumbing hadn't yet come to Golkana. We were shown into the clubroom of the local branch of the Women's Democratic Organization. It was lined with treadle-operated sewing machines and looked more like a traditional women's club than the local headquarters for the female militia. "No, no, all of these women are defenders of the revolution," insisted Sohaila, introducing me to their commander, Feroza Fidaie, a gray-haired woman who told me she was forty-five, but looked fifteen years older. Dressed in baggy white pants, a navy and white polka-dotted *kameez*, and navy veil, with silver bangles on both wrists, she could have been a work-worn grandmother. But Fidaie not only claimed to have fought at the front in 1980 and 1981; she had also recently been elected to Afghanistan's Grand Assembly. She had been widowed and had lost one of her six sons under President Amin, whom she called "CIA," just before Karmal took office. Fidaie brought out the Enfields, folding commando-style AK-47s, and Soviet Papasha machine guns, which were given to the group by the state. I asked what sort of training the women received. "No training, it isn't necessary: all women learn how to fire a gun in their villages." I pointed out that so did men, but they also received military training. "We are breaking tradition just by having these women's defense groups; we must move slowly." Didn't it seem odd, I asked, that the guns were supplied by the state, that the women were willing to die for the state, but the state didn't want to train them how to use the weapons? "It isn't necessary," they insisted. "Not so long ago," said Fidaie, "Marogoul here killed a counterrevolutionary. She shot him as he tried to enter her house when her husband and son were away. She was able to shoot well enough to do it in the dark."

A little later, I asked the women to pose with their Kalashnikovs for a photograph. Of the four armed with the machine guns, only Fidaie knew how to extend the folding butts. It was left to Kamal to show them. Their lack of basic knowledge about their weapons made me wonder how much of a role the Women's Defense Groups really played. That the groups existed at all, signified a change in the status of women in Afghanistan—a change that invariably takes place, however, when a nation is at war. Looking around Kabul, one could see that it was a society consisting mostly of the elderly, the young, and the women. And with most of the men away fighting either with the *Mujahideen* or in the army, more opportunity was open to the women. Next door to the Women's Defense Group, literacy classes were being held. Before the war, Afghanistan's literacy rate had been only 15 percent. Outside the large cities, few women or men had the opportunity to go to school. Now in this simple mud classroom, fifteen women between eighteen and sixty were sitting on the floor reading aloud from mimeographed primers. "In the Revolution, the power is with the people," they chanted over and over again. The class, which was six months old, was taught by a young woman who hadn't graduated from high school. She showed me the arithmetic textbooks. They were filled with illustrations of tanks, tractors, and happy workers. "Great claims have been made in the battle against illiteracy," one Western diplomat told me. "But six years after the invasion, there are still only 1,917 women registered in literacy classes outside Kabul. And by the regime's own admission, 90 percent of the female population is still illiterate."

Unless a woman is a college graduate and a party member, there are not many jobs open to her. One of the larger employers is the state-run Bagrami Textile Mill, on the outskirts of Kabul.

The conditions and benefits described by the mill's president, Abdul Rahim, as we sat in his office decorated with large photographs of Babrak Karmal and Anahita Ratebzad, sounded excellent. "Our fifteen hundred workers get fifty days' paid vacation a year and three months' paid maternity leave. We supply free transportation to and from the city, two meals a day, a company clinic, youth club, and Friendship Room, and a free kindergarten."

Conditions began to seem less than ideal during a tour of the factory floor. Opening the double doors to the factory, one was stunned by the noise of the machines, which made speech, even shouting, impossible and hurt the ears. The heat from the machines made the vast room oppressive. The air was thick with cotton filaments, which dimmed the already dim light, and made it difficult to breathe and see. None of the machines had a noise hood; none of the workers was supplied with face mask, eye goggles, or protective ear covers. Employees, some of whom looked as young as eleven, worked ten-hour shifts, six days a week. When we left, three of the factory executives came out holding their ears and complaining of the noise.

I was asked whether I would like to see the factory kindergarten. As we drove out of the textile mill, we could see the first of that day's returning helicopter gunships landing immediately behind the factory. A jet flew overhead in the direction of the main airport trailing a thick plume of black smoke, suggesting that it had been hit. The kindergarten was located a mile away from the factory, in a stark three-story building set back from the road. Parking near the highway, we picked our way over the unfinished driveway. "There are fifty of our workers' children here," the factory guide told me. Inside I was shown into a sparsely furnished room where four toddlers were napping. The director, who was also the total staff, was a young girl of nineteen. Looking at the bare cement walls and floor, I asked if the kindergarten was still under construction. I was told no: it was fully operative. I asked to see the other rooms. "It isn't necessary; the other children are all home sick." A quick stroll down the hallway showed the other rooms completely empty.

Outside, I looked at Sohaila quizzically. It was becoming apparent that the DRA needed a little more practice on giving Western journalists guided tours around the achievements of their revolution. As we walked back to the jeep, Sohaila surprised, and also endeared herself to me when she quietly admitted, "There are only four children in the kindergarten because we don't have the budget. Because of the undeclared war, all our budget goes to the military." But then she quickly reverted to the party line: "Before the revolution, the cares of women with children were not attended to. Now they are."

Before the revolution, conditions for women depended on where they lived. In Afghanistan's few cities, girls were educated, and many went to college. The majority had discarded the all-enveloping *chadori;* they had been encouraged to do so by the king several decades before. And although arranged marriages were still the norm, love matches were becoming common. In Kabul, it was not unusual to see boys and girls out strolling together.

In rural areas, however, a women's existence was very different, and her position in life was defined at birth. When a son was born, the event was celebrated with the firing of guns and a feast. With the birth of a daughter, there was silence. Friends and relatives expressed their sympathy. I frequently met men who would tell me they had "three children and four daughters."

From the moment of birth a girl was taught to be invisible. Their heads would be covered from the time they were toddlers; many were wearing full-length *chadoris* even before puberty in the presence of men other than their immediate family.

The *chadori* is a garment I grew to detest on the occasions I was required to wear it when traveling with the *Mujahideen* in Pakistan and being smuggled past checkpoints. Made of silk, nylon, or heavy cotton, they weighed several pounds and were suffocating. One never felt the sun or a breeze touch one's skin. The embroidered eye grill, which measured four by one and a half inches, meant one could only see directly ahead. Going up or down stairs or walking over rocky terrain was a frightening or painful exercise. And yet the *chadori,* or the more modified head veil, is not stipulated by the Koran. The paragraph that refers to feminine dress and behavior says only, "And tell the believing women to lower their gaze and be modest, and to display of their adornment only that which is outward, and to draw their veils over their bosoms." Both the *chadori* and *purdah* were merely fashions borrowed from the Persians and persistent in the Muslim world since then.

Outside the cities, if education were available, it was restricted to boys; I remembered meeting women who had never
held a pencil. A woman's world was mostly limited to the confines
of her home, behind high *purdah* walls, unless she was required
to work in the fields. Her day began at daybreak, when she rose
to pray, and continued until well after dark. Firewood and water
had to be fetched, sometimes involving treks of many miles.
Every meal took several hours of preparation. Men and boys ate
separately and before the women, who divided what remained;
consequently, malnourishment was far more common among
girls than their brothers. And in addition to household chores, the
average woman had ten children to care for. Their rights were
few, and even a visit to a neighbor required permission from their
husbands.

A village girl was often engaged as an infant and married by
the time she was thirteen or fourteen. In most cases, the first time
she would have seen her husband was during the wedding ceremony when a mirror was held under her veil so she could see his
reflection. Once married, she was required to live with her parents-
in-law. If she failed to become pregnant, her husband would take
a younger, and hopefully more fertile, wife. He was entitled to
four wives and was supposed to treat all of them equally. Divorce
was the prerogative of the male only. If a woman had been divorced by her husband, she was permitted to have her children
live with her until the boys were seven and the girls nine. Then
the husband assumed custody.

Since the war, some of the restrictions for women have become relaxed both in the cities and in the villages, and mostly out
of necessity, such as the formation of the women's defense
groups. But although Moscow and the PDPA have claimed to
have brought a new equality for Afghan women, many things
haven't changed. In court, for example, the evidence of one man
is still considered equal to the evidence of two women. And divorce still can be initiated only by a man, but now it is decided in
the woman's presence instead of in her absence, as before. The
custody of children continues to go to the father, "although we
want to change that," Aziza Pewiston, a woman lawyer, told me.
"Eventually, we hope to take into consideration which parent can
benefit the child more, and what the child wants."

For Sohaila, too, as progressive as she considers herself, her choice of husband will be made by her father. The same is true for her twenty-five-year-old sister, who is studying economics in Leningrad.

"That doesn't sound as if the revolution has brought about equality for women," I told her.

"It is our custom," said Sohaila shyly, also acknowledging that for the same reason she had never had a boyfriend. "I will get married in about three years' time, when I am twenty-six or twenty-seven, when my father thinks it is time."

Blushing and giggling, Sohaila admitted that when she was graduated from college, there were four men who wanted to marry her. Her father turned them all down on the grounds that she was too young. "My favorite was Wahid, who worked in the Foreign Ministry. He was a friend of my brother's, and he used to write poetry to me. But my father found out and was furious. He forbade Wahid to come to our house. I told my father I liked him, but my father said, 'You can marry him if you like, but you will never see your family again.'

"Wahid married someone else, but they were divorced after nine months because he could only talk about me. Now that he is divorced, of course, my father will never let me marry him."

Until Sohaila does marry, she will live at home with her parents in their Microrayon apartment. Her father is an official in the Ministry of Banking; her mother is illiterate. I asked her which she considered more important to her, her religion or her politics. "Oh, politics, of course."

"Do you want to marry a party member?"

"I would prefer it, but it isn't necessary. But if he isn't a party member, I don't want to have to explain all the time the party's ideology to his parents."

The war has also caused a curious reversal for some Afghan women. A number who were living Westernized life-styles have reverted to more traditional customs. It isn't unusual in Kabul to find educated families whose women, particularly the young ones, are wearing the *chadori* for the first time in their lives. "A number of girls have been abducted and raped by drunken Soviet soldiers," one told me. "The *chadori* gives us some protection." There are also refugee women in Pakistan who now find their lives circumscribed, whereas before they weren't. One woman who found herself in this situation was Sameen, whose home had been in Kabul. I had met her in Lakti Banda refugee camp in Pakistan. We sat talking on the dirt floor of her simple one-room mud house. Her clothes were tattered, patched, and muddied. Despite the desperate poverty of Sameen's life, there was a grace and dignity to her every movement. Her slim, tall figure made her seem more like a model than the peasant her clothes suggested. As she prepared tea for me, she laced it with honey she could ill afford and I didn't want, but she did it anyway. It was a gesture of hospitality, and Sameen had nothing else to offer a guest.

"I was not like this before the war," said twenty-six-year-old Sameen, brushing her purple *kameez* with her hand as if to rub off the mud. "I wore Western clothes, had my hair styled regularly. Now look at me. Today I live in *purdah*. I cannot go out unless I am covered by a veil. Before, we had a beautiful house, and now . . ." She stopped speaking, and my eyes followed her around the empty room, with its cracked and flaking mud walls. "Here there is no electricity, no bathroom, no running water, no kitchen. I'd never cooked on an outside cooking fire before.

"But what I really miss are my books," Sameen, who has a bachelor of science degree, said quietly. "But more than wanting books for me, I want them for my children. I want my children to have an education, to have a future."

Sameen's husband, Faiz, a civil servant, was forced out of his job after the invasion. They fled to Pakistan with their two children, leaving behind everything they owned, when word reached them that Faiz was going to be arrested. In that uprooting, Sameen was plunged into an anachronistic existence with which she still hadn't come to terms. By pure luck of the draw, the camp to which Sameen and her family were relocated was one ruled by fundamentalist mullahs. "Living in *purdah* is very difficult for me," said Sameen. "Perhaps if you are born to it, it is easier. But I wasn't. Even the little everyday things like fetching water are more difficult. The path to the well is very steep and I've fallen many times. Wearing a veil, I cannot see properly.

"There are also many things I can no longer do. Last year, for example, I tried to start a school here. Our camp doesn't have one, and I wanted my children to be able to read and write. I also thought it would be a way to put my education to good use." No sooner had Sameen started the school than the mullahs closed it down. They were outraged at the idea of a woman teaching. For several months, as punishment, Sameen and her family were ostracized.

When I left, Sameen covered her face with her veil and accompanied me a short distance down the track outside her house. "I'm sorry I can't walk you to your jeep," she apologized, "but there are men in it. The people here wouldn't approve." After we said good-bye, I turned to watch her pick her way slowly back up the rocky trail, so as not to stumble, as the veil gently flapped around her. Sameen's sad shrouded figure seemed a perfect metaphor for her country.

But it isn't only women who have been plunged back into traditional customs. Dr. Abdul Rassoul, one of the leaders of the Union of Afghan Mujahideen Doctors in Peshawar, was typical of the men who had also been affected. After the invasion, the thirty-five-year-old cardiologist had been invited to practice in Europe, first in Germany and then in Holland. But he returned to work with the *Mujahideen* in 1981. A thoroughly modern man right down to his Westernized appearance, we met just after he became engaged to a woman he had never seen and who had not been permitted to attend the couple's engagement party. "In Kabul, I would have chosen my own wife. Her personality, her appearance, and her education would have been important to me. In the circumstances I now find myself in, there is no opportunity for me to meet women. So I told my mother to find someone for me." Rassoul's mother did: a twenty-five-year-old student of physiotherapy whom he would marry twenty days later.

Wasn't he curious about how his fiancée looked?

"I asked my sister to find out for me," said Rassoul, describing a method Afghan men have used for centuries to get descriptions of their brides. "My sister told me that she is not so beautiful like a movie star, and not so ugly. She is ordinary looking, and a quiet girl. And that is fine.

"What I need in a wife today is someone who understands my work for the *Jihad*, who will accept that I lead a dangerous life. She also needs to know that while today I have a salary, tomorrow . . . things may change."

One woman in Afghanistan who has long enjoyed an independence her country's women have yet to experience is Anahita Ratebzad. But in addition to that freedom, she lives a luxurious life-style few Afghans of either sex are able to maintain today. I met her for the first time in the large mansion that had once been President Daoud's office on Sadarat Crossway. Our jeep parked behind her silver Mercedes 350 SL, with its black tinted windows. I was shown into a large, elegant room furnished with Western antiques and chandeliers. It overlooked a formal English-style garden in full bloom, with rose bushes surrounding the swimming pool. Exquisite floral arrangements decorated the room, and the table was laid for tea with fine china English style, and bowls of nuts, dried fruits, and sugared almonds Afghan style.

The woman who came to greet me was as elegant as the room. Dr. Ratebzad, age fifty-four, was much more attractive, slimmer, and more feminine than she photographs. She wore a maroon silk two-piece dress, her only jewelry a diamond ring and a platinum Swiss Longines watch. With short slightly graying hair swept back off her face, discreet makeup, and a generous mouth, which smiled readily, she seemed more like the wife of a successful European lawyer or doctor than the most powerful woman today in Afghanistan. Behind her was a large colored photographic portrait of Babrak Karmal, the only one I had seen that flatters him. Karmal, of course, is the man with whom Ratebzad's name has been aligned romantically, in a relationship that is reputedly almost as old as their political association. Married at the age of fifteen to the man who became the king's personal physician, she had three children with him. The couple separated twenty-five years ago but never divorced.

"I first met Babrak Karmal when I was very young. He was the first person to influence me politically; he was so full of enthusiasm and patriotism. So I followed him." Their fortunes have run together ever since. In 1965 when the People's Democratic Party of Afghanistan began, she was one of its first party members; that same year she founded the Women's Democratic Organization. When Karmal fell from grace in 1978 and was made ambassador to Czechoslovakia—this kind of appointment being a traditional third world method of exiling political opponents—Ratebzad became ambassador to Yugoslavia. Both returned to power together a year later.

With me that day, Ratebzad wanted to talk about peace. "The situation in the world is getting very tense. It is even more dangerous than it was during World War II. The first measure of people in the progressive forces of the world is to guarantee peace. The Soviet Union has made a peace proposal, but the other side doesn't want to cooperate. It is the fault of Reagan. He is a cowboy and used to putting ropes around the necks of animals; now he wants to put a rope around the necks of people.

"The people of the world want peace. They want freedom. Their needs are very simple—they want simple lives, simple houses, simple food—yet look how many people are dying from hunger in Africa, in Latin America, even in the United States. I was in the United States studying. I was taking English lessons at Columbia University. I remember seeing whites and negroes dying on the streets of New York because they didn't have enough to eat. Little children lying dead on the street. Dogs were walking around; they wanted to eat them." Ratebzad spent five years in the United States from 1949 to 1954. She told me she holds a nursing degree from the University of Michigan, but the college has no record of this. Later in Kabul, she earned an M.D. and became a professor of preventive medicine.

I asked her when we could expect peace in Afghanistan. "We are on the steps of having it. We have tried to have face to face peace talks with our neighbors, but unfortunately, Pakistan does not want it. You know, Pakistan can't survive; even with the atomic bomb the United States has given it, it won't remain Pakistan. We have also tried to have good relations with Iran. We've gone halfway to meet them, but they don't move. So now, we will close the borders with these two countries. With the borders closed, the counterrevolutionaries will be cut off from their supply of weapons from the imperialist countries.

"The reactionary forces don't approve of our revolution. They don't want us to have a better life. When Richard Nixon came to Afghanistan when he was vice president, he said our country didn't deserve anything. Let's keep them as a history museum, he said. The United States wants to keep us in darkness, in tribalism and feudalism."

I asked Dr. Ratebzad whether Afghanistan hadn't exchanged one master, feudalism, for another, the Soviet Union. There was a large Soviet presence in her country, I said; Soviet soldiers were dying in Afghanistan. When did she expect to see an end to this situation?

"Let me put it like this," she replied; "years ago when Sweden was in trouble with Great Britain, it asked France to help.

Cuban soldiers are living in Angola, even though Angola is a long way from Cuba. It is done out of friendship. We have never had trouble; we have only had help from the Soviet Union from the first day of our independence during the time of Lenin until now. I remember my mother telling me when I was a small child, the Soviet Union is our great uncle."

"It doesn't seem very 'helpful' to Afghanistan, however, for the Soviet Union to pipe, for example, all your country's production of natural gas for use into their country," I said. "Many people would call that exploitation."

"Let me tell you, no one besides an Afghan can understand this." She laughed. "Right now, we don't have the possibility of using this gas. So why shouldn't it be piped to the Soviet Union? We don't have the equipment to use it. Before the revolution, nobody wanted to use the gas. After the revolution, when we wanted to build industries that would use it, we found ourselves facing the undeclared war. All our money, all our budget, all our human resources are going to that great animal Reagan. He is just swallowing them. When we wanted to start utilizing our gas, the United States, China, Pakistan, and other reactionary forces like the Arabs stood in front of us and said you cannot. You don't know how many schools, installations, factories, roads, and homes have been destroyed, how many human lives been taken. We were going to build up Afghanistan, and these imperialist forces destroy everything. Nobody but an Afghan can understand that the Soviet Union isn't exploiting us. Our relationship with the Soviet Union has grown up from a friendship to a brotherhood. There is a good relationship between our two parties, our two governments, and our people—they are really helping us as much as we want."

"We have been talking about peace today; what about human rights in your country?" I asked. "There have been two major reports published this year documenting human rights violations in Afghanistan, accusing your regime of carrying out atrocities."

"Well, those reports, I'm sure, were produced under the influence of the imperialist and reactionary forces. If the people from the UN and the special monitoring agencies want to come here with an open mind they can see the situation in this country for themselves."

"The International Committee for the Red Cross would like

to come, but your government doesn't permit them to. They came once at the beginning of the war and have been trying to return ever since, but you've refused to let them."

"Who said that?"

"The International Committee for the Red Cross said that."

"I don't think this is true. It is like when the United States gave $280 million to the counterrevolutionaries and gave them land-to-air missiles, which were made in the United States. The BBC and the Voice of America both said that the United States had not been the provider. When the Red Cross came here the first time we showed them everything. We took them to Pul-i-Charki prison; they found everything to be favorable. I think the Red Cross doesn't want to come here, and they blame us. We didn't know you. You just called me, and I talked to our Ministry of Foreign Affairs, and we contacted our embassy in New Delhi, and you are here. Since this is the case, why do you believe we wouldn't let the ICRC come?"

"If, as you seem to feel, there are no human rights violations in your country, why have so many Afghans fled as refugees?"

"It is true we made a few mistakes at the beginning of our revolution. It was a mistake to try to bring people by force to literacy classes, particularly the women. Our peasants didn't want to have their women seen by strange men.

"A mistake was made with land reforms. When people lost their land, they ran to Pakistan and Iran. Many ended up in the hands of the counterrevolutionaries. They were simple peasants, ignorant people, and they were deceived by the counterrevolutionaries. So we lost some of our people. But the majority of Afghans in Pakistan are nomads, 2.5 million of them. The remaining one million are mostly aristocrats who lost their comfortable lifestyles in the revolution, which is why they left Afghanistan. Just a few are deceived peasants. But Zia likes to keep all these people and call them refugees. This way, he receives international funding, which he then passes on to the leaders of the counterrevolutionary groups."

As our interview wound down, I switched from the political to the personal and asked Dr. Ratebzad why she had never divorced. "Because I never wanted to get married again. . . . My husband was chosen for me by my family."

"Did you love him?"

She laughed, embarrassed, and then shook her head. "Well, from far away. But why didn't I get married again? I find taking care of the people of my country, being busy with the revolution, building a new country for the coming generations, all these are so many things to do, you never think of a new husband. You are so tired by the time you come home, you want to be alone in your bed."

My last question was to ask her how she would describe Babrak Karmal. "Comrade Karmal has a great sense of humanity. He can never sit without thinking of the people and their suffering. And he always teaches his colleagues that nothing is more delightful than to think about others' suffering, and to be able make them happy.

"He is also such an honest man, and he always likes to have around him very honest colleagues and comrades. He will compromise on everything except his principles. All he wants is to be in the service of his people. He really loves Afghanistan."

That not all of Afghanistan felt the same way about Babrak Karmal had been violently apparent two nights before my interview with Ratebzad, when fighting broke out on the grounds of the presidential palace. The city was twenty-five minutes into its official 10:00 P.M. curfew when heavy machine guns started blasting away at the palace. "It was incredible," said Ed Hurwitz, the U.S. Chargé d'Affaires, as we sat drinking orange juice in the garden of the American Embassy residence. "The palace is just down the road, and I could hear everything clearly; so could diplomats from the French, Italian, Turkish, and Chinese embassies, who are even closer. The machine gun fire went on for about half an hour; it was extremely fierce. We wondered whether it was an assassination attempt or an attempted coup. Then at about 11:00 P.M. the tanks arrived. We could see their tracer rounds. In all, the fighting went on for about ninety minutes. Then it abruptly stopped."

As always in Kabul, there was no official comment on the palace attack in the media the next day, although rumors quickly circulated that Karmal had been injured. Later, I would learn that fourteen people died in the battle, but Karmal was unhurt. Although the Kabul media never covered anything that suggested the regime was not totally beloved, they were quick to show the United States in a bad light at every chance. My second week in

Kabul, when a Bakhtar Airlines plane carrying fifty-two passengers crashed in bad weather between Kandahar and Farah, the newspapers, radio, and television all carried stories for days accusing the *Mujahideen* of shooting it down with Stingers supplied by the United States. That the *Mujahideen* did not have Stingers, and even if they did, a passenger plane would not be strategically important, was, of course, irrelevant.

By the time I left Kabul, I had overdosed on anti-American propaganda. But even at the airport there was no escaping it. Plastered over the walls were posters depicting a smiling Reagan dressed as a cowboy, with his hand resting on boxes of U.S. ammunition, while at his feet sat an Afghan child who had lost his legs in the war. Beneath the posters milled two hundred Afghan youngsters, between fifteen and twenty-three, who were en route to Tashkent and Moscow to study.

Leaving Kabul was a lot more difficult than getting in, I discovered in a three-day battle to get an exit visa. After being bounced from one ministry to another, none of whom seemed to know how to issue exit visas to nondiplomats, I finally received it. But my troubles weren't over, I learned shortly after saying goodbye to Sohaila at passport control. Going through security, my hand baggage was thoroughly searched. And although my American passport wasn't discovered, two hundred dollars' worth of Indian currency and film were. An extremely officious female security guard started shouting at me in Dari. Trying to remain calm, I responded that I didn't understand. This made her shout louder. Grabbing my wallet with the rupees and my camera bag, she waved me through security. As far as she was concerned, both were confiscated, and there appeared to be no appeal. I refused to budge. I didn't much care about the money, although I had declared it coming in and it was noted in my passport, but I was determined not to be separated from my film. I lunged for my camera bag. As we both pulled at it, she lost her temper and struck my arm. Without letting go, I retreated into being very British and began to demand in a loud voice that I wanted to speak to an official who spoke English. Finally, our ruckus had the desired effect. An English-speaking security official came over to find out what all the fuss was about. I explained that I had been a guest of Anahita Ratebzad's, that she knew I had been using my camera, and that I would be more than happy to telephone her, if he wanted me to. Just as before, Dr. Ratebzad's name had a magic effect. After a few words from her superior, the female security guard sulkily returned my possessions. I was waved onto the plane with the beginning of a splitting headache from those last few minutes of tension.

The Air India plane took off on time, after flares had once again been dropped to divert *Mujahideen* missiles. As with our arrival, we gained height by corkscrewing up. My last glimpse of Kabul was of Pul-i-Charki prison. Circling round and round, we stayed directly over it for about five minutes. The design of the prison makes it look like a segmented cake from the air. Built during the Daoud era to house five thousand prisoners, Pul-i-Charki, which has been described as a charnel house of torture, now holds thirty thousand. As we circled over the jail, I thought of Fahima Nassery, a woman I had met in Peshawar who had been an inmate of Pul-i-Charki twice, and every day she had spent there showed on her face. Nassery was thirty-seven years old but, with her deeply lined face, and her hair pure white at the temples, looked fifty. Her gaunt figure, haunted expression, dark circles under her eyes, and chain smoking, the latter very unusual in an Afghan woman, suggested without her having to articulate it that here was a person who had known pain and fear.

In 1981, Fahima had been a math and science high school teacher. She had also helped to organize demonstrations against the Soviet invasion, and she had distributed "night letters" for the *Mujahideen*. Early in the morning of April 23, she was home with her three young children. Her husband, an official with the Ministry of Planning, was away on business. There was a knock at the door and her seven-year-old daughter, Mina, answered it. "Sixteen men and one woman, all Afghan, came into my house. They cut open pillows, mattresses, quilts, carpets; they broke apart the toilet and looked inside; they destroyed everything in the house. Outside were four Russian soldiers with guns. They searched my house from early in the morning until 2:00 P.M. Eventually, they found some of the night letters, and they also found my *Mujahideen* ID card. They asked me why I hated the Russian party. I told them all of the Afghan population hated the Soviets." Fahima was taken to the KHAD office in Sheshdarak, a suburb of Kabul. Her three children, ages three, six, and seven, were left alone.

"They put me in a room where all sorts of loud music was

playing, Farsi, Pushto, European music. So much different music, it was playing very, very loud. It went on for hours and hours; I thought I would go crazy. Sometimes, in other rooms, I could hear men and women screaming."

At 10:00 P.M. she was interrogated by two female Afghan guards under the guidance of a Soviet male adviser. "They slapped me several times in the face; then they left. But people kept coming in all night to stop me from sleeping." At 7:00 A.M. she was given tea and bread, the first food and drink she had received since her arrest. Six hours later, she was transferred to the secret police headquarters in Sadarat. "They left me in a small room with bloodstains, bloody handprints on the walls. The room was overrun with rats and insects. There was a terrible smell.

"By now I was very frightened. I didn't know what they were going to do. My fear was like an internal torture. I didn't know if anyone had found my children. And my mother has a weak heart, and I was afraid she would have a heart attack. I was afraid they were going to kill me. And I kept hoping I wouldn't give any names. I kept telling myself, a nation who lives standing, should die standing.

"At 10:00 P.M. the second night I was taken to a clean room; it was well furnished, with carpets on the floor. The guards had my notebook, and they kept asking, who are these names; what is your organization? I said they were the names of my friends, but they didn't like my answers. They started to beat and kick me and pull out my hair. They pulled out big handfuls." Fahima lifted her veil to show where her hairline had receded in places. "They continued to question and beat me until 5:00 A.M. Next door, I could hear the cries of small children and the screams of adults.

"On the third night, again at 10:00 P.M. they came for me. This time, they put a big metal hook around my neck. There was a man in the room with a stethoscope. Two men took off my shoes and made me put my feet on the floor. Then they gave me an electric shock. My whole body went into spasm. I could feel the pain in my head, in my ears. They kept repeating it. My body would jerk and then I would fall on the floor, half unconscious. They'd stand me up, slap me; the women would pull my hair. Then they'd begin again with the electric shocks. It went on for hours." On the fourth night, after several hours of electric shock treatment, Fahima suffered heart arrhythmia. The torture was halted on that occasion.

During her interrogation, Fahima was always questioned at night to deprive her of sleep. The only nourishment she received was a meal of tea and a small piece of black bread once a day. The electric shocks were always administered by men, the physical beatings by women.

"The next night, they continued to question me, but this time they made me stand on one leg. When I fell down, they punched me and pulled out my hair. Then they took me into a room near the toilet; it had a bath in it with blue water inside. They made me stand in it. The water came up to my knees; I don't know what it was. It didn't have an odor, but it burned. It felt like a million needles. They made me stand in it four times that night. My feet became very swollen; my skin began to peel. I was shaking very badly. I could hardly stand. They held me by the front of my head." Fahima's legs are permanently scarred from the chemical bath.

"At one time, I couldn't open my eyes, they were so swollen. I had severe headaches, I couldn't walk, and I kept blacking out."

Fahima was tortured continually for twenty-five days. Her worst night was the fourteenth. As she began to talk about it, she started shaking. She fumbled for a cigarette, and her hand trembled too much to light it. "They took me into a different room; it was badly lit, but I could see the bloodstains everywhere. The stench was overpowering. On the floor were amputated fingers." Fahima broke off. "I'm sorry, forgive me; this is very difficult for me." She closed her eyes as if to block out the memory, and began to gnaw on her fist. It was several minutes before she could continue. "There was a stretcher on the ground with a body on it. The face was covered. The guards said to me, these are the fingers of your men, your lovers. They pointed to the stretcher and said go and look at his face. You used to live with such people; now you can stay with him." Fahima began to cry and shake her head nervously. "I can't talk about it anymore."

At the end of her four weeks of interrogation, Fahima was transferred to Pul-i-Charki prison, where she was housed in a cell that measured nine by twelve feet with between fourteen and twenty-five women, one as young as fourteen. The cell was con-

stantly wet from a broken sewer pipe that ran through the middle
of it, and it was overrun with vermin. Skin sores and lice were a
common problem, but a minor one compared to the aftereffects of
torture from which most prisoners were suffering. And finally at
Pul-i-Charki, Fahima received three prison meals a day: a thin
vegetable soup in the morning, the same with rice at lunchtime,
and a piece of bread in the evening. Four months after her arrest,
she was sentenced to one year's imprisonment and one and one
half years' close surveillance. Because of her arrest, her husband
was interrogated and two of her sisters were also jailed but
released after seven months.

When Fahima was freed, her family and friends recommended that she leave the country. "I didn't want to leave Afghanistan," said Fahima. "I wanted to stay; I love my country.
And anyway, it would have been difficult; I was closely watched."

On May 22, 1984, she was arrested again. Three KHAD officials came to her home. "Through the window, I could see a car
and two military jeeps. I knew I hadn't done anything wrong, but
my heart was racing." Once again, she was taken to KHAD headquarters. "That evening they came and told me they had found a
lot of evidence in my house. I knew it wasn't true, that if they had
found something, it must have been planted. But they said they
had proof, and I would be condemned to death. They showed me
photographs of my children and told me they had been put in an
orphanage. And they said they had imprisoned my husband and
my family. They kept telling me I was going to die. They kept up
this mental torture for a month. Then they put me in a cell with
other women. After six months they released me. I was never
tried."

After her second release, Fahima and her husband, Ahmad,
fled with their children to Pakistan. "When I left Afghanistan, I
left my whole life behind. I wanted only to live in my country."
Fahima's son, Yama, now eleven, and her oldest daughter suffer
from emotional problems dating from their mother's first arrest.
"My daughter Mina is very bright. It is because of her I became
involved in organizing anti-Soviet demonstrations in the first
place. Twice in her school, because of her top marks, she was put
on the list to be sent to the Soviet Union for twelve years. I said
I didn't want to send her, and I was told I must; otherwise it would

Author (centre) with Mujahideen shortly before their assault on Ali Shier.

Above: Freedom fighters at Khost sorting U.S. supplied ammunition, much of it dating back to 1949.

Below: Commander Fatah Khan going over final battle plans.

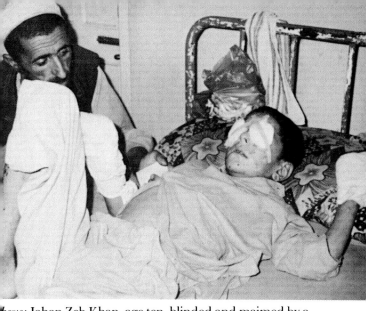

above: Jahan Zeb Khan, age ten, blinded and maimed by a Soviet bomb shaped like a toy.

below: Wakil conducts a funeral service for two youths who died in a bombing attack on Zazi.

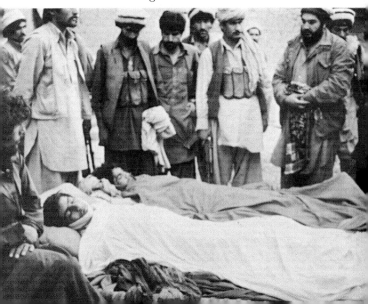

Above: Tor (left) and Humayoon with the skull of a Russian sold

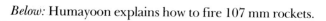

Below: Humayoon explains how to fire 107 mm rockets.

Above: The Mujahideen pray before their attack on Malgai in Jalalabad.

Below: The freedom fighters open fire on a Communist base with a Dashaka.

The author in Afghan dress, ready for the road.

Left: Hamid stands guard with an ancient 303 Enfield rifle.

Below: Wakil training Mujahideen to use heavy arms.

A forlorn refugee camp, targeted by Soviet aircraft during the mujahideen attacks in ... (A Deltic

be considered as being disloyal to the party. I told them she was sick and kept her at home. That was when I began to become politically involved. I didn't want Afghan children to grow up as Russians."

7

The Coming of Age
of a Guerrilla

Before the plane from Kabul had landed in Delhi, I decided that in trying to slip back into Pakistan, my persona non grata status notwithstanding, I would attempt to do so through Karachi, even though it would mean a journey of some eighteen hundred miles to Peshawar, instead of the direct route of five hundred miles. I reasoned that Karachi was a much bigger airport than Lahore, and although they may have received notification of my expulsion, a chance I would have to take, in Lahore it was possible that one of the handful of immigration officials would recognize me. After all, it had only been two weeks since I had been tossed out on my ear. My plane touched down in Karachi at the same time as several other full flights. The arrival lounge was chaotically crowded, and the lines through immigration were dense and long. As luck would have it, an energetic official decided to speed things up and started moving down my line with visa stamp in hand. Instead of the ponderously slow grilling most tourists receive on entering Pakistan, I was given a prompt tourist visa, no questions asked. Elated, I bought a ticket on the next plane to Islamabad, the Pakistani capital, knowing that if I flew into Peshawar, my name would be on the passenger list forwarded to the Intelligence department. In Islamabad, I checked into a hotel and, even though it was 2:00 A.M., telephoned NIFA to let them know I was back. A sleepy Wakil told me to stay in my room and someone would pick me up the following day.

Late the next afternoon, Hamid arrived. He seemed pleased to see me, having assumed after my two weeks' silence that I wasn't returning. I burbled something about playing tourist in India to explain what I had been doing. He cautioned me to check out of the hotel as quickly as I could and meet him in the parking lot as he had spotted two Peshawar Special Branch officers downstairs. They were probably accompanying a visiting dignitary. On the drive to Peshawar, Hamid told me Wakil wanted us to arrive in the city after dark. "This way there will be less risk of anybody spotting you," he said, explaining that the *Mujahideen* offices and residences were frequently under surveillance. Wakil met us in Peshawar. Greetings over, he told me, "When you are in Peshawar, I'm afraid you are going to have to live as if you are under house arrest. You can't go out, make or receive phone calls, or mail anything. And to be frank, the less time you spend in Pakistan, the better. For that reason, I've arranged for you to leave for Afghanistan tomorrow. A party is going to Jalalabad Province; you will go with them." "Okay," I said, although I would have loved a day to catch my breath. I had just spent twenty hours traveling from Kabul; now I was to return to a region only forty miles from where I'd started. My destination was also a curious coincidence. I had told Sohaila I wanted to travel outside Kabul and had requested a visit to Mazar-i-Sharif close to the Soviet Union. Not surprisingly, that had been refused, but I had been offered a visit to the Soviet-held city of Jalalabad. The tour was to demonstrate to me that life was normal there, that there was no fighting or *Mujahideen* in the vicinity. On the day we were due to leave, I was hit with a virulent twenty-four-hour stomach virus and was too ill to travel. At the time, I had been disappointed—there had been no opportunity to reschedule the trip. Now I was to travel to the same region with the *Mujahideen*, who were delighted to show me that, indeed, there were freedom fighters and fighting in Jalalabad.

We left the next morning before the sun was completely up. Wakil didn't join us. He was going to Quetta, 350 miles southwest of Peshawar, I guessed to take delivery of an arms shipment, although he refused to discuss it. The man in charge of this trip was Said Mohammed, a twenty-four-year-old commander who had early earned a reputation for himself as an excellent military leader. The illiterate son of peasant farmers, he commanded the respect of many men twice his age despite the fact that all of his communications with headquarters had to be written for him and that he signed them with a thumbprint. Said Mohammed looked as unprepossessing as his background: a muscular young man, of average height, his straight lank hair constantly seeming in need of cutting and combing, his clothes always giving way at the seams. He was one of the few *Mujahideen* I met who were beardless, although he was proud of his trim mustache. His large mouth was invariably worn in a wide grin, displaying several broken teeth. What Said Mohammed lacked in formal education, he made up for in bravery bordering on daredevilry and a pure hatred for the Soviets. He also was an instinctual tactician. There were very few military operations he conducted that didn't succeed. But although he may be intrepid, it is unlikely that Said Mohammed will live to be middle-aged. "He's a commander who isn't satisfied with just commanding," said Wakil. "He always wants to be out front. We've told him repeatedly that he's a lot more useful to us alive than he is as a dead hero, but he doesn't change. Commanders like this die young." The *Mujahideen* have lost a number of excellent commanders for this reason. "They always tell us it isn't the Afghan way for a commander to stay in the rear," explained Wakil. Wakil had recently lost a close friend, Dadmir, the same way. Dadmir had been one of NIFA's most valued commanders. A group of us were watching "Hansel and Gretel," part of the American television series *Faerie Tale Theater*, on Peshawar television one evening when the news came. Earlier, I had been highly amused at the sight of ten tough freedom fighters engrossed in Joan Collins and Ricky Schroder's reenacting this Grimm Brothers children's story. The fairy tale continued to play incongruously and ignored in the background as the messenger told us Dadmir had been killed. "I feel as if my brother has died," said Wakil at the time. In the darkened room, I was probably the only one to notice his eyes fill with tears.

Almost as stunning as Dadmir's death had been the reaction to it. When the Soviets pulled back, they had taken Dadmir's body with them, a tactic they use to demoralize the *Mujahideen*. The commander's wife, sisters, and other female relatives had been so outraged at being deprived of giving Dadmir a proper Muslim burial that they had launched a counterattack in an attempt to reclaim his corpse. The women had failed in their unprecedented efforts, when the *Mujahideen* had disarmed them and insisted they retreat to safety.

As we left Peshawar, Said Mohammed explained that we were to take a roundabout route to get to his base because I was a potential security risk. We would be using an almost unknown trail to the border, which was virtually impossible to discern among the rocks and boulders. After that there would be a two-day walk. On this trip were the commander's older brother and deputy commander, Lal Mohammed; Hamid and Tor; Rohullah, the young son of a schoolteacher; and Humayoon, a former major in the Afghan army and missile specialist. The commander wanted Humayoon's expertise for a particular assault he was planning against one of the larger bases in his area. Also with us was Omar, a twenty-two-year-old freedom fighter with a different kind of specialty, but one that was just as useful as Humayoon's. Omar had a talent for being conscripted, and then almost as soon as he arrived at a military base, he decamped with as many weapons as he could lay his hands on. His record so far in a single desertion was twenty-two Kalashnikovs and three hundred grenades. Multiply that by the numerous times he had been conscripted and he was a forager *M*A*S*H* would have envied. Omar had also become quite facile at persuading his fellow conscripts to desert with him with their weapons. Yet despite these talents, he was considered slow and somewhat simple by the *Mujahideen* and was invariably the butt of their teasing. And it was probably because of this that Omar, a handsome young man about six feet, four inches tall, with shoulders as broad as a weight lifter, was most comfortable with young children, who flocked to him like some turbaned pied piper.

On route, we stopped at NIFA's armory to pick up several boxes of ammunition, ten R-107 mm rockets, and machine guns for Hamid and Tor. With these new supplies, the eight of us, plus a driver, my pack, and the other guns, our small Japanese jeep was so crammed it was impossible to move. At the border, we stopped at one of NIFA's safe houses for lunch, bowls of what looked like boiled goat's fat floating in greasy water. The smell and appearance of the food made me lose my appetite, even though I was warned I should eat because there would be nothing later on. After lunch, the commander tried to rent donkeys to carry the ammunition, but there were none available. There would be the following day. He decided to stay behind until then, but felt it was safer to send us ahead. We would make the first leg of the journey by tractor (these were used like local buses in this part of the country), and after that we would walk. Waiting for the tractor, I drew a crowd of curious villagers. "This boy is very white," said a teenage boy, pointing at me. "Did you keep him locked up away from the sun?" "Is he going to *Jihad*?" asked another. Hamid told them I came from the Panjshir Valley, which was why I looked different, and that I was a rocket specialist, and a very good fighter. They seemed satisfied by the explanation.

An enormous tractor arrived, sounding just like a tank, and as we clambered up onto it, competing for any foothold, I realized it was Russian-made. It seemed ridiculous to be going to war against the Soviets on a Russian-made tractor, but perhaps it was no more bizarre than the United States–supported Afghans being fired at by Soviet tanks built in the Kama River Truck Factory, the world's largest such plant, with Ford Motors and Mack Trucks know-how. Although the licensing agreement between the United States and the Soviet Union in the seventies had stipulated that American know-how not be used to manufacture military vehicles, U.S. intelligence reports soon showed that it had.

The tractor rumbled across an arid valley churning up as much dust as a dust storm; it was a constant struggle to keep my cameras and contact lenses free of it. At the foot of a small peak, the tractor reached the end of its route. Walking up the steep incline, we passed six men and their heavily laden donkeys coming down. The animals' loads of brightly colored rolls of fabric were so wide that we had to scramble off the trail to let them pass. "Contraband, they are smugglers," said Hamid, who also cautioned me not to talk. "These people come from Kabul and sell their goods in Bara, in Pakistan [a busy market town where vendors also openly sold hashish and cocaine]. Some of these smugglers also make money selling information to the KHAD; they report on any *Mujahideen* movement they see. If these people are informers, they will be very pleased to tell the KHAD we have a foreigner with us."

After thirty minutes, we reached the summit, and when I did, I groaned. I had assumed this small peak would be the same distance down as it was up. But the view before me was stunning. We were at the top of a dramatic mountain range. Jagged peaks stretched for miles until they disappeared into the distant blue of the horizon. Immediately in front of us was an almost perpendicular drop of thousands of feet. Well, at least our route is downhill, I told myself, as I began to follow the *Mujahideen* down the boulder strewn track that appeared so tenuously hewn out of the granite face it seemed in danger of sliding off the mountain. The path, little more than twelve inches wide, switchbacked so often, the vista swung back and forth dizzyingly. I didn't dare look down. I kept telling myself, "If you fall, fall to the mountain side." If I lost my footing and fell the other way, I would plunge over the edge. The sun shining in our faces and reflecting off the rocks was near blinding, and with every step down, my toes banged painfully against the end of my boots. After four hours, my ankles and knees felt like jelly and we were still only halfway down. "I need a break," I told Hamid, as I sank to the ground. Tor looked at me in disgust or embarrassment and stepped over my prone body. Tor, who was invariably in front during any of the *Mujahideen* marches, had lungs and leg muscles that a marathon winner would have envied. While I rested, the others prayed. All too soon, we were moving again. Several hours later we arrived at a small stone village, carved out of the mountain face. Looking around at the peaks that rose up on all sides, I felt as if I'd been transported to Tibet. A fierce-sounding wind was beginning to blow through a nearby gulley. It was an inhospitable place, due both to its natural surroundings and to the people themselves. The region was mostly rock face, and I couldn't see how the villagers supported themselves. Even their source of water was four kilometers away. Why had a community grown up here? Parched from our hike, I waited for the villagers to come and greet us as they normally did and offer us tea. But no one moved. The doors to the small stone houses stayed closed. Only a few curious small boys came to stare.

We made our way to the village mosque, the traditional resting place for visitors. Humayoon told one of the children to fetch water. The boy disappeared but didn't return. After about thirty minutes, Lal Mohammed angrily ordered the remaining boys to fetch the village head. An elderly man slowly shuffled toward us. After he was told this was no way to treat visitors, we were given water begrudgingly, but that was all. We stayed long enough to drink it and then left. Hamid told me this village had once had a bad experience with freedom fighters, but he wouldn't elaborate, and now they tried to discourage any of them from stopping. "But it wasn't our party," he said. "And they shouldn't treat us all like that. We are fighting for their freedom, too, and if they don't realize it on their own, they must be taught it is so." We continued to walk. Rohullah was beginning to limp; his new sandals and the rocks were badly lacerating his feet. I promised to bind them for him when we stopped for the night. I could also hear Omar, a heavy smoker, panting; that was unusual with the *Mujahideen*, who no matter how steep the trail never seemed to become breathless. By now the sun was setting, and it was hard to see the path. I asked Hamid to walk nearby. I knew if I could talk, I wouldn't constantly dwell on falling. I commented that Tor seemed very different from the year before, less fun, more hotheaded. "He's more difficult to get on with," said Hamid. "He's often very tense, and sometimes when you're with him it is as if a curtain comes down, and you aren't there." I also knew that in the last few months, Tor had been volunteering to be in front on every operation. It was as if he had a death wish.

At 9:00 P.M. we reached a large village where we were to spend the night. This one was as friendly as the other one had been hostile. We were shown to an open-side mosque with straw on the floor. The villagers told the *Mujahideen* that their elders had been invited to Kabul to take part in a tribal *jirga*, a grand assembly. The regime was offering large sums of money to any village that would help close the border and refuse to assist the freedom fighters. They assured the *Mujahideen* that they hadn't sent anyone. Tea was soon brought, and shortly afterward I crawled exhausted into my sleeping bag too tired to eat.

I woke with a start. It was still dark. I thought it was dawn, but it was only 11:00 P.M. Humayoon and Lal Mohammed were on their feet and yelling, and I saw Tor reach for his Kalashnikov and heard him slip off the safety clip. Were we under attack, being robbed? "What the hell is happening?" I asked. Omar cursed. And Hamid and Tor burst out laughing. "Yes, we're being attacked," said Hamid, "by fleas and mosquitoes; the mosque is full of them." Always plagued by mosquitoes, even on picnics in the States, I'd only been vaguely aware of them. The *Mujahideen*, however, claimed they were more disturbing than all-night rocket attacks. They dragged their blankets into the courtyard and bedded down again. But not for long. At 3:00 A.M., the local mullah arrived and very loudly began to call the faithful to prayer, although his enthusiasm seemed more to impress us than his congregation. Lal Mohammed gave the order to move out. No water, no tea, no breakfast. But this time I was given a donkey. The boy we had rented it from would accompany us to bring it back. Our route in the dark was no different from the previous day's, straight down and straight up, and I was grateful to be riding. Hamid walked alongside me, asking me the correct definition of English words or synonyms for *divagate* or *collateral* to add to his already vast vocabulary. Never a morning person, my brain refused to function, and I grunted at him. Five hours later we arrived at a village on the edge of the fast-flowing Kunar River. The water looked milky from the speed of the current and the churned-up silt. We were invited to stop for cookies and tea and again heard that Kabul had been offering large sums of money to villagers in the area who would inform on the *Mujahideen* or refuse them passage through their region. Here, too, we were hastily assured that the offer had been turned down. But how long, I wondered, or how large the offer, before someone finally accepted it?

Breakfast over, we began to walk along the cliff that edged the river. With us was a villager carrying a large wooden pole frame to which were lashed four inflated cow carcasses. I assumed the contraption was some kind of water carrier. "No, this is our boat," explained Hamid. "It is!" I exclaimed, grateful I could swim. Because of the shortage of wood and other building materials, boats constructed from decapitated cow carcasses had been made in this region for hundreds of years. The skins, which were tied with rope at the neck and at the leg stumps, lasted for three years if they were greased, said the boatman. Such boats had two major flaws, however. They were extremely unstable and often capsized, pitching the passengers into the water. Since many Afghans cannot swim, drownings were a regular occurrence. The other handicap was that with the weight of the passengers, particularly with weapons, the carcasses quickly became deflated, and they had to be steered to shore every fifteen minutes and blown up again. From my point of view, there was another problem with the boat. When several people sat on it, it sank up to the poles, which meant that one rode with one's rear end and feet in the water. The Afghans didn't seem to mind, but I spent my time trying to keep my cameras and pack dry. The boat was also difficult to steer in fast water because it had no rudder. The boatman either swam alongside it or paddled with his feet. Either way, with a river like the Kunar, there was little steering possible, the vessel went with the fierce current. To cross the river, we walked almost half a mile upstream from where we wanted to land on the opposite bank—the current carried us that distance downstream. Here the river was split in three by large sandbanks; we crossed the first and widest part in relays on the boat. The last two channels we waded across. Since my boots were already wet, I kept them on, a mistake, I learned later, as they tightened on my blisters as they dried.

Until now, we had seen little war damage in this province, but on the other side of the Kunar River that changed abruptly. As we continued to walk, every village we passed through had been deserted after heavy bombing. Few houses were left intact. "They were driven out two months ago after the planes came," said Lal Mohammed. "The tanks and soldiers left this area only yesterday, the people in the last village said." He went on to explain that this side of the river had been very heavily mined by the military. "We used to have a big base near here; they wanted to make sure we didn't come back." The *Mujahideen* did come back, however, and lost two of their commanders to those mines when they were trying to clear the area for their men. Lal Mohammed pointed to the nearby field where the commanders had died just weeks before. Without realizing it, the guerrillas had come across a seismic mine, one of the newer types that are being used in Afghanistan and that are set off by vibration. Commander Pesho saw the mine and warned his men it was there. He was eight feet from the device when it detonated, killing him and another commander who was standing nearby. Frequently such deaths occurred because the mines are booby-trapped. I remembered meeting a nineteen-year-old mine specialist, Abdul Matin, in a Peshawar hospital. He had lost his entire right arm and left hand and been deafened in his right ear when he was trying to clear an area of mines for his colleagues. "Often they have more than one layer," he told me. "I thought this one had two, it turned out to have three."

"In this area and around the base where we are going you mustn't go walking by yourself," Hamid warned me. "The *Mujahideen* try hard to clear the mines but they do it by sight and they could miss some." "What sort of mines were they?" I asked so I'd know what to look out for. "In this area, they scattered a lot of butterfly and toy bombs, and they buried a lot of the larger antipersonnel mines. It was one of those that killed the commanders." "Could the larger mines be detected in the ground?"

"Sometimes yes, sometimes no. Sometimes you can see small mounds of earth with rocks on top." Great, I thought, in this rocky terrain they'd never be detectable. The concern about mines was apparent even when I wanted to use one of the ruined houses as a latrine. Hamid checked the rubbled area first to make sure it was safe before letting me go in.

We followed the Kunar for some time, enjoying the narrow stretch of vegetation it supported in the otherwise arid valley. In the early afternoon, we turned away from the river and began to climb again. Now the terrain resembled scree desert. Half an hour later, I could make out four small tents pitched at the foot of rocky hill. Two *Mujahideen* came out to meet us, shooting their Kalashnikovs into the air in greeting. This was Daka, Said Mohammed's base and home to sixty freedom fighters. It was a godforsaken-looking place, set on rock and overlooked by granite cliffs, with the barren mountain range we had just crossed rising behind it. Nothing grew here, and the heat just reflected off the rocks, turning the region into an oven where the temperature in the day never went below 110 degrees and at night below 90, when a hot wind blew, sucking any humidity from the air. There were two things the camp had in abundance, however: biting flies and dust. This land was so barren that it was strange to see the Kunar River in the distance, as if it were some kind of mirage. Without it, of course, this camp could not have survived. All our water came from there, and the men hiked down to the river five times a day to wash before praying. The water in Daka was stored in old gasoline containers, and our drinking supply, which was already full of silt from the fast-flowing river, also had a strong gasoline smell and taste. I jokingly remarked that it must be the water that supplemented the *Mujahideens'* meager diet. It wasn't very long before I was fantasizing about large glasses of iced orange juice.

The *Mujahideen* in Said Mohammed's camp spent three-month stints at Daka, making three or four raids a week on the nearby bases when they had the ammunition. The main Jalalabad Highway was just across the river, and it was protected by a string of small bases. Three kilometers from where we were was Landai Khyber garrison, which housed twelve hundred troops and a number of Russian advisers and their wives. During their time at Daka, the *Mujahideen* lived mostly on *nan*, potatoes and raw onion, and tea. Their only time off was five days every three months when they were permitted to return to their families in Pakistan. With these conditions, any army in the world would have had an uprising, yet the commander's men were a cheerful bunch. And they were delighted to see me—a visit from a foreign journalist made them feel they weren't forgotten by the outside world.

Exhausted, I was unable to match their exuberance. We had covered eighty kilometers in two days over rough terrain, and I hadn't eaten anything in thirty-six hours. Even now, I was so tired and dehydrated all I could do was drink eight cups of tea. Hamid admitted that he had had no idea that the route we had taken was as tough as it had proved to be, for which I silently thanked him. That evening Said Mohammed arrived with the rockets and ammunition; he'd taken the more direct and much shorter route. With considerably more energy than I had, the commander blithely began planning the next day's assault. I decided that battle or no battle, I wasn't going anywhere the next day. Then Humayoon discovered that the two mortars were defective, and the operation was postponed until we could borrow some from the nearby Younes Khales Resistance group. In Peshawar, one was constantly hearing the seven *Mujahideen* groups' being accused of factionalism, of squabbling among themselves, or of competing for arms, and while this certainly happened, this was not the last time I would see the different political parties borrow weapons from one another or plan battle strategies together.

That evening, dinner consisted of *nan*, boiled potatoes, and raw onion, but much of the week we were reduced to eating just raw onions and bread. With the villages emptied, there was no other food available in the area. After the meal, the men, many of whom were Kuchi, former nomads, began to sing their tribe's traditional songs at the tops of their voices. They were joined by two full-throated tenors from the top of the opposite ridge, where a guerrilla Dashaka was posted. The sound must have carried for miles. "Aren't they afraid the bases will hear them?" I asked the commander. "The bases can hear them; they know we are here, but they never come out at night unless we attack them." "What about during the day?" Said Mohammed smiled. "We want them to come out and fight. That's why we're here. And it's easier for us once they leave the bases."

Most of us turned in by about 9:30 P.M.; except for singing, there was little else to do once it got dark. It seemed that I had only just cleared the rocks out from under my sleeping bag when there was a bloodcurdling howling no more than a hundred yards from where we were attempting to sleep. I sat bolt upright and froze. "Wolves," said Rohullah calmly. "They come around every night." Almost immediately, I had a desire to urinate, which didn't surprise me—I've often felt my bladder had a perverse sense of timing all its own. It took me an hour to find the courage to get up and walk away from the camp. And then I only went as far as decency and darkness obliged me to. I wasn't sure what I more afraid of, the wolves or the mines. Weeks later, Tor admitted that he had felt the same way about getting up in the night at Daka.

I awoke the next morning covered in insect bites. Even though I had slept fully dressed, it was hard to find a part of my anatomy that wasn't adorned with angry red welts. I'd been bitten so often on the face that one eye was swollen closed, making me resemble a prizefighter. The itching couldn't have been worse if I'd spent the night wrapped around a poison oak tree. The *Mujahideen* laughed when they saw my appearance. "Looks like the flies found a good deluxe foreign restaurant," yelled one. Tor promised to see whether the camp's first-aid kit contained any antihistamine.

Beyond the tent a young boy was busy baking the breakfast

nan. Noor Jhan was eleven years old and looked impossibly young to be an experienced killer. But he was. "He's a good cook, but he's a good freedom fighter, too," said Lal Mohammed. "He's very strong and can walk as far as any of the *Mujahideen.*" Noor Jhan had first seen action a year ago in Laghman Province. Armed with a 303 rifle he had been deployed to cover the *Mujahideen* so they couldn't be attacked from the rear when they ambushed a convoy of Soviet and Afghan tanks. "There were two hundred of them and only sixty of us," he said proudly. "I fired my first shots that day." In that engagement, four freedom fighters died. "I was sad my friends died but happy we won." Noor Jhan, who stood about four feet, nine inches, and probably weighed less than one hundred pounds, had been at school in Peshawar with his seven brothers and sisters when a *Mujahid* uncle came to visit. The boy left with him. Did he understand the politics of this war? I asked. "It isn't hard," he replied. "The Russians came here to Afghanistan. They claimed to help us. But it isn't true. We had a peaceful life here before."

Had he seen any Russians? "Seen them! I've killed many. You want to see their bodies, or what's left of them? The animals have mostly eaten them. I'll show you where we killed a lot of Russians three months ago. It's not far from here. We call it our butcher house."

Noor Jhan was referring to a gorge about a mile away from the camp. One hundred *Mujahideen* had been retreating from the advance of two thousand Soviet and Karmal troops who were attempting to clear the area of guerrillas. Knowing the gorge was closed at one end, the freedom fighters allowed the Soviets to chase them into it. Then, goatlike, they scaled the deep sides of the defile and doubled back on the enemy. As we entered the gorge, with Noor Jhan leading the way, the scorch marks on the rocks told of fierce fighting. About a quarter of a mile in, we came across the first skulls. Tor picked one up on the end of his machine gun and waved it at Humayoon, Hamlet fashion. "These are the kind of Soviets I like best," he said. Baby-faced Noor Jhan chimed in, "The last time I came here, you could see the brains; they were yellow. The wolves have been eating them." As we continued up the gorge, the tattered remains of uniforms were strewn around. So were human bones, where they had been dragged by the animals. Only the knee-high Soviet army boots were left intact. I'd seen all I wanted to see. "Let's get out of here," I told Hamid as I shivered despite the heat. On the way back, we heard the first heavy artillery of the day. "There are BM-21s just at the back of this mountain. Sometimes I think they fire them just to let us know they are still there," said Rohullah.

When we returned to the camp, most of the men went down to the river to swim. As a woman, I was told I couldn't join them, but I envied the men the chance to cool off. Tor stayed behind, saying the river was too dirty to swim in. I didn't point out that he'd been drinking it ever since we'd arrived. Said Mohammed brought out a large sack of medications. They were a mixture of leftover pills and ointments in containers in a variety of languages —French, English, German, Norwegian. I was asked to translate the instructions on the ones I could read, and Tor wrote their contents in Dari on the packages. Although I could read the French and German ones, my medical lexicon in both languages was small. The first one I pulled out was a French liquid antibiotic marked to be given intramuscularly, not intravenously. What happened if you did it the other way around? I wondered. I also came across some painkillers that were mislabeled antibiotics. It was anybody's guess how many injured or sick *Mujahideen* had been made worse after being administered medication that looked as if it might help. And the *Mujahideen* love medicating themselves. The moment a first-aid kit was brought out even the toughest freedom fighters would line up with real and imagined complaints: anything for a pill, a little personal attention. Tor told me he dispensed vast quantities of vitamin C capsules, which he used as panaceas, because the men refused to go away empty-handed. But Raies's complaint wasn't imagined. His left foot was badly swollen. He'd dislocated it during an assault on their last operation. In typical *Mujahideen* fashion, Raies had continued to fight; only on the way back did he have the decency to pass out from the pain. Tor professionally bandaged it for him and told him to rest it. But he knew the man wouldn't. He also dressed a number of festering blisters that left me amazed that their owners were still able to walk.

The next few days were passed similarly. In the heat of the day, the men swam in the river and spent a lot of time dozing. Each morning for several hours we would hear the sound of heavy artillery nearby, the direction it came from changing from time to time. But everyone tuned it out as if it were *Mujahideen* Muzak. It was always in the background, but since it wasn't aimed at us, no one reacted to it. Occasionally, a MIG or a reconaissance plane passed overhead. But from the perspective of our sweltering canyon, the war that week seemed slightly removed, almost as if it had gone on hiatus. Shape was given to the day only by the five regular prayer sessions. In the late afternoon, as the temperature dropped a little, men desultorily began cleaning and checking weapons. But even that task seemed more occupational therapy than essential. On one occasion, Humayoon, who had been trying to repair one of the defective mortars, thoughtfully woke me up from a nap before he fired it. He knew how loud it would sound in our canyon and didn't want to frighten me.

I had purposely not brought any reading material because the freedom fighters never had any except the Koran. Although I was never without a book at home, here I found that reading cut one off from the *Mujahideen.* In this mostly oral culture, I found the Afghans loved nothing more than to talk. Sometimes we talked politics. Rohullah, age twenty-one, had been a twelfth grade science major when he'd been conscripted. He'd escaped after two months and joined the *Mujahideen.* Intelligent and introspective, he spent one afternoon plying me with questions: Who did I think would win in Nicaragua? Did I see any difference between the foreign policies of Thatcher and Reagan? How did I feel about the difference between Carter and Reagan? The Afghans fight Russia because they want to preserve their religion; why does the West fight communism? Was it because we were Christian, or was it simply because we wanted to protect our way of life? We talked about the birth of communism, and Rohullah launched into a surprisingly knowledgeable discourse on the roles of Marx, Lenin, Engels, and Trotsky. Here was another young mind that would have done well in college. "When all of this is over, on that day of happiness, then I will go to university," he said. "But by then, it will be too late. I will be an old man, a burden on society."

Often, however, I found that because I was a woman, the Afghans told me about their fears. Humayoon, age twenty-eight, whose shock of blond hair and bushy beard made him look like a sixties hippy, rarely spoke except to Tor. But one afternoon he sought me out and started talking about his family. He had two children under two and also supported his parents and three sisters and a sick brother in Wardak Province. He hadn't seen or heard from them in seven months and wasn't due for any leave until next April. There had been a lot of fighting there recently, and he didn't know whether they were safe. "Sometimes I think my babies will forget me," he said quietly, almost to himself.

As a major in the Afghan army, Humayoon had been based at Shindand Airbase and had seen the Soviets enlarge the runways so the strategic bombers could land and take off there. "It was then I realized how important Afghanistan was to the Soviet Union," he said. Humayoon joined the *Jihad* shortly after. His normal role was Dashaka, Zigovak, and missile instructor at NIFA's training camp. I had watched him in operation there. The camp, started and run by Brigadier Safi, had trained some eighteen thousand men, three thousand a year, in guerrilla warfare and had gained a wide reputation for its demolition course. I had been horrified at conditions there when I first saw the camp. The tents were set up on rocks, even though there were trees in the area that would have provided some shade, and the sun beat down mercilessly twelve hours a day. The temperature had been 130 degrees when I was there, and four men had died of heat prostration that week. Many of the others were covered in sores: infected mosquito bites, Tor told me. "Why were the conditions so lousy?" I asked Safi. "Could anyone really learn anything here? "Two reasons," he said curtly. "The main one is lack of funding. I have three and a half rupees a day to feed each of these men, for example; that's the price of a Pepsi Cola, and it gives them a diet of little more than five hundred calories a day. Commando training requires four thousand to six thousand calories a day. The second reason is that the conditions here are no different from the conditions they'll have when they're fighting." Having seen Daka, I realized Safi wasn't exaggerating.

Humayoon was a good teacher, and many of the *Mujahideen* owed their skills to him.

Another afternoon, Hamid came and sat next to me. Solidly stoic and apparently even-keeled, Hamid never showed his emotions. He had probably learned to internalize his feelings when he'd first left Kabul and his family at the age of sixteen. I was aware that he had been so distraught then that he'd spent his first four months in Peshawar without leaving his room. Similarly, tough-as-nails Omar had taken an overdose of Valium during his early days of exile. Accident or misery? No one had ever been sure, and once it was over, Omar had refused to to talk about it.

But this particular afternoon, Hamid was in pain, and I guessed his ulcer was acting up again. "You know, the war has changed me. I never used to worry. . . . Ever since we've been here, I keep thinking how our family used to spend every winter here in Jalalabad Province on my grandfather's farm. I used to spend hours riding with my grandfather on his tractor when I was a small boy. He was my favorite relative. I could talk to him about everything, and he always listened. . . . I miss him very much. Sometimes I wonder whether he is still alive. I haven't seen him since the *Jihad* began."

"If he wasn't, don't you think your family would find some way to let you know?"

"No, I think my father wouldn't want to upset me."

But it was my conversation with Tor that surprised me the most. We'd been at Daka almost a week, and the base one morning was all but deserted with most of the freedom fighters' swimming. Tor joined me under one of the threadbare flysheets where I was trying to shelter from the blistering sun and write up my notes. "Mommy," he began. "I feel very sad." Tor had started calling me "Mommy" during my first trip to Afghanistan, when he'd been particularly cute on one occasion, and I'd jokingly told him I was going to adopt him. As I got to know him better, I realized that he had been very close to his own mother and the rest of his family, and to have no contact with them was very painful for him. Tor was obviously trying to re-create a family for himself, which was probably why he and Hamid seemed like brothers. Now he began to say, "the night before we came to Jalalabad I learned a good friend, Sikander, had been killed. He was the last of my six close friends who joined the *Jihad* with me when I joined. He took the paramedic course with me. Sikander was a very fine medic; he had an excellent brain. I loved him, loved all six like brothers. Now they're all dead, and I'm left.

"I keep trying not to think about it; otherwise I will go crazy. But last night I dreamed about Sikander. In my dream, he came to me and put his arm around my shoulder and said, don't be sad: 'I'm not dead.' But I knew he was. Then I woke up. And I keep asking myself why was he killed and not me? Why am I still living?"

It was obvious from Tor's expression that these were rhetorical questions; that I wasn't supposed to reply, just listen. And I also realized I wasn't surprised by what he said next.

"You know, Mommy, I'm never afraid in the *Jihad*, when we fight. I want to be martyred."

"Aren't you more useful to the *Jihad* alive than dead?"

"Afghanistan has many young men like me to be useful. Anyway, I died five years ago when I left Kabul. My soul has gone to heaven; this is just my body. If I die, it is finished. People will say, 'he was a brave freedom fighter; we can be proud of him.' It is an honor to be martyred."

"Are we talking about martyrdom or suicide?"

Tor smiled a brief crooked smile, "We are talking of dying.

"If God wants me to die, I will die. If God wants to take my arm or leg, he will take it. Five years ago, when I was in Mazar-i-Sharif, bullets were falling like rain. I was frightened and I wanted to run. I was sure I would die. But I remembered my mother saying the night I left home, 'Never run. You are an Afghan; never die with a bullet in your back. Fight to your last drop of blood.' It wasn't my time to be martyred. I was only shot in my left foot and got a flesh wound on my left knee. I couldn't walk for two months; it was very painful. Since that time, I have never been frightened. But I think I will die in the *Jihad*. Why should I live? I have no parents, no home, no education. I was going to be a big doctor, a surgeon. I was always first in my class. . . . Now I have no future."

He looked so anguished, and in need of comfort, that I wanted to hug him. But I knew any display of physical affection would outrage the other Afghans. So I settled for reaching for his hand and held it briefly. Then almost immediately I watched the vulnerability disappear; his face went blank. The curtain Hamid had mentioned came down. Tor got up and silently walked away. I didn't see him again for several hours, and when I did he was camp jester again and making even taciturn Humayoon laugh with his Puckish humor. As I looked at Tor, I remembered teasing him some time before: "Be serious; you're always kidding around," I started. "No," he'd corrected me. "I maybe be laughing on the outside, but often on the inside, I'm crying." And then he'd laughed at himself.

The following morning the commander announced that the borrowed mortars had arrived. "We leave tomorrow evening," he told us. "The base we are to attack is Malgai Tana. But there are two small bases nearby as well as the large one, Landai Khyber. The moment we start hitting Malgai, we can expect to be counterattacked by these other bases," he explained. "For this reason, Humayoon will take eight men and the rockets and shell Landai Khyber." This way, Said Mohammed hoped the troops in the garrison would be fooled into thinking the *Mujahideen* numbered far more than they did. "When we shell Landai Khyber, they will think the *Mujahideen* are going to storm their base; they won't have time to worry about Malgai. The big base has BM-21s and helicopter gunships, and we want to keep both of these away from our real target." Said Mohammed's plan was an optimistic one. Humayoon would have eight R-107s, one for each man with him, and as was invariably the case, the rockets lacked the firing tubes. "You have to be very careful when you aim them," the commander told Humayoon. "Close to the base is a village. If your rockets are off-target you will kill innocent people." After briefing the major, the commander and a small group of men left to check out where he wanted to place his heavy guns and mortars and to decide on the retreat routes.

Since we were in for a long hike the following day, I decided I wanted to cool off at the river, even if Islamic decorum decreed that as a woman I could not swim in their company. The route down to the river took us through another bomb-ruined village, the ground around it strewn with shrapnel and pieces of shell casing. Once again, I was warned to walk where the *Mujahideen* walked in case of mines. "We found many antipersonnel mines here." When we reached the river, our swimming party consisted of about fifteen of the mostly younger and therefore more flexible *Mujahideen*. They decided that if they swam fully dressed and I swam fully dressed nobody could object. I waded into the Kunar up to my neck before anyone could change his mind, and my baggy Afghan pajamas ballooned out behind me. The cool water felt wonderful after a week of living and sleeping in the same clothes with only a small jug of water with which to wash. The river's current, even close to the edge, was so strong it was hard to stand upright. Most of the men struck out for an island in the middle. I wanted to join them, and although I was a strong swimmer I wasn't sure that I was powerful enough to make it across and back. And if I weren't, I risked being swept downstream perhaps to land on the bank near the Soviet base 1½ kilometers away. But the teasing of the freedom fighters made me finally try it. "You'd better double tie your trousers," Hamid yelled; "the river's so strong I nearly lost mine." He was right; the speed of the water clawed at my clothes as I half-swam, half-battled across. Half a dozen hands stretched out to pull me ashore. I struggled to catch my breath, while they mocked Tor still standing on the opposite bank. I felt as if I'd completed a hazing rite. The island's beach was black oozing mud and I sank to midcalf in it. Standing there, and over the roar of the river, I suddenly became aware of the sound of engines.

"Hamid, can you hear that noise; what is it?" I asked.

The *Mujahideen* abruptly stopped talking. And Hamid, whose hearing is extremely acute, listened for a moment. "Tanks," he announced at the same time as we saw them. No more than half a kilometer from where we'd been cavorting on the riverbank a line of tanks was heading toward the highway, marking its route with a trail of dust. "I think we should return," said Hamid. So did I. Fifteen Kalashnikovs on the far bank was decidedly undermatched for what looked like double that number of tanks. The swim back was just as tough as before, but there was added incentive this time. As we were putting on our sandals for the hike to the base, we heard voices coming toward us on the narrow trail that paralleled the river. But their owners were obscured by the seven-foot rushes that edged the water. The *Mujahideen* picked up their guns and waited. The foliage parted and a group of about ten travelers with baggage and a guide found themselves facing us. Both parties were surprised to see the other, but ours obviously had the advantage.

"Where are you going; where have you been?" Rohullah asked. The guide said they were from Kabul; they had paid two hundred rupees each for him to take them to visit relatives in refugee camps in Pakistan. The road was closed, so they were making their way overland. While the guide was explaining, the women brushed past us and moved on down the path, more from fear it seemed than from propriety. The *Mujahideen* didn't stop them. Most of the group were old men safe from conscription and women with several children. But the freedom fighters were suspicious of one boy of about eighteen. They frisked him at gunpoint and then searched his baggage, a large cloth bag. It contained one change of clothing and two enormous Korans. This satisfied the younger *Mujahideen*, whose average age was about seventeen, and they wanted to let him go. But Hamid and Rohullah disagreed. "A boy his age would have trouble getting past all the checkposts without being conscripted," said Hamid. "It doesn't make sense. He could be an informer."

Rohullah told the younger *Mujahideen* he wanted to take the youth back to base for more questioning. A short argument broke out. To my surprise, the teenagers prevailed. The guide and boy scurried away. It was then that the tanks began shelling the area around the road. The whine and the thump of the rockets made it difficult to converse.

"Why did you let them go if you feel that way?" I asked Hamid. The boy's freedom to travel and his lack of papers had also struck me as odd. And I felt uneasy that the youth had had a clear look at me. Without my turban I was obviously female and foreign. Neither Hamid nor Rohullah could explain why they had given way to the younger *Mujahideen*. "I think it was a mistake on our part," said Hamid uncertainly. He would worry about it for the rest of the day.

While Hamid and Rohullah discussed whether they should go after the boy, a white-haired old man with a long gray beard came shuffling along the same path. But unlike the earlier group, he was pleased to see us. He said he'd been traveling with the same party but couldn't keep up because he'd recently had an appendectomy and wasn't "as strong as I used to be." The old man sat down stiffly, pleased for a chance to rest, and offered us homemade *khajor* cookies that are traditionally given to a son when he goes into the army or to someone going on a long journey. They were stale but sweet and tasted good after our week-long diet of *nan* and onions. The man explained he was on his way to visit his two sons, both of whom were freedom fighters.

"The *Mujahideen* have closed the Jalalabad Highway to traffic since yesterday," he told us. "They posted the area, saying the road would be closed for six days, which is why we had to come this way. There are 150 cars and buses stopped on the highway.

I counted them. They can't go forward and they can't go back. It's dangerous for those people. They get caught in the middle of the fighting." The old man awkwardly got to his feet and tried to press more cookies on us. "God will bless you," he told Hamid and Tor. "You are fighting a just and holy war." Then he continued his slow and painful hike.

When we returned to the base, the commander was waiting for me. Word had gotten out, he said, that he had a foreign journalist at his camp. He'd been to Kama Daka village close to Landai Khyber base and the villagers were asking him about me. "They said you were a photographer, so someone must have seen your cameras, and they knew you were an American. And if the village knows a *feranghi* is here, they will know it in the base also. I think it is good we are leaving tomorrow." Afghanistan's bush telegraph has always been highly effective. Wakil had warned me that it wasn't safe for a foreigner to stay in one place very long because word quickly spreads, and that even in regions loyal to the *Mujahideen*, the KHAD intelligence was very good. This information left me feeling very jumpy for the rest of the day. And I wasn't the only one—the peace of the camp was disturbed by the first voice I had heard raised in anger since I'd arrived. The man who was shouting was addressing no one in particular, but he was becoming increasingly outraged and vocal. And I realized I hadn't witnessed such a scene since New York, where they are tragically common among the deranged street people who frequently berate invisible adversaries. "Ah, yes," I was told by way of explanation, "the man has a mental problem."

"What do you mean?"

"Sometimes he is happy, sometimes very angry, for no reason. But he's a very good Dashaka operator." The man's paroxysm of anger would not have looked out of place on a schizophrenic ward.

"Is he a reliable Dashaka gunner?" I asked, thinking of the mayhem he could cause if he chose to point his antiaircraft gun down at the base, for example, during one of his outbursts.

"Oh yes, he's a very good fighter. He's been in the *Jihad* for four years." Had he been ill before, I wondered, or was he suffering from war neurosis? What happens to a shell-shocked guerrilla who witnesses one too many of his friends or family die or suffer? The *Mujahideen* gently humored the man, and finally he calmed down. He looked exhausted afterward. No one but me seemed disturbed by the man's behavior.

Shortly after this scene, several *Mujahideen* arrived, dragging the spent casings of BM-21s, each one weighing forty pounds. They would carry them back to the border and sell them for scrap metal. The going rate was 100 rupees ($6.25) for eighty pounds of metal. A factory in Lahore recycled the Soviet casings into building materials. It seemed hard work for small returns, but the guerrillas are mostly unpaid, and their scrap metal earnings helped them support their families.

I noticed young Noor Jhan, whom Tor had quickly dubbed Baby Jhan, was wearing *kohl* around his eyes, a local treatment for eye irritations, which were a common problem with the mini-dust storms. "But tomorrow I will wash it off. If I am martyred, my dead body must be clean," he told me matter-of-factly. I turned away from him too distressed to continue the conversation. What kind of war was this when kids young enough still to be in the Little League talked calmly about dying?

That evening, Tor helped lighten my mood by reciting Persian and Uzbek poems to us. I couldn't understand a word, but his voice was as honeyed as Richard Burton's at its best. He held his audience spellbound. "You want a poem about *Jihad?*" he asked the gathering of *Mujahideen.* "No, about love," came the response. "Ah, don't ask me about love; my heart is so full of love it will explode. You want to put mines in my heart? I am lovesick," the ham in him quipped before he launched into a Persian poem full of romantic imagery that would have put Byron to shame. I looked at these men, who didn't see a woman for months on end, who lived in a culture where women were frequently hidden from them, and who, if they were single, were forbidden the company of females except relatives. How did they handle sexual feelings, or just plain desire for affection? So far, I had certainly seen no suggestion of homosexuality. And the lack of privacy would have made that difficult. I knew the male hand-holding common in Muslim countries was merely a sign of friendship, although I had seen more than one Western male jump at the sight of two bearded *Mujahideen* with machine guns slung over their shoulders and linking little fingers with each other. On my first visit to Afghanistan, my photographer had positively blanched the first time Tor had walked alongside him and taken his hand in his.

I finally got around to asking one of the more outgoing freedom fighters whose English was good enough to broach the touchy subject of sex and the single guerrilla. "Of course, I would like to get married some day. And there are some days when I would like it more than others . . ." he said with a throaty chuckle that made him seem like any twenty-year-old ruled by his hormones. "But in my culture and in *Jihad* it is impossible to have a girlfriend. I would like one. If I think about a girlfriend, what do I do? I just go crazy. It will give me a headache. I can dream, and then I have to open my eyes. Here are the rocks, here are *Mujahideen*, here are guns. No girl. No, it is better I don't dream. In Peshawar, if I want to go on a picnic, if I want to go to the cinema, I go with male friends.

"Before the *Jihad*, my father saw me talking to a girl after school. I was just talking to her . . . for about five minutes. But when I got home, he beat me. He told me it was good it wasn't the girl's father who had seen me. He said he might have killed me. I learned not to talk to girls.

"Of course, it doesn't stop our feelings. We still have them. But as a good Muslim I won't make love to a woman until I am married. That may not be true for all of the *Mujahideen*, but it is true for the ones I know."

The following day the commander called me over while he shaved in hot tea, the only hot water available, and with a razor blade hooked over his index finger for a lack of a razor. He told me I would be with the Dashaka and mortars during the battle. "They will be two thousand meters away from the base. It is safer than the front until they locate our position and begin to fire back." He explained they always tried to knock out the Dashakas and mortars first. "But there is no safe place in battle. This is war; you may perish; we all may perish. Also, if we have to retreat, we have to retreat very fast. It will not be easy." He delivered those words in a manner that made me feel I was about to sky dive and was being cautioned that I couldn't sue the parachute packers if something went wrong. He looked at me to see whether I were still going. I told him yes.

We pulled out at 6:00 P.M. after evening prayers as the sun began to set. We could only move freely at night to avoid detection on this route. Before leaving, every freedom fighter passed under a silk-wrapped Koran, a blessing for the battle. The heavy weapons were lashed to five large donkeys and a mule. Our caravan of fifty men snaked along the valley. Humayoon was coming with us. He'd decided he couldn't bring Landai Khyber under attack and guarantee the safety of the village since they were so close together. The commander laughingly said, "Anyway, our propaganda will be as successful as the rocket attacks. Someone in the village will inform the base we are going to attack. They will be on guard the whole time, too busy to worry about Malgai." Our journey was to be a two-hour walk and then a forty-five-minute climb, I was told. During this time, there was to be no talking and no smoking, Said Mohammed ordered. We would be passing close to several bases, and it was possible any one of them would send out night patrols. Our feet on the loose slate clattered noisily to my ears. We hadn't gone very far when a baby donkey, no higher than my hip and braying loudly, caught up with us. It was impossible to turn it back. The foal was still nursing, and its mother was carrying one of the mortars. We began to climb and I cursed this country that never seemed to have any flat terrain. The baby donkey continued to whinny, the noise echoing loudly. "It's a KHAD spy," joked Omar. "If it continues, I will slaughter it," responded Lal Mohammed. "Does he mean it?" I asked Hamid, my Western love of animals written across my face. "Of course he does. If it doesn't stop, it will cause all of us to be killed. A donkey isn't important."

Fifteen minutes later, halfway along the caravan, there was a sound like a small rockfall. Stage whispers carried the news back to us. A donkey carrying one of the mortars had fallen over the edge. It had missed its footing in the dark, something I was always afraid of doing. The donkey's fall had been broken by a ledge about fifteen feet down. In the dim light of a pencil flashlight, the animal was still moving. "I hope it hasn't broken a leg?" I said, my Western sensibilities once again showing through. "I hope it hasn't broken the mortar," replied Hamid. Several freedom fighters scrambled down onto the ledge and talked soothingly to the trembling donkey. As they pulled it to its feet, one of the *Mujahideen* yelped in pain—his finger had been badly smashed between the mortar and the rocks. The *Mujahideen* manhandled the animal back onto the narrow path. Apart from minor cuts, abrasions, and fear, it seemed to have escaped serious injury. But Hamid was angry. "You see, this is our situation," he said bitterly. "We have no proper transportation, no facilities. And we are trying to fight a superpower." We continued our trek. The darkness now was almost total. The moon hadn't yet come up, and the mountain towering above us would obscure it for several hours to come anyway. The shadowy silhouettes of the rocket-propelled grenades carried by the *Mujahideen* in front of me looked like Roman spears. I stumbled constantly over rocks I could not see, a problem the *Mujahideen* did not seem to share. I strained in the dark to see the trail, expecting with every step to follow the donkey and plunge over the edge. Suddenly, the sky in front of us lit up. I almost screamed aloud as a shell roared overhead and exploded some distance behind us. "Jesus! What is happening? Have they seen us?" I rattled at Hamid. Poor Hamid: since he was my most reliable interpreter, I often endowed him with omnipotent powers and assumed he knew everything. As always he patiently tried to answer my questions. Now he said, "No, I don't think they've seen or heard us. Often the bases just do it for their own security. It makes them feel safer." He appeared to be right. The *Mujahideen* kept moving, and sporadically, the shells would arc across the sky. The commander moved down the line. "The password tonight is 'loudspeaker number five,'" he said and disappeared into the gloom. After two and a half hours, Said Mohammed brought us to a halt. Optimistically, I hoped it meant we were nearly there. I should have known better: Afghan estimates of time that a journey will take are always considerably shorter than the reality. I was never sure whether that was meant to encourage a foreigner, although it always had the opposite effect on me as I was unable to pace myself, or whether it was because to most Afghans, time wasn't important. But when the commander stopped us, we hadn't even reached the halfway point. Said Mohammed took seven men and told us they were going ahead to scout and act as mine detectors. We were to keep advancing as long as we didn't hear anything from them.

Six hours from the time we started out we found ourselves at the end of a ravine. We unloaded the donkeys and tied them to convenient boulders. Our route lay straight up a rock cliff that rose several thousand feet above us. Even goats would have found it hard going. In my opinion, this was mountaineering pure and simple, and no human should have attempted it without ropes, which, of course, we didn't have. But not only did the Afghans scale the face with ease; they also lugged the heavy weapons and their own machine guns up it, too. Hamid and Rohullah grabbed my hands and dragged me with them, my feet scrabbling for footholds. Halfway up was a series of rock steps, almost terraces; we stopped on the largest. This was where we would spend the night. But the surface was far from flat, and it was difficult to find space enough for all of us to stretch out and sleep. It was not a comfortable night. And when the *Mujahideen* woke in the gray dawn to pray, I was happy to abandon attempts to sleep. After prayers, the men spread out, looking for a water supply. My bottle had been emptied early the night before. Now all of us were feeling dehydrated, and this would only get worse as the sun climbed. Baby Jhan located what appeared to be an old rain puddle about four feet by two, and a few inches deep. The puddle was an entire ecosystem, filled with frogs, tadpoles, beetles, and assorted aquatic insects I didn't recognize, and little red worms I wished I couldn't see. This was breakfast, and it didn't look appetizing. I yearned for a water filter; my water purifying pills had long since run out. Finally, my thirst got the better of me, and I scooped up tiny handfuls, trying hard not to ingest any wildlife.

The assault party moved out early. The rest of us were told to make ourselves comfortable—impossible—because we wouldn't be leaving before 2:00 P.M. The attack would begin at 4:00 P.M. Hamid, Tor, Humayoon, and I settled under a stunted thorny bush. As the sun started to get hotter, it gave minimal shade. By 10:00 A.M., however, the shade had disappeared and the rocks started becoming too hot to sit on. We kept wetting turbans in the puddle and sitting on or under them, but they dried within minutes. We tried to doze, but raging thirst quickly woke us. Tor complained of hunger, and suddenly like giggly kids we started tormenting ourselves with fantasies of meals we'd have back in civilization. Tor salivatingly described platters of Kabuli pilau and glasses of freshly made buttermilk. Humayoon said he'd settle for a pack of cigarettes, and all I could see was a long row of glasses containing iced orange juice or iced coffee. I didn't articulate it, but thoughts of iced drinks turned to thoughts of air-conditioning, and soon I was asking myself why was I there. Why was I sitting under a broiling sun halfway up a mountain in a country most people couldn't place on a map waiting to witness a war that had nothing to do with me when I could be back in New York in a nice comfortable office? Was I nuts? Was the Afghan refugee's statement "A nation is dying, and the world should know" reason enough? At that moment, hungry and thirsty and becoming more miserable by the minute, I wasn't sure. There was only one thing of which I was sure: the Afghans deserved to win this war, if only because it was so damn difficult to get to each battle. I decided, too, that if this were to be one's last day on earth, this would be a hell of way to spend it.

Then almost as if he'd been mind reading, Tor suddenly asked me, "Why are you here? Why did you come?" I shrugged and asked him the same thing, "Why are you here?"

"Me? I don't have good life. This is all my life. If I die, it's okay. But you have good life. And all the time I think I don't want you to die." Brains too addled from the heat, I murmured, "Well, thank you. It's your turn to wet the turbans."

At 1:30 P.M. we began the last two-hour climb. In the 110 degree heat I was forced to stop every fifteen minutes. But Baby Jhan leaped from rock to rock like the kid he was, the 303 rifle across his back almost the same size as its owner. We reached the top, and I could clearly see the base two thousand meters away on top of a small hill, its red flag getting the same response from the *Mujahideen* as it would have from a tormented bull. Humayoon immediately began setting up the Dashaka, its location having been selected two days before. The gun turret protruded through a natural V in the rocks, affording the gunner some protection, but there was no level ground around the gun, and maneuvering out of one another's way without dropping over the edge was difficult. Runners arrived from the two mortar locations to say they were set up and ready. I chose a spot twenty feet lower and off to one side of the gun. From my position, it was easy to spot the assault party moving into position on a ridge below us.

At 4:05 P.M. Said Mohammed fired our Dashaka, the signal to begin. The noise was deafening, and before the reverberation had died away, one of our mortars fired about five hundred yards to our right. Our Dashaka fired again. Two shouts went up: the first mortar had scored a direct hit. The wall of the base closest to the flag had been hit, the dust mingling with the smoke as it rose into the air. The second shout was in anger. Our Dashaka had jammed; the ammunition belt wasn't feeding into the gun properly. Humayoon struggled to free it. It fired two or three bursts and then jammed again. Two minutes after the *Mujahideen* opened up fire, Malgai's guns fired back. Their large mortars fell far short of where we were. A Dashaka gunner I didn't know managed to get the heavy machine gun going again, but it would only fire intermittently. Time after time, the cartridges jammed. "Fire, you son of a bitch," bellowed Hamid, as an enemy mortar screamed over our heads and exploded with a loud crump behind us. Cursing, Said Mohammed yanked the ammo belt from the gun. Then, anger quickly dissipated, he patiently began checking every cartridge to make sure it was properly loaded. Said Mohammed's base didn't have the belt feeder machines I had seen at Khost, and when the task was done by hand, jamming was a frequent problem.

While the *Mujahideen* struggled to get the Dashaka going again, I stayed clinging to the small crest I'd chosen, watching through binoculars the advance of our assault force. There was no ground cover at all between them and the base. And they marched upright along the ridge as apparently relaxed as if out for an afternoon stroll, while the heavy guns from the *Mujahideen* and Malgai blasted away at each other over their heads. It was an astounding display of courage or foolhardiness or maybe both, and without their ardent religious faith, I wondered whether they could have done it. Once they were closer to the base, they would also be walking straight through Malgai's protective minefield.

Our Dashaka started up again, and this time it didn't jam. The gunner was enveloped in a cloud of smoke, and our ears were assaulted by the noise. After each salvo, the noise continued to echo through my brain, deafening me for about a minute. Then enemy fire started coming at us from two different directions. "The other bases are firing back also," yelled Hamid. "Look, they are firing everywhere, even up in the sky." This amateur display by the enemy delighted the *Mujahideen* around me. Lal Mohammed grabbed the megaphone. "Death to the Communists. Long Live Islam," he yelled, the *Mujahideen* around the Dashaka and stationed at the mortars picking up the chorus: "*Allah o Akbar; Mordabad Shuravi,*" God is Great; Death to the Soviets.

At 4:40 P.M. another of our mortars scored a direct hit. Flames shot up from the base. But Malgai continued to retaliate. Their shells whistled overhead and hit the mountain behind us.

The next strike I felt rather than heard. A mortar crashed into our ridge, about seventy-five yards to my left. The debris rained harmlessly down ahead of us, and the rocks I clung to bucked and dipped like the ground in an earthquake. I was ordered down from my position. "I'll be fine," I tossed back, too keyed up to want to move. "The commander says it's not a request; it's an order. Do it!" Hamid shouted at me. Unaccustomed to the tone in his voice, I complied. The commander was right. Now that the base knew our location, their guns were directed straight at us, but aimed a little too low every time. As the rockets ploughed into the mountain face below us, our perch vibrated almost constantly. My stomach tightened, and I told myself that the one good thing about not having a square meal in more than a week is that at least you can't shit in your pants from fear.

The *Mujahideen* began to take it in turns to fire the Dashaka. Tor, even without his glasses, managed to hit what looked like an ammunition tent. It exploded, sending flames shooting into the sky, and continued to burn with the noise of a thousand firecrackers. He danced in delight and then roared, "Down with the enemies of God and Islam."

Shortly after five, the commander borrowed my binoculars. The advance party was getting closer to Malgai, and he wanted to make sure he didn't shoot his own men. At 5:55 P.M. the rat-a-tat of Kalashnikovs began. The assault force were close enough to use their guns. The men around me fell silent as we all strained through the fading light to watch their progress. Nobody said it, but we knew we were waiting for the small crump, the explosion that would mean one of them had stepped on a mine. At 6:07 P.M. the first man reached the base and disappeared from our sight behind it. Said Mohammed fired another volley from the Dashaka; "for their morale," he grinned. Answering mortars came back at us. We ducked as they whined safely over us, and I realized the commander had chosen this spot well. A direct hit to knock out our gun would have taken tremendous skill or heat-seeking missiles. As it was, everything was falling short or long.

Ten minutes after the assault force disappeared inside the base, the commander told me to start back. "It's getting dark now; you won't see anything. All the fighting is taking place inside Malgai. And it will be difficult going down the mountain in the dark. And if the helicopters come ..." Hamid, Omar, and I started back down. Hamid was deaf in his right ear from the noise of the Dashaka and stayed that way for forty-eight hours. Because the mortars were still strafing the route we had come up, we followed the bed of a dried-up mountain stream, which dropped so abruptly it must have been more like a waterfall in the spring. "This way we won't get lost in the dark," said Hamid. Several times we reached dead ends, probably from rock falls, and were obliged to scale them. Suddenly, Hamid and Omar slipped the safety catches off their guns. And then Omar, who was leading, let out a blood-curdling bellow. I stopped breathing, and at the same time I could feel my heart race. "What is happening?" I whispered at Hamid. "There could be anybody around here," he replied. "Omar was just seeing whether he got a response." He did: seconds later a stray mortar exploded near us with a thunderous racket. We kept going, with my clutching on to Hamid's arm as I stumbled behind him, aware with every step that blood from my heels and battered toenails was soaking my socks. Finally, more by accident than design I felt, we made it back to the terraced base where we had spent the night. A gleeful Baby Jhan and Tor were there before us. Several hours later the assault force, all of them and uninjured, arrived, carrying large wooden cases, their booty from Malgai. All I wanted to do was return to Daka, but the *Mujahideen* wanted to show off their plunder: boxes of Soviet-made grenades and AK-47 ammo; several Russian-made teakettles, which the Afghans always claim are superior to their own; bread, sugar, china cups, I.D. cards, and money. When they'd stormed the base, they found it empty. The Afghan troops had beaten a very hasty retreat. "There was a meal on the table, good grapes," said Raies, who produced a bunch he'd carried back for me. I was touched by his thoughtfulness. After the week's diet privation, they tasted like ambrosia. "The troops had just been paid, so we took their money," added Raies gleefully. A simple, illiterate farm laborer, he had clothes and sandals more tattered than most worn by the *Mujahideen*. "Then we found two containers of gasoline and poured it over the mattresses and set the place on fire."

Fearful of a helicopter attack, the *Mujahideen* stayed at Malgai long enough to ensure the fire they set was raging, and to take the red flag from its pole; later they would tear the flag into strips and use it to clean their guns. "Communist flag is very good for cleaning *Mujahideen* guns," said Baby Jhan. The return journey to Daka went by in an exhausted haze for me. I was given one of the donkeys to ride but kept sliding off it as I just didn't have the energy to hold on. We entered Daka with Lal Mohammed leading the donkey with one hand and holding me upright with the other. I felt as if I could sleep for a week. We got three hours' rest. Then Said Mohammed woke us up. "There is bound to be retaliation today," he said. "They know she is here; if they send helicopters I don't have enough men to protect her. She must leave; it isn't safe for her to stay."

8

Russia's Vietnam?

It was agonizing to put my boots on three hours after taking them off. My feet were not a pleasant sight that morning. The large oozing blisters on my heels had bled, burst, and bled again. My toes looked as though I had been trying to dance *en pointe* without prior practice, in essence the same kind of battering my feet had been subjected to as we climbed down the mountain for hours the night before. Both large toenails had been half-torn from the nail beds. They began bleeding again from the slight pressure of socks being pulled on. I was also feeling light-headed from lack of food and sleep and utter fatigue. But *exhaustion* was a word that didn't seem to exist in an Afghan's vocabulary. I slowly got to my feet and began to pack. I wasn't looking forward to our two-day journey back, particularly the mountain range that stood between us and the border. But Lal Mohammed promised to rent a donkey for me once we'd crossed the Kunar. I repaid his benevolence when we reached the river. This time we were to travel downstream for more than an hour, and as we waited for the boatman to inflate his cow carcass boat, Lal Mohammed looked more and more nervous. "I hate these things; I can't swim," he said, embarrassed. "Don't worry," I reassured him grandly. "I'm a former lifeguard; if the boat capsizes, I'll be happy to save your life." In the condition I was in then, however, if the boat had gone down, I probably would have sunk with it.

In the large village of Menzawara, the deputy commander kept his word. While we rested in the shade, he negotiated rates for the largest donkey I have ever seen. The beast was already loaded with four huge cartons of contraband cigarettes. I was to ride on top. Apparently, Menzawara was a smugglers' way station. Dozens of bootlegged televisions, bales of fabric, and cigarette cartons from Kabul were stacked on the river beach waiting to be transported over the mountains to Pakistan. The forty thousand Red and White cigarettes that would serve as a seat for me had been manufactured in Pakistan and shipped to Afghanistan for sale under the government monopoly; now they were being smuggled back to Pakistan. It was while we were in Menzawara that a NIFA messenger caught up with us. I was not to return to Peshawar. Instead, headquarters had decided to grant my earlier request to interview some of their Soviet prisoners of war but only on condition I agreed not to reveal their location. I agreed. Until three months before, most of the *Mujahideen* parties had kept their Soviet prisoners in camps around Peshawar. They had learned the hard way that when they were held inside Afghanistan, intelligence leaks often led to Soviet attacks in an effort to recapture their men. But in late April, an incident at Jamiat's Zangali Badaberah supply depot fifteen miles south of Peshawar forced the freedom fighters to move their prisoners back into Afghanistan. Jamiat had been holding twelve Soviets at Zangali, but during evening prayers the POWs had killed a sentry and attempted to seize control of the camp. In the fierce fighting that ensued, the Soviets retreated into the ammunition depot. Shortly afterward, the depot was reduced to rubble in a powerful explosion that rocked the camp and was heard in Peshawar. All twelve died, although whether it was by the *Mujahideen* hand or by their own remains unknown. But, charged Vitaly Smirnov, the Soviet ambassador to Pakistan, "this incident shows the increasing use of Pakistan territory by foreign countries to create a military center where they train Afghan bandits thrown out by the government." In Moscow, an outraged *Izvestia* ran a lengthy article quoting an apparent eyewitness survivor who alleged the POWs were "kept in chains and shackles, and cruel torture and subtle humiliations were used to try to incline them to treachery. However, our servicemen resisted with pride and dignity. . . . Then a cruel skirmish began. Our small detachment of Soviet servicemen annihilated more than 100 counterrevolutionaries and Pakistani soldiers. But the forces were too unequal. The Pakistani soldiers gunned the defenders down at point-blank range."

A jittery Pakistani government, who never officially acknowledged the presence of any *Mujahideen*-held prisoners of war, promptly ordered Resistance groups to remove all Soviets from their territory. The Resistance complied. Prisoners were now kept at secret locations inside Afghanistan and moved frequently to avoid detection. At the beginning of the war, few *Mujahideen* took Soviet prisoners. Unless the captives were Muslim and willing to fight with the Resistance, most were executed on the spot. As one commander explained, "Guerrilla warfare, by its nature, means we move around constantly. We had nowhere to hold prisoners and often didn't have food to feed our own men. Prisoners meant we had to deploy men to guard them, share rations that were in short supply with them; and, of course, they were also a security risk." The situation began to change when François Zen Ruffinen, a lawyer with the International Committee for the Red Cross, was posted to Pakistan in 1982. The slightly built Swiss, who speaks eight languages, honed his negotiation skills for POW well-being and exchanges in Hanoi during the Vietnam War, in Iran in 1980 for the U.S. hostages, and in the Middle East for Israel and the PLO. When he became director of ICRC in Peshawar, he began secret monthly "public relations" classes for Afghan commanders. Using Koranic law, which stipulates fair treatment of prisoners of war, the Red Cross also explained to the freedom fighters that slaughtering prisoners would only "harm the image of the *Mujahideen* when you want to be considered for foreign aid." Unless they began to take prisoners and treat them decently, the Resistance would be perceived as savage killers, the commanders were told. Zen Ruffinen also organized regular first-aid courses in war injuries for the commanders, who would then go back into the field and teach what they had learned to their *Mujahideen*. Gradually, the public relations classes began to have an effect. "Now I am negotiating with the seven-party Resistance coalition to permit the Red Cross to visit their Soviet POWs inside Afghanistan and report on their conditions," he said, although such visits would be considered "illegal trespass" by the DRA.

Occasional accounts still surface of POWs being treated less than humanely, particularly by Gulbuddin Hekmatayer's group Hezb-i-Islami, whose prisoners have been reportedly chained up in caves, tortured, and then executed. And Resistance judge Malawi Abdul Bari of Kandahar claims to have executed twenty-five hundred prisoners, who were shot, decapitated, hanged, or stoned to death.

The two Soviets I was to meet had been prisoners of NIFA for four years. We would travel for several days to reach them, on foot and by jeep. As we arrived at the base, the first person I saw was a man wearing leg irons who smiled sadly at me as he hobbled from one building to another. But Hakim Gul was Afghan, not Russian; a member of Babrak Karmal's Parchem party, he was accused of being a ranking KHAD official at Khost. Gul, age thirty-seven, was also a well-known Afghan singer who could be heard frequently on Radio Khost. Captured two and a half weeks earlier, he had not yet been interrogated but protested his innocence to me repeatedly. The *Mujahideen* treated him with contempt, and it was hard to assess whether their loathing stemmed more from his alleged KHAD position or because his broadcast songs were all proregime, even though Gul insisted to anyone who would listen, "They forced me; I am innocent; I am innocent." The two Soviet prisoners enjoyed a rather different standing, not unlike the way I had noticed Naeim, the young Afghan boy who had been trained as a Russian spy, was treated by the *Mujahideen*. They were not trusted, but they'd been around so long they were almost part of the scenery. The ordinary *Mujahideen* shared their cigarettes and exchanged badinage with them, although the freedom fighter officers were less friendly. Garek Dzhamalberkov, age twenty-five, and Nikolai Balabanov, twenty-three, had defected from the Russian army to the Resistance. They both claimed to be Muslims despite the tattoo that completely covered Nikolai's chest, which made it seem unlikely in his case at least. The tattoo depicted an onion-domed Russian Orthodox church and was framed with several crucifixes. Despite their claim, however, NIFA had never permitted them to fight alongside the freedom fighters as a number of defectors did. Yet neither of the Soviets was shackled as was the Afghan prisoner. And dressed in the same *shalvar kameezes* the freedom fighters wore, they were difficult to tell apart from the *Mujahideen*. Both men said they had defected because the conditions in the Soviet army were brutal and because they could no longer stand the savagery of their own troops against the Afghans. Their story was one that was repeated frequently by Soviet POWs. Sent to Afghanistan, often without any formal training, and after being told they were fighting Americans, Chinese, and Pakistanis, conscripts would learn on arrival that the only foreign troops in the country were their own. Their disillusionment soon grew, when they realized they were waging war against an enemy who for the most part were ill-equipped peasants who all too often were only trying to defend their livestock and their crops. And because of their lack of training, conscripts were often quickly captured. One eighteen-year-old who was taken prisoner by the *Mujahideen* had been in the army just two weeks before he was caught. He was picked up by the freedom fighters when he was sent to buy cigarettes for his corporal in a nearby village. Others are captured when they leave their bases to buy drugs. As with American soldiers in Vietnam, the Soviet army has a serious drug problem in Afghanistan, where in much of the country marijuana grows like a weed, and the opium poppy is so frequent in some provinces that it could almost be the national flower. It is now estimated that 60 percent of all conscripts in Afghanistan are drug abusers. As Soviet prisoners frequently say, "Hashish helps you forget you are far from home and afraid of dying." But these are not the only reasons the Soviet army in Afghanistan has a major morale problem.

Life in the Soviet army has always been one of hardship. Soviets are conscripted at the age of eighteen and serve two years, during which time they do not receive any home leave. After he is discharged, an enlisted man stays on reserve duty until the age of fifty and is required to take periodic refresher courses. Conscientious objection is forbidden. College students may defer service, but only sons of high-ranking party officials are able to avoid conscription if they can prove they are serving the country in a different capacity. Once drafted, the Soviet recruit quickly learns that discipline is tough. Officers, NCOs, political officers, and the KGB all monitor behavior, and firing squads are employed even in peacetime. Despite such controls, desertions and AWOL incidents are frequent, and the suicide rate is twice that of the general population. And even if a conscript is not posted to a war zone, life in the Red Army can be hazardous to his health. During peacetime exercises, for example, a 3 percent casualty rate is considered acceptable, and deaths are not uncommon.

Soviet troops in Afghanistan suffer additional privations. They complain of shortages of everything from basic foodstuffs to ammunition. Other hardships include poor sanitation in tented camps, which leads to the high incidence of hepatitis, typhoid, cholera, and malaria; virtually no recreational facilities; and harsh treatment at the hands of superiors.

Food is a major cause for complaint, and conscripts say that many rations are marked CONSUME BEFORE 1965, or that food is moldy or maggoty. Many troops have been observed exchanging or selling weapons for fruit and vegetables. Their monthly salaries of nine to fifteen rubles (eleven to nineteen U.S. dollars), issued in credit notes they can only spend in Red Army canteens that are emptied by the officers, leave them no choice. In fact, Soviet troops have been described as the "neediest soldiers in the world." Not surprisingly, weapons, ammunition, spare parts, and batteries are also exchanged for drugs. One diplomat reported that a Soviet soldier had sold his Kalashnikov for less than one dollar worth of hashish. Asked if he would be disciplined for selling his rifle, he replied that it wasn't his: he had stolen it from a storehouse. Lack of food and money has also led Soviet soldiers to plunder Afghan civilian homes and steal anything that can be sold, from transistors to clothing and jewelry. Most troops say they just want to survive their two years of active duty and then go home.

Soviet officers have the thankless task of trying to motivate a mainly conscripted army to fight an unpopular war. But there are compensations for careerists. An officer serving in Afghanistan receives between 700 and 800 rubles a month, instead of the normal 250 rubles a month, and each year he serves there is the equivalent of three years served elsewhere. And unlike for the conscripts, for whom alcohol is forbidden, vodka is also available to Red Army officers. But rampant alcoholism among the Soviet brass is responsible for many breaches in army discipline, which all too often go uncensored. For brutally beating a conscript, for example, an officer may receive only a caution, or the incident may even be overlooked.

Because of low troop morale, the Afghan war is increasingly said to be Russia's Vietnam. But although there may be some similarities, it is a long way from being that. A major reason of course is lack of public accounting. The Kremlin does not have to answer to an electorate on any of its activities, and it has always been able to control the dissemination of any information completely. Until recently, the Russian public received almost no news of the war or the Soviet presence in Afghanistan. In fact, in the beginning of the Soviet occupation, Moscow denied outright that their troops were there. And draft boards required all recruits to sign statements swearing they would not discuss the war when they were discharged. Dissident Andrei Sakharov ran afoul of the Kremlin when he spoke out against the invasion. But then the first of the zinc coffins and the death notices began to arrive, the coffins for the officers, and the latter for enlisted men, who were frequently given mass burials in Afghanistan. And then the planeloads of wounded began to return. By late 1986, the death toll had risen to an estimated 25,000, with between two and three times that number wounded. With approximately 140,000 Soviet troops inside Afghanistan, and 40,000 also engaged in the war but based just across the northern Afghan border, it was becoming hard to maintain a news blackout. Of the 2 million Soviet troops, more than a quarter had now served in Afghanistan. Suddenly, in the sixth year of the war, Mikhail Gorbachev allowed the state-controlled media to do a surprising about-face that startled the Soviet public. On radio and television and in the newspapers, reports began to appear on the heroic struggles of the Soviet forces inside Afghanistan who were "defending our motherland."

For the first time, public demonstrations against the war occurred, but nothing on the scale of the antiwar movement in the United States during the Vietnam War, and they were quickly quelled. On two occasions in May 1985, parents of conscripts to be sent to Afghanistan publicly protested. One demonstration was in Tbilisi, Georgia, and the second, just days later, in Armenia. On each occasion, dozens of parents were arrested by secret police and charged with "hooliganism," a crime that can carry a prison camp sentence.

Today the Soviet Union is spending an estimated $12 million a day, $4 billion a year, on the war in Afghanistan, and although the United States also spends comparable amounts on its favored friends—$10 million a day, for example, on Israel—the U.S. economy is twice as large as the Soviet Union's. And as world oil prices dropped in the winter of 1985–1986, the Soviet Union's economy began to nosedive. Approximately 70 percent of the country's hard currency is derived from the exporting of natural gas and oil. They rely on such exports to finance imports of food and new technology from the West. If oil prices do not recover quickly, and they are not expected to, the Soviet Union will lose billions, and this in turn may force them to slow up the manufacture of weapons and reassess their presence in Afghanistan.

Many analysts feel that the present situation in Afghanistan is a military stalemate and that for the Soviets to win this guerrilla war in the difficult terrain that the country presents, a massive escalation of troops would be required. Rahim Wardak, chief of staff of the Afghan Resistance, who held the rank of general before the war and was trained in the United States, Soviet Union, and Egypt, is among a number of military specialists who estimate that 500,000 to 1 million troops would have to be committed to the Afghan war. "It will take this many men to defeat the counterinsurgency," he told me. And for the Soviet Union to commit this number of forces would mean a tremendous increase in financial cost during a period of economic downturn, and the troops would have to be redeployed from their European and Chinese theaters, something the Kremlin is unlikely to do. And even if they were to increase their military presence in Afghanistan substantially, sheer numbers do not guarantee success, as the United States learned—it had 500,000 troops in Vietnam at the height of the war.

"The Soviet invasion of Afghanistan was a mistake and we knew that before we began," Arkady Shevchenko, the highest-ranking Soviet official to defect to the West, had told me in Washington, D.C. "As early as the midseventies, the Central Committee was receiving intelligence reports that said that Afghanistan would not be an easy country in which to install a Communist regime, both because of their deep religious beliefs and because of the expected resistance." KGB reports also recommended against it. And two years into the war, Soviet diplomat Yuri Velikanov stated, "For us, Afghanistan is an embarrassment. There were mistakes when we went in, and we are looking for ways to get out." Shevchenko, who was personal adviser to former Foreign Minister Andrei Gromyko and head of the UN Political and Security Council Affairs, added: "There was a conflict of opinion in Moscow. The Foreign Ministry, which tends to be pragmatic, warned against attempting to Sovietize or communize Afghanistan; they even pointed to the Muslim Basmachi uprising in Soviet Central Asia in the 1920s and how long it lasted. [The Basmachi uprising was the largest and most persistent resistance movement to Communist rule in Soviet history. Many fled across the border into Afghanistan and resettled there.] But the Central Committee, which is more ideologic than pragmatic, has a tendency to ignore reality. Their leadership was made up of old men like Brezhnev, and the invasion was born out of their fear of change. The stability the country achieved after the Khrushchev turmoil, they wanted to preserve at any cost. And they saw the situation in Afghanistan as something that could change the internal stability of the Soviet Union. Had Mikhail Gorbachev, a younger man, been leader at the time, I do not believe the Soviet Union would have invaded Afghanistan. As we now see, it was a failure, a mistake and a serious miscalculation."

But although the invasion may have been a mistake, the Soviets have also gained from the war. According to Major Joseph Collins, an associate professor at the U.S. Military Academy and a specialist in Soviet studies, the Kremlin built an army for World War III on the plains of Europe. "The majority of Soviet servicemen only saw mountains for the first time in Afghanistan. At the beginning they did not perform well in a counterinsurgency role in the mountains of South Asia. But since then, they have improved. In the areas of weapons and personnel, Afghanistan has been a prize, though a very expensive one, for the Soviet military," said Collins. "Training deficiencies have been detected and combat experience, though it tends to be fleeting, will ensure a more seasoned Soviet army. Particularly significant has been the performance of Soviet pilots. We can be assured that the Soviets will hone their fire support skills to a fine edge in Afghanistan. If nothing else, Soviet command cadres in future conflicts will be better able to control their air and ground firepower."

One of the crack units that really honed their combat skills in Afghanistan are the Spetsnaz, the elite heliborne commandoes. Composed only of volunteers, and distinguished by their striped sweaters, they began to show up in Afghanistan after the regular army was seen to perform poorly in the harsh Afghan terrain and climate. Skilled in seek and destroy tactics and silent killing techniques, the Spetsnaz are frequently dropped at the rear of *Mujahideen* attacks and cut-off retreat routes. Supplied with sophisticated night-vision equipment and silenced pistols and submachine guns so the Afghans can't tell where the fire is coming from, they now often ambush the ambushers at night, a development that has perturbed the freedom fighters who were used to moving at night because the regular troops prefer to stay in their bases after dark. Some of these elite forces have become so skilled in mountain warfare since arriving in Afghanistan that there have been a number of reports of their scaling steep mountain faces and wiping out Resistance groups bivouacked for the night in locations so treacherous to reach in the dark and considered so safe from sudden attacks sentries hadn't been posted. The Spetsnaz also enjoy tactical flexibility that is denied regular troops, who are obliged to take orders from a central command that may be hundreds of miles from where the operation is taking place. Because of such rigid prearranged planning, *Mujahideen* report many incidences of convoys' heading to areas already evacuated and ignoring retreating freedom fighters they pass en route because they had been ordered to attack the emptied area. This blind obedience to orders was a factor the Resistance frequently used to their advantage. And so were the other weaknesses in the Soviet army, which were characterized by their own military critics as being "oversupervised, lacking initiative, and addicted to cookbook warfare, which uses battle recipes."

"But the Spetsnaz are a real problem for us," said Rahim Wardak. "They now have six to eight battalions of them in Afghanistan. Often they wear the same clothes we wear and look like us. By the time we realize they're Soviet, it's frequently too late."

But fortunately for the Afghans, the average Soviet soldier

is not a highly trained Spetsnaz but a reluctant, unenthusiastic conscript like the two prisoners I had come to visit. Garek and Nikolai were also reluctant to be interviewed. POWs since 1981, they had long ago wearied of being war trophies. Their only interest in me at the beginning was whether I had brought cigarettes or books or magazines in the Russian language for them. Both men knew enough Farsi to converse with the *Mujahideen*, but they couldn't read the language. The empty days passed slowly for them. I found myself apologizing for my oversight. Nikolai shrugged philosophically; Garek was plainly annoyed. An underweight young man, with dark brown hair, low bangs, and a thin, short beard, Garek had the appearance of an ascetic, but angry, monk. Because of his hostility, I suggested to the freedom fighters that I interview the two men separately. I hoped it would be easier to establish rapport with them individually. Before I could propose I start with Nikolai, the *Mujahideen*, always willing to help, ordered him to leave. I was left with the taciturn Garek. We sat on the ground to talk, and immediately a cloud of biting flies settled on us. Tor, who spoke Farsi better than Hamid, offered to translate, and when Tor's English failed, Hamid assisted, a cumbersome method by which to conduct an interview, but there was no other choice. Although a number of the *Mujahideen* who had been trained in the USSR spoke Russian, these interviews had been set up so unexpectedly that there hadn't been time to arrange for one of them to join us. Now the language difficulties would serve as a constant trigger for Garek's anger. Frustrated when he couldn't make himself understood, he would erupt into what appeared to be outbursts of sarcasm. Tor would patiently wait for him to stop and then begin again.

Throughout our conversation, Garek chain-smoked tensely and rarely looked at me. From Dushanbe, Tadjikstan, about one hundred miles north of the Afghan border, he said he had dropped out of school in the tenth grade to avoid conscription. "I spent three and a half years moving from city to city, staying with friends, so the military wouldn't find me."

"Why were you so eager to avoid conscription? The Afghan war hadn't yet begun."

"My father was a pilot; he died in jail," replied Garek, as if that were explanation enough. When pushed further, he said it happened when he was very young, and he didn't know why his father had been imprisoned. "My mother refused to discuss it with me or my sister."

But in September 1980, when he was twenty, the army finally caught up with him. "I was in the army six weeks, given a uniform, given food, and that was all. Then I was sent to Afghanistan. I didn't receive any weapons or any training before I came here. The night before we left, we were just told we were being sent to Afghanistan, but they didn't say where. One officer told us, 'You will pass two years there, and then you will go back to your country, if you are still alive.' All of us recruits got very drunk that night. I passed out; I think most of us did. The next thing I knew I was in the back of a truck. Two and a half years later, we reached Mazar-i-Sharif, in northern Afghanistan.

"The unit I was in was assigned to house-to-house searches in the city. We were told we were looking for Chinese, Pakistani, and American mercenaries, but we soon learned that wasn't true. In fact, it became a joke among the men. We were also told that if we found any Afghans with guns, we must kill them." In a culture where virtually all male adults possess guns, mostly ancient rifles, this order meant open season on slaughtering Afghans. But when the officers weren't present, Garek insisted, many Soviet troops ignored the order.

"If you didn't receive any weapons training, how were you expected to use firearms?" I asked him.

"All Soviet schoolchildren, boys and girls, are taught in the fifth grade when they are twelve; it's normal. I was trained how to use an AK-47, and a heavy machine gun." As we talked, two jet fighters soared overhead, so high they seemed the size of crows. Garek didn't even look up. If he was afraid of being bombed by his own planes, he didn't register it.

Garek stayed in Mazar-i-Sharif for six months, where the living conditions for the troops were deplorable. Billeted forty to a tent—only officers received adequate housing—enlisted men froze through the harsh winter. The men complained of always being on the move but never being told where they were going, and they also complained of the lack of facilities. "The whole time we were there we never had a chance to have a bath. The lack of hygiene caused a lot of health problems, men had open sores, and the rotten food made a lot of people sick. We never had enough to eat, never saw fruits or vegetables; a lot of men suffered from vitamin deficiencies. Dysentery was a problem, and it seemed like one out of two of us had jaundice at some time." Garek said that medical care, when it existed, was poor. "Often the doctors didn't know what was wrong, or they would order a man back on duty when he could barely walk and was bright yellow."

Discipline frequently collapsed in the base, also, with fighting breaking out between the different ethnic groups. A conscript from Soviet Central Asia, for example, resented taking orders from a Ukrainian officer. "And the officers drank heavily and were very brutal; they would pick on us," said Garek. "If they didn't like the way you looked at them, you got beaten. If you didn't move fast enough, they beat you up. I saw a man shot on the spot because he disobeyed an order. Sometimes we felt the officers treated us no differently from the way they treated the enemy. When things got too rough, we'd smoke hashish. We couldn't get vodka; that all went to the officers. We'd buy the hashish from the villages, trade it for ammunition. Some men were using heroin. I started using hashish to help me forget some of the cruelty I saw. The officers were brutal to us, but they were so much worse to the Afghans. The first time it happened, I was disgusted, but I thought it was an isolated incident. Two Afghan prisoners were brought in. The officers pushed them around a bit, playing with them, the way a cat does with a bird. Then they tied them together, back to back. They bent over them and the men screamed. As the officers stood up, I realized they had cut off the men's testicles. Then they tied dynamite to their arms and blew them up."

Garek said he turned away to vomit and afterward realized he wasn't the only one to do so. "I hadn't seen such cruelty before, but it got worse."

As he spoke, the anger that was present earlier was curiously absent. His voice was monotonal as if he were trying to remove himself from the experience. Only a tic in the side of his cheek betrayed any emotion.

The worst occasion was after the Soviets received a report that four trucks transporting raisins had been stopped and searched by freedom fighters close to the village of Rabatak near the Soviet border, about 1½ kilometers from their base. A convoy was sent out to intercept the *Mujahideen;* Garek was part of it. "When we reached the place, we saw a group of men but they disappeared into the village. The houses were a barrier to the tanks, so the officers ordered the tanks to plough into them. They were just one-story and made of mud. It was easy. We rolled right over them. People were buried alive; you could hear their screams over the noise of the tanks." The soldiers rounded up any male in the village who wasn't killed on the spot. They were taken back to the base.

"There were thirteen prisoners in all. Our officers tied the men's arms behind their backs. Then they took one of them and blew him up with dynamite in front of the others. They seem to like to do that. After that, at gunpoint, they forced the twelve men to lie down on the ground in a line. Then they drove a tank over them.

"I watched them do it; I couldn't move. It was an inhuman act. I couldn't understand why they did it. They didn't even know if they were freedom fighters; they could have just been men living in the village. I was ordered to bury them. But there wasn't much left to bury. There was snow on the ground, and it was bright red with blood. You could see bits of human flesh on the tank treads."

Garek and some of his colleagues started to dig in the frozen earth. "It took us a long time; the ground was so hard. Before we finished, some of the officers returned. They were drunk out of their minds. One of them had a long knife and cut off the head of one of the corpses. He held it up by the beard and kept staggering around shouting 'I've caught a fish; I've caught a fish.' He asked for a big dish, which somebody brought him. Then he put the head on it, poured gasoline over it, and set it alight. He was laughing deliriously the whole time. He said he wanted to see an Afghan head in ashes. The man was so drunk, he didn't remember any of what he had done the next day.

"It was after I witnessed that incident, that I knew I wasn't going to stay."

When Garek stopped speaking, the freedom fighters around him fell silent also. After a minute or two, one of them suddenly addressed him. "You're a Russian; why are Russians so brutal?"

Garek stared down at the ground. He didn't reply. I had asked a similar question of Arkady Shevchenko in Washington. As we sat in his large, comfortable home in an elegant part of the capital, the expensive beige and rose pink furnishings seemed a strange setting for a discussion of atrocities in Afghanistan. And the Persian miniature depicting the Afghan national game, *Buzkashi*, the forerunner of polo, seemed equally out of place. I had explained to Shevchenko that I had covered a number of wars, yet I was horrified at the level of brutality being carried out on a large scale by the Soviets in Afghanistan. "Normally, when such atrocities take place," I said, "it is under the order of a man generally considered to be unbalanced, such as Idi Amin or Pol Pot. But in Afghanistan this is not the case, yet there have been frequent massacres, teenage girls have been thrown out of flying helicopters, young children have been set on fire in front of their parents. Why is this happening? I find it hard to believe the Soviets are any more inhumane than the rest of us."

"I don't think the Soviets are any more inhumane, either, on an individual level," he replied. "But there are two things you have to understand. Firstly, the Soviets are angry and frustrated. They have suffered losses, which they didn't expect to happen, so some of the brutality you can put down to human nature. But secondly and most importantly, the Soviets employ terror as a means to win a war, to frighten the population and to intimidate them. In the West, you don't understand this, but it is not alien to the Soviet philosophy. They did it to their own people in the twenties and thirties under Stalin. Such an attitude has existed since Lenin's time, since the Red terrors in 1917 when they eliminated class enemies, which included children, women, anyone who was considered a class enemy. The Communist regime is based on this philosophy, and it was reinforced by Lenin. Terror, mass terror of the enemy was the philosophy from the beginning. And the West, since it doesn't share this kind of morality, doesn't understand it. They didn't even when it was taken up by Stalin. Don't think that Soviet leaders would easily depart from this approach."

"So if a Soviet officer carries out a massacre of fifteen hundred people on the scale of the one carried out in Laghman, for example, he can do so without fear of the kind of censure Lieutenant Calley received after My Lai in Vietnam?"

"I do not believe an officer in the field would do such a thing on his own, without an order coming from the top. They can kill a few or torture some on their own, but fifteen hundred people, that order would have to come from Moscow. It would be part of a terror campaign, and that campaign would be approved at the highest level. Do you think the Central Committee doesn't know that Soviet dissidents are being placed in mental hospitals? Do you think they really believe the dissidents are insane?

"When the Soviet Union signs an international law or the Geneva Convention, it is mostly done to protect their image. It is part of a big game. The Soviets frequently sign such agreements without meaning to implement them. We did the same thing when we ratified the Biological Weapons Convention in 1972. I was part of those negotiations, and we did it knowing full well that we would not destroy our biological weapons, and with our complete understanding that we never intended to stop producing them."

Shevchenko, a lieutenant colonel in the reserves at the time of his defection, explained that the Soviet army is the best prepared army in the world in chemical warfare and that there was no intention on the Kremlin's part to change that: "Every man in the army is trained in chemical warfare; even the smallest unit is equipped and prepared for any contingency." In addition to this, today's Soviet military has a corps of 120,000 chemical specialists, compared with about 6,000 in the United States. Its estimated stockpile of half a million tons of chemical weapons includes hydrogen cyanide, mustard gas, and persistent nerve agents, such as the particularly lethal Soman and VR-55, whose effects can linger for weeks. Soman, an agent the Red Army favors, has been described by the Pentagon as being "tasteless, colorless, and odorless. One lungful or a drop on the skin, and every muscle in the body contracts, the heart seizes, and breathing stops. Some victims die in minutes; others writhe on the brink of death for hours." The Soviet Union, one of the signatories of the 1925 Geneva Protocol on chemical warfare, maintains that the law provides only that a country should not be the first to use chemical weapons but that it can resort to chemical warfare if it is the victim of a chemical attack. Obviously, the Afghan Resistance are not in a position to use chemical weapons against the Soviets for the simple reason that they don't possess any. And yet chemical weapons have been employed numerous times by the Soviets in Afghanistan since the invasion. And unfortunately for the Afghans, their climate is ideal for its use, as the British discovered in 1919 when they first used it there.

As a letter to the British War Office dating from that period attests: "In Afghanistan, the heat of the sun distinctly favours its [a chemical weapon] use, as evaporation from the ground will be much more rapid, and more toxic atmospheres will be created. As a consequence inflammations will be more severe and they will appear sooner; while profuse perspiration will encourage blistering, and skin lesions will have a tendency to become septic."

The first reports of chemical agents being employed in Afghanistan, particularly trichothecene mycotoxins that induce blistering, vomiting, dysentery, and ultimately death, occurred as early as 1980, one year after the Soviet invasion, with a cluster of such incidents in 1981–1982. Mycotoxins are manufactured from wheat fungus, and Soviet scientists began seriously studying them in the 1930s because fungal growths on poorly stored grain had killed thousands of Russian citizens. Since 1982, American, French, and Afghan doctors all report treating victims of chemical warfare in Afghanistan. Chemical warfare, of course, makes no distinction between soldier and civilian. And once used, they also offer no choice of surrender.

Shevchenko defected in 1978, so he had no actual knowledge of chemical weapons usage in Afghanistan. "But I would expect them to use it," he said. "It's much cheaper than conventional warfare, and it would give the army an excellent chance to test the agents under real conditions. Remember also, there are no mechanisms for international inspection if they do employ it."

Although Shevchenko had no direct knowledge of chemical weapons being employed in Afghanistan, I spoke to a number of people who had. General Rahim Wardak was one of them. He had witnessed the aftereffects of a lethal incapacitating agent in Wardak Province in 1982. "A small group of *Mujahideen* were dug in on top of a hill, and for two days were engaged in fierce fighting with a Soviet unit. Because of the freedom fighters' superior position, the Soviets had taken quite a beating. We'd seen them drive away two truckloads of wounded and dead. Finally, the Soviets fired gas rockets at the *Mujahideen* position. All seventeen of our men were killed immediately. Death was so instant, they appeared frozen in position; one man's hand still held the apple he was eating. And what was uncanny about this incident is that there wasn't a physical mark on any of them." The Chief of Staff has also received a number of reports of contaminated water supplies in various provinces. "In Hazarajat, in the middle of the country, we found the bloated corpses of animals in the water after contaminants had been employed. For the most part, it appears that the Soviets use chemical weapons when they are losing badly. Although, on occasion it does appear they use them to test them, too. For example, recently, we've come across chemical bullets being used in the newer AK-74 guns."

Chemical warfare engenders fear in even the most seasoned fighters. It was certainly one of my concerns the whole time I was with the *Mujahideen* in Afghanistan. But for the Afghans, there is another demoralizing aspect. "Devout Muslims believe that when someone dies in a holy war, his body does not decompose," explained Wardak. "Some of the agents being used in Afghanistan rapidly accelerate decomposing. We've found bodies where the flesh is separating from the bones within hours of death. The psychological effect this has on the *Mujahideen* is horrifying."

When Soviet troops are captured, Wardak said, they invariably have their gas masks with them. "Normally, an ordinary soldier hates carrying any extra equipment. If it isn't necessary, he throws it out. But the Soviet troops hang on to their protective clothing. And they know we aren't going to be using chemical agents against them."

An American physician, Dr. Preston Darby, who spent two months inside Afghanistan in 1985 for the International Medical Corps, saw patients who had apparently been exposed to new chemical agents in the Panjshir Valley region. Reporting to Congress on his return he said, "These agents include a tar-like material that burns severely. The Afghans were unable to rub it off and the tar would stick to their hands and start burning their hands if they rubbed it. They tried to remove it with twigs and leaves." The Texan physician also treated a twenty-eight-year-old Afghan freedom fighter with advanced anaplastic bladder cancer. "This is an extremely rare form of cancer to find in a man this young. Normally, we would conclude that he had been exposed to a carcinogen in his workplace. Since that is not the case here, I suspect he was in an area where chemical weapons were being used."

Mohammed Nabi, a veteran Afghan pilot who defected by flying his SU-7 fighter jet to Baluchistan in Pakistan, witnessed large-scale chemical weapons storage depots at Soviet-held Shindand and Bagram airports in Afghanistan. Trained in Byelorussia for nearly five years and fluent in Russian, Nabi had been an instructor for SU-22 and SU-7 fighter jets. Based at Shindand, in southern Afghanistan, he described the strategic airport as having "runways three thousand meters long, and fifty meters wide. There were underground rocket silos there, and the airport was ringed with tanks armed with S9 antiaircraft guns. There were also large storage areas there for chemical weapons. We were told what they were and we were also told the area was off-limits. But troops wearing protective chemical weapons clothing were a common sight at Shindand.

"On one occasion, there was a raid on a *Mujahideen* base fifteen kilometers from the airport. During the chemical bomb attack, the pilots inadvertently bombed their own men. Several injured Karmal troops were brought to Shindand; their bodies were black and swollen. All later died."

When Nabi was based at Bagram airport outside Kabul, he said an area there was also given over to storage of chemical weapons and that he had seen decontaminating equipment.

The Soviets first experienced the effectiveness of chemical weapons as a terror tactic when they themselves fell victim to them at the hands of the Germans during World War I. Having suffered a half million casualties, one in ten of whom died, to chemical warfare during this period, Soviet leadership began to stress the importance of such weapons after the war. During the 1920s and 1930s a great deal of research and development took place in the field, and the first military chemical academies were established. At the end of World War II, the Soviets captured and relocated to the Soviet Union two German nerve agent production plants and stocks of chemical agents. Today, according to a Department of Defense report, there are nine chemical weapons storage depots spread across the Soviet Union. And almost all Soviet conventional weapon systems ranging from mortars to long-range tactical missiles have compatible chemical ammunition or warheads. An M-8/HIP attack helicopter, for example, can be equipped to carry up to 1,650 pounds of chemical munitions on each wing. And virtually all combat and combat support vehicles have chemical agent filtration systems installed in them.

In the Soviet Union, the Shikhany Chemical Warfare Proving Ground, which is equidistant from Moscow and the northern Caspian Sea, is one of their primary chemical weapons test areas. Until the Afghanistan war, the Soviets had had to rely on simulated testing at Shikhany, or third-hand reports of usage by client forces in countries such as Laos and Cambodia. The war in Afghanistan has given them the chance to assess first-hand the chemical weapons' effectiveness and what, if any, safety improvements for their own men need to be made.

Captured Soviet soldiers often reported their fear of using chemical weapons. Many had heard of incidents in which their own men had been injured using them.

□

"There are many ways to kill a man in war," Garek Dzhamalberkov told me. "The clean way, and our way. And from what I witnessed in my six months in the army, I knew I didn't want to be a part of it. I was disgusted by what I saw. We were killing people, we were killing animals in Afghanistan, we were covering the country with blood. I'm Muslim; I couldn't keep killing other Muslims." Garek's revulsion at killing fellow Muslims was a problem the Soviet army had first faced at the beginning of the war. For reasons best known to themselves, the Kremlin had ordered that the first troops sent into Afghanistan be Muslims from Soviet Central Asia. They may have thought there would be some advantage because there was less of a language barrier or cultural difference, but the decision backfired on them badly. Islam proved to be a unifying force that transcended national borders. Soviet Muslims had access to the Koran for the first time, and they bought up as many copies as they could find. And to the distress of the Red Army, Koranic law and not Kremlin dictate began to prevail. A number of Soviet Muslims were caught leaving caches of weapons and ammunition for the *Mujahideen*. And others, like Garek, chose to defect. By the second year of the war, Soviet military strategists had realized their mistake, and they began sending European Russians.

Like other Soviet Muslims before him, when Garek decided to defect, he had already made contact with the *Mujahideen* and had been smuggling arms to them. Betrayed by an informer, he was jailed and tortured. "This is what they did to me," he said, the anger back in his voice. Pushing back his sleeves, he thrust both arms out at me. "Look! This is what they did." Both arms were deeply scarred by a series of slash marks that stretched from wrist to elbow in the same way a sausage is scored. "I was sent by force to Afghanistan. And when I decided I didn't want to slaughter people, this is what they did. They used razors."

It was while he was in prison that he met Nikolai Balabanov, who had been incarcerated for the same crime. Both men were under death sentences. "We knew we had to escape before they could ship us back home," said Garek. "After all, if we tried and failed, we didn't have much to lose."

Pretending they were suffering from diarrhea one night, they attacked a guard in the poorly monitored latrines, stole his Kalashnikov, and escaped. "We were stealing a jeep when a captain tried to stop us. We fired at him—I think we killed him—then we drove off. We hadn't gone far when we ran into some *Mujahideen* who yelled at us to stop. They encircled the jeep. As I began to get out, I realized one of them was holding a hand grenade. He looked like he was going to throw it. I was convinced I was going to die. So I started praying very loudly. When they heard I was praying to Allah, they put down their guns." For the first year and a half of their imprisonment, both men were kept by the *Mujahideen* in Kunduz Province. Then they were transferred to Pakistan. After the Jamiat explosion they had been taken back to Afghanistan and were now constantly moved. Garek, although underweight and listless except when his anger overtook him, seemed to cope with imprisonment better than Nikolai. In fact, the first time I saw Nikolai, I was shocked by his appearance. A man of about five feet, ten inches, he told me he had weighed approximately eighty kilograms, about 176 pounds, at the time of his defection. Now, he looked like a walking cadaver. His clothes hung in loose folds on him, jutting out sharply where they hit his protruding collarbones and shoulder blades. The tops of his arms were substantially thinner than mine; he looked as if he weighed no more than 110 pounds, and he frequently trembled. Nikolai's cheeks and eyes were sunken, and his skin had an unhealthy waxen appearance. And with his dirty blond hair cut in a medieval pageboy style, his coarse features, and a mouth full of rotten teeth, he resembled a figure, albeit an emaciated one, from a Brueghel painting.

When I had first seen both men, but particularly Nikolai, I

had asked one of the commanders why they were so thin. "There is food for their stomachs," he told me. "But when a man doesn't know his future—and a prisoner of war doesn't—when he has no hope and low morale, then there is no food for the spirit. And this is why he gets thin." And indeed, twenty-three-year-old Nikolai did seem to fit that description. From Alma Ata in Kazakhstan, about 150 miles from the Chinese border, he'd been an electrician before being conscripted into the Logistics Unit of the 45th Division. His father had died when he was a child, and he'd lived with his mother, a factory worker, and his younger sister. He began to shake and his eyes filled with tears as he talked about them. "My mother didn't know I was in Afghanistan; she thought I was serving in Russia. The last time I heard from her was five years ago." The tears rolled down his cheeks as he said, "I have to forget about them; I can't think about them. I know I will never see them again. I can't go back; I would be killed."

"Do you regret defecting?"

"I couldn't stand what we were doing. I saw villages destroyed with heavy bombardment: everyone and everything was destroyed. I couldn't stand it. I remember our commander said to us, 'We will occupy Afghanistan and make it Communist. And we will also do the same to Pakistan; just wait a while.' And when we caught Afghans, I saw an officer cut off a man's nose, cut off his fingers. Somebody asked him what he was doing and he replied, 'I'm playing.' When I defected, I thought the freedom fighters would let me join them; I thought they would let me fight. Now all I do is sleep all day and think all night. Sometimes I think I will become an old man here. Other times I think I'll be dead in three years or mentally deranged. I've thought of suicide. The nights are worst; they're the loneliest."

"Have you ever thought of escape?"

"Escape! Escape to where? When I was in Pakistan, where would I have gone? If I escape in Afghanistan, I'll only get caught again by other *Mujahideen*. There is no escape for us."

Yet six months later, Nikolai would attempt to escape after a report circulated that ten POWs had been killed when the *Mujahideen* holding them came under an attack. Rather than be hampered with the prisoners as they retreated, the commander apparently shot them. Panicked that a similar fate could be his,

Nikolai managed to escape. He got as far as Peshawar before being picked up and sent back to Afghanistan, where he is more closely watched than he was before.

Other defectors have been more trusted by the *Mujahideen*. One East German, a twenty-five-year-old who had been studying in Kabul, fled the city and managed to make contact with a group of NIFA freedom fighters. Born in East Berlin, he now fights with the *Mujahideen*, speaks passable Pushto and Dari, and uses the name Ahmed Jan. But he hasn't forgotten his mother tongue, as West German television viewers saw last year when he was filmed taking part in a Resistance operation. Ahmed Jan declined to give his real name to protect his family, who still live in East Germany.

A more unusual defection to the Resistance was that of an East German female. Twenty-four-year-old Kerstin Beck was a linguistics student at the Faculty of Language and Literature at Kabul University when she escaped from the city in March 1984. From Muecheberg, East Germany, she was the daughter of a driver in the Ministry of Foreign Affairs. She had been a student of Asian Sciences specializing in Afghanistan at Berlin University. In September 1983, she was one of seven students to be sent to Kabul for advanced Pushto and Dari studies. In an interview with Afghan journalist Faizl Akbar, who was director of Kabul Radio until the invasion and now runs the Afghan Information and Documentation Center in Peshawar, she said, "We were taught that the people of Afghanistan were Communist and that they themselves had established a Communist regime. But it was quickly apparent to us that the Kabul regime was not in control of the country. And it was also obvious the Soviets weren't. We could hear shooting nearly every night in the city, and two months after I arrived, the first secretary of the Soviet Embassy was shot dead in daylight in front of a shop. The staff at the East German embassy told us about it when they informed us that we were not free to move around the city any longer, that it wasn't safe. We were limited to the university, to Microrayon, and to the areas of Wazir Akbar Khan where we lived and to Shahrenaw. The rest of the city and the bus service were off-limits to us."

Beck began to think about making contact with the *Mujahideen*. "I knew the borders between Afghanistan and Pakistan were porous. I thought I might be able to reach Pakistan and, once there, apply for asylum to West Germany. Afghan students at the university helped me get in touch with the Resistance."

Beck spent several days traveling from Kabul to the Pakistani border with the Harakat *Mujahideen* party. "I witnessed burned and bombed houses, and lifeless villages along the entire route," she said. "All the residents had either fled to Pakistan or been killed. I passed through villages that had been bombed just the day before I reached them. Cultivated fields were abandoned. During that journey, I saw a destroyed Afghanistan. This was the same country the Soviets and the Karmal regime called a flourishing and progressive Afghanistan." Beck was admitted to West Germany shortly after arriving in Pakistan.

In addition to Eastern European defectors, the Soviet satellite countries have apparently supplied troops to Afghanistan. The most frequently reported are Bulgarians, Czechs, and East Germans. There have also been occasional accounts of commandoes from Cuba, South Yemen, and North Vietnam. During the International Human Rights in Afghanistan hearings in Oslo in 1983, testimony given stated that a helicopter shot down in Faryab Province was found to have a Bulgarian crew, and that for some time a Vietnamese unit was based at Kabul Airport. Chief of Staff Wardak also said that Vietnamese troops, easily identified by their appearance, had been seen in Kunar Province. "Soviets use foreign forces to create the impression that what they are doing is an international endeavor," explained Shevchenko. "This is why Hungarian and East German troops were used, for example, in the invasion of Czechoslovakia. In this manner, the Soviet Union is able to demonstrate that what they are engaged in is supported by all Communist communities throughout the world."

In an effort to encourage troop defections, the U.S. Senate Task Force on Afghanistan at the end of 1985 suggested setting up an underground railroad to Pakistan to help Soviet troops to desert. Congressman Don Ritter, Pennsylvania Republican, proposed that Voice of America broadcasts could convey the existence of such a railroad to Soviet troops stationed in Afghanistan. That the Voice of America is unlikely to be heard by many Soviet troops in Afghanistan, because it is jammed regularly, did not dampen enthusiasm for the proposal. Even when it isn't jammed, few soldiers have sufficient privacy to risk tuning in. The underground railroad seemed a rather clumsy method to drain the Soviet army. The proposal was also rather ironic, considering that at the time, thirty-three Afghans who had fled their country's regime and traveled to the United States to apply for political asylum were languishing in the U.S. Immigration and Naturalization Service's detention center in New York.

Such a program would not help the POWs like Garek and Nikolai. During their early imprisonment when they were still in Pakistan, both men expressed desire for political asylum in the United States. But their requests, conveyed to the States on several occasions, never received action. Now, their existence is purgatorial.

When I left their temporary prison base to return to Peshawar, I went to say good-bye to them. Garek, sullen as usual, continued to stare at the ceiling and didn't even look up as I spoke to him. Nikolai painfully rose from his *charpoy* and shuffled outside with me. Although he had never actually been confined behind bars, he had an institutional stoop and gait. Despite the emotional emptiness both the Russians felt, Nikolai still had a gentleness, a sensitivity to him. I had noticed it the day before when a very young stray kitten wandered into the camp. The Russian spent an hour cajoling it to come close enough so that he could pick it up and stroke it. Watching him then, it was apparent that he needed the contact a lot more than the cat. Now as we said good-bye, he noticed a sunflower behind where we were standing. One of the few flowers in that dry and dusty region, its stem had been damaged and the large yellow bloom hung down from its own weight. Nikolai squatted in the dust and tried repeatedly to straighten it, his need for something beautiful in his life pathetically obvious.

9

Hunted

Do it again. Okay, not bad. Try it again." I was sitting on the floor of my room in Peshawar with Tor demonstrating how to load and strip a machine gun. Wakil was poised above us, watching me struggle with the gun parts and trying to wrestle them into submission. "One more time," said Wakil. "I think you're getting the hang of it."

"Are you sure this is something I really need to know?" I asked him. "I'm here to report on this war, not fight in it."

"Tomorrow's trip is the most dangerous so far. We're going as far as Bamiyan; that's the center of the country. A lot of the journey will be flat. If something goes wrong, there's nowhere to retreat to. It would be useful if you knew how to use a Kalashnikov."

"But I've never used a gun in my life. I'm not sure I could bring myself to use it, even if I had to."

"That is for you to decide. But we're going to be traveling in Soviet-held territory. And in Ghazni Province where we'll spend the most time, there are a lot of helicopter gunships. Recently we lost thirty *Mujahideen*, when several helicopters just descended and killed them. One month ago, two vehicles were stopped, the passengers were taken on board, and then they were thrown out of the flying helicopters. You might be glad you know how to use a gun."

I said nothing. It seemed ridiculous to tell a freedom fighter that I loathed guns, and that at home I was even opposed to hunting.

We were leaving the next day, September 26, for a trip to five provinces, Paktika, Ghazni, Bamiyan, Wardak, and Zabul. Wakil would be heading up an intelligence-gathering team. We would be gone about five weeks. Once again, I had touched down just long enough in Peshawar to scrub off the grime.

Kalashnikov lesson over, Wakil opened a paper sack and tossed a faded gold *chadori* at me. "You'll wear that tomorrow," he said. "It's a ten-hour drive to the border this time, and there are too many checkpoints to risk driving you through with your face showing." The *chadori*, which exposed only my feet, was dirty and patched. "That is good; you are meant to look like the peasant wife of our vehicle's driver. If it was too new, the Pakistanis might be suspicious." I spent the rest of the evening painting my feet and ankles with the dye I'd used to turn my hair black. Even though so little of me showed under the *chadori*, my skin is so pale that if I had been ordered out of the jeep and an observant Pakistani militiaman had noticed my feet, he would have been instantly suspicious. "She looks like a dirty nomad," pronounced Hamid when he saw me. My boots and male clothing had been stashed out of sight under one of the seats.

The *chadori* was stifling hot, and the band of the head section soon began to give me a headache. It was annoying, too, to have one's vision restricted to a narrow field straight ahead. There were two benefits to wearing it, however: it kept out a lot of the dust, and dressed as a woman, I sat up front in the small Japanese jeep in comfort, instead of being crammed in the back. But it did mean that I had to keep remembering to avert my face, even though it was completely covered, every time we went through a checkpost or village. This kind of modesty is difficult for an eternally curious Western journalist. "I may look, and possibly smell the part," I said from the recesses of the smelly *chadori*, "but what if someone talks to me?" "Don't worry; they wouldn't dare to speak to a woman wearing a *chadori*; it just isn't done," said Wakil. "They will always address 'your husband,' and if necessary, your husband will tell you what to do."

We drove four hundred kilometers south of Peshawar. Shortly before the NIFA border office, we were stopped and had to get out of the vehicle while it was checked. I stood off to one side, with my back to the men as I had seen the women do, while the men did the talking. A few minutes later, Wakil barked something curtly at me in Dari, which I didn't realize was addressed to me because I didn't understand it. Still role-playing, Hamid came over and prodded me angrily back to the jeep. "Sorry," he said once we were inside, "but I had to pretend you were a little bit stupid."

At the NIFA office in a small village, we were met by Saied Mohammed Amman, a former science professor at Kabul University, whose wife had been killed in Ghazni, where we were heading, nine months before. He ushered us inside a small courtyard. Because of my *chadori*, I was quickly led into the women's quarters completely out of sight of the men, where I would stay in *purdah* until we left the following day. It amused me to think that when I arrived anywhere wearing men's attire and a turban, even though my gender was known, no one objected to my sleeping with twenty or so men. Now, because I was dressed as a woman, I would be treated as one. But *purdah* was a lonely experience, although I was surrounded by a constant crowd. None of the women spoke English, and my limited Dari was soon exhausted. I spent the rest of the evening smiling till my jaw ached while they smiled back at me. Finally, I started tearing up my notebook to make origami animals, paper airplanes, and strips of dolls for the children by the light of a small oil lamp until my imagination ran out. Then someone produced a transistor radio. The only English-speaking program turned out to be Radio Tashkent, which was promoting tourism and ended by wishing all their young listeners "the opportunity to travel." For most young male listeners in Tashkent, of course, their opportunity to travel would probably be limited to Afghanistan once they were conscripted.

Eventually, I was shown into a small room with a *charpoy* in front of a window without glass, which permitted access to the many bats. The bats, creatures I detest, swooped and dived over my head like swallows until I became too tired to keep an eye on them and fell asleep. It seemed only a few hours later that I was wakened; it was still dark. The women embraced me and then prayed over me; they found it strange that I was willingly returning to what they had fled from. Wearing the *chadori*, I rejoined the men. This time the jeep was joined by a pickup filled with *Mujahideen*; it also contained three large cartons of medications for Tor, who would function as a doctor on this trip. I noticed, too, that there were enormous jerricans of fuel lashed onto the backs of both vehicles. There were no gas stations where we were going, and this was not a journey on which to have an empty tank. I was introduced to a quiet young man, Said Amin Jhan, who came from Ghazni and would be our mechanic. "If a vehicle breaks down where we're going, it could cost us our lives," said Wakil. "I hope you're a good mechanic, Amin Jhan," I said.

Thirty minutes after leaving the NIFA base, we passed through the border, the first vehicle through it that day. On the Afghan side, a long camel train of refugees was patiently waiting for the chain gate to be opened. They had lost quite a few of their number two days before when they were strafed by jet fighters for what they believed was a reprisal attack after a *Mujahideen* assault on a base. Almost immediately the road became a barely discernible trail, which vanished altogether more often than it was visible. The sun was just beginning to come up, promising another hot day, when Wakil stopped the jeep and told me to change into my *Mujahideen* clothes. With no convenient boulder to duck behind and an audience of twenty freedom fighters, I discovered another use for the *chadori*: it made an ideal changing tent.

The countryside ahead of us was a vast rock plain that met a brilliant blue sky as large as any in Kansas. The vista was interrupted only occasionally by wide buttes and cliffs that brought to mind Victorian prints of the Australian outback. It was a somber and lonely scene, and we were the only things moving in it. There was no sign of habitation. Southern Paktika could not have been more antithetical to the lushness of its northern neighbor Paktia.

When we resumed our journey, Wakil was driving the jeep, something he would do for the duration of the trip, no matter how long the days. As we careened over the jolting surface, which looked as if it had been thrown up by an earthquake or attacked by a giant pneumatic drill, he battled with the vehicle as violently as any skipper of a boat would during a heavy storm. Now that I was dressed as a man again, I was delegated to a seat in the rear so that Nazar Jhan, commander of Ghazni Province and our guide, could sit up front. But no matter where one was sitting, riding in the jeep was a miserable experience. My knuckles were quickly rubbed raw from my hands being wedged between the canvas roof and supporting strut in an effort to stay upright and prevent myself from being thrown from side to side. Even though we tried to brace ourselves, some part of our anatomy was always crashing into a metal edge of the jeep or a weapon. And from the time we started until we stopped, we churned up so much dust that it was like traveling in our own private dust storm. Despite covering our faces as tightly as possible with our turban ends, bandit-style, so as to expose the minimum amount of flesh without asphyxiating, we still breathed, ate, and sweated dust for hours on end. Within a couple of hours we all looked as if we had been liberally dusted in chalk. I soon learned to ride with my eyes closed most of the time, to protect my contact lenses. The overpowering stench of gasoline from the jerrican lashed to the rear of the jeep, which couldn't be properly closed, added to our discomfort. Yet Wakil insisted it was less tiring to drive than be driven. Later he would admit that in countryside where we were visible for miles and therefore vulnerable he wanted to be "in charge."

Most of the morning passed the same way. Then someone spotted black smoke in the distance, and we all tensed. But it turned out to be a large tractor-trailer that was belching fumes. As it crossed the empty horizon, it brought life to our isolation in the same way distant Bedouins do in the desert. Shortly afterward, we spotted several pickups moving toward us. One of the men in our lead pickup tracked the small convoy's movement with binoculars. *"Mujahideen,"* he soon yelled. We stopped and waited for them. As always when Afghans meet one another when traveling, each party greeted the other enthusiastically. The commander of the arriving group could barely stand. Ashen-faced, he was helped from his vehicle and eased down to a nearby flat rock. It was obvious from the speed with which Wakil leaped from the jeep that he recognized him and was concerned. The man was

Salman Gailani, the nephew of NIFA's leader and commander of Paktika Province. The natural assumption was that Gailani had been injured in the assault he had just led on a large Soviet base. But the thirty-five-year-old commander was suffering from a severe attack of malaria, a disease that felled, and even killed, many *Mujahideen*. Malaria, which had been virtually eradicated in Afghanistan before the war, was now a major health problem in the country, affecting an estimated 40 percent of the population. Omar had almost not joined us on this trip because he was also recovering from a recurrent bout of malaria.

As Gailani briefed Wakil on conditions farther ahead, we learned that it had been the commander's operation that had led to the reprisal attack on the refugee train we'd passed at the border. In the same attack, six helicopters had bombed two trucks transporting goods to Pakistan. Once we left Gailani's unit, there was one depressing but telling change in the scenery—graves. Numerous graves, some with flags denoting martyred *Mujahideen*, lined the route.

At 1:00 P.M. we took a break to stretch our legs, rub off the dust, and ignore our rumbling stomachs. It might have been lunchtime, but, typically, we weren't carrying food. Parked at the foot of a butte, which afforded a few feet of shade, most men checked their guns and refilled Kalashnikov magazines. Wakil decided it was time for me to learn how to fire the machine gun I'd stripped and reassembled the night before. Sitting down Afghan-style, I reluctantly raised the Chinese-made machine gun to my shoulder, but I delayed firing it. "She's afraid of it," laughed Aga Mohammed, a former brigadier in the Afghan army, who still wore his uniform jacket. He was right; I was afraid of the recoil. Having stood next to numerous Kalashnikovs when they were fired, I had felt the ground beneath me vibrate. I wasn't sure I wanted to fire a gun that powerful even though the AK-47 was switched to single-shot from automatic. I closed my eyes and strained to squeeze the trigger. There was minimal kickback. From the laughter, I realized my shot had gone far wide from the rock I'd been told to aim at approximately 250 meters away. "Not surprising: you had your eyes closed," said Wakil. He showed me how to sight the gun. I fired again. Much to my surprise, the rock I was aiming at shattered. Four more rounds were all on target. "Hey, I'm good at this," I said gleefully. "Yes, now you know how to kill," said Hamid quietly behind me, bringing me back with a start to the purpose of what we were doing. I quietly handed the gun back to Wakil.

Near the end of the afternoon we reached a small adobe village, the first settlement of any kind we'd seen all day. We stopped outside an open-sided *chaikhana*, teahouse. The place was decorated with posters of Massoud. The Panjshir leader's face had been superimposed on Sylvester Stallone's Rambo body. Massoud, who is wiry, had suddenly sprouted bulging biceps and was clutching an M-16 instead of an AK-47. The *chaikhana* was bare except for the posters, unless one counted the hordes of flies, which I did out of curiosity when the men went to pray. They averaged four per square inch, a head count that made me glad we had ordered scrambled eggs to eat and nothing that had been sitting around uncovered for hours. When the *Mujahideen* returned, I learned that the village was actually a Resistance stronghold. The place had a feel of the O.K. Corral except that all the cowboys strolling down the main street were holding hands. While we ate, Wakil said we would be traveling until about 3:00 A.M., twenty-four hours from the time we'd started out.

We continued in the dark, driving without lights and losing the track frequently. We stopped once to pray and to defuse the rear brake lights so their red glow wouldn't pinpoint our presence. Shortly after midnight, we saw the lights of Khierkot Garrison, which Salman Gailani had just attacked and which housed three thousand troops. Half an hour later, a freedom fighter on a motorbike traveling in the opposite direction from us told us we were on the road that led directly to the garrison. Was that our intention? It wasn't, of course, but without lights, maps, and proper roads, it wasn't surprising. We made U-turns. He offered to lead us to the *Mujahideen* base we were looking for and explained that tanks often patrolled this area at night. But the only activity we saw were occasional flares sent up by the fort. While the flares hovered in the sky, they shed enough illumination for Wakil to be able to avoid crashing into the largest rocks, but our speed never exceeded ten miles per hour. Finally, about four kilometers from the garrison, we pulled into a ghost town of a village. It had been abandoned after heavy bombing three years before. Now the *Mujahideen* used it as a camp. We parked the vehicles in animal stalls and picked our way through the dark, narrow lanes. The deserted, gutted village was eerie. The moving shadows atop several walls were patrolling freedom fighters.

We were led to the top floor of a large two-story house, one of the few buildings left intact. As we stepped into the darkened room, we stumbled over the bodies of sleeping *Mujahideen*. They made room for us on the mattresses spread over the floor, and someone fumbled for the oil lamp. Before it was lighted, I was sprawled in a corner, trying to open my sleeping bag. Wakil didn't even seem tired, his stamina prodigious. "That's nothing," said Hamid. "I was with him about a year ago when he drove over such terrain for two days and two nights with only two thirty-minute breaks." As we waited for someone to bring tea, we learned that two days before, four helicopters had encircled two local shepherds in nearby fields. While two choppers continued to circle, the other two gunships landed and their crew robbed the shepherds of their cheap watches and what little money they had and then took off. Muggings by helicopter were a common occurrence in this region, and we would hear about such incidents almost daily.

After a couple of hours' sleep, we were roused again. Wakil told me planes had been flying overhead for the last hour and he felt they might be gearing up for something. I'd slept so heavily I hadn't been aware of them. There was also nothing separating us from the garrison but rock plain, easy for tanks to cross. "Here if the tanks come out, you fight until you are dead; there is nowhere else to go," said Wakil. Because of the village's unprotected position, we were going to pull back to the *Mujahideen* headquarters in the foothills a few kilometers to our east. Two of the local freedom fighters squeezed into the jeep with us. "The men are in the mood to attack, and they will if they don't recognize you," said one. "Also, the *Mujahideen* have heavily mined the route to our base. Unless you know the safe way, you'll never make it through."

He was right: the slalom course he forced us to follow had no apparent logic to it, and although he insisted there were stone markers visible to the initiated, I was unable to detect any. As our jeep climbed, our guide yelled to invisible sentries, who bellowed back. Finally, the route became too steep to drive, and we stopped several hundred yards inside a deep gorge. The jeep was quickly but thoroughly camouflaged with fallen scrub, and we continued on foot. The canyon made a forty-five-degree turn, and we saw the stone rooftop of several small dwellings built into the mountainside. Perched all over the steep cliff, like so many nesting birds, were about two hundred grinning freedom fighters who were watching our progress up the incline. This base was home to eleven hundred men. They were excited about Wakil's visit; they didn't get many visitors from the Peshawar HQ. The *Mujahideen* had attacked Khierkot again the night before, and many men, including their own commander, hadn't yet returned. Because of this, Wakil decided to move on after the obligatory tea, to Konak, a *Mujahideen* mountain fortress several hours' hike away. Built by Commander Toth Ghazi, whose name inspired respect in this region, the fortress had been carved out of the mountain itself and was an impressive piece of engineering. The series of rooms that were connected by a stone walkway were complete with chimneys and stoves necessary for the harsh winters here. Ghazi was also in the process of excavating a room that would be large enough to house two hundred men. The place resembled a miniature Colditz Castle, where British POWs were held in Germany during World War II. But Ghazi's ingenuity didn't stop there. He had also built a canal to redirect a mountain stream into his base for a ready water supply, and he burned pine chips to produce resin, which fueled the base's lamps. His men had also continued to farm the fields abandoned when the villagers fled. We were offered an excellent meal of barbecued goat, a gustatory treat after the boiled meat that was normally proffered if meat were available.

As we sat in a smoke-blackened room carpeted with thick quilts, Ghazi told us that jets and gunships bombed to within a kilometer of where we sat but never came back this far. "And even if they did, they'd have to flatten the mountains to reach us." From the surrounding peaks, all of which had Dashakas and Zigovaks on top, there was a superb view of Khierkot Garrison below. We could see the tanks as they left the post to patrol.

The fifty-seven-year-old commander, with a ready gapped-tooth grin, was as tough as one of his mountains. In the last six years, he'd been shot sixteen times and still had enough shrapnel left in him to set off a metal detector. On one occasion, he said, he was shot twice and collapsed in a pool of blood. "The forces thought I was dead. They took my gun, shot my horse, then someone stood on me while he bayoneted me. But I didn't move. Then they left. I lived because God wanted me to live." Ghazi's four sons are fighting with him. "The oldest has been shot three times so far," he said proudly, seeing the wounds as badges of honor.

Because of Ghazi's hospitality, we stayed longer than Wakil had planned. He wanted to be under way the moment it became dark, and already the sun was beginning to go down. The return hike to the jeep would have to be made at top speed, something I didn't relish in the mountains. Ghazi made a suggestion I heartily seconded: his youngest son, Tawiz, would take me back to the jeep by motorbike. Tawiz, dressed completely in black, seemed as fierce and as dour as his father was friendly. He looked through me as we were introduced and glowered at the scenery as we said our good-byes to his father and as I climbed on the back of his 250 cc bike. He appeared so hostile that I thought it wiser not to hold on to his waist or shoulders. Tawiz took off with a jolt, and we began down the mountain on a narrow track that appeared to lead directly to the garrison. As we twisted and turned, the sinking sun flashed off the bike's two mirrors, signaling our presence clearly to anyone below. I tapped Tawiz on the shoulder and suggested in sign language that he turn the mirrors inward. He considered my advice for what seemed an inordinate amount of time and begrudgingly did so. That he did not like taking instruction from a woman was obvious.

Just as I thought we were destined to drive straight to Khierkot, he turned overland, and the ride now became a dirt-bike race for one. His hostility notwithstanding, I clutched to his waist as we swerved and skidded over the terrain. Several times he nearly lost control of the bike. After an hour, with the light almost gone, it became obvious Tawiz was lost. I thought we'd come lower than we should be, but Tawiz didn't agree. We continued in the same direction. Finally, we came to a small hamlet. Several men were standing outside talking, and after a long discussion in which they pointed in two different directions, Tawiz took off again, none the wiser. Half an hour later, two large motorbikes headed toward us. They were driven by *Mujahideen* sent out to look for us. We followed them back up the mountain. By the time we returned to the base near the jeep, Tor, Humayoon, and several others had already arrived. Wakil and the rest showed up shortly afterward. This camp's commander, Adem Khan Jalal Khiel, had returned in our absence and insisted we stay to dinner. Wakil wanted to move on, but he also didn't want to offend him. I noticed the little goat I had seen tethered outside a tent that morning had gone. In its place was a bloodstain.

Adem Khan had attacked Khierkot the previous night with missiles. He had just received a report from inside the garrison —most forts had Afghan informers inside them—on the casualties they had inflicted in the last few days. "One Russian, six Karmal artillery officers, and forty Karmal soldiers dead," he intoned to Wakil. "One doctor wounded, and the head administrator wounded. His fifteen-year-old daughter killed." What about the *Mujahideen* casualties? "A few injuries, nothing serious," he said. Once again, the surprise element of a guerrilla attack appeared to give the *Mujahideen* the advantage despite their paucity of numbers and arms.

We left immediately after we'd eaten. The temperature had dropped rapidly, and it was now quite chilly. Three motorbike outriders with RPG-7s accompanied us to guide us through the mined region and check for patrolling tanks. "There are small ones here and they move very fast," we were told. We were heading toward YahYa Khiel, a town of forty thousand close to the Ghazni border. Adem Khan had said that vehicles hadn't moved out of the town on our intended route north because of a report that a large Soviet convoy of three hundred tanks and APCs was in the region. "If that is the case," said Wakil, "we will have to stay in one of our safe houses. We will have to remain secret; you won't be able to go out."

We reached YahYa Khiel two hours later. In the large adobe town, the houses all had high mud walls of fifteen to twenty feet and were built to resemble small fortresses. The market was vast, and many of the stores had goods piled up outside. "Coming here is like going to Kabul; there are plenty of goods. The people have stayed; they haven't become refugees. They have a connection with the government."

"So how safe are we coming here?" "Oh, they're sympathetic to the *Mujahideen*. Many are *Mujahideen* at night." This apparent contradiction was common in Afghanistan. Be loyal to the regime during the day and fight it at night. Yet as we passed groups of men standing outside the houses talking, I wondered what they made of a jeep traveling without lights. And I wondered which of them we could trust, and which we couldn't. We zigzagged for nearly an hour through the narrow streets of the town. Adem Khan told us the original house he'd planned for us to stay in was too dangerous. He was taking us to the outskirts of YahYa Khiel. "Somewhere where you can leave in a hurry if necessary," he said. The house we stopped at suggested a wealthy owner. Entering through enormous metal gates set in a thick adobe wall more than two stories high, we found ourselves in a large courtyard. The house, built in an L shape, extended the length of two of the four walls. From the porch roof, tobacco leaves hung to dry. Animal stalls for cows, goats, and donkeys filled a third wall. In the center of the courtyard were vegetable gardens and fruit trees. A tractor sat next to the well. We parked alongside it. This was the home of Deputy Commander Azib Khan.

We were shown into a large baronial-type hall that was just inside the gates. The hall was the most luxurious room I'd seen in an Afghan house so far. Fifteen feet high, it had a carved wooden ceiling, and the floor was covered with an enormous red and black carpet. In the corners stood brass spittoons and ornate chillum water pipes. The windows were built just under the ceiling, giving the hall a churchlike feeling. They were built that high so that visiting men would not be able to see the womenfolk working in the courtyard. Deputy Commander Khan, a tall, turbaned man of thirty-eight with a mustache but no beard, was a traditionalist, who would tell me he had two children and three daughters. And he insisted I sleep in the women's quarters, even though it meant waking them to do so. He was a pompous man, and I found him hard to like.

After a segregated breakfast, I incurred Khan's displeasure by rejoining the men. I was just in time to learn that the convoy we had heard about had been on its way back from Kabul when it was ambushed twenty-five kilometers from where we were. Local intelligence said the convoy was fearful of another attack and was waiting for reinforcements. Since the attack, no vehicles had entered or left YahYa Khiel; the townsfolk were too afraid to move. "Unlikely to be a force of three hundred tanks or APCs then," I said to Wakil. "Anything that size wouldn't be afraid of an ambush." Wakil agreed.

All morning freedom fighters arrived to greet Wakil, the

bush telegraph having already broadcast his presence. One of them brought a report that paratroopers had landed nearby. That account was one Wakil believed to be accurate. Another of the visitors, thirty-year-old Shahwali, had heard we had a doctor with us. Newly married, he told us his twenty-year-old wife was sick. She'd had a lot of pain for three days, he said, and YahYa Khiel, like most of Afghanistan today, was without a doctor or hospital. "You'll have to go with Tor to examine her," Wakil told me. "The husband won't let Tor examine his wife; you'll have to do it." I said I'd be happy to try, but I felt about as qualified to do that as I did to use a Kalashnikov. As it was daytime, I was told to pull my turban low over my eyes and cover my nose and mouth with the end of it. Someone wrapped me in a large *patou*, which covered me almost as effectively as a *chadori*. It was then Tor discovered that one of his three cartons of medication, the one containing all his antibiotics and most of his surgical instruments, was missing. Apparently, it had been left behind at the first village in which we stayed. Wakil was angry and berated Tor for his lack of responsibility. Not knowing what might be wrong with our patient, I went to fetch my own supply of antibiotics. I'd purposely brought 500-milligram Keflex, a powerful full-spectrum antibiotic that I'd hoped would knock out most bugs, but I hadn't expected to be practicing medicine. Tor and I were driven to Shahwali's house, a twenty-minute motorbike ride away.

I was shown into a small room where a young woman and her mother were sitting on the floor. Tor remained outside. Both women were covered completely in veils. The slimmer of the two was Shahwali's wife. But she wouldn't let me near her because she assumed I was a man. After explaining, I told Tor I needed him to be in the room to translate; otherwise I couldn't communicate with her. We played out a farce of Tor, the medic, sitting in the back of the room, while I, the layman, asked the patient questions and examined her. The latter wasn't easy. She refused to look at me and kept her face completely covered because of Tor's presence. From her symptoms it sounded to me as if she had a severe attack of cystitis, uncomfortable but not serious. Keflex, I knew, worked on bladder infections. I also suggested she stop drinking tea for a week, but drink plenty of water. Feeling more like a "barefoot doctor" every minute, I told her she'd also feel more comfortable if she could take a warm bath. Her husband and mother couldn't have been more grateful. They gave both of us presents of silk scarves and a bottle of shampoo.

Westerners traveling with the Resistance are invariably assumed to be doctors. After word got out about that visit, it was difficult to persuade people otherwise. By the time we returned to the deputy commander's house, there was a line of patients waiting. As I walked into the courtyard, a woman thrust her dehydrated infant at me. Dehydration caused by diarrhea from gastrointestinal infections is a major killer of children under five in Afghanistan. I knew Tor still had the rehydration salts in his medical supplies. I told the mother I wasn't a doctor and pointed to Tor. The look she gave me suggested as clearly as if she'd said it, what earthly use was I? But others refused to be convinced. A woman of about twenty-six asked to see me in the women's quarters. I kept insisting I wasn't a doctor, but she wouldn't take no for an answer. Once inside the house, she showed me a large protruding mass about two inches above her navel. I had no idea what it was. It could have been a hernia or cancerous tumor for all I knew. She told me it only hurt after she'd been working all day. I shrugged and repeated "Ni doctor. Ni doctor" in pidgin Dari. Then she pointed to her mouth and opened it to grin. The condition of her teeth would have horrified any Western doctor. Her gums were a bleeding mess, many of her teeth were missing, and although she was still very young, her gums had severely receded. I could only guess at advanced pyorrhea or possibly massive vitamin C deficiency. I went in search of Tor to tell him what I'd seen.

From my description of her symptoms, Tor said it sounded like a tumor and that she needed to be hospitalized for tests, which meant going to Peshawar. The only hospitals operating in Afghanistan now are in Soviet-controlled cities, and not places where *Mujahideen* families would risk going. "Her chances are not good; it is unlikely anyone will take her there," he said. "For her mouth, all I can do is give her vitamin C tablets."

The days at YahYa Khiel passed similarly with Tor's treating the men, and my practicing medicine without a license on the women. Although tumors were beyond my diagnostic skills, I realized that my Western knowledge of medicine and first aid enabled me to treat a vast assortment of minor maladies. The house also was constantly full of *Mujahideen* reporting to Wakil. The size of the stationary convoy had gradually been downgraded to an accurate ninety tanks and APCs. Finally, we received the report we were waiting for: the convoy was pulling back. "Good, we leave tonight," said Wakil. "Are we sure the report is correct?" I asked. "The longer we stay here, the less safe it becomes," he replied. "Too many people already know there is a delegation from NIFA here."

That evening, Khan served a whole boiled goat. The head was served intact, with eyes, skin, and brains. Considered a delicacy, it was offered to me. I gagged. "Wakil, tell them anything you like, tell them I'm sick, but make an excuse for me—I can't even look at it."

"Just try it; it's good," said Wakil, digging in with relish. "The eyes are particularly good, very sweet," he added, offering me one. "Just don't eat the black part." I groaned and declined. There was a repeat performance when he reached the brains. By now Tor and Hamid were enjoying my discomfort and began to eat my portion of the head with exaggerated enjoyment. I fixed my eyes near the ceiling so I wouldn't have to look at the food.

After dinner, we listened to Babrak Karmal on Radio Kabul. His speech was a precedent for the president. For the first time he admitted that all was not well within his regime, by calling for unity between the two Communist factions, his own, the Parchemis, and the Khalquis, the opposition. He also told administrators to cut down on corruption in their offices and to get outside Kabul and not just concentrate their efforts in the city. The *Mujahideen* jeered when Karmal finished. "The Communists have the mud walls of the capital; we have the rest of the country," said one. By ten o'clock, Wakil had changed his mind about leaving. "The truck we're waiting for hasn't arrived," he said. I crawled into my sleeping bag. What seemed like a few minutes later, I heard Wakil say, "Jan, come quickly; we're leaving." I inwardly cursed. Someone who needed eight hours of sleep a night to function properly, in Afghanistan I was lucky if I averaged three or four, and that night I hadn't had thirty minutes. I hurriedly packed, went out into the frigid night air, and stood shivering as the *Mujahideen* opened an extra ammunition box and divided it among themselves. Wakil and Commander Nazar Jhan got into the front of the jeep. Hamid, Humayoon, Amin Jhan, and

I climbed into the back. Tor chose to ride in the captured Soviet truck with fifteen local *Mujahideen* armed with RPG-7 grenade launchers and Kalashnikovs.

As we drove out of YahYa Khiel, Wakil was deep in conversation with the commander. I asked Hamid whether he knew where we were heading. He didn't, which wasn't unusual. On trips like this, invariably only the senior officers knew exact destinations for security reasons. The ordinary freedom fighters followed their commanders without question, totally unperturbed about their lack of information. But it drove me crazy. Just as I liked to know how long I would be hiking so I could pace myself, in a war zone, I also liked to know a little about where I was heading. "What difference does it make?" Hamid asked me. "If you're told it's dangerous, it may be safe by the time you arrive. If you're told it's safe, you could die."

We drove without lights, but they weren't necessary. The full autumn moon was bright enough to cast shadows as sharp as those at midday. The scenery was bathed in brilliant silver light that made the ground look snow-covered. The Afghan sky was alight with stars. But I was in no mood to appreciate the scenery. I was cold and tired and for several days now had not been feeling well. On trips like this one, bouts of diarrhea were to be expected, but the one I was suffering from now was not responding, as earlier attacks had, to the powerful medication manufactured in Pakistan. And even when I wasn't being offered goat heads, the sight and smell of food were making me feel nauseous. I assumed I had picked up some kind of bug from the water we'd been drinking in Jalalabad.

In addition to wishing I were in bed, I couldn't help feeling we were moving too early. I wished we'd waited another day to confirm the report of the convoy's movement. And the bright moonlight made me uneasy. Although our jeep was khaki and blended in with the scenery during the day, the large moving shadow it cast that night must have screamed "Bomb Here" if seen from the air, particularly since the Soviets had recently announced that traffic in the region was no longer permitted to move at night, that they would "shoot to kill" at any vehicle that did so. I asked Wakil whether the new ruling or the full moon bothered him. "You crazy bum," he responded. His colloquialism made me chuckle despite his tone. "If they tell us to surrender, do you think we will?" His only comment on the moon was a curt "This is a war, not a picnic."

About thirty minutes into the drive we spotted headlights moving toward us. At the same time a small spotter plane, flying at about four thousand feet, paralleled our route but some distance from us. Both our vehicles braked to a halt. A hurried conference took place, and the men in the truck climbed down and fanned out, RPG-7s at the ready. They were worried that the lights belonged to a tank. "The truck will go ahead," said Wakil. "If they stop it, they will find it empty except for the driver. If they fire, well, we'll know we've got problems." As we talked, I could see the *Mujahideen* slowly advancing on foot toward the lights. The jeep didn't move. As the oncoming vehicle neared us, we could see that it was a truck. Our men yelled at it to stop. It turned out to be transporting goods. "Sons of bitches," muttered Wakil, "driving with their lights on. It's a good way to get killed."

We continued on. Whether from nervousness or too much tea, I became aware that my bladder was uncomfortably full. But the area we were in was so exposed that I didn't think it was a good idea to ask Wakil to stop. As if he were reading my thoughts, Wakil told us that in this region recently a local commander with an ammunition truck and a small convoy of seventy men had been ambushed at night by a helicopter gunship that had landed and lay in wait with its lights off. It opened fire so quickly that thirteen men died and eleven were injured before they knew what had hit them.

"Over there, look," Amin Jhan's voice broke in urgently before Wakil could finish what he was saying, "Helicopter!"

"Where?"

"Over there," he said, pointing through the right window of the jeep. The blinking navigation lights of the chopper could be seen clearly as it flew a similar route to that of the earlier spotter plane. We were driving west; the helicopter seemed to be traveling northwest to southeast. From its snub-nosed silhouette, we could see it was a gunship. We kept driving. "It doesn't seem to be moving," Hamid said. We craned to keep it in sight, something that was difficult to do from the back of the jeep, where the Plexiglas windows were opaque from dust. Wakil drove half-hanging out his open door so he could get a better view. "Oh, shit," he said in English. "It's changed direction. It's following us." Slamming the door, he floored the jeep. The truck did the same thing. But Wakil swerved around it and raced ahead. My head smashed against a metal crossbar, and I clutched for handholds. Behind us, I watched the truck slam on its brakes; the men poured out and began to run. As they did, Humayoon and Amin Jhan grabbed their weapons and dropped out of the back of our jeep. The helicopter stayed right on our tail. It was approximately two thousand feet up, and the same distance behind us. We bucketed over the track, doing about eighty miles per hour. Any faster on a surface like the one we were on, and Wakil would have lost control of the vehicle. I braced myself for the helicopter to fire, but it stayed in exactly the same position behind us. "We're a military jeep; maybe it thinks we're one of theirs," I said to no one in particular. "It'll find that out very quickly on the radio," replied Hamid. Wakil swerved into a dried-up riverbed. As the jeep lurched, my jaw smashed into the metal bar across the back of his seat. My head rang, I tasted blood in my mouth, and I expected to come up spitting teeth. I realized I'd cracked a tooth, but my tongue reassured me everything else was intact. "If we can get to those mountains. . ." said Wakil. But we all knew we didn't stand a chance in hell of reaching the distant peaks. The jeep was skidding all over the place. The motion of the helicopter right behind us seemed effortless. I wondered how well they could see us, how effective their damn nightscopes were. My teeth hurt, but I found myself clenching them, and every muscle ached as I hung on for dear life. The effort helped numb my fear.

"There's a village up ahead," said Wakil. "If we can get there . . ."

"I can't tell, is it my imagination, or is the gunship closing in on us?" I yelled over the roar of the engine.

"It might be planning to land ahead of us to stop us reaching the village."

Wakil searched for an incline up from the riverbed toward the village. Twice he had to reverse when the banks were too steep. We were like a tramcar forced to stay on its tracks. As the helicopter came closer, Wakil suddenly crashed the jeep into the highest four-wheel gear, an action meant to be performed when the vehicle is stationary. The gears made a loud grinding noise, but they caught. The jeep shot up an almost vertical five-foot bank. The twenty-foot walls of the village were only two hundred yards ahead. Wakil careened around the first of the fortresslike houses, twice bouncing off the adobe walls. In the center of the village, he parked under a cluster of trees. "Get out, now; get out," he barked. I fumbled for my pack. "Leave it; leave everything. It will only slow us up. Just get away from the jeep. But stay under the trees." We piled out. The gunship hovered over the edge of the village where we'd entered. Staying in the shadows of the buildings, the three men began to slowly move toward it to get a better view of what it was doing. The HIND-24s are designed to hold thirteen heliborne commandoes but in practice have been known to hold quite a few more. If it were going to land and disgorge its passengers, the freedom fighters wanted to know. "Wakil," I stage whispered, "I'll be there in a minute." Bowels loosened by fear, I needed a pit stop. Ducking behind a house, I told myself, "Well, at least you won't embarrass yourself like another American did recently." Caught in a bombing attack, he'd been so frightened that he'd defecated in his pants. The freedom fighters still chuckled over the incident. As I squatted in the dust, the blinking stars didn't look so different from the helicopter. Then I realized one of the stars had red navigation lights. "Jesus!" I said aloud. Our helicopter was not traveling alone. Clinging to the shadows, I edged around the buildings to catch up with the *Mujahideen*. "There's a second one over there," I said. "That makes three in all then," said Hamid, pointing to another helicopter I hadn't seen that made the third point of a triangle over the village. "Oh shit!"

"I know this village," said Nazar Jhan; "we have *Mujahideen* here." He led us through the souklike lanes. Wakil stopped suddenly. "I think we'd better get the pack and hide it. If they search the village and find a pack belonging to a Westerner, the villagers will suffer." He ducked back to the jeep to get it. Then Nazar Jhan led us to a small house on the southern edge of the village. He pounded on the door. Nothing happened. He continued to knock. I realized the village was uncannily quiet: not even a dog was barking. Only the clatter of the gunships' blades disturbed the night. Wakil stuffed the pack into a pile of straw in an animal stall. I stopped him long enough to grab extra film, and the painkillers, then I bade good-bye to my possessions. Hamid headed up the stairs that ran up one side of the house, leading to a flat roof used for drying corn. Wakil and I followed him. The door downstairs finally opened, and Nazar Jhan disappeared inside.

On the roof, in the shadow of the chimney, the three of us searched the sky for the gunships. They hadn't moved. They were hovering about one thousand feet above the ground and appeared to be stationary in the sky. "Oh Christ, here come two more," I said, pointing to the far side of the village. The village of about one hundred houses was encircled. Watching the two new helicopters join the other three, I felt like an animal being hunted by a pride of lions that knew the location of its prey and was just waiting for it to panic and break cover. I couldn't stop myself from thinking about the radio conversations the gunship crews would be exchanging about us. And I didn't understand why they hadn't yet fired.

I began to torment myself with myriad silent questions. What were they planning to do? Were they going to land and conduct a house-to-house search for us? It was a stupid thing for me to focus on, and I found myself growing colder than the night warranted. My hands were icy. "Now what?" I asked nervously, aware that my question was fatuous but needing to ask it anyway. Neither Hamid or Wakil responded. The first helicopter moved off slightly. "I think it's returning to the truck," I said, watching it head in the direction we'd come. "Pray for the *Mujahideen* then," said Wakil. I found myself doing just that, and I thought of Tor and Omar and the other men I'd become fond of. We waited for gunfire. But there was only silence. The helicopter gained height and began to circle slowly. "What the hell is it doing?" I said, keeping up a nervous barrage of questions. "Parachutes," responded Hamid. "Look, there's something white dropping from the helicopter; I think it's parachutes." My eyes strained to make out what his could see. "Shit! Are you sure?" That could only mean Spetsnaz troops. We had one Kalashnikov, a 303 rifle, and Wakil's Soviet pistol. "No, I'm not sure, but I think so."

"If they landed Spetsnaz near our truck, wouldn't we hear shooting?" I asked. "They prefer to take us alive; they learn more about the *Mujahideen* that way," said Wakil bitterly. "I think they were looking for us. They knew a NIFA delegation was traveling in this area." Suddenly his voice grew less tense. Wakil looked at Hamid and then said calmly, "If they land . . . I told the men before we left, if anything happens, we fight to the death, no excuses, no exceptions. . . . I'm not going to be taken alive. I'll fight the best I can and use my last bullet on myself." For the first time since I'd met him, he looked as young as he was. "I feel the same way," replied Hamid.

"Great, fabulous," I screamed internally, having no idea how I felt about being captured. If there were senior officers on board, I might, as a Western journalist, make it back to Kabul, a war trophy like Nikolai and Garek. If not . . . I thought of the Soviet ambassador's threat after Abouchar's arrest. And I knew I'd rather die with a bullet than be pushed from a flying gunship. I also knew I didn't want be to be the sole prisoner. I said as much.

"I can't make that decision for you," said Wakil, leaving me fully aware of what his own was.

From below, Nazar Jhan called Wakil. All three of us went downstairs. The commander was with a short stocky man. "You can't stay here," he said. "You must leave. The gunships will send for reinforcements, probably tanks, or they will wait until light; then they will search the village. They'll find you if you stay. And they'll slaughter the villagers for hiding you." Why haven't they landed so far, I asked. "Because they are uncertain what they'll find here," explained Wakil. "This village could be a *Mujahideen* stronghold. They normally wait until morning before they attack."

"There's a *Mujahideen* base about four hours from here," said Nazar Jhan. "We can try to make it there."

"How do we do that?" I asked. "Walk," said Wakil.

"Won't we be seen the moment we leave the village?"

"We don't have a choice." Although I was apprehensive about leaving the shadows of the village, any action was better than waiting for the gunships' next move.

"Get her pack; it isn't wise to leave it here," instructed the commander. Hamid dug it out of the straw. The villager put it on his back. He was coming with us as our guide.

The commander explained that we were to leave in two groups, so as to minimize the gunships' chance of spotting us. The villager led the way through the narrow adobe streets to the opposite side from where we'd entered the village. One by one our party ducked out for pit stops; I wasn't the only one whose bowels were affected by tension. Our guide chose a point farthest from two of the helicopters. "We leave from here," he said, pointing across the flattest field I'd seen in Afghanistan. The fields were separated by shallow irrigation ditches no more than a few inches deep. There was nowhere to hide: no bushes, no trees. Behind us, the lights of the helicopters continued to blink. The commander and the guide left first, taking the Kalashnikov with them. They walked briskly across the first field. We were left with the 303 rifle, a gun the British first used just after the Boer War, and Wakil's Russian pistol, which held eight rounds in its magazine. I thought of the hand grenades Tor and Omar always carried and the RPG-7s. Normally, the jeep was full of weapons; tonight for some reason they'd been loaded in the truck. Wakil slipped the safety catch from his pistol and handed it to Hamid. "Let's go," he said.

We moved out fast, stopping short of running for two reasons. Too sudden movement would be easier to spot from the air, and we had a lot of ground to cover and needed to pace ourselves. The path we followed glistened white in the moonlight. Never had I felt so exposed. Like a child, I longed to be able to separate myself from my shadow. Concerned about the same thing, Wakil ordered us to cut through the fields, since the soil didn't reflect the light so well. The cornstalk stubble was sharp and ankle-twisting. I stumbled constantly over the uneven terrain. And every time I did, I glanced back nervously, waiting for the chop-chop-chop of the gunship rotars to sound closer behind us. As I did, I wondered what kind of night vision these helicopters were equipped with. I hoped it was low light television, which was quick to cause eye fatigue and not high-tech thermal imaging, which would be able to detect even our parked jeep through the trees.

For the first time since I'd been traveling with the freedom fighters, I found myself leading. I was aware my energy was solely due to adrenaline. My fight or flight hormone had never functioned so efficiently. But I began to wonder how long it would last. Would my stamina suddenly drain away and leave me unable to go on? "Helicopter, another one," said Hamid, stopping abruptly. We halted behind him. A sixth gunship flew across us and headed toward the village. "Oh fuck, no!" my voice sounded shrill to my ears. I had a sudden desire just to stop and wait to be picked up, the way I'd felt in childhood games of hide and seek when the tension became too great. Being hunted down this way was like being awake in a nightmare that wouldn't end. We started moving again. I became aware that I was panting heavily. I suddenly realized I was hyperventilating and was also feeling close to tears, reactions I couldn't afford right then. I found myself beginning to pray for us and for the *Mujahideen* in the truck. Then out of nowhere a line from a gospel song I remembered from Sunday school came into my head: "Do Lord, Oh do Lord, Oh do remember me. . . ." Mindlessly, I repeated it over and over like a mantra. Its repetition had a soothing effect, and I heard my breathing regulate itself. I was still frightened, and I still glanced backward repeatedly, but the rising hysteria had subsided.

Now I was only aware of the chafing of the rough cotton fabric of my baggy Afghan pajamas against my legs caused by the friction of moving so fast. I tripped again and went down on one knee. Wakil helped me to my feet and continued to hold my hand. I wasn't sure whether he did it to stop me from constantly falling or to make sure I kept up, but human contact had never felt so good.

Ten minutes later, Wakil pulled up sharply. "There, ahead, Hamid, what do you see?" He pointed to a distant shadow. Hamid's eyes were the most acute of us three. "I don't know. It's too far."

"I think it's tanks," said Wakil, pulling us down into the dust. We squatted. The shape didn't change or grow closer. Behind us the gunships were still poised over the village like birds of prey. We waited five minutes; then Wakil cautiously proceeded. We followed him. A dull tension headache tightened its band around my head. After a couple of hundred yards, Wakil suddenly laughed wryly. "Bushes, my tanks are bushes." Once we passed the large cluster of bushes, I relaxed slightly. They concealed us from the view of the helicopters. And by the time we'd walked beyond their cover, we'd be difficult to spot. As long as they didn't start circling. . . .

Wakil, however, didn't ease up on the pace. At 4:00 A.M., we finally arrived at the tiny village that had been our destination. As we reached its outskirts, a man came out to greet us. He'd been looking out for us and had recognized Nazar Jhan. "We were expecting you hours ago," he said. "What happened? We were getting very concerned. Why are you on foot? We were told you were in a jeep." He led us to a small house just inside the village wall. The owner's sheep had been herded into the small fenced yard in front of it. As if expecting to be fed, the animals moved en masse toward the gate. I tried to move them back, to push my way through. "Excuse me, sheep, excuse me," I found myself saying inanely. Then I began to giggle uncontrollably.

10

A Deadly Game of Chicken

Still giggling, I staggered up a short flight of stairs and into a tiny adobe room, hitting my head on the low doorway as I went. In the dark, I fell over a small boy who had been sleeping under a pile of quilts. His father lit an oil lamp and called to his wife in a back room to make tea: Afghan hospitality functions around the clock. Sipping the scalding tea, I felt safe for the first time since we'd left the jeep. Being in a house, albeit a mud one, gave me a curious sense of security, even though intellectually I knew it was false. And then, as if someone had yanked a plug, every ounce of my energy drained away. Pulling one of the quilts over me, I asked, "Since it's 4:30 A.M. now, do you plan to get up at 5:30 to pray?"

"Of course," said Wakil. "It was probably our prayers that kept us safe tonight."

"Not just yours," I replied. "I think mine helped a lot, too."

At seven o'clock I was wakened by the sound of children crying, cocks crowing, and other assorted farmyard noises. Wakil had spent the same two and a half hours listening to tanks. I hadn't heard a thing, having slept the sleep of the exhausted. I went outside to splash water on my face. The yard that had been full of sheep when we arrived was empty now. The soft edges of the whitewashed adobe houses were pleasing to the eye, and the paint seemed fresher against the brilliant blue of the sky. I watched the women go about their chores, carrying water, baking *nan*, and from time to time shyly smiling over at me. It was an arcadian scene. And like a child who is afraid of the dark but grows brave with the day, I felt the dread of the previous night begin to diminish.

Throughout the morning, the *Mujahideen* from our truck began to arrive and were taken in by a number of the forty families in the village. Once again, I was impressed by the bush communication. "It's not that clever," said Wakil. "That they knew we were coming here last night, for example: when we're traveling in areas like this, we send messengers on ahead. If you arrive unexpectedly, well, you might be mistaken for someone else and get shot." Among the visitors was a local mullah who spent a long time talking to the commander and Wakil. He told them that two days before in a nearby village, a helicopter gunship had landed. A frightened nine-year-old boy had started to run. The soldiers told him to stop. Panicked, the boy kept running. The soldiers felled him, killing him instantly, with a volley of machine gun fire. Incidents like these had caused up to 40 percent of the population in this region to flee as refugees. And it was why a man I could see ploughing with a bullock-drawn plough just beyond the village was tending his fields with a rifle slung across his back.

While the men talked, I dug out of my pack a small traveling Bible a religious friend had given me before I left New York. I had always intended to read the Bible from cover to cover but had never gotten around to it, and when I was traveling with the freedom fighters there seemed little time to read. Now I opened it at Genesis. The life it described didn't sound very different from the one I was watching in the village. The *Mujahideen* asked me what I was reading. When I told them, they seemed pleased I was reading my "Koran." In their eyes that meant I "wasn't *kafir*," an "infidel" or unbeliever. One of them asked, "If she is killed in our *Jihad*, does it mean she is martyred?" automatic passage to paradise. They deliberated on the question for some time, finally deciding only a Muslim could be martyred. Tor came over and said, "I want you to answer one question, to answer it honestly. Were you afraid last night?"

"Yes, of course, I was afraid. I'm normal."

"What kind of afraid, of death or capture?"

"You know, Tor, I was so damn busy being scared I didn't have time to think about it."

"For me I want to be martyred, not captured. I am not afraid to die, but if they capture us, they torture us very badly. To die with a bullet is better."

"When they capture us, they put us on television," added Hamid. "This demoralizes the *Mujahideen* and is very bad for our families who see it. And when they kill us afterward, our families die inside also."

By the afternoon, all our *Mujahideen* were accounted for except two. Humayoon and Amin Jhan were missing. I remembered what Wakil had said about the Soviets' preferring to take the *Mujahideen* alive, that they learned more that way because the prisoners could be tortured until they talked. Captured *Mujahideen* were transported to Kabul, often given show trials that were televised, and then taken to Pul-i-Charki prison, where they were executed once they were no longer useful. Reports that had been filtering back in the last year had detailed exsanguination as one of the methods of execution, a bizarre manner of killing prisoners that was attributed to the shortage of blood for transfusions and the increasing number of Soviet casualties. I remembered being with Wakil in Peshawar when word had come that two of NIFA's men had been picked up by the KHAD in the capital. "They're as good as dead," he said sadly. "In fact, they'll wish they already were." And so would their families and friends if they talked under torture.

I thought about Humayoon and Amin Jhan: quiet Humayoon, who supported his parents and four siblings, including his invalid brother, and who hadn't seen his two babies for so long that he was afraid they wouldn't know who he was, and kind, gentle Amin Jhan. Clean-shaven except for a trim mustache, twenty-two-year-old Amin Jhan wore an embroidered *khuwalie*, pillbox hat, instead of a turban like the others. A handsome young man, with a dimpled, shy smile, he blushed easily. Thoughtful and sensitive, he danced attention on me so often that Wakil referred to him teasingly as my pet. It was Amin Jhan who noticed if I wasn't well enough to eat the food the villagers supplied and begged treasured eggs to scramble for me. He always made sure I had the warmest, cleanest quilt at night. He cleaned the dust off my seat in the jeep, and he even plucked thorns from a patch of grass before I sat down. In the rigors of a war zone, such cosseting was rare, and I cherished it and was fond of him.

Always fascinated by things mechanical, Amin Jhan had been the kind of kid who could fix anything. He had wanted to be an engineer; instead he'd become a freedom fighter at sixteen after several hundred tanks had attacked his village, which stood on the main Ghazni-Kabul highway near Qarah Bagh. They shelled the village all day, while fighter jets dropped napalm bombs. When it was over, three hundred people, virtually the entire community Amin Jhan had grown up with, were dead, many of them burned alive. Two years later, while still only eighteen, Amin Jhan was made a group commander with one hundred men under him.

Now both Amin Jhan and Humayoon had disappeared, and I felt heartsick. The *Mujahideen* prayed for their two companions: *"Inshallah,"* God willing, they would return. If they didn't: "This is war; it is God's will." Every man in the room had experienced such loss before, of a colleague, a friend, a relative, some like Tor, many times. I looked at Tor; Humayoon had been close to him, but his face registered nothing.

At 5:30 P.M. sixty *Mujahideen* from surrounding villages appeared to meet with Wakil. The men gathered on a platform just outside the village wall that served as an open-air mosque. As they arrived in small groups, I noticed only three of them had Kalashnikovs. There were a number of 303s, one RPG-7, and a 12-bore shotgun, more useful for bringing down ducks than the sixty-foot-long MI-24 gunships. A good third of the men were unarmed. They were the worst-equipped *Mujahideen* I had seen. An elderly man with tendrils of white hair escaping from his turban, who was obviously a leader, greeted Wakil and then launched into an impassioned plea. Patting his ancient 303 rifle he said, "We do what we can, but we need Kalashnikovs. And even they are useless against gunships and MIGs. And we need a regular supply of ammunition. Unless we get better weapons, we are like helpless children against the godless invaders of our country." The man's face flushed, and his bottom lip began to quiver as he talked. He struggled to control his emotions but lost. His voice shook as he said, "We are willing to die to free Afghanistan, but don't ask us to throw away our lives." Then tears rolled down his cheeks. Angry in his embarrassment, he brushed them away impatiently with callused, work-worn hands. "Unless we get decent weapons, we can't beat the enemy; we are just sacrificing our lives with no gain."

Listening to the man and aware there were no new weapon supplies destined for this region, Wakil's frustration and distress were evident. A freedom fighter sitting near us turned to me and said bitterly, "Your government says it is supporting us, says it is sending us the weapons we need. Where are they? Why don't we see them here? For every man we have fighting, there are ten or more waiting for arms. We can't fight gunships with rocks."

Washington had finally acknowledged that fact at the beginning of 1985, when they had approved putting into the covert pipeline Swiss-designed 20 mm Oerlikon antiaircraft cannon. Capable of firing one thousand rounds per minute, with special armor-piercing shells and adaptable for ground-to-ground as well as antiaircraft combat, the Oerlikon seemed to be the *Mujahideen's* answer to Soviet gunships. But just as the CIA giveth, it also saw fit to take away—the agency had chosen a gun that weighed a hefty twelve hundred pounds and could only be transported in carts by teams of mules. Since most Afghan mountain trails are too rough and steep for carts, the guns have to be used in a fixed position—useless in a guerrilla war that requires mobility. The first four Oerlikons that were sent in on "an experimental basis" were all lost when the freedom fighters were forced to retreat in a hurry and were unable to take the time to remove the guns. Soviet gunships landed and picked them up. They were later displayed on television. The freedom fighters have also lost some of their Dashakas and Zigovaks heavy machine guns in similar fashion when MI-24s trailing boat anchors have plucked them from mountain peaks. This ingenious method proved effective enough to give birth to a brief-lived rumor of a new kind of helicopter equipped with powerful magnets. After the Oerlikon incidents, the *Mujahideen* pleaded again for the shoulder-held, heat-seeking Stingers, which weigh only thirty-five pounds, although Washington sources now say the Stingers are not as accurate as they were originally thought to be.*

The village meeting broke up, and a rare despondency fell over the *Mujahideen*. The men split up and went their separate ways. Suddenly, as if the location, not the mood, were depressing, Wakil stated that we would move on again that evening, once it became dark. The moment he spoke, I realized that emotionally I wasn't ready for another nighttime session of hide and seek with Soviet gunships. It was too soon. I could have used a break between the two journeys, particularly since I doubted there had been a brighter moon all year. I said nothing, but for me the fear of the known was considerably worse than the fear of the unknown had been. And then, as if I weren't jittery enough, Wakil made me feel worse by announcing, "Tonight's trip is very dangerous, more than last night. We are crossing the Ghazni-Kabul highway, which is in Soviet hands and is policed day and night by tanks. We have to travel along it for several kilometers. This whole area is heavily patrolled by gunships and tanks. For this reason, I've arranged for the local *Mujahideen* to be stationed along our route. They will check that their area is clear before we move into it." I was nervous before his caveat; now my dread had returned. And it didn't diminish when the truck that was transporting us arrived. The ancient vehicle had the noisiest, throatiest engine I had ever heard, and that would announce our presence as effectively as spotlights. But it was the best the impoverished area could produce. The driver who came with the truck was

---

*In March 1986, information was leaked to the Washington press stating that 150 Stingers were quietly approved for Afghan and Angolan insurgents. An outraged congressman, Lee Hamilton, the Indiana Democrat who is chairman of the Select Committee on Intelligence and who was concerned about such weapons falling into the hands of international terrorists, announced that he would try to pass a bill to cut off aid to the guerrillas if that decision were not reversed. But all the talk of Stingers transpired to be nothing more than just talk. Later that summer, after being confronted by four leaders of the Afghan Resistance coalition, Reagan admitted during a meeting with the *Mujahideen* in the White House that, in fact, the Stingers had not been put into the pipeline.

Then in September that year, Hamilton's bill to block Stingers for the freedom fighters was defeated. Two months later, the Resistance quietly received the first shipment of the heat-seeking weapons.

almost as much a handicap as the vehicle. Slow to comprehend and to react, he seemed unfamiliar with the truck, which kept cutting out on him, and with the region, in which he kept getting lost. Repeatedly, he turned on the full beams to locate the lost trail. I sat next to him in the cab, and ignoring my groans and protestations, he waited until one of the *Mujahideen* riding in the back hung head down through his window and bellowed at him before he turned off the lights. After a nerve-wracking half hour of this pantomime, Wakil ordered him replaced. I went back to imagining every twinkling star the lights of a helicopter gunship.

When we halted to replace the driver, Wakil mentioned that we were heading back to the village where we'd left the jeep and would pick it up if it were still there. It was, and sitting in it were Humayoon and Amin Jhan. I became as enthusiastic as any Afghan in my greeting of both of them. Even in the dark, I saw Amin Jhan blush when I hugged and kissed him. The two men explained that when they dropped from the back of the jeep, the helicopter was right behind them, and they had had to get out of sight. They had originally planned to join the *Mujahideen* who had leaped from the truck to take up firing positions. But everyone had disappeared from view. They decided to make for a cliff some distance away that would give them some measure of protection. It was then that they saw the other gunships head toward the village. "One stayed over our truck for an hour, just swinging back and forth," said Humayoon. "That our truck was a Soviet one might have confused them at first until they discovered that none of their own was in that area." Convinced, as we had been, that the gunships would eventually land so troops could conduct a house-to-house search, Humayoon and Amin Jhan stayed near the village, hoping they might be able to draw fire if necessary. When the helicopters finally left, the two *Mujahideen* assumed they would be replaced by tanks. They stayed hidden until it became apparent that this was not the case. Then they ventured into the village to see if they could learn what had happened to us. In doing so, they found the empty jeep, which was minus its key since Wakil had taken it. They were pondering their next step when we arrived.

I was delighted to exchange the antiquated truck for the jeep, but after the beating it had taken the previous night, we couldn't get it to start. The engine spluttered and died as if the battery were flat, but it had been new when we'd started out. "Everything is probably full of dust," said Amin Jhan as he peered under the jeep's hood. I felt myself becoming more and more uneasy as he tinkered with the engine. The village stayed curiously locked up, as if the inhabitants didn't want to acknowledge our presence. Like me, they were probably aware that they had had a lucky escape the previous night. Amin Jhan was not having a great deal of success. The men pushed the jeep into the open, and then nudging it with the truck, they tried to jump-start it. The engine would catch, the jeep travel a few yards, and then it would cut out. By now, I would have been happy to abandon the vehicle. I had visions of the thing breaking down at a crucial moment. But this was the jeep's maiden voyage; it had just been donated by a British journalist, and Wakil had no intention of leaving such a valuable item behind. After half an hour, Amin Jhan proved his title of mechanical wizard was deserved: the jeep began to purr.

We were under way again less than half an hour when we spotted headlights. They went on briefly and were immediately turned off. This happened three times, and on the last occasion, we could clearly see men jump from the vehicle. We cut our engines, and our *Mujahideen* climbed down also. Several of our men began to walk slowly, Kalashnikovs at the ready, toward the oncoming vehicle. Tor, I noticed, was out in front again and offering himself for target practice. Once again, he was lucky. The other vehicle was a full ammunition supply truck for another Resistance group. They had thought we were enemy troops. Both sides were relieved to find the other were *Mujahideen*. In their delight, they took precious minutes to greet one another. They pumped hands, kissed cheeks, and hugged so enthusiastically that it seemed as if they had known one another for years, and every relative had to be inquired about. I just sat in the jeep wishing I were miles from Ghazni. I felt that way some time later, when Wakil slammed on the brakes of the jeep and began to berate the freedom fighters in the back of the truck for smoking. Their lighted cigarettes were a double security risk, he told them: the red glow could be clearly seen for some distance, and they were sitting on top of a giant jerrican of gasoline, which didn't seal properly. They obeyed him immediately and without question. But discipline among the freedom fighters was quirky, I had already learned. They would often sing or laugh loudly on dangerous routes, and the cacophony seemed the most strident closest to an enemy base. When I had first traveled with the *Mujahideen* I had thought it was lack of awareness, but I soon realized it was pure bravado.

Throughout the drive, shadowy figures mostly on bicycles would suddenly appear at the side of the route. They were the *Mujahideen* from local villages who had been alerted of our journey and had been deployed to check out the safety of their particular region. Their presence was comforting, although I was nervous enough to hope their assignment had been carried out thoroughly. As we got closer to the Gudar River, which we had to cross, the number of bicycles increased. I could soon see why. In the bright moonlight the tank tread marks crisscrossing the ground were as visible as they would have been in the day and were evidence of the heavy tank traffic in the area. "This is a favorite place for tank ambushes," said Wakil. Without testing the depth of the water, the driver of the truck drove the vehicle straight into the river. It got about halfway across and bogged down on the muddy riverbed with water coming up to the bottom of the cab. The *Mujahideen* leaped into the frigid water and began pushing and yelling. The driver responded by energetically revving the engine; one way or another it seemed destined to flood. The noise from both truck and men would have alerted a tank convoy up to five miles away. In the midst of the racket, I sat in the jeep, expecting enemy shells to find us at any moment. After ten minutes, the truck moved forward. Five yards later, it became stuck again. The drama was played out all over again, and finally the truck jerked and hiccuped its way to the far bank. With the jeep, the *Mujahideen* were more cautious, testing the depth of the water and wandering farther downstream until they found a firmer bottom. We made it to the other side with no problem and drove off, only to discover that the truck wasn't following. The drivers of both vehicles began to bellow instructions at each other. As the truck didn't respond, Wakil became more stentorian. Each time he raised his voice, I sank a little lower in my seat. We were sitting in the middle of Soviet-held territory, and the *Mujahideen* were making enough noise to waken the dead. Finally, I suggested it might be more efficient, if not prudent, to go over and find out what the problem was before every garrison in a ten-mile radius around us had turned out. When Wakil did so, he discovered that the men in the truck had been trying to persuade the *Mujahideen* bicycle guard to join us. Not surprisingly, the latter only wanted to go back to their village and catch up on their sleep. I wished I could join them.

Not far from the river, we pulled into a bombed-out school. We were close to the Ghazni-Kabul highway and would stay there until Amin Jhan, now on home territory, and another *Mujahid* had checked that the road was clear. Two bikes were produced from the gutted school, and Amin Jhan and his colleague cycled bumpily over the fields toward the tarmac road. As they did, a half-dozen flares lit up the sky some distance from us, and the thud of BM-21 shells began exploding every thirty seconds, from what sounded to be the direction of Ghazni city. I shivered in the chill night air and, for the umpteenth time that evening, wished I were back in New York. After about half an hour, we heard the short toot of a whistle. "That's it; get going," said Wakil to the truck driver. Coughing and wheezing, the truck followed the route the bicycles had taken. We could see it clearly until it reached a line of trees that edged the highway; then we listened as the rasping engine grew fainter and fainter. Once it was off the road, the bikes would repeat the performance and come back for us. They'd been gone almost thirty minutes when we heard the whistle again. Wakil ordered us back to the jeep. "We'll be on the highway about eight minutes," he said. "Once we cross it, we'll be close to *Mujahideen* territory. We can relax." We reached the trees. Amin Jhan and the other man pulled out of the shadows. They gestured us forward and then began to pedal furiously after us. The road in both directions was clear. I willed it to stay that way. Under any other circumstances, I would have enjoyed the ride. It was the first tarmac road I'd driven on outside Kabul, and it was a delight after the bone-jarring journeys we'd had so far. As it was, I closed my eyes and didn't open them again until I felt the jeep turn off the road. We stopped to wait for Amin Jhan to catch up with us and then drove through a deserted village. "This was my home," he said, as we wound through the devastated community. Suddenly, he indicated to Wakil to stop. Jumping down from the jeep, he disappeared inside a walled garden. He returned ten minutes later with his *patou* full of apples. "It was my uncle's orchard: the best apples in Afghanistan," he said, dumping several pounds of the fruit into my lap. He was right; the crisp green apples were the best I'd ever tasted, and they were juicy enough to quench our thirst after hours of swallowing dust.

Two hours later, we pulled into a tiny hamlet of half a dozen houses. Too keyed up to sleep, I sprawled in a corner of the dusty room in which we were quartered and talked in a low voice with Tor until the *Mujahideen* trying to sleep complained. "I want to go my home," said Tor.

"To Kabul?"

"Yes, by highway it's very close, two or two and a half hours' drive. In a few days, October 8, it will be four years exactly since I left my family."

"When did you last visit them?"

"That day. I've never seen them again."

"Couldn't you go at night, secretly?"

"No, my house is very close to a KHAD office. Too many people know I am *Mujahid*. It wouldn't be safe for my family."

In the morning, we discovered we were staying in the house of a man who had been released from Pul-i-Charki two months before. "Don't write my name; don't write my name," he implored. "The next time they arrest me, they said they would kill me." Faizl, as I agreed to call him, had worked in the government Press and Publications Department. Arrested one day at the office, he was charged with antigovernment activities: "They said I permitted counterrevolutionaries to visit me and stay at my house." He was interrogated and tortured at a KHAD office for three months and then given a rare trial. "It was a five-minute trial, and in that time they decided the futures of thirteen people." He was sentenced to six years. "The prison conditions were as bad as the physical torture," he said. "We had 145 to 150 men in our cell, which measured ten by three meters and was meant for twenty people. There were cots up to the ceiling. There was so little space we had to move or pray in rotation. We had nothing to read, nothing to do. They often turned off the electricity, and we were rarely allowed to leave the cell. Even to go to the bathroom, we were made to wait on rotation. One man, Jalladin, who was sentenced to fifteen years, went insane after being tortured. He lost so much weight, he looked like a stick. All day long, he banged his head on the bars and screamed, but they ignored him.

"There were boys as young as fourteen; they were called 'little donkeys.' But there were also Pakistani and Egyptian pris-

oners, and a French mechanic who was serving sixteen years."
Faizl had no information on why a Frenchman was imprisoned at
Pul-i-Charki; he only knew that he had been there since the beginning of the war. Pakistanis and Egyptians have been known to
fight with the *Mujahideen;* in fact, the Resistance group headed
by Rasul Sayyaf and which is a party championed by the Arab
states, has frequently numbered Egyptians among its freedom
fighters.

When Faizl was released, he knew he would be watched, and
if he stayed in Kabul, his chances of being picked up again were
high. He decided to return to his family home in Ghazni. Despite
Faizl's visible nervousness, he was a brave man. Although the
KHAD doesn't make empty threats, and he almost certainly risks
execution if arrested a second time, Faizl's home was soon being
used as a safe house for traveling *Mujahideen.* Kalashnikovs and
grenade launchers were stacked against his living room wall like
so many brooms. (Three days after we left his village, Soviet
troops in six tanks and three gunships arrived to search it. Apparently, word had gotten out that there was a doctor visiting, and
the Russians knew that meant either *Mujahideen* or foreigners.)

I stepped outside to explore the hamlet, the smallest and one
of the poorest communities in which we had stayed. Immediately
in front of the house was a narrow meandering stream that fed
a water-activated flour mill about a mile away, which served half
a dozen communities in the area. Paddling down it were a dozen
mallards, the sun glinting off the emerald green feathers of the
males. On the far side of the stream were the village's fields. Old
women and tiny children were digging up onions and white car-
rots for the winter. Behind us were hills that changed color with
the light; now they were sienna red. It was a bucolic setting,
intruded on only briefly when I was ploughed into by a small girl
in hot pursuit of a runaway calf. I joined her in the chase, but the
calf was as frisky as a lamb and too fast for the pair of us. We
both sank on our haunches on the bank of the stream and inspected each other. She was joined by a friend. Both girls, about
age seven, were veiled. "Why does she smile at everyone?" the
owner of the calf asked Wakil, who had just finished his morning
ablutions for prayer.

"Because she can't speak to them in their language."

"But she shouldn't smile at every man; it isn't right." Her

companion chimed in, "What language does she speak, the language of the ducks?" "No, no," said the girl with the calf. "She speaks like a small bird; wait and see."

Wakil was amused. "Quack, quack, quack," he said, teasingly flapping his elbows at me. With our newfound young friends we went to join the brigadier and Amin Jhan, who were sunbathing on a grassy bank at the edge of an onion field. It was about eighty degrees, but the breeze had a freshness to it that hinted at autumn. We stretched out in the sun, and I felt myself unwind. We'd been there about fifteen minutes when, without warning, the air was filled with a terrible noise, like the roar of an enraged animal. As if out of nowhere, two jet fighters screamed over the water mill and flew straight in front of us so low they felt as if they skimmed the rooftops. "Run," shouted Amin Jhan; "run for the the trees." No one needed telling twice. We made the thin line of trees, just as the jets, MIGs, circled back, glinting black against the blue sky. "They'll probably bomb this time," said Wakil. I leveled my camera. Amin Jhan stopped me. "If the sun reflects off the lens . . ." The planes shrieked past us and disappeared over the hills, gone as fast as they had come. I was left stunned at the way they had appeared. "They were on top of us before we even heard them," I said, uncomprehending and unnerved. I was more familiar with the reverse—we would occasionally hear planes and the thud of bombing, but the sky would stay empty. At those times, I assumed the jets were traveling too high and too fast to be seen. Could the hills behind us have deadened the noise of that morning's MIGs? No one seemed to know. But the tranquility of the morning had come to an abrupt end. Now every crow in the sky would look like a jet. And now also I became very aware of the highway just four kilometers away that I had chosen to tune out earlier. The trucks and armored vehicles moving on it were suddenly very visible. An hour later, we heard the distant pounding of bombing. "Ghazni city," said Amin Jhan.

Throughout the afternoon people from the outlying area began to arrive, having heard the *Mujahideen* had brought a "doctor" with them. Soon there were fifty people waiting to see Tor, and I was pressed into service. An old man complained of chronic nosebleeds. I told him most of us had the same problem, which was true, and blamed it on the dryness and the dust. The best we could do was to give him vitamin C tablets, which would help a little. He was happy just to get the tablets. My next patient was a two-year-old boy whose mother said he had had a runny stool since the summer. I asked her what she was feeding him. He was breast-fed, she replied, but now that she was working in the fields in the morning, she couldn't nurse him and had been giving him cow's milk. "Maybe he's allergic to cow's milk," I said, more guesswork than diagnosis. I remembered a medical article I had read that had recommended goat's milk in such a case. It couldn't hurt. I suggested she try it and start feeding her son a little solid food.

An elderly judge who knew Wakil came by. "Did you bring my false teeth?" he demanded with a gummy grin. "You said last time you would." Wakil shook his head. "Next time, old man, I promise," he replied. "Well, at least he's not asking for machine guns," he added in an aside to me.

Tor called me from an adjoining vegetable storeroom he'd been using as an examining room. "I need your help," he said. His patient was a commander of about thirty who had a badly infected knee. The man had fallen during a military operation a week before and hadn't cleaned the wound. Now his knee was nearly twice its normal size. The joint was so swollen and the skin stretched so tightly over it that he couldn't bend it. He said it throbbed so much that he couldn't sleep. The knee was red and angry looking and hot to the touch. "I must drain it; otherwise the next step is septicemia, and that will kill him," said Tor, more certain of his medical vocabulary than he was of his everyday English. "It's dark in here; I need you to hold the lamp and hand things to me when I ask for them." Tor began liberally smearing the man's knee with bright orange tincture of iodine. Having lost his surgical knives at the onset of the trip, he picked up a specially sharpened and sterilized Swiss army knife. "Hold your leg still," he told the commander. Tor began to cut into the side of the man's knee. I bit my upper lip; the commander briefly closed his eyes but otherwise didn't flinch. Foul-smelling pus mingled with blood from the wound. I heaved. Tor kept cutting. I retched again. "I'm sorry, Tor; I can't stay," I said, putting down the lamp and rushing from the room. Outside, I leaned against the wall, gulping the cool evening air, my "barefoot doctor" mantle in tatters at my feet.

Having watched Tor treat dozens of patients under primitive

conditions, with primitive equipment, and rarely with the appropriate drugs, I was full of admiration for what he was capable of doing. So was Wakil, who a few months before had arrived in the village of Chardehi, near Kabul, just after it had been bombed. A twelve-year-old boy had had both legs severed at the thigh by a large piece of shrapnel. Lying in his own blood, he saw his father die in front of him. Wakil found the boy bleeding profusely but still conscious. He was screaming, "I'm going to die; please don't let me die." Wakil picked him up and carried him back to Tor, who made tourniquets from strips of turban. That was all he could do; he had no painkillers, no other supplies. The boy continued to scream, "I'm going to die." "You're not going to die," Wakil told him repeatedly, "You're much stronger than you think." The child traveled four days tied to a horse and by jeep before he reached the Red Cross hospital in Peshawar. "We didn't even have aspirin for his pain," said Wakil. But because of the attention of one paramedic, the boy lived instead of succumbing to shock, loss of blood, or mass infection.

Standing there, I became angry as I recalled a conversation I'd had with a State Department official, a special assistant to an under secretary. I had asked him why $2 million appropriated by Congress for medical assistance inside Afghanistan was finally spent a year later in Pakistan. "There's no point in sending such aid inside," he told me. "The Afghans are an uneducated bunch. They wouldn't know what to do with it; it would just be wasted." I'd been livid at the time, but the official had said much that day that made me angry. He felt that the month-long first-aid courses offered by ICRC to the Afghan commanders were adequate, even though I informed him that the *Mujahideen* were given a handful of bandages, a small bottle of disinfectant, and aspirin on graduation. I would have liked the man and like-minded bureaucrats to have stood in the Red Cross hospital the day the wounded from the Khost offensive began to flood in. I will never forget the Afghan brought in with a hole almost twelve inches square and nearly one inch deep gouged out of his back by shrapnel. I was amazed that he was still alive, as was François Zen Ruffinen, the hospital director. That he'd survived a three-day journey in that condition was little short of a medical miracle. But he was lucky in one regard: he'd made it to a hospital. Eighty percent of the wounded freedom fighters die of their injuries before they can be properly treated. During the Vietnam War, thanks mostly to the work of the med-evac teams, only 15 percent of injured U.S. soldiers died. A med-evac team in Afghanistan is a donkey if you are lucky, a stretcher made from tree branches or guns and turbans if you are not. A wounded person may take three weeks or more to reach Pakistan or find one of the few foreign teams of traveling doctors like *Médecins Sans Frontières*.

What Tor had just done for the commander was minor surgery, of course, but his patient would have been a lot more comfortable and a lot quicker to heal if the *Mujahideen*, who treat civilians and fighters alike, were supplied with basic medical supplies.

□

The *Mujahideen* spent that evening competing with one another to see who could strip and reassemble his machine gun fastest when blindfolded. One of the most dexterous was a young mullah-in-training, Abdul Rehman, who had joined us the day after the helicopter chase. His had been the sole RPG-7 I had seen at the outdoor mosque meeting. Dressed in the white of his calling, Abdul, age seventeen, would train for another fourteen years before he could consider himself a mullah. From Randakhail in Maqor, he had become a freedom fighter a year before after his house had been searched by the Soviets. During the search, his fifteen-year-old sister, with whom he was very close, was kidnapped. "We never saw her again," he said. "She was very beautiful. Do you know what happens to girls like that, when they are taken away by the soldiers? They are defiled and then killed." It wasn't far from Maqor, in an isolated stretch of country, that three gunships landed near a nomad camp and abducted four girls. As the helicopters flew over a nearby village, the clothing of the girls was tossed out. Some time later, the girls' naked bodies followed. While Abdul was training to be a man of God, he had every intention of avenging his sister.

The following day brought several pieces of bad news. Our antiquated truck had finally died. We also learned that *Mujahideen* had engaged in hand-to-hand fighting in Ghazni city the previous night. Planes and helicopters had started to bomb the city even before dawn. "Wherever they saw a house with light, they bombed it," said a Resistance informer. That night also the river area where our truck had bogged down had come under heavy attack. "The forces are out all over, blocking all the roads." The man also brought with him several more accounts of helicopter mugging attacks in the area. Most of the time, the booty totaled little more than a few hundred afghanis, a cheap watch or two, and maybe a transistor radio. It hardly seemed worth the effort.

"We can't stay here," said Wakil, "and we obviously can't go toward Kabul through Ghazni city. And we couldn't go south now if we wanted to." Wakil decided to keep going north to Bamiyan and western Wardak, and then head southwest to Kandahar. But until we could replace the truck, we couldn't go anywhere. A large jeep was promised, and it finally arrived at the end of the afternoon. Both jeeps were loaded with care: twenty-two men and their weapons had to be accommodated. At 7:00 P.M. we started out for Qal'a-i Khan, near the Bamiyan border. The vehicles bounced over the rutted fields. Almost immediately Hamid and I were hit with severe cramps. Every thirty minutes, we had to ask the jeep to stop, crawl over the tangle of humanity in the back of it, and drag ourselves off into the dark. Soon Hamid was moaning aloud. More to keep up my own spirits than his, I teased him that now he knew how a woman in labor feels. "No, no, it's much worse," he insisted. "Nonsense," I responded, "it's much less." Neither one of us, of course, had the slightest idea of what we were talking about. And in the next few days, severe stomach cramps became my normal state of being. I was consumed with a weakness I hadn't felt before; even being a passenger in the jeep was exhausting. There was a fever that came and went and a constant feeling of nausea, and the smell of food disgusted me. There was also a more vivid awareness of my viscera than I had ever experienced. My attention had never been more inwardly focused. I recalled someone's saying, "This is Wardak Province." "Mmm," I mumbled. Several fever-wracked days later, someone else pointed out the Hazarajat Mountains, which cut across the center of the country and rise to thirteen thousand feet. I was aware of little more than Wakil's frequent *Mujahideen* briefings and the concerned faces of Amin

Jhan, Wakil, and the other freedom fighters peering at me from time to time. Tor pronounced it unlikely I was going to die. I was less convinced.

Hamid and I began functioning again at about the same time, except that although my symptoms abated, they never completely disappeared. The attacks of diarrhea would flare up suddenly and explosively, leave me exhausted, and then subside somewhat. It was a health problem that was inconvenient and enervating, both hazards in a war zone. I promised myself that when we reached Peshawar, I would have a few lab tests.

I knew we were heading south again the night we found ourselves driving into heavy shelling. Less than one and a half kilometers from the route we were taking, it suddenly began to rain mortars and rockets. The sky was alight, and our jeep vibrated with every thud. We kept going as if it were nothing more untoward that we were driving by than building construction blasting. We stopped to pick up a local guide near Maqor airport, which housed fifty gunships and three transport planes. He was to take us to the base of Commander Akhtar Mohammed. As Fidel Castro had done during his guerrilla days, Commander Mohammed slept in different locations nightly for security reasons. Driving up to the village, we saw the shadowy silhouettes of men jump from the walls surrounding it and crouch down into trenches a few yards in front. "Stop, stop," yelled our guide. "If you go any farther, they'll shoot. Let me go ahead and identify you." The guide left his gun with us so he would be seen to be unarmed. Several minutes later a tall, large-featured man in his fifties came to greet us. Because of his soldierly bearing and air of efficiency, I wasn't surprised to hear that Mohammed had been a high-ranking officer in the police force before the war. He was also "very strict on discipline" with his *Mujahideen*, which was probably just as well. Mohammed commanded an area that had the largest Soviet garrison in the province sitting in it. Maqor, which was manned by six thousand, many of them from the elite Rieshkhur Division, was Command Headquarters for the region. A few minutes' drive down the Kabul-Kandahar highway was a large barracks that had been an American-built hotel, not unlike a Holiday Inn, originally used by the highway construction staff. "It's the most comfortable barracks the Soviets have," he said. We sat long enough with the commander to take tea and learn that he was planning to attack the garrison the next day. "We've got twenty rockets; they've got one hundred tanks and nearly sixty gunships in the region. Unless we are very lucky, we can't do a lot of damage, but it keeps them off balance." Then he decided to move us to another village. "Too many people saw you arrive here," he said, "and this close to the garrison, we have to beware of informers." He drove us back into the hills into what felt like a far-flung outpost.

The following morning, Wakil was asked to conduct a formal inspection of *Mujahideen*. Several squads arrived on foot, marching smartly behind the black flags of NIFA. With sand-colored, adobe homes built like small fortresses behind us and the marching *Mujahideen* in front, a newly arriving visitor would have been forgiven for thinking he had stumbled on a turn of the century scene when the British Empire still ruled much of this continent. The crisp turnout of several hundred guerrillas on parade in the broiling sun was too much for one man. An epileptic, he suffered a severe seizure, and as he fell to the ground in spasm, the barrel of his AK-47 smashed into the face of a man standing nearby, gouging a jagged hole in his eyebrow. Blood spattered both men. Tor was ordered to fall out in a hurry and administer first aid.

Just after the parade broke up, a spotter plane flew low over the village. Five minutes earlier it would have witnessed a line several hundred yards long of heavily armed *Mujahideen*, which would have made the pilot's morning reconnaisance trip very worthwhile. When the spotter plane came back twice in the next half hour, the commander decided that it was time to disperse his men and to move us on.

We left for another "safe village." We were moving so often, I was beginning to feel like a criminal on the run, and safety had long ago become relative. The constant moving was affecting Hamid, too, but for different reasons. "We're in the middle of my country, and yet we have a home nowhere in Afghanistan," he said angrily. We drove for ninety minutes, and throughout the journey we could see the Maqor garrison in the valley below us. When we pulled into another anonymous village, Wakil ordered me to follow two local men. "Leave your pack in the jeep," he said, driving off with no further explanation offered. I assumed I was being taken to one of the houses there, but the men struck out at a brisk pace across the fields. I trailed behind them, glancing over my shoulder repeatedly for the rest of our party. But only Tor appeared. "What's happening; where are we going?" I shouted to him. He shrugged. Our companions couldn't help; they only knew they were to take us to a village up in the hills.

An hour later we arrived at Bangal Khiel, a handful of houses set down in barren stony hills. Once again, I was left wondering how the inhabitants supported themselves. But some distance from the village, the land was fertile enough for them to grow grapes and almonds, they explained. Just as I was beginning to think that Tor and I were to spend the night alone with the villagers, Wakil arrived with several of the *Mujahideen*, but without Hamid. "He took the jeep to a neighboring valley," explained Wakil. "If anything goes wrong, it would be easy to cut off our escape route from here." That statement, along with Wakil's preoccupied air, made me suspect that he wasn't telling me everything. The light was beginning to fade when we heard rumbling. The noise was approaching the village. After the peace of the afternoon, the sound was chilling. "Tanks," said Wakil, grabbing a grenade launcher and rushing outside. The rest of us scrambled to our feet to go after him. As we did, the sound enveloped us and we clearly heard the clatter of the rotating blades of helicopters. Wakil ducked back inside the house as six gunships no more than five hundred feet up flew over us. From the windows of the house we watched them head toward the garrison. I was never able to look at gunships without thinking about the devastation they had just wrought or were about to carry out. In their versatility—their ability to hunt their prey, to hide in gullies, to land at whim—they were far more threatening than jet fighters. I wondered what it felt like to fly something that was so efficient at annihilation.

I awoke to a commotion the next morning. Pulling on my socks and boots, I followed the *Mujahideen* out to the trail leading into the village. The small crowd fell back as the commander strode up. A new group of *Mujahideen* had arrived carrying the bodies of three dead freedom fighters. All in their early twenties, the corpses were riddled with bullets. They had been cut down that night when they had attempted to ambush tanks moving on the highway. Now they were being returned to their villages, which were above us. The commander and Wakil left with the men bearing the bodies, to pay their condolences to the families of the dead men. While they were gone, *Mujahideen* began to load

107 mm rockets onto the backs of donkeys. As I watched the weapons being loaded, a wizened old woman dressed completely in black began to berate me in a shrill voice. "You people should give us better support, better weapons. We can't finish this war with these rockets. Either help us with proper equipment or solve the war peacefully. Afghanistan is on fire. Your country is watching us burn." By now, I was familiar with this kind of anger directed at me as an American and a symbol of the Afghans' frustration. There were no words that would make her feel less bitter. I took her hand in mine and held it. She clutched it hard, began to cry, and left.

Under the supervision of the brigadier and Humayoon, the rockets were being moved into place on two peaks commanding excellent views of the garrison. Because of the heavy air activity, the operation had been postponed to the following day. But the men would stay overnight in position. Tor was ordered to go with them with a supply of bandages so that, if necessary, he could stop any bleeding. Hamid volunteered to join them. I was left alone with the villagers, who went about their daily tasks. I went out to sit under a solitary hawthorne tree in front of the shell of a house that had been bombed two years before. It had been a long time since I had spoken to a Westerner or had a chat with a woman. And I realized that in the last few days, there hadn't been a lot of English conversation, either. My knowledge of Farsi and Pushto was growing, but not enough to converse. And translating every word was as exhausting for the interviewer as it was for the interpreter. In the last few days tension had been growing among the men. The easy camaraderie seemed to be waning. And that morning, Wakil had been uncharacteristically snappish. For the first time I felt isolated and alienated.

In search of company, I stopped to watch two small children playing inside a courtyard. The older child, a girl of about four, took one look at me and began to scream hysterically. "She thinks you're a Russian," said Wakil, who had come up behind me. He soothed her, but it took a while for the child to feel comfortable enough to let me approach her. Once she did, I fell back on an old favorite and began to make paper dolls in lieu of conversation.

All day long, helicopters and reconnaissance planes flew over. At twilight, the commander told Wakil and me that we were being moved again. "Once we attack the garrison tonight, retaliation will be swift," explained Akhtar Mohammed. "This is not a good place to be." We retreated farther back to an equally small settlement, Sangar, where we were met by several angry dogs that had to be restrained by their owners. Shortly before 11:00 P.M. Tor came through the door of the house where we were to spend the night. Grimy and exhausted, he flopped down next to me. "Too many helicopters. The brigadier postponed the operation again." An hour later, the brigadier, Aqa Mohammed, and Humayoon returned. The brigadier was wheezing heavily, an asthma sufferer in recent years; the steep, seven-hour climb in the hot sun without food or water had taken its toll. "We counted twenty-four gunships landing at the garrison," he told Wakil. "And from what we could see they had at least seventy-two large tanks and sixty of the smaller and faster BMD tanks." The brigadier knew the garrison well, having served there. "They also have at least forty-eight cannons, sixty-three mortars, thirty-six Dashakas, and the same number of Zigovaks." I asked him exactly how much of a dent he thought twenty rockets without their firing tubes to ensure accuracy would make on such a stronghold. *"Inshallah,"* he replied, adding that they'd only received the 107s a year ago and had found them effective.

Aqa Mohammed, who had been a career officer for seventeen years, had served time in Pul-i-Charki for trying to even up such a disparate balance of arms as the one he now faced. Since the beginning of the war, he had regularly smuggled arms and ammunition out of the garrison in his military jeep and had kept half the Resistance supplied in the area. In 1983, he was arrested after two freedom fighters revealed under torture that he was their contact. Tortured himself for two months, he kept insisting he was innocent and said the same thing at his trial, claiming he had only been named because of personal animosity. Because of his rank and family connections, his case was adjourned for review. Seven months later, and after several heavy bribes, he was released and immediately joined the *Mujahideen.* Now he said, "We'll try again tomorrow. If the gunship activity is as heavy as today, we'll have to assume word has leaked out. We'll postpone the operation for a week."

We were roused at the crack of dawn again: "Get your things together; we're moving." I cursed. We changed villages so frequently now that I had become totally disoriented. Getting up in the night to find the latrine area on the edge of the village, I'd become so confused that I had twice walked into the wrong house. We turned north and walked for thirty minutes to yet another village, Tangai. All hell suddenly broke loose behind us. The garrison had opened up fire, and it sounded as if Bangal Khiel were being shelled. The noise reverberated around the hills, and the ground underneath us began to shake. We were taken to a house in the middle of the village. As before, I found myself feeling safer with a roof over my head even though I knew I was no better protected than if I had stayed in the open. I could only imagine I was responding in the same way an animal does when it instinctually returns to its lair when frightened. The shelling continued all morning.

Spotter planes circled the area constantly like so many vultures. And because of them we were unable to leave the house. It was while we were holed up that the commander told us his *Mujahideen* had just detained three old men. They had followed us to every village we had visited in the last couple of days, ostensibly buying goat skins. The *Mujahideen*, however, thought they were informers who were reporting back to the garrison. Elderly men and women were often used by both sides for this purpose because they could normally travel unhindered and without raising suspicion.

Around noontime, the shelling ceased. Shortly afterward we learned what had happened. Bangal Khiel had received several direct hits. The two little girls I had played with the day before were dead. So were their parents. They were the only fatalities the village had received. I was devastated. Try as I could I couldn't block out images of the children, one skinny little four-year-old with scabbed knees and tangled brown hair and her toddler sister, lying as limp as the paper dolls I had made them twenty-four hours ago. I was assailed with emotions, but the predominant one was guilt. If the garrison had gotten wind of our presence in the village, and that seemed the only explanation for Bangal Khiel to be shelled, we were the reason two children and their parents were dead. A tiny community of simple mud houses whose residents scratched a living from stony, ungiving land had been laid waste because we happened to pass through it. "For God's sake, Wakil, how can you stand it?" I asked him through my tears. "What do you do with those feelings?" Wakil looked at me and then came and sat on the carpet next to me, all sign of his earlier irritability gone. The other *Mujahideen* looked on, unable to understand what I was saying, and concerned anyway, not having seen me cry before. "I understand how you feel," said Wakil gently. "It isn't easy for us either, knowing civilians are bombed because they help the *Mujahideen*. But I've also been back to some of those villages after an attack, and I've spoken to parents who lost their children. I've never found one who blamed us or who told us to stay away. They understand what we are doing. You mustn't forget it, either."

His words were meant to comfort me, but I was too raw. There also was no time for grieving. The commander was convinced the ceasefire was only a lull and wanted to move us on again. Only Humayoon and the brigadier were to stay behind; the commander needed their missile expertise when he eventually attacked the garrison. We said a hasty and sad good-bye. I had become fond of both men. I never saw either one again.

This time, because of the risk of reconnaissance planes, the commander split us up into small parties, which were less likely to raise any interest if seen from the air. I left with Amin Jhan, fifteen minutes after Hamid, Tor, and Omar. We were heading for Shah Alam Khiel, an hour's walk away across foothills with zero cover. Halfway there we spotted a gunship. Out in the open, my first inclination was to look for a ditch to throw myself into. Amin Jhan was less concerned. Shaking his head as if to say don't worry, he kept walking. I had no choice but to follow. Before we reached Shah Alam Khiel the shelling began again as the commander predicted, only this time it sounded closer and was accompanied by the deeper crump of bombing. We made the village just as the first of the afternoon's spotter planes came over. Amin Jhan guessed from the direction of the explosions that they were hitting Sangar. "It seems as if they're attacking all the villages we've stayed in," he said quietly, articulating aloud what each of us had been thinking. I wondered how long it would take for the bombing to catch up with us. It began to feel as if we were playing some deadly game of chicken. We sat in an empty, dirty room and waited for the rest of our group. The four *Mujahideen* took advantage of the time on their hands to pray. I sat off to one side so as not to come between them and Mecca. As Omar prostrated himself in prayer, a hand grenade fell out of one of the magazine pouches of the belt fastened across his chest and rolled across the floor. The men continued to pray, ignoring it. Weapons and prayer had been part of their lives for too long.

While they prayed, I timed the frequency with which the reconnaissance plane passed overhead. Like an angry bee, it buzzed over us every fifteen minutes, a pattern that seemed ominous. I worried about Wakil and the others. We had no idea where they were when the bombing started up again. Four hours later, as the light was fading, a small pickup arrived. After a hurried conference with the driver, Hamid told us we were going with them. Where was Wakil? I asked. "I don't know," replied Hamid, "but the commander wants to evacuate us." We climbed in and drove to yet another village. Wakil wasn't there, but the commander was, as was a large crowd of villagers, all of whom looked understandably tense. As I had observed so many times before, news traveled fast in this land with very little modern communication. And this region was too close to the Soviet command base for local inhabitants to bait the enemy too often, or too much. "Stay in the pickup," I was told in a manner that discouraged questions. An hour later, our van and the commander's left. We drove in the dark, bumping slowly over a rutted cart track. I had the distinct impression we were moving in a large circle. The commander finally said he was taking us to Wakil, and he wanted to make sure no one knew where we were going. A little while later, we drove up behind our jeep. Wakil was in a nearby house. For security reasons he'd taken a completely different route from the way we'd come. We moved out almost immediately and traveled throughout the night. We were heading to Zabul Province. A plane flew by shortly after midnight, and my heart skipped a beat, but the aircraft didn't appear to see us and kept going. We passed several farmers working in their fields by the light of small oil lamps. Because of the helicopter mugging attacks, they were too afraid to farm during the day. Twice we became lost and had to pound on doors in two villages for directions. The nocturnal pounding must have been terrifying for the residents because middle-of-the-night callers usually meant a visit from the KHAD.

It was after 4:00 A.M. when we pulled into a large, prosperous village. We parked under some trees, while the commander went to rouse one of his contacts. We were told to drive the jeep and pickup into what looked like a large adobe barn. It had garaged three trucks until a bombing attack destroyed them the previous year. Our vehicles were quickly covered with rags. Machakhan, our host who owned the building, indicated we should move quickly into his house, which he shared with his large extended family. He said he wasn't sure of the loyalty of all the villagers.

I was shivering from cold and lack of sleep. My health had nosedived again. The severe cramps had returned, signaling that my gastrointestinal bug was back with a vengeance. I was aware from the way my clothes fit that I had lost a lot of weight. Some kind of eye irritation, probably caused by the dust, also forced me to remove my right contact lens. Viewing the world through one lens caused a minor equilibrium problem. I felt miserable and wanted only to crawl into my sleeping bag and sleep for several days. But that was hard to do in a room with twenty *Mujahideen* all drinking tea and catching up on the local news. Then a man in his twenties came in and said something to Machakhan, and the mood in the room changed abruptly. A five-year-old boy, one of Machakhan's grandchildren, had just died two rooms from where we were sitting. Sick for seven days, he'd expired as we were arriving. That explained why the family had been awake when we drove up: they'd been tending the child. The boy had died of measles, a common childhood killer in Afghanistan since the war because children suffering from malnutrition lacked the strength to combat what were usually minor illnesses.

Wakil offered the *Mujahideen* to dig a grave for the child. Machakhan refused. "It isn't necessary; we have sufficient men. Pray with us; then you must sleep."

I asked Wakil whether it would be better if we moved to another house, whether we were intruding on the family at this time. "No, it is better that we stay; it wouldn't be right to leave now." But he cautioned us to be quiet; no loud talking or laughing.

Later that morning, Tor learned there was an epidemic in the village. "I went to fifty houses; everyone had at least one sick child," he said. "But it isn't measles; they're all suffering from diarrhea, malnutrition, and very high fevers. There's very little I can do. I just don't have the right medications." Tor became angry and then depressed. "But even if I had medicine, I could cure these children, and then bombs would kill them."

I spent the day curled up on a mattress in the corner of the room, feeling lousy but knowing my health problems were minor compared to those in the village. In the afternoon we heard sporadic bombing, and later we learned that helicopters had dropped twelve bombs on a village four kilometers from where we were. Then, just outside the village, they had killed the occupants of a pickup with incendiary bombs. The van was burned so badly that it was impossible to tell how many people had been traveling in it. A little later, a report came in that a second pickup truck, a favorite vehicle of *Mujahideen*, but also of farmers, had been fired at. It was obviously open season on pickups, and Wakil decided we would leave later that night. I groaned at the thought of another night spent on the road.

Just after sunset, Wakil said he was going to the village mosque to preach. "Is that wise?" I asked him. "We've already been told the loyalty of all the villagers isn't certain. There's a base close to here. It would only take someone a few minutes by motorbike to tip them off." I didn't understand why we'd been under virtual house arrest all day for security reasons, and now he was about to stand in a crowded mosque, announce who he was, and preach a sermon. "I will be talking about the importance of *Jihad*," he said, considering that explanation enough. "We will be gone by the time the forces can react. And if they do come, we will fight them. We know this terrain. We know where our strongholds are; they don't."

"And if they bring helicopters?"

"Look at the night. It's a very dark, windy, and dusty night. Helicopters don't like this kind of weather. And we are close to the mountains; that also makes it difficult for them in the dark." I hoped he was right. But it did seem to be tempting the fates. He was gone a long time, and I was relieved to see him return, but I was dreading the trip. Wakil wanted to drive back to Pakistan without stopping. "It's less dangerous if we drive straight through and don't stop," he said. The trip would take twenty-four hours, another jolting journey that was tough on healthy passengers. And by now, I was far from healthy. The burning fever I had developed left me alternatively bathed in sweat and trembling from cold. I felt about as weak as a baby. But I was in a vehicle, and that was better than walking or riding a donkey. And in the eyes of the *Mujahideen*, I was well off and there was no cause for complaint. "Are you sure we have to do the trip without stopping?" I all but whined. "No, we can stop," said Wakil impatiently. "But if we do, the chances are very good the crows will eat our flesh in the desert of Afghanistan."

We made it to the Pakistani border in twenty hours. It was a drive I would rather forget. Wakil pulled into a small camp of refugees who would cross the border in the morning. I had to be helped from the jeep. I passed out in a tent, and because of my condition, Wakil decided we should stay overnight. I vaguely remembered his telling me to change into the *chadori* for the drive back to Peshawar. The *chadori* was caked in dust, having been stuffed under a seat in the jeep since we'd left Pakistan. But I was beyond complaining. In Peshawar, Tor helped me up to my room. I collapsed on the bed fully clothed and as filthy as the *chadori* I'd just taken off. Tor covered me and left. Wakil returned a little later with orange squash and some two-week-old newspapers. "We can take you to the hospital tonight, if you like." "No, no," I replied, "tomorrow."

After he'd left, I idly picked up the English language *Muslim* and began to skim it. As sick as I felt, having been out of touch for nearly a month, the journalist in me craved information. At the bottom of page six was a headline that made my skin crawl: SOVIET COPTERS ATTACK NEWSMEN. The story went on to read, "A U.S. photographer traveling with a reporter killed in Afghanistan has reported that the attack was carried out by four Soviet helicopters." The Soviet ambassador's threat at the time of Abouchar's arrest had finally been made good. Charles Thornton, a fifty-year-old reporter for the *Arizona Republic*, had become the first American to die in Afghanistan. A chill hit me as I read the story dated October 6, and I couldn't tell whether it was fever-generated or whether it was the awareness that Charles and I had been doing the same job at pretty much the same time. The only difference was, his luck ran out, mine held.

Migratory Genocide

had never met Charles Thornton, but I did know the photographer, Peter Schlueter, twenty-nine, who had been traveling with him. Peter and I had met in January when I had been in Phoenix, Arizona, lecturing on Afghanistan. I also had discussed the war on a local television program, and it was after that the *Arizona Republic* sent a reporter with a photographer to interview me. Peter had been the photographer. When the journalist left, he stayed on and told me he wanted to cover the war in Afghanistan and asked how I had gone about setting up such an assignment. I explained and shared some of my contacts with him. Then in August in Peshawar, shortly before I was expelled from Pakistan, Peter had learned I was in town, and we had spoken briefly on the phone. I had asked him whether he needed any help or introductions. He told me he didn't, that their program was set. I knew he and Charles were accompanying an

American doctor and male nurse who wanted to establish a clinic in Afghanistan. The medical team and *Republic* staffers had chosen not to travel with any of the established *Mujahideen* groups; instead they had elected to go with an independent commander. Indications were now strong that their truck had been ambushed, that the Soviets had been tipped off about their presence.

Thornton's group was on its way back to Pakistan about forty miles from the border in Kandahar Province on the night of September 19, when four Mi-8 helicopters landed in front of their truck and troops started firing. Charles, a father of two teenage boys, died in the first burst of bullets, after being shot in the head and chest. Peter dived out of the truck with tracer fire bursting all around him and crawled into a nearby ravine. His only injury was a twisted knee incurred after falling down the side of the ravine. But news of what had happened only reached Pakistan in October because Peter took two weeks to get out of Afghanistan. By the time I learned about it, he had already been flown back to the States.

When a correspondent covering a war dies under fire it sets off an eerie chain reaction within the rest of the press corps. Suddenly, their invincibility is replaced with something close to superstition. Instead of believing that a colleague's death is like lightning—which may strike again in the same place, but is unlikely to do so immediately—they begin to see it as an omen that another one will shortly follow. I had seen it in El Salvador; now I was experiencing it myself. Such emotions have little logic, of course, because the risk of death or injury is present the entire time a journalist is in a war zone. But reporters couldn't function if they dwelt on that, and so they don't, until something happens to one of their number that forces them to do so.

In bed with knees drawn up against severe stomach pains and fighting constant nausea even though I hadn't eaten for days, I battled with my demons. I was due to make one last trip inside Afghanistan, and I kept remembering the sign tacked up on the foreign press center wall in San Salvador, which began, NO STORY IS WORTH YOUR LIFE. I believed it then, and I believed it now, but finally I also convinced myself that it wouldn't happen to me.

When Wakil came to see how I was feeling the following day, I told him I would still be going to Kunar with him, as long as I could shake my bug. The mountainous province of Kunar is just below the Wakhan Corridor, a narrow finger of Afghanistan that extends to China and was depopulated and then annexed by Russia at the beginning of the war. Kunar had taken a severe beating by the Soviets partly because it was one of the major weapon routes into Afghanistan for the *Mujahideen*, partly because of its proximity to this strategic region. The Soviet Union has always been very nervous about its large eastern neighbor. According to Arkady Schevchenko, this nervousness was a contributing factor to the invasion, a fear that internal changes in Afghanistan would cause increased Chinese influence there. "Moscow was concerned about the growing strength of the Chinese and the security of their own border," he said.

"If you are planning to go to Kunar, you'd better see a doctor today," said Wakil. We waited until after dark, since I didn't want to run into Pakistan's Special Branch, and Tor drove me to see Dr. Abdul Rassoul of the Union of Afghan Mujahideen Doctors. Rassoul, the cardiologist who had just become engaged to a woman he had never seen when I had first met him, had been Tor's teacher during his year-long paramedic course. Each man had a great deal of respect for the other's capabilities, and they were good friends. "Tor would have made a very good surgeon," said Rassoul, "if his education hadn't been interrupted. He has a natural talent and a first-rate one for medicine." A few lab tests later and Rassoul confirmed what Tor had suspected. I had amoebic dysentery, which can be fatal if untreated, is damn uncomfortable, but is also curable with modern drugs. I had probably contracted it from the water I'd drunk in Jalalabad, said Rassoul as he handed me a prescription. I also had a corneal ulcer in my right eye caused by dust under the contact lens. This meant I could wear only one lens, not an ideal way to view the world.

The next couple of days were the only time I didn't resent my informal house arrest in Peshawar. I was too weak to do anything but rest. Because Afghans feel that to leave anyone alone is the height of bad manners, Wakil, who always put in long days at headquarters whenever he was in Peshawar, deployed Hamid or Tor to sit with me. Most of the time my companion was Tor, who in between watching me nap wrote or recited Persian poetry for me and then painstakingly translated it into fractured English. If I had the energy, he gave me Dari lessons, but my linguistics skills were considerably less than his, and he often laughed uproariously at my excruciating accent. He also told me a lot of stories about his childhood. He talked about his older brother, twenty-three-year-old Gul Agha, who had been bedridden in recent years because of kidney disease, and of his seventeen-year-old twin brothers, Sattar and Hakim, one of whom took over the high school boxing champion title that was Tor's until he joined the Resistance. He particularly missed Mahnaz, his thirteen-year-old sister, who hero-worshipped him long before he had become a freedom fighter. But it was a photograph of his mother and youngest brother Baryali, age seven, that he carried with him. "Baryali is like my twin; he looks just like me and has the same personality," said Tor. "The last time I saw him, the last time I saw any of them, was the night I left to join the *Jihad*. I took with me the clothes I was wearing, and ten thousand afghanis [eighty-three dollars] my mother gave to me. I said goodbye and I never saw or heard from them again." Tor stopped talking, looked down at his hands, and began to crack his knuckles loudly and methodically. The cracking signaled as efficiently as Morse code that he didn't want to talk about his family any more.

The two days I stayed in bed I was aware of a great deal of activity on the floor below. Each afternoon, dozens of turbaned commanders arrived for lengthy meetings. Peeking out of the window as they arrived and left, I felt like a kid who peers through the bannisters at the party below. Confined to the second floor, behind closed-curtain windows, and unable to go out, I began to feel more and more as if I were living in *purdah*.

Although I thought I was being discreet as I watched the outside world through a chink in the curtains, someone was obviously aware that my curiosity was getting the better of me. When the *Mujahideen* finally left on the evening of the second day, and I went downstairs to sit for an hour in the high-walled garden, I found a hand-printed note in Dari and English tacked to the office door: NO ADMITTANCE. That was assured anyway by the the hefty-looking padlock affixed to the door. Later I learned the meetings were joint military planning sessions attended by commanders from several of the *Mujahideen* parties. The door was locked because maps outlining the following month's offensives in Khost were plastered all over the walls.

We left for Kunar the following morning. Although the two days in bed had helped, I still felt a long way from being well. And when the grime had been washed off, I looked it, too. For the first time, I was glad to don the *chadori*. Once it was on, no one could see how pale and drawn I was. The route north took us through Swat, a scenic part of Pakistan that reminded me of the foothills of the Swiss Alps. As the road wound higher, the temperature turned cooler. The valleys we passed were verdant and fertile, and even the mountain slopes were a lush green, a refreshing change from the usual parched countryside. Late in the afternoon, we reached a small village, just inside Kunar, where we were to spend the night. Commander Malik Azdarai came out to greet us and hurry us into the walled compound of his home before any curious eyes noted our presence. A tall man with a handlebar mustache and intelligent eyes, he organized tea with the speedy efficiency that marked everything he did. As we were drinking it, he produced an enormous logbook and handed it to Wakil. It contained the biographies of all his men, including their special skills, their performance under fire, the weapons they had been issued, and the quantity of ammunition they had at any one time. The log also recorded every operation his men had been on, the number of "martyrs" his force had suffered, plus an account of enemy casualties. It was an up-to-the-minute analysis of the *Mujahideen* strength in that area and something the Soviets would have found very interesting reading.

The logbook that Wakil said he'd never seen any other commander undertake was kept so meticulously I expected to find that Azdarai had been a businessman before the war, but he'd been a farmer, no doubt a successful one. But perhaps he had to be, as he had two wives and seventeen children to support. And it was because of his older wife, forty-five-year-old Shirina, that the commander, despite his own excellent reputation, was best known. In a province known as the "abode of warriors," Shirina had demonstrated that women, even those who live behind the veil, can be worthy of that title. In their own village, Parnosona, deep inside Kunar, the inhabitants had been surprised by a Soviet attack one morning before sunrise. "They landed paratroops around the village and circled us with helicopters and planes," said the commander. "I had sixty men, armed only with AK-47s and 303s. At first, we were lucky: the Soviets killed a lot of their own men with their bombing. But soon we were fighting hand to hand. We were heavily outnumbered, and it looked very bad for us. Suddenly my men realized my wife was fighting with them, and it gave them courage." It also encouraged the other women to join her, even though most were armed with only daggers or sickles. Using a 303 Enfield, Shirina killed four Soviet soldiers before the villagers were forced to retreat. The women who had nothing with which to fight threw themselves into the river and drowned rather than be raped and tortured. The villagers abandoned Parnosona after that attack.

We left the next morning before it was light. There were thirty of us, including the commander, in two vehicles, our jeep and a pickup. The drive through the snow-capped mountains was spectacular: the air was brisk, the slopes covered with pink heather. Here and there were small clusters of conifers. A month later, the track we were winding ever upward on would be under three feet of snow. The occasional houses clinging to the edges of the inclines that we passed had their flat roofs covered with corncobs drying out for winter consumption, and providing easy feasts for the families' chickens. At the top of one peak we stopped for a light breakfast of *nan* and walnuts. Once again, I couldn't eat. The sight and smell of food had nauseated me for three weeks, and the night before in the village I had discreetly covered my nose with my hand during the evening meal so that the odor of boiled goat wouldn't make me vomit. From the way my clothes now fit me, I estimated I had lost between fifteen and twenty pounds since I had first become sick. The only food, strangely enough, that I seemed able to eat was grapes, and they were hard to come by. Wakil told me that in Afghanistan, invalids were often put on four-day grape diets to "purify the system."

On the long drive, I noticed that Tor only had two magazines with him for his AK-47 instead of the standard minimum of four. And of those two, one had only five bullets although it should have contained thirty, and the other was more than half-empty. And he was carrying no spare ammunition. I surprised myself by chewing him out for his oversight, if that is what it was. "What's the matter with you; are you crazy?" I asked him angrily. "Are you planning on throwing the empty gun at the enemy? Or do you want to die?" Tor turned the full force of his Puckish grin and charm on me. "No problem, Mommy, no problem," he said dismissingly. The other men sitting nearby watched the interaction with curiosity without understanding what was said. "Tor, sometimes I think I value your life more than you do," I said, fighting down a desire to shake him. "It's too late now," said Hamid quietly. "Somebody will have to share with him."

At midday, the vehicles came to a halt. Our route was now too steep for anything but walking. The snow-crested Hindu Kush—Killer of Hindus—mountain range, which rises to twenty-four thousand feet, soared up ahead of us, lofty despite the fact that we were nearly fifteen thousand feet up ourselves. To the south, the peak of Spin Ghar—White Mountain—could just be seen in the bordering province of Jalalabad. "Our summer house was at the foot of that mountain," said Wakil nostalgically, chewing on a piece of stale *nan*. "I miss that place so much, the times when our family were all together. The last time I was there, I was a boy."

While the vehicles were driven away from the village to be hidden in the woods, I was shown into a one-room stone house to change, and my women's clothes were stowed in a corner until we returned. Dressed as a man again, I was relieved to be able to put on my parka. Despite the brilliant blue of the sky, the temperature was cool, and I had been chilled under the silk *chadori*. Wakil pointed out our route for the day. I grimaced as he indicated the three peaks we had to cross. He laughed as he saw my face. "Kunar is a difficult province; it's all mountains," he said. "But we're kind to you; the beginning is downhill." He was right: a thousand-foot steep climb down. As we picked our way down the dried mud cliff, I was glad to see that all the *Mujahideen* were sweating as freely as I was. The sharp descent was also hell on my damaged toenails, but they were the least of my problems, I thought, as I stared up at the first of the mountains we had to cross. It rose ahead of us as steep as the cliff we were climbing down and considerably higher. Crossing the valley floor, I found myself surprisingly short of breath despite the flat terrain and after thirty minutes was forced to stop at a small village. The rough stone and timber houses were large enough to shelter families and their animals in the harsh winter months. Leaning against a wooden trough that channeled a mountain stream through the village, I put my breathlessness down to my general state of health but was surprised at how long I took to stop panting. We began to climb, and I soon found myself unable to keep up. Wakil and the commander dropped back to me. "Go at your own speed," said Wakil, taking in my bright red face and obvious distress. "We won't make our destination tonight, but I'll send some of the men on ahead and explain." "I don't understand it," I told him. "The slightest exertion is leaving me breathless, and I feel dizzy, light-headed, and have a pounding headache." We continued on up, with my wheezing alongside him in a manner that was distressingly reminiscent of my childhood asthma attacks. Don't look up, I told myself; just keep putting one foot in front of the other.

We passed four *Mujahideen* coming down carrying a man on a stretcher hand-fashioned from branches and blankets. The man's face was covered with a quilt and I assumed he was dead, but the stretcher-bearers told us he was injured. Victim of a helicopter gunship attack in the region that was our destination, he had three bullets in his left leg and one in his left side that had smashed his ribs. He was considered lucky, the bullet in his chest apparently missed his lungs, avoiding a wound that would probably have been fatal without immediate medical attention. They'd been walking for four days, and it would be another three before the injured man reached a hospital in Peshawar. They lurched on down the mountain, every step no doubt agony for the man they were carrying. My own difficulties seemed insignificant by comparison, and I started off with renewed determination. Unfortunately, the spirit may have been willing, but the flesh was definitely not up to the task that day. All too soon I was gasping for breath again. Then, looking at my hands that were now swollen to almost twice their size from water retention, I finally realized what my problem was. "I think I may be suffering from altitude sickness," I told Wakil. Wakil looked at me quizzically; like most Afghans raised in the mountains, he wasn't familiar with the concept. I tried to explain that my body was used to functioning on a higher concentration of oxygen than was available at that altitude, and that before I could climb any more mountains I needed to take a day or two to acclimatize. "After that, I should be fine," I said. Wakil looked doubtful but agreed to split the party. Half the men would go forward—the RPG-7s they were carrying were needed ahead—and half would stay with me. Wakil explained that fifteen men were the minimum security force he felt happy with in that area. The commander returned with us to introduce us to the village where we would stay.

The village was in a glorious location, in a natural bowl surrounded on all sides by mountains. In the north, one peak gave way to another peak, and to another, in serried rows as far as the eye could see. The community was spread out, each house standing on several acres of vegetable garden. Because there was no flat ground, all farming was done in a series of steps. Once again, every roof was covered with drying corn for the winter. It was a placid scene, making it hard to believe that the village had come under gunship attack eight days before. Two *Mujahideen* had died in the bombing, and several children had received shrapnel wounds. Now, however, *charpoys* were dragged out of houses and grouped on a flat roof for us to rest and catch the last of the day's sun, which gave more visual comfort than physical as the temperature had been close to freezing since 3:00 P.M. The *Mujahideen* peeled off ammunition belts and tossed them on one of the beds along with their Kalashnikovs. I flopped thankfully onto one of the free *charpoys*, wrapped myself in quilts, and watched the sun sink behind the mountains. Small boys joined the village elders as they exchanged news with the *Mujahideen*. About an hour later, I was wakened from a seminap by angry shouting. The *Mujahideen* had been moving their weapons inside the house for the night, when Omar had discovered that two of his full magazines were missing. Three young boys who had been hanging around all afternoon were suspected of stealing them. They denied it vigorously.

"Why would they bother?" I asked Wakil. "Aren't their fathers supplied with ammunition by Commander Azdarai?" "A loaded AK-47 magazine is worth six hundred rupees [forty U.S. dollars] in the bazaars in Pakistan; that's a lot of money here," he replied. The shouting became increasingly heated, with the villagers, outraged that their guests should have had something stolen, joining the commander in berating the boys. The three skinny youths, ages fourteen, ten, and seven, continued to declaim their innocence. The ten-year-old, Ahmad, shook his head and laughed in a manner small boys have always employed when trying to convince adults they aren't guilty of some infraction and are still hoping that winsomeness will win the day. It was an error of judgment. The commander and a villager grabbed his arms and marched him into the house, slapping him as they went. We could hear his voice rising shrilly: "I didn't do it; I didn't; you can ask my friends."

Restraining the fourteen-year-old, the men turned to the

youngest boy. "Unless the magazines are returned, the military committee will hang this *Mujahid* for losing his ammunition," they told him, pointing to Omar, who now looked as uncomfortable as the boys. The child burst into tears. "But it isn't fair," he said between gulps. "It's not his fault." The men continued to lambaste the boys, in an effort to browbeat an admission out of them. The teenager, Abdullah, was less easily cowed: "I'm not guilty; I didn't steal them." A hand smashed across his face. "The other boy is guilty," he glowered sullenly. Ahmad's weepy protestations could still be heard from inside the house. He was dragged back outside, trying to jerk his head out of cuffing range. An elderly man with a white beard who was obviously a village elder joined the fray. Without raising his voice, he said something that made the entire group fall silent. I asked Wakil to translate it for me, but he refused. I pressed him to tell me. He looked at me irritated and then replied coldly, "What he said was if they have stolen the ammunition, they must be shot."

"You've got to be joking!" His face assured me he was not.

The commander addressed the crowd. "To steal such things is the work of the enemy. We use these weapons to fight the Soviets. Whoever steals our means to do this are helping the Soviets. They are no better than spies, and like spies, they must be shot." The group agreed. The boys froze. I felt a wave of nausea hit me that had nothing to do with my dysentery.

"For God's sake, Wakil, they are children!"

"Remember Niaem? He was a child, too. Do you know how many *Mujahideen* lives he cost? He was lucky he was caught by a party who knew about Russian indoctrination. Other groups would have shot him on the spot."

I looked around and realized word of what was happening had obviously spread throughout the village. Small knots of adults had downed their farming tools and were silently watching the proceedings. On a nearby ridge, veiled women stared down at us.

Panic in his voice, Ahmad, his face still streaked from tears, suddenly burst out, "I didn't steal anything, but we have a magazine at our house; I will give it you." Everyone began talking at once. It was obvious that the boy's offer was seen as an admission of guilt. The villagers began calling for the death sentence again.

"Wakil, surely you can intervene. . . " I asked.

"If you kill such a child, thousands more will learn about it. Such stealing will not be repeated."

Ahmad was marched away to his home at the top of the ridge. His father was away fighting; the veiled women watching us were obviously his relatives.

"The magazine, when he brings it, will tell us whether it was stolen," said the commander.

I turned to Wakil. "Do they have serial numbers on them? Do you keep a record of them? Is there a way of telling?"

"No, they are not numbered. But I can tell if they are similar, or if they are the same age."

"It doesn't seem a very accurate method . . ."

The men returned, still dragging the boy, and handed Wakil the magazine. He turned it over in his hand, inspected it closely, and then compared it to the remaining magazines in Omar's ammunition belt. The commander repeated the same action. The tension was palpable. A more prudent person would have stayed silent. I wasn't prudent. "Is it one of Omar's?" I asked. I expected to be snapped at. But the harsh expression on Wakil's face disappeared, and he suddenly looked as young as his age again. "I don't know," he said simply. "I'm not sure." The element of doubt did not impress the other villagers. The magazine shouldn't have been in his home, they insisted. If it weren't stolen, why was it there? The commander told them he would make a decision in the morning. The boys were sent home.

□

Wakil looked at me; he seemed tired. "Yes, I will try to intervene. The parents must be told to punish the boy. But if he has done something like this before, it may not be possible to stop the men. In war, justice is harsh." He turned to Omar, who, despite his towering height, appeared almost as small as Ahmad. "Give me your gun," he ordered. Omar flushed and fetched the Kalashnikov. "If you can't keep your ammunition, you don't need a gun." He handed it to the driver of the jeep. "Here, it's yours." The other *Mujahideen* looked embarrassed. In a Resistance that is chronically underarmed, in which men wait for several years for a machine gun, to strip Omar of his gun was effectively to emasculate him. His face, and those of the other *Mujahideen,* registered the harshness of the punishment. A subdued crowd drifted into the stone house to sleep. And, for once, there was little conversation.

Despite the bitter cold, I stayed outside with Wakil. The star-filled sky seemed close enough to touch. He stared off into the distance, the tenseness of the way he held himself suggesting that this was not a life he had planned for himself nor would have wanted for the three boys who had just been harangued for the last two hours. Without looking at me, he intoned as if in answer to my unasked question, "Omar will get his gun back eventually but not until he has had at least two trips inside. He doesn't know that, of course, and I won't tell him." We walked silently back into the stone house together, picking our way over the sleeping forms of *Mujahideen* huddled under quilts. The freezing temperature, the continual barking of the village dogs, and the rats scrabbling in a large pile of dried corncobs intended for winter fuel that were stacked in the corner of the room where we were spending the night all conspired to make sleep difficult. Shortly after 2:00 A.M. I was wakened by intense stomach pains. I threw on my parka and, shivering, staggered outside. A wave of pain hit me that made me sit down. It began to radiate, and my hands went numb. I doubled over whimpering. The attack subsided long enough for me to catch my breath, and then another wave hit me. The pain was so severe that I began to wonder whether it really were my stomach or whether I were having a heart attack. For the next forty-five minutes, I suffered repeated intense attacks. Finally, they subsided. I vomited violently and was left with barely enough energy to crawl back into bed, where I lay shivering and exhausted. Two hours later, before it was even light, we had visitors. An old man carrying a silk-wrapped Koran and a boy of about eighteen arrived to see the commander. Ahmad's grandfather and cousin, they had come to plead his case. "For the sake of this book, forgive the children. Don't shoot them," beseeched the old man. "We were guests here, at home here," said the commander. "I recruit my *Mujahideen* from this village; this is my territory. If something like this can happen in your village . . ." Then he changed his tone and became avuncular: "Maybe you noticed how effective a few disciplinary actions are. A few slaps on his face, a few slaps on his arse, and he revealed where the magazine was."

Ahmad's grandfather, his ancient turban looking as old as he was, continued to hold the Koran in front of the commander. "We know he did wrong; forgive him this time on this Holy Book. We guarantee there won't be a next time. If there is, we will bring up his past, and no mercy will be given." The commander was silent for a few minutes, while the rest of us watched from our *charpoys* in the gloomy light. Finally, he spoke. "The boy must be punished. The first penalty is he must live away from the village for one month. Another village will teach him discipline. Then his parents must be fined; twenty thousand afghanis should make them teach their son not to steal." The old man nodded his head: the decision seemed just to him, even though the fine represented two years' income for these mountain folk. He kissed the commander's hand, thanked him profusely, and, muttering at his companion, hurried away. I followed them out just as two MIGs flew overhead. While their trail of vapor still hung in the sky, they flew back again. After morning prayers, Wakil commented on my pallor and I told him what had happened during the night. "I think we should turn back," he said. "I don't think you will have the strength to go on. If we do, we may end up carrying you out." Still feeling weak, I didn't argue.

☐

On the outskirts of Peshawar, Wakil turned off the main road into the city. The jeep bounced over the unpaved track and came to a halt underneath a railroad viaduct at the edge of a foul-smelling wasteland. "I noticed refugees arriving here recently; I want to see what they need." A quarter of a mile away, on what resembled a pebbled beach, several hundred Afghans had settled. As we drew closer, it became apparent that what had first looked like small, misshapen tents were crude shelters made of sacking, ancient horse blankets, even old clothes. The refugees who came out to greet us, mostly women and children, had recently arrived from Kunduz, a northern province just below the Soviet border. It had taken them a month to walk there. They had arrived twenty days before. They were excited by my arrival, assuming I was a relief worker, the first they would have seen. The women's faces dropped when it was explained that I was a journalist. "Why isn't anyone helping us?" asked Nikbakhta, a forty-year-old mother of five, who tugged at my clothes insistently to get my attention in the crowd that surged around us. "We have nothing, no food, no medicines. Look, this is what we are eating." She pointed to some rock-hard *nan* covered with green mold that was stored on top of one of the shelters under a piece of plastic. She had placed it there two days ago when a heavy rainstorm had caused the nearby canal—which looked like an open sewer and which they were forced to use for drinking water—to overflow its banks. Their camp had been flooded to a depth of twenty inches, accounting for the stench in the area. "Even the graves were washed away," she said, pointing to a nearby burial ground where they had buried their children who were too weakened by the journey to survive the conditions they met in Pakistan.

Recently widowed, Nikbakhta said they had left their village after a bombing attack that killed eighty. She stood four feet, ten inches, her matted hair framing a nutbrown face that was haggard, her cheeks hollow. She looked frail and old, yet her appearance belied her strength. "It was a difficult journey without our men, but we had to come here"—she paused—". . . I didn't know it was going to be like this."

As we were talking, I became aware of Hamid, squatting on the ground holding a skinny boy I guessed to be about nine, who was sobbing so heavily the front of Hamid's tunic was wet. Hamid rocked him back and forth in an effort to calm him. "What's wrong?" I asked. "I asked him where his father was," replied Hamid. "He told me he was dead, that the Russians came to their village during Ramadan. His father was working in the fields, and they captured him. . . ." The small boy looked up, his eyes red from weeping. "They drove the tank over him," he screamed at me. "I saw it, I saw them do it. I was standing there. They drove their tank over my father. Why? Why did they do that?" The strident sound of his own voice seemed to make his outburst subside. He hiccuped twice and wiped his nose on his sleeve. He didn't expect an answer.

"You must be the father of your family now," Hamid told the child, Sarihullah, who was in fact twelve years old. Sarihullah looked at him. Pointing to Nikbakhta, the boy said, "My mother did not look old like that in Afghanistan. It happened when she came out of our house and saw my father's body on the ground."

Wakil, who had been assessing the needs of the refugees, joined us. "The problem with these people is they are not registered as refugees," he said, shaking his head at the conditions there. "Nor will they be while they stay here. The Pakistani government stopped registering refugees in Peshawar in 1982. There are too many Afghans here. They want them to settle in other areas away from the border, but the Afghans want to stay as close to their homeland as possible."

"So what will happen to these people?" "If they are lucky, one of the camps will eventually register them. If not, they will have to move, or they will have to share the rations of registered refugees. I can bring them basic supplies—tents, quilts, food—but we don't have enough to do it on a regular basis." Tor interrupted. "If you think this is bad, I will show you Munda camp tomorrow. It's much worse than here, and much bigger. Some of the people in Munda have been there a year, and they still aren't registered."

Munda is an hour's drive from Peshawar. To call it a refugee camp is a misnomer; it is a long way from being a place of refuge. In Munda, the six hundred families who had fled the Laghman massacres found they had exchanged one hell for another. Munda is a rag city, whose entrance is marked by a large cemetery, a depressing but apt symbol for the camp. As we parked the van in the blistering sun, all I could see was row after row of meager shelters made from the few remaining clothes these refugees had managed to bring with them. They gave no respite at all from the searing heat or the clouds of flies. Munda was also a silent camp: no children ran up to check out visitors or played in the dust. In the 128-degree heat, no one moved. As I walked between the rows of the pathetic patchwork hovels, children lay pale and still on the ground. Few of these families even had bedrolls. Some of the youngsters stared at me hollow-eyed, too listless to turn their heads and watch my progress or flap away the flies that covered their faces. Their distended stomachs and stick limbs told of their hunger. "The heat is killing our children," one man told me. "We've buried twelve in our section of the camp in the last couple of weeks. One died yesterday from dehydration; he was six months old. Others are dying from diarrhea and vomiting. Most of them have open sores."

Conditions such as these have given the Afghans in the Paki-

stani camps the second highest infant mortality rate in the world
—only Liberia's general population's is higher. According to a
study conducted by the federal Centers for Disease Control in
Atlanta, 156 Afghan refugee children die in every 1,000 in the first
year of life, and an additional 225 per 1,000 will die in the following four years. These tragic figures mean that one Afghan child
out of every three in a Pakistani refugee camp will not reach the
age of five, an appalling statistic in what is usually considered a
controlled environment where medical care is supposed to be
available. But it isn't just children who suffer in the camps: birth-
related deaths among Afghan refugee mothers are the world's
highest. The study, sponsored by the UNHCR, concluded that the
high death rates could be prevented by proper medical care. The
four main causes of death among Afghan refugee children, for
example, are diarrhea, easily avoided with inexpensive rehydration salts; malaria; measles; and tetanus, also all preventable.

The 342 Afghan refugee camps in Pakistan are mostly built
on wasteland that local people have never been able to farm. The
early arrivals were housed in mud houses, but the Pakistan authorities have since forbidden the construction of them "because
it gives the impression the refugees are here to stay." Most Afghans are now housed in tents that are sweltering in Pakistan's
summers and freezing in the winters when the temperatures drop
below zero. Registered refugees are supposed to receive monthly
rations of fifteen kilograms of wheat, 900 grams of edible oil, nine
hundred grams of dried milk, six hundred grams of sugar, and
thirty grams of tea. Frequently these supplies are interrupted or
rations are incomplete. In theory, a cash allowance of fifty rupees
(U.S. $3.30) is also supplied per refugee per month to purchase
vegetables or some kind of protein. In reality, it is rarely received.
Each family is also allotted twenty liters of kerosene per month
for cooking, but like food rations, supplies are often disrupted.
When they are, the refugees have to cook with wood, which is also
in short supply. Young children must often walk five to six miles
in search of enough twigs to cook the one meal a day on which
most families exist. And water, too, is a major problem, particularly in the summer, when the camps' shallow wells often run dry.
The water allocation is supposed to be twenty liters per person,
but it is rarely that because there is a shortage of water tankers

to distribute it. And twenty liters for all your needs—drinking, cooking, bathing, and laundering—is soon put into perspective when one realizes that fifteen liters of water is expended every time an American toilet flushes.

With conditions such as these it isn't surprising that health problems and sickness in the camps are severe. Cholera and typhoid outbreaks occur occasionally. Currently in the camps tuberculosis is at a critical level: 30 percent of children and adults alike are infected with it. And young children also die from malnutrition. Chronic depression, too, is a major problem in the camps, where activities of any kind are few and far between, and where income-generating programs have been cancelled because of fund cutbacks.

Foreign relief agencies, such as the United States–based International Rescue Committee, the British Save the Children Fund, the Swedish Committee, the Saudi Red Crescent, and the international church group Inter-Aid, do what they can, but it is never enough. How can it be? Seven years after the invasion, half of the world's 10 million refugee population is Afghan, and three-quarters of them live in Pakistan. And daily the refugees continue to arrive in a forced exodus that has been described by Louis Dupree, America's leading Afghan scholar, as migratory genocide.

If the conditions are bad for registered refugees, for the unregistered new arrivals they are desperate. Hungry, ill, exhausted when they arrive after their arduous journey out of Afghanistan during which their caravan may well have been used for target practice by gunships and jets, they are uncomprehending when they find themselves faced with bureaucratic snafus and lengthy delays before they can receive assistance. Told that the area in which they have arrived is no longer permitting refugees to settle, too many simply do not have the energy to move on to new camps near the Punjab on the other side of the country. Some Afghan officials report delays in registration of up to eighteen months. In Munda, the families living in the rag city had been waiting two months. They had been told it would take another seven months to process them. And until they were registered, they would not receive food, tents, bedding, buckets for fetching water from the well, or even medical assistance. Once they had sold their meager possessions, they existed purely on the charity of other refugees who were willing to share their limited food rations.

As I wandered past one tattered lean-to, a newborn infant caught my eye. The child was lying on a small pile of dirty rags, his mother trying unsuccessfully to keep him cool by fanning him with her skirt. The baby's skin hung in shriveled folds from its tiny frame, an ominous sign of advanced dehydration. And the child was covered from head to toe with large, angry-looking pustules. The infant looked as if he weighed no more than three pounds. He was fifteen days old, his mother told me, and for the last week had had diarrhea and wasn't nursing properly. "Of course, he isn't properly fed," snorted Tor. "How can she feed her baby when she isn't getting enough to eat herself." The child's mother, Busjana, had five other children. She had walked from Afghanistan heavily pregnant and had given birth to the baby, Noorallah, five days after arriving. A survivor of the Laghman massacre, she was now watching the more insidious massacre of Munda. "Why haven't you taken your baby to the clinic that visits here?" I asked her. "I did, they said they couldn't treat my baby because I don't have a refugee card yet. They told me to keep him cool by sprinkling water on him; then they sent me away." She grew angry. "Sprinkle water on him! We don't have water to drink; how can we do this?" I turned to Tor, "If this baby doesn't get medical assistance soon, he will die." "Yes, many have," he said soberly.

"She must take him to a hospital. We will drive her to Peshawar."

"Unless you take the baby yourself, it is possible the hospital won't accept him."

"Fine, so I'll go," I said furiously, more than willing to become an "ugly American" and battle any hospital official. "Explain to the mother; let's get this kid out of here."

As we drove back to Peshawar, I thought of Kachaghari, the showplace refugee camp that Western officials interested in the "Afghan problem" are taken to see. Kachaghari is fifteen minutes' drive from the center of the city, Munda just an extra forty-five minutes farther out. In Kachaghari, there were neat rows of adobe homes, schools, a hospital, several income-generating programs, even driveable roads. In Munda, children were dying because of a lack of two dollar buckets for families to supply themselves with water, or because bureaucrats were slow in their paperwork. The politics of death are never very pretty, but as far as the Afghans are concerned, Western politicians and relief experts haven't had to see them in action.

We took the child to the large Khyber Hospital. Hamid knew one of the doctors in admissions, and Noorallah was admitted to the nursery and treated right away. He had a temperature of 104 degrees and was suffering from malnutrition and dehydration; the boils were attributed to a severe staphylococcus infection. The doctor said the child would recover with treatment, but that the sepsis from the boils would have killed such a young infant if he had been left untreated.

Later that evening, Hamid, Tor, and I were still angry about the conditions we'd found at Munda. Mild-mannered Hamid surprised me. "We've got to do something, tomorrow!" he demanded of Wakil over dinner. "No matter what it takes, we've got to get a truckload of food out there immediately. The conditions in that camp are criminal." Wakil promised to do his best. And by noontime the following day he had persuaded the Inter-Aid Committee to give him ten tons of wheat flour, five hundred kilograms of cooking oil, and twelve buckets. "There's no tea or sugar this time; they just don't have it," he said, as he arrived in the loaded truck to pick us up. The truck was mobbed when we returned to Munda. The hungry refugees were so desperate not to be overlooked that they made it difficult to unload the food. Once the supplies were given out, and the crowd began to disperse, it was possible to see a young boy sitting in a wheelchair who had been waiting patiently in the horde for Wakil to be free. It was Bangul, the twelve-year-old whom Wakil had brought back to Peshawar after both the boy's legs had been severed at the thigh by shrapnel. "See, I told you you weren't going to die. I said you were strong, didn't I?" Wakil teased him, when Bangul wheeled himself slowly over the uneven ground to the Resistance official. "And just as I told you that, and I was right, now I'm going to tell you, you don't have to stay in that chair; you can learn to walk on false legs."

"I tried, but it hurts."

"You didn't try enough. You can be walking next time I come to Munda, if you really want to. It will be much easier for you to get around out here."

At the end of the afternoon we all felt good to have done something to help the residents of Munda. But what happened when the flour and the oil we delivered ran out? Then what? I wondered.

"It's been particularly bad in the last few months," Mervyn Powell, a forty-eight-year-old program officer for the United Nations High Commissioner for Refugees in Pakistan, told me. "The major offensive in Paktia this summer meant twenty thousand refugees were unregistered, and the Pakistani registration process is rather cumbersome. Backlogs soon build up." Powell admitted that implementation of refugee programs is a problem in Pakistan. "We pay the government seven and a half million dollars for implementation and administration costs, but they won't even tell us how many people they employ. We believe it is between seven thousand and eight thousand people, but we aren't sure." Since donor countries don't like to donate to this fund—"implementation" has zero public-relations value back home—the United States is the main underwriter of this cost. But sadly, the money is not always well spent. "This may surprise you, but because of lack of proper implementation, we have never been able to spend all the funds allotted for the Afghan refugees. It's a crazy situation. In the North-West Frontier Province last year, 11 percent of our budget had to go unspent because the Pakistani authorities weren't implementing the programs properly. In Baluchistan, which has one-fifth of the refugees, the figure was tragically much higher—50 percent. We've had wheat spoil just because it sits in a depot too long before it is delivered to the camps. There are water shortages because drivers of the tankers frequently disappear for a few days." In 1983, after allegations of corruption, the Pakistan Commission for Afghan Refugees dismissed or suspended nine hundred employees (approximately 11 percent of the total staff) on charges of "theft, negligence and absenteeism," but obviously the problem has not gone away.

Powell pointed out also that there were emergency rations available for unregistered refugees, that the situation I had seen in Munda should not have occurred. "Pakistan's civil service doesn't have the exclusive rights to incompetence; it's present everywhere," he said. "However, there are problems here." Other relief officials also claim that a sizeable sum of the Afghan refugee funding is going to upgrade Pakistani villages and tribal areas.

In addition to the bureaucratic inefficiency or corruption, the Afghan refugees had just been hit with a major cutback in funding. "Unfortunately, for the Afghans, there are fashions in anguish, and Afghanistan is sadly not a fashionable tragedy right now," he explained. "They were eclipsed by Africa when the Ethiopian famine caught the media's imagination.

"Sudan, Ethiopia took 30 percent of our global funds of $360 million this year. So we've had to curtail our activities in other areas. The allotment for Afghan refugees was $57 million last year, one-sixth of our global funds. This year, that figure was slashed to $41 million. It's a financial nightmare. We received a cable saying that we had to cut all programs that did not pertain to 'sheer survival.' So, income-generating and self-help programs have had to go. Carpet weaving training centers for boys have been cut. We've had to defer the tuition of teachers." The last is particularly lamentable. There are 2 million children in the Afghan refugee camps and schools for only seventy-six thousand. A generation of children are growing up uneducated.

"On a more personal level," added Powell, "these budget cuts mean we can no longer supply cloth for clothes and shoes as we did until last year. And the twenty liter kerosene allotment per family is being cut in half. Kerosene is very expensive."

To be an unfashionable tragedy cost the Afghans dearly. "Maybe somebody at UNHCR's headquarters needs a lesson in arithmetic," one relief agency official told me. Afghans may make up 50 percent of the world's refugee population with the number growing daily, but only 12½ percent of UNHCR's funding was being spent on them.

But budget cuts were not the only new difficulties facing Afghans in Pakistan. As Powell put it, despite the cumbersome bureaucracy, "the host country, Pakistan, has shown a tremendous and remarkable tolerance in absorbing the world's largest group of refugees. However, because of the vast numbers involved, that hospitality is now beginning to wear thin at the edges." The absorption of a force of refugees equal to the population of a sizeable country has caused General Zia considerable loss of support among the Pakistanis. The Afghans' sheer numbers have disrupted local economies, and some Western diplomats fear they could endanger Pakistan's political stability by feeding internal and external threats. That the camps are often used as *Mujahideen* recruiting bases is, of course, well known to the Soviets, and the increasing number of jet bombing incursions inside Pakistan, with growing loss of Pakistani life, are attributed to this. There is concern that the camps will one day be attacked in the same manner; for the same reason, the Israelis bombed Palestinian camps inside Lebanon.

"The changes in Peshawar since 1980 are sizeable," a former Kabul University professor told me. "The huge influx of Afghans has put tremendous pressure on the Pakistani lower classes, where unemployment was already high. The refugees, unable to survive on the relief aid given them, are more and more forced to start their own businesses—tailors, vegetable stands—and undercut native prices. Rents in the city have soared—a three-room house that cost one thousand rupees in 1980, now costs three thousand rupees per month. Naturally, this sort of thing causes tension between the Afghans and the Pakistanis. But increasingly, there is concern that we may be here to stay, and it is being made clear our welcome is drying up."

The professor talked about the restrictions on the Afghans in Pakistan, who cannot own property and cannot vote. Single men cannot live in the city. "It is also difficult, even for the well-educated living outside the camps, to continue their education. The colleges don't want them. There are four Afghan students in Peshawar's medical college, which has a student body of five hundred. Each of those students, star pupils in Afghanistan, had to battle for several years to get admitted."

Afghans are advised not to complain publicly about the problems of refugees. Hassan Olasmal, editor of the *Mujahid Afghan Olas* newspaper, was arrested and jailed in July 1985 after publishing a series of articles that focused on corruption in the Pakistani bureaucracy and materials' not getting to the refugees. "He has not yet been charged with any crime, nor has he been permitted any visitors," said the professor. There are increasing reports also of Afghans' being harassed by police on the street, arrested, and held until family members pay bribes.

Hamid's younger brother, Shamsullah, age fifteen, who

along with another brother, Wahid, sixteen, had newly arrived from Afghanistan, fell foul of such treatment while I was there. He was still shaken and bruised from his beating when I saw him. A good-humored, energetic boy, he had been on his way to 6:00 P.M. prayers at the Mahabat Khan mosque in the Chowk Yadgar section of Peshawar when he was stopped by five police officers. "They asked me where I was going and I told them," he said. "They asked why I had been looking around me. I told them I hadn't. One hit me across the face and back with the butt of his rifle. They said I was a refugee and had no right to walk on the street at this time, which I knew wasn't true. One wanted to search my pockets. Before you do that, I told him, I want to see your hands. I was afraid they might try to plant hashish in my pockets."

Wahid and Omar were also on their way to the mosque but were one hundred yards behind Shamsullah when they saw what was happening. Omar tried to intervene, and the officers became angry. The same man who struck Shamsullah tried to smash his gun across Omar's chest, but Omar, considerably larger than the fifteen-year-old, grabbed the rifle and held it. "Then they all became furious and beat Omar very badly," said Shamsullah. "When he was on the ground, they grabbed him by the arms and legs and dragged him and me to the police station, which was about three hundred yards away. On the way there, they asked me for money. I told them I didn't have any. Then they locked us in the jail. Wahid saw what happened and ran to fetch Wakil. If he hadn't, we would probably still be there."

When Wakil arrived and introduced himself as a Resistance official and the boys' uncle, there were apologies all around and offers of tea. "I told them I didn't want their tea and asked them why they had picked on an innocent boy like that. I said that if the police continued with that kind of behavior, the day may well come when the Afghans retaliate.

"It's very sad. Shamsullah had just arrived in Pakistan; now he will see all police here as brutal and corrupt because of this one experience." But police harassment of the Afghans is a purely Afghan problem. Of far more concern to the Pakistani citizens are the growing incidents of the Afghan-Soviet war being played out in the streets of Peshawar. Explosives planted in Peshawar are killing and maiming Pakistanis two or three times a week now.

The Pakistani people have begun to grow weary of the "Afghan problem" that appears to have no end in sight, and they have also become disenchanted with President Zia's ever-growing dependency on U.S. economic and military support, financial aid he won in the first place because of his Afghan policies. Benazir Bhutto's return to Pakistan in early 1986 gave the country an alternative leader behind whom to rally. The thirty-two-year-old popular opposition leader whose father, Zulfikar ali Bhutto, was overthrown by Zia in 1977 and hanged two years later, is heir to her father's Pakistan People's Party. Suddenly there is talk of the first female leader of a modern Muslim country. Benazir is Leftist-leaning. And her brother, Shahnawaz, who died a slow and painful death after being poisoned in Cannes in July 1985, organized the Al-Zulfikar terrorist group to give armed resistance to Zia's military dictatorship. The organization was headquartered in Kabul and was supported by the regime as well as Libya's Qaddafi. It was Al-Zulfikar terrorists who hijacked the Pakistan International Airline plane from Lahore to Kabul and then on to Syria in 1981, thereby triggering mass arrests in Pakistan of Zia's political opponents and causing the president to pass restrictive martial laws. Although Shahnawaz had exchanged terrorism for jet-setting before he died, Pakistan still has many agitators who have relations with Moscow. In August 1985, fifteen Pakistanis, who were returning home from Kabul, were captured in Jalalabad equipped with brand-new Soviet AK-47s supplied to them in the Afghan capital for terrorist activities back in Pakistan.

Afghans naturally are concerned by Benazir Bhutto's ascending star. The PPP takes the position that Pakistan should not fight what they see as the United States' war against the Soviet Union in Afghanistan. They have long called for recognition of the Afghan Communist regime and acceptance of Afghanistan's being in the Soviet sphere of influence. And although the party is strongly opposed to the presence of Soviet troops in Afghanistan, they would also like to see covert aid to the *Mujahideen* ended. Another requirement of Benazir's party is that Afghan refugees leave Pakistan.

As Pakistan increasingly seems less of a refuge for the Afghans, many of them begin to think of third country resettlement. But unlike the acceptance of Indochinese refugees, few countries seem anxious to take the Afghans. In 1983, according to the

UNHCR, the United States resettled 1,692. Turkey took 381, France 115, Australia 65, Canada 49, West Germany 37, Italy 18, Switzerland 10, United Kingdom 7, Denmark 5, Sweden 4, New Zealand 3, and Austria and India 2, for a total of 2,390. This acceptance rate has not changed substantially since then, and is infinitesimal for 5 million refugees. And although the U.S. administration is sympathetic to the Afghan refugees' cause, the State Department's Bureau for Refugee Programs does not reflect that. The quota for refugees from the entire Near East Asian region, which includes Afghanistan as well as Iran, India, Bangladesh, Pakistan, and all Arab countries, totals a mere 6,000 a year. Curiously, the quota from Indochina, which has been as high as 165,000 a year and now stands at 45,500, has only been three-fifths filled since 1980. Many experts feel that even without increasing the number of refugees into the United States, the existing admission quotas should be adjusted to take into consideration the fact that one in two of the world's refugees today are Afghan.

In desperation, a few Afghans have traveled to the United States with false papers in an effort to apply for political asylum. Once in the States, they have found that the welcome mat for "huddled masses yearning to breathe free" does not apparently extend to them. Instead, they found themselves quickly incarcerated in the Immigration and Naturalization Service's holding center in Manhattan. The majority of these Afghans have been freedom fighters who fear for their safety in the uncertainty of Pakistan. An ever-burgeoning industry in Pakistan, for sums as high as U.S. four thousand dollars a head, has grown up to produce false passports and "safe passage" to the West. Ironically, some of the Afghans apprehended in New York were en route to Canada when their planes transited through JFK airport, and they were required to clear immigration there. The plight of these Afghans, some of whom had been imprisoned for fourteen months, came to light when they staged a hunger strike. Prior to this, six Afghans had been quietly deported from the United States in 1985. Three had been sent back to Pakistan, where they were arrested for illegal entry on arrival and imprisoned. Three others were "sent into orbit," shuttled around by airlines until a country agreed to take them in. Two of those sent into orbit were Roashan Amunallah, twenty-five, and his eighteen-year-old brother, Obeidy, from Kandahar. In Afghanistan, the two freedom fighters had been jailed, tortured, and nearly killed by the Communist regime for their political beliefs. Their older brother, a *Mujahideen* commander, had already been killed by the Soviets. Marked men, the brothers fled their homeland. In May 1984, they paid a Pakistani travel agent in Karachi five thousand dollars for Air Lanka tickets to Colombo, Sri Lanka, and a Korean Air Line flight to JFK. They were arrested on arrival and spent ten months in New York's immigration jail before going on a hunger strike, which led INS agents to begin referring to them as "troublemakers." On March 29, 1985, the "troublemakers" were placed on board a KAL flight to Seoul. Korean authorities didn't know what to do with them and put them on a KAL flight to Hong Kong. From Hong Kong they were shuttled to Taiwan and back to Hong Kong. From there they were returned to Seoul and on April 1 were flown to Colombo, but Sri Lankan authorities refused to permit them to enter. Instead, the brothers were flown to Saudi Arabia, which in turn sent the men back to Seoul. Korea had already made it very clear it didn't want the two Afghans and arranged to fly the brothers to Kabul via Japan and India. Returning the two freedom fighters to Kabul, of course, was a certain death sentence. The terrified brothers resisted so strenuously that the Koreans cancelled the flight and the Afghans lived in the transit lounge of the airport for ten days. They were finally allowed to enter West Germany and apply for political asylum.

"The tragedy with the Afghans jailed by INS is that in Pakistan they were turned away by U.S. authorities who would not permit them to file applications to come to the United States as refugees even though they had offers of sponsorship or employment," said Arthur Helton, of the Lawyers Committee for Human Rights in New York, who led the battle to free the Afghans pending their political asylum hearings. "Knowing that the U.S. administration supported the freedom fighters in Afghanistan, these people made their way to America, where, to their great astonishment, they were met with imprisonment." It was all the more surprising, therefore, to hear U.S. senators suggest the formation of an underground railroad to encourage Soviet soldiers fighting in Afghanistan to defect and apply for political asylum.

On January 10, 1986, the INS released thirty-three Afghans pending their hearings. "Exactly twenty-four hours later, however, another Afghan refugee arrived at JFK asking for political asylum," said Helton, "and he was immediately incarcerated in the INS jail. And so the whole process was begun all over again. By June of 1986 there were four more." Obviously, however, political asylum affects only a tiny handful of Afghans. The majority want only to return to their homes, but not until the Soviet presence has disappeared from Afghanistan.

At the end of 1985, the United Nations General Assembly voted an overwhelming 122 to 19 to adopt a resolution demanding immediate withdrawal of Soviet troops from Afghanistan.* It was the widest margin—only the Communist countries voted against it—of the now seven similar measures passed since the 1979 invasion. The latest UN vote demonstrated that third world opposition to the occupation, rather than fading with time, continues to gain momentum. This impetus is of major concern to the Soviet Union as it poses a barrier to normal Soviet relations with third world countries, as well as with China and the United States. And because of this, many Sovietologists were optimistic that the seventh round of negotiated peace settlement talks, conducted by UN Under Secretary General Diego Cordovez in the summer of 1986, would finally make headway. But once again, the talks broke down.

The "proximity talks," which first began in 1982, have Cordovez shuttling back and forth between two hotel suites housing the Pakistan and Afghanistan delegates, because Pakistan insists that direct talks would mean they recognize the Soviet-backed Afghan regime, something they refuse to do. Cordovez has attempted to draw up a framework for a political solution, which involves four "key instruments": troop withdrawal, noninterference and nonintervention (a cessation of U.S. and other aid channeled to the Afghan Resistance via Pakistan, even though the Soviets would continue to send aid to the government in Kabul), international guarantees to maintain Afghanistan's independence, and the return of refugees. Such an agreement hinges, however, on the Soviet demand that support to the Afghan Resistance be halted before the Russian troops withdraw, something that is unacceptable to Pakistan, and even more unacceptable to the United States. As Dr. Elie Krakowski, special assistant to the

*In November 1986, the UN vote was 122 to 20 in favor of a Soviet withdrawal.

assistant secretary of defense, says, "Moscow has always demanded the cessation of outside support to the Afghan Resistance precede any consideration of a Soviet troop withdrawal. The so far nonnegotiable nature of that demand, its 'unconditional surrender' character, by now should have been obvious to all. Moscow is in fact saying that the only way it will ever withdraw is when the Afghan Resistance has been eliminated. In other words, Moscow will remove its troops when there is no longer any reason for their being in Afghanistan. . . . The hints of withdrawal timetables are designed to undercut outside interest and support by encouraging the belief that increasing restraint by the outside world is the only way to a negotiated settlement."

In July 1986, in what was seen as a pre-summit move to influence public opinion abroad and growing antiwar sentiment at home, Gorbachev announced he would withdraw six thousand Soviet troops from Afghanistan. But outside the Soviet Union, the move was seen as a purely cosmetic one since three of the regiments to be pulled out were antiaircraft forces, which were not needed in Afghanistan in the first place as the *Mujahideen* do not possess aircraft. In the past also, when announcements of troop withdrawal from Afghanistan were made, it transpired that they were "routine rotation of troops." In one case, in 1982, six thousand troops were withdrawn, and were replaced shortly after by nine thousand new soldiers. Gorbachev's latest announcement was also seen as a move to placate the Chinese, who continue to call for Soviet withdrawal from Afghanistan, at a time when the Soviet leader is spending considerable time trying to improve Soviet-Chinese relations.

A major stumbling block in any negotiated peace discussion, of course, is the *Mujahideen*, who have never been invited to the negotiation table. "We have not been briefed on any of the talks," said Mohammad Gailani, the son of NIFA's leader, "and we will not negotiate with the puppet regime in Kabul. We will deal only with the Soviet Union. They are the ones who invaded our country. Our conditions for a peace settlement are very simple: a complete withdrawal of all Soviet troops and a government of our choosing.

"The Soviets talk about a one- to two-year withdrawal period. This is completely unacceptable to us. Withdrawal should take one to two days—that's how long it took them to come in."

Whenever another round of Afghan peace talks has begun,

however, the Soviets have launched a major offensive in Afghanistan to coincide with it. It happened in the summer of 1985, and again in the spring of 1986 when fifteen thousand troops began a fierce offensive a week before the talks opened. After intense bombardment of Paktia Province, Russian forces overran a key Resistance stronghold in Zhawar. The mile-long underground complex was a major training and storage site for the *Mujahideen*. Soviet newspapers claimed their troops killed two thousand freedom fighters and wounded four thousand in the operation. There was also a marked increase in Soviet arms shipments to Afghanistan at the same time. Moscow obviously concurred with Thomas Gouttierre of the Center for Afghanistan Studies at the University of Nebraska when he said, "The day the last Soviet soldier leaves Afghanistan will be the last day of the Afghan regime."

But while diplomats dicker, the Afghans, who many feel are caught in the crossfire between two superpowers, continue to die, and much of the world prefers not to notice. As I was getting ready to return to the United States, the Washington-based Committee for a Free Afghanistan contacted me and said they wanted to invite two young *Mujahideen* for a year-long nationwide lecture tour of American colleges. "If college students can hear what is happening in Afghanistan from young people their own age, maybe we will be able to raise public consciousness in America, to make Americans care," Mary Spencer, their administrative director, told me. I suggested Hamid and Tor, both because they had moving stories to tell and because they had both spent a quarter of their lives fighting a war. And as the Resistance chief of staff, Rahim Wardak, had told me earlier, "A protracted guerrilla war is tough on the guerrillas. They don't get weekends and vacations. War-weariness is very debilitating." And while he may not have agreed with me, Tor seemed to display symptoms of that, and I thought the break would be good for both of them.

With formal invitations to the States, visas for Hamid and Tor were speedily obtained, despite the fact that since both were displaced persons they obviously couldn't get passports; their only travel documents were papers issued by the Pakistani government, which confirmed that they were refugees.

Hamid and Tor were to fly to the States with me when I returned at the end of October. Used to moving at a moment's notice and with little or no idea of their destination, the two young guerrillas exhibited the same aplomb about their first foreign trip. The idea of a year-long lecture tour in a foreign language on the other side of the world perturbed them not at all. Hamid only wondered whether he'd like flying. Accompanying us on the trip would be Said Mohammad Raza, the deputy commander whose arm was missing four inches of bone, whom I had met in the Ebneseena Hospital shortly after my arrival in Peshawar. After I had told the Committee for a Free Afghanistan of the commander's constant pain and the possibility of Reza's arm being amputated, they had contacted the Borgess Medical Center in Kalamazoo, Michigan, who had agreed to perform a bone graft free of charge.

On my last day with the freedom fighters, I helped Hamid and Tor pack for their trip. I chuckled when I saw Hamid, true to form, trying to squeeze four bulky dictionaries into his suitcase, and no amount of persuading would convince him to leave any behind. As we were sorting clothes, his brothers, fifteen-year-old Shamsullah and sixteen-year-old Wahid, put aside the exercise books in which they were doing their homework and asked Hamid and Tor for their Kalashnikovs. To me, the two teenagers, sprawled on Wakil's *charpoy*, their favorite place to study, looked far too young even to be entrusted with guns. Only the day before Tor had been teasing Wahid about his minute inspection of his chin in a mirror—something he did every day in case the beard he longed for had suddenly sprouted overnight. As the two older *Mujahideen* agreed to turn over their machine guns, I realized Hamid's younger brothers were the same ages he and Tor had been when they had joined the Resistance. But it was still hard for me to accept that by the following month, Shamsullah and Wahid would have accompanied Wakil inside Afghanistan on their first operation.

Later that afternoon, Hamid and Tor left the house to go on a round of good-byes. I remained with Wakil drinking green tea. Holding the delicate cup with both hands, he stared at the tea for a long time. Then very quietly he began to talk about Hamid, the nephew he treated as a son. "Hamid was just a boy when he left Kabul. He had everything then: he had a mother; he had every opportunity. The Soviets took it all from him. He lost everything." Then almost silently, Wakil began to weep. "Now he is leaving again. I love both these boys as if they were my own. They have been my family. I will miss them very much. Because of the Soviets, our families have been broken up. We are pushed from one country to another. . . ." He tried to control his tears, but he was unable to do so. His whole body began to shake. He had contained his feelings for so long, had forced himself for six years not to show his pain; now suddenly, he was unable to control those emotions.

To see the man I had leaned on for the last three months, the man in whose hands I had entrusted my life crying was difficult for me. I didn't know what to say to comfort him. My first instinct was to hold him, but I stopped myself because of his culture's taboo against my doing so. But watching this strong man's anguish was too much for me. Putting my arms around his shoulders, I searched for something to say. "Don't cry," I pleaded, as I began to cry with him. "You will see Hamid and Tor again. We are only borrowing them, not keeping them. I promise you you will see them again."

Wakil looked up at me, tears streaming down his face into his beard. "I hope you are right," he said, "but who knows who will still be living when they return."

12

Letter to Moscow

On the flight back to New York, I began to feel that a journey into Afghanistan to write about the war had to end in Russia. In my hand baggage I was carrying thirty-five letters found on the bodies of Soviet soldiers by the *Mujahideen.* Given to me by the guerrillas and Faizl Akbar, the head of the Afghan Documentation Center in Peshawar, such mail, along with other personal documents, was collected for intelligence purposes by the Resistance after operations. The package of letters from home to soldiers in the field also included driver's licenses, army salary cards, Komsomol (Young Communist League) membership booklets, three maps of Afghan provinces without legends in accordance with Soviet concern about information's falling into the wrong hands, a prayer that began "May the blood of God in heaven preserve you from all harm," and a diary—the paper detritus of these young men's lives. The Komsomol cards contained identification photographs of the owners, all skinny, callow-looking boys who appeared young enough still to be in school. I shouldn't have been surprised, therefore, when a high school transcript that had arrived after one boy had been drafted was tucked inside a letter by his mother, but I was. Without membership in the Komsomol, the adolescent version of the Young Pioneers, no Soviet youngster will be admitted to college. As I looked at the photographs in these cards, these soldiers stopped being anonymous war casualties, faceless corpses. I began to wonder what sort of lives had been cut down, brought to a premature end in the formidable terrain of Afghanistan. But it was the diary I found myself staring at the longest. The edges of the pages of the cheap plastic-covered notebook were stained brown where its owner's blood had dried on the paper. Before I could look at it, I had to prize apart each page gently. Inside were a number of sketches, among them one of an Aeroflot plane flying from Kabul to Ashkhabad in Soviet Central Asia and a date I would later learn (when I had the diary translated) was the conscript's demobilization day, May 7, 1983. On the next page was a drawing of a long-haired girl, whose name was Zoya, framed in a large heart with a caption underneath that read "I'm waiting for you." The diary's owner had also penned several poems that he'd decorated with flowers. One titled "Who'll celebrate May '83?" expressed his yearning to get out of the army. He'd signed his own name, Barkandai, underneath and inscribed the poem "in memory of Orgeshov," no doubt a fallen colleague. Another called simply "Aphorisms" was written for his girlfriend. It read:

> I owe my motherland
> Give me a kiss, my darling
> Don't cry . . . from parting
> Point out 24 months on the calendar
> And you'll see May '83 will
> come quickly
> If it is our fate,
> We'll have a Komsomol wedding
> Don't cry like an old woman
> Don't let bitter tears cover your face.

Barkandai died before he was able to celebrate his May demobilization. It was not his fate to have a Komsomol wedding.

The more I held the diary, or looked at well-handled snapshots of young women, obviously wives and sweethearts, that had fallen out of the pages of the personal papers, the more I wondered about the conscripts' families in the Soviet Union. How much did they know about the war in Afghanistan? How did they feel about it?

The official Soviet version of the war in Afghanistan was a fascinating mix of contradictions, evasions, apparent wishful thinking, fantasy, and skillful propaganda. If Russians accrued their knowledge from the Soviet press, they must have been very confused.

Twenty-four hours before the Soviet invasion of Afghanistan, the national newspaper, *Pravda*, which means "truth" in Russian, published the following story under the headline SOVIET TROOPS IN AFGHANISTAN?—"PURE FABRICATION":

> Recently Western, and especially American, mass news media have been disseminating deliberately planted rumors about some sort of "interference" by the Soviet Union in the internal affairs of Afghanistan. They have gone so far as to claim that Soviet "military units" have been moved into Afghan territory. All these assertions are pure fabrication, needless to say. It is common knowledge that relations between the Soviet Union and Afghanistan are based on a firm foundation of good-neighborliness, noninterference in each other's internal affairs, and equal, mutually advantageous cooperation.

It went on to say that the Soviet Union had never infringed on Afghanistan's "sovereignty and national independence, is not now doing so, and never will." Eight days later, the same newspaper was explaining its military presence in Afghanistan "as a limited Soviet military contingent, which will be used exclusively to repel armed interference from outside. The Soviet contingent will be completely withdrawn from Afghanistan when the factors that make this action necessary are no longer present." The outside interference the story referred to was the "undeclared war by Pakistan, China and the United States," a convenient Kremlin invention. *Pravda* justified the Soviet Union's move by citing "the provisions of Article 51 of the United Nations Charter, which provides for the inherent right of a state to individual or collective self-defense to repel aggression and restore peace. The fabrications that imperialist propaganda is spreading these days about 'Afghanistan's occupation by Soviet troops' have nothing in common with reality." The next day, January 1, *Izvestia* reported that "CIA agents are training Afghan rebels in the area of the Afghan-Pakistani border, under cover of the Drug Enforcement Administration and the American Asia Fund."

Later that year, on August 12, the Soviet media accused another American of operating undercover. This time it was CBS-TV's Dan Rather. Under the headline WHO'S HIDING IN THE GUISE OF A JOURNALIST? Rather was denounced as being an "Afghan Lt. Calley." In bizarre, identical accounts, *Pravda* and *Izvestia* both commented on Rather's report from Afghanistan early that year in March when he went behind enemy lines disguised as an Afghan, a report that earned him the sobriquet in the United States of "Gunga Dan." Quoting an Afghan newspaper, they accused Rather of participating in the murder of three villagers while he was in Afghanistan.

> The counterrevolutionary bandits sought to intimidate the villagers to prevent them from supporting the new revolutionary authorities. The innocent workers were brought into the square, and then one of the American journalists got into the action. He commanded the bandits first to torture the unfortunates, to stone them, and then to cut off their heads. All this bloody violence was captured on film by the Americans, who wanted to make a "vivid film" about the Afghan mercenaries' struggle against the revolutionary government of Afghanistan.
>
> Such are the facts. When they are compared, it becomes perfectly clear (and the Afghan press is absolutely right in drawing this conclusion) that CBS-TV commentator Dan Rather took a direct part in the sadistic murder of three Afghan workers. So, a bloody crime was committed. There are witnesses. The name of one of the criminals is known. However, there seem to be no signs of any intention to bring charges against Rather. The widely known case of Lt. Calley—the brutal butcher of My Lai—automatically comes to mind.

The article went on to suggest that CBS was merely a "cover," and that Rather was really "an agent for one of the American special services." A month later, *Izvestia*, in an article titled THEY'RE PROTECTING HIM, was still writing about why Rather should be extradited and brought to trial for his war crimes.

But duplicity would appear to be a specialty of *Pravda*. Shortly before the Dan Rather tale, the newspaper had run an article detailing TROOPS MOVE OUT, "INTERNATIONAL DUTY DONE". It quoted Afghans as being "grateful to the Soviet soldiers who came to our aid when times were hard for us." The article didn't say that this troop withdrawal was normal personnel rotation, and *Pravda* did not report on the troops who arrived to replace them, nor did it mention that Soviet forces had increased from 85,000 when the invasion began to 100,000 by that time or that there were now 1.4 million Afghan refugees in Pakistan who had fled their homeland.

The following year, 1981, when the U.S. State Department accused the Soviet Union of employing chemical weapons in Afghanistan, *Pravda* ran a story stating that Afghan counterrevolutionaries were using chemical weapons manufactured in "the federal laboratory in Salisbury, Pennsylvania." A year later, in the cultural newspaper *Literaturnaya Gazeta*, in purple prose that the more sensational tabloids would have been embarrassed to use, the Soviet public were treated to a lengthy feature titled INCUBATOR OF DEATH.

It began: "We have succeeded in exposing a plan by Washington's intelligence service to cause a catastrophic outbreak of infectious diseases among the Afghans. Under the guise of combating malaria, American biologists recruited by the CIA and stationed in Lahore are breeding poisonous mosquitoes, *Aedes aegypti*, that transmit deadly viruses to their victims." It went on to detail "the sinister experiments that bacteriologists from the University of Maryland had been conducting in Lahore." The research was headed by David Nalin, the U.S. consul in Lahore, and University of Maryland's Prof. Richard Sakai, the article said. So that the publication's audience would have no doubt that these two men were bad guys, Nalin was described as having "roguishly darting eyes in a fat, greasy face glowing with the light of keen intelligence, cunning and resourcefulness." Poor Professor Sakai didn't get off so lightly: "The reptilian smile on the thin lips of Sakai's bony, ascetic face looked half insane to me. Had he already lost his mind from the brain-damaging vampire kisses of *Aedes aegypti?*" the author asked himself after forcing his way into the lab to witness said "sinister" experiments.

The reporter summed up:

> Just who are Sakai and his bosses? Mad sadists? Yet they are spiritually akin to the apparently psychologically normal cannibal professor Samuel Cohen, who designed the neutron bomb for the purpose of turning Western Europe into a lifeless Pentagon base. The American professor Edward Teller, "the father of the hydrogen bomb" who has called for incinerating the socialist countries in a shower of thermonuclear warheads, is another of the same sort. None of these professors, however, are insane from the medical standpoint. They are war criminals.

Just who the two men in the article are wasn't hard to discover. Sakai is a geneticist from the University of Maryland and Nalin is not a U.S. consul but a physician who at the time of the article was with the National Institutes of Health in Bethesda, Maryland. Both men were in Pakistan working on a fifteen-year-long NIH-sponsored study of malaria and other viruses.

By 1983 when the Soviet scorched earth policy had begun and there were now 2.8 million Afghan refugees living in Pakistan, *Sovetskaya Rossia* ran an upbeat feature on how the Afghan people had grounds for celebrating because the Afghan economy was booming. DOLLARS AND BULLETS ARE POWERLESS was the headline.

A year later, to the embarrassment of Moscow, several Soviet soldiers, unhappy with what they witnessed in Afghanistan, had defected to the *Mujahideen* and made their way to the West. In December 1984, *Izvestia* explained away one such incident by reporting that two Soviet soldiers were "seized in Afghanistan, drugged in Pakistan and taken to London against their will. . . . Using the dirtiest and basest methods of pressure—blackmail, juggling of facts, psychological and physical coercion—the Western special services, through their henchmen, tried to turn Soviet citizens into traitors to the homeland."

Things changed dramatically in 1985. The war was obviously to be a protracted one, Soviet casualties were climbing, and the antiwar demonstrations, as tiny and as quickly suppressed as they were, had begun. Suddenly, the Soviet press began to compare the Afghan war to "The Glorious Patriot War," World War II, in which they lost 20 million, and which even now is still able to strike a deep emotional chord in the Russian population. Almost overnight, war heroes in Afghanistan were being lauded, and twenty-two men were quickly created "Heroes of the Soviet Union" for their bravery and automatically received the Order of Lenin, the country's top civil award. As one Western diplomat remarked, "Once you start making heroes of the men who die there, it gets harder to back away and say it was all in vain." The youth paper *Komsomolskaya Pravda* devoted almost an entire page to a story called "Duty" that detailed the shabby treatment given to Aleksandr Nemtsov by his home town authorities after he became a paraplegic in Afghanistan. For two years his plight was ignored until finally officials were fired or reprimanded for their indifference. The public outpouring of letters in response to the article was reported for several months.

For the first time, Soviet television began to show combat scenes. Reports no longer insisted that Soviet troops were in Afghanistan merely to assist the "Afghan Revolution" or to rebuild the country: now they were engaged in fighting the enemy —the counterrevolutionaries. Letters were published from mothers of conscripts like the one in *Pravda:* "I don't hide the fact that the pain of parting was great, but outwardly I kept calm. . . . The memory of what we went through during the Great Patriotic War lives on in every Soviet family. But one cannot live on memory alone while evil exists in the world. We must actively fight for peace; good must defend itself! . . ." Articles commenting on the military training advantages afforded by actual combat began to appear. Then in November 1985, *Pravda,* reporting on the death of the *Arizona Republic* reporter, Charles Thornton, described him as a saboteur who carried out a "barbarous act of destroying an Afghan airliner with fifty-two people aboard with a missile of U.S. manufacture" shortly before he was killed himself. There was no mention of their earlier articles accusing the *Mujahideen* of shooting down the plane.

Just what did the Soviet public themselves really believe? The letters taken off dead Russian soldiers in Afghanistan that I brought back with me gave some idea.

When I had them translated, the letters, which came from all over the country, were in Russian, Ukrainian, Turkmen, Uzbek, and Azerbaidzhan. Considering the heavy self-censorship that is pro forma in Soviet society and the fact that many of the letters were perused by the military censors, I was surprised at just how often Afghanistan was mentioned. A number of the letters hinted at the fears of families and friends, like the one from Irina Brastvitskaya in the city of Shchilkovo to Mikhail Vladimirovich Chuvilkin.

Hello Misha!

I've been hearing for some time now that you're serving in Afghanistan, and I was afraid it might be true. Now that it's confirmed by your letter, I'm terrified for you, terribly. I simply can't imagine all this. But if you think of us and our decent little city (in our province there are so many picturesque spots), it will be a bit easier for you.

Lest the letter become too thick and have no place to be kept, I won't write a second page. So goodbye. Don't be sad. Be careful and prudent. Beat the foe of our homeland and hurry home.

Irina

Or the one from the Gorelov Family in Reutovo near Moscow to their son Nikolai.

Hello dear son, Kolya!

Greetings from Mama, Papa, sister Vera, Olya, Nadya, Zhenya, Anechka. We all wish you in your difficult military duty success, and most importantly, good health for the long years 'till your return.

Dear son Kolya, watch out for even the little mines, and be on your guard when you're at your post. Of course it's difficult, but with difficulties, don't let your courage fail and . . . things will go better for you.

We wish you, my son, good health, success in your service, a speedy return home, and the very happiest frame of mind. . . .

With our greeting, Mama and Papa

Other letters complained of conditions in the army. A common problem was infrequency of mail, and as one mother in the city of Florita wrote to her son, Vitaly Patrakiva, it was compounded by theft from letters containing cash.

Dear son,

Finally you've written that you've received a letter from home. A long time has passed, but in the meantime I got your letter. In two letters I sent you two envelopes—Air Mail—if the censor hasn't meddled and taken them out. You know how I doubt the order in the army so much that nothing could surprise me. Until now, I thought there should be order there like nowhere else, but I see disorder of the kind you'd really have to look for at home. For the half a year since you moved from your area, I've had only one letter sent back with the address struck out. But last week you'd already left there. I sent a registered letter, and not only did it not come back, but it disappeared completely. They know, of course, that there is still a receipt, but again it seems they're looking for money —may their pockets be always empty. I'm very sorry.

But don't be bitter; don't lose courage. That is very bad, all the more because you are expected to endure fire. For in Afghanistan these days, no one stays the same for long. You will be tempered. First by cold, then by heat.

Write more often. I kiss you,

Mama

One young soldier, Valera Alekseevich Sholokhov, did more than complain in his letters home. He went AWOL for two months, causing his parents to fear he was dead; four months later he was. On his body, thirteen letters from his parents were found, a moving account of the last few months of his life. One from his mother, Nina Mikhailovna, read:

My darling son, what a commotion you have caused in our house and village. The unit you serve in has been looking for you. What tears, weeping and despair you've caused our family and friends. We didn't think you were alive; we thought you had perished. Papa cried about you so much that he could not find a place for himself. We wrote a letter to your unit and sent a telegram saying that you were not at home, and asked them to notify us if you appeared. And then we received the letter.

They wrote that you were absent without leave from the 24th

of May to the 6th of July; that you are not disciplined, not willing
to work hard, not dependable; that you are not familiar with the
military equipment and are not interested in knowing; that you
don't know anything about weaponry; that you are not cooperating
with your line officers; and that you don't go to *politzanyatiya*
[political indoctrination classes]. This letter upset us even more
than the first one, in which they notified us that they were searching
for you.

Picture the person, the organization, or the unit which would
need a person like that. What would you do with them? We know
the military life is hard for you, but it's hardest for us, your parents.
Did we really want to have a son like this? Other parents are
rewarded with gratitude for the good upbringing of their children.
And those parents are 100 times worse than us.

Dear Valera, please understand that everywhere discipline
must come first and foremost. Don't go off on the wrong track.
After all, you know how hard your father and I have worked.
Remember that we didn't even have a house. Everything is built
upon our honest and hard-earned kopecks. Do you remember how
my hands ached, but look how hard I worked. We kept a cow to give
you and Sveta milk; we've had pigs and hens. This wasn't easy.
Work, work, work! Always work! These days everything is possible
if you love work, and you'll be useful wherever you go. In our
country, work brings honor.

Valera, the most terrible thing in a man's life is if someone
wants to get rid of you. Learn to obey. It's necessary wherever
you go.

Valera, your father, Sveta, and I hope that you will not dis-
grace us; that you will serve with integrity; that you will listen and
come to know all that modern warfare demands.

All you have left is one more year to serve, so serve it with
integrity and ask for forgiveness from those whom you wronged.

Write to us and tell us, if you can, where you were from 5/26
to 7/6. Don't do that again.

We hope you will complete your service well and will come
home with your head raised high and proud.

We await your letters—write more frequently.

And please thank your superiors for letting us know that you
are alive. For we thought we would never see you again.

So my son, stay alive and well.

Mama

But it was the love letters that were the most difficult to read, women pouring out their hearts to lovers, husbands, they would never see again.

To: Vladislav Egorov

My lovely essence, I miss you very much; my feelings, dear, cannot be expressed in a letter, not these affairs of the heart. We're having such a beautiful spring, about which much is written. This time of year has a special effect on me, but right now I would give up everything to be with you. You alone are dear to me.

Only a little time remains before we meet again. The time is flying it seems to me. But still I must admit that I live for you. I'm really afraid of just one thing, which I'm constantly trying to put out of mind. I'm constantly afraid you might not be protected against stray bullets, especially on foreign soil. I ask you, my beloved, to pardon me that I haven't treated you the way a girl should.

Vladyuskha, my dear, I beg you to take care of yourself and remember that you are awaited. I love you and I will always love you all my life. With this I'll stop writing.

Lyuba

The most poignant was found on a soldier, Sergei Yurevich Viflyaitsev, from Gubskaya Oblost, who died when he had less than six days left to serve.

Seryozha, it has already been a long time since we received a letter from you. You only have a little more time left to serve. Today is already the 21st of March, and at most six days remain until your arrival, and when you get my letter you will already be getting ready to leave for home. I think I still have time to write a letter before the end of March, and then I will be awaiting your arrival home.

Seryozha, if you only knew how much I want to see you, how much I miss you. Don't worry about us. Everything is going well. Take care of yourself so you come back healthy. Seryozha, we're awaiting your arrival home before your birthday. Good-bye. I'm waiting. I love you and kiss you.

Zoya, and daughter Svetochka

Studying the correspondence, I finally came to the conclusion that I would travel to the Soviet Union, taking some of the letters with me, and attempt to locate and interview the families who had written them. The decision was considerably easier than putting the process into motion. "How do you plan to set it up? You can't write or call ahead, even if they have telephones, which is unlikely, unless you want the KGB to meet you," friends with contacts in the Jewish dissident underground told me. "What you are trying to do isn't very wise," a Russian émigré acquaintance cautioned. "You don't know if these families are good Party members. And even if they aren't, they'll never talk to you; they'll be too afraid. There are articles in the Soviet Penal Code that strictly forbid what you are trying to do, and this would certainly be considered 'anti-Soviet agitation and propaganda.'" "How will you get the letters in?" asked a colleague, who knew the Soviet Union well. "They scrutinize even the magazines and books you carry in and often confiscate them. How do you think they'll react if they find these letters on you?"

But there were more practical considerations before any of their fears had to be considered. I didn't speak Russian and needed an interpreter, someone fluent enough to cope with the sensitivity of talking to the families about the men who had died, families for whom perhaps Russian was a second language. The more than one hundred ethnic groups in the USSR speak eighty different languages although Russian is required and the majority of Soviet citizens are fluent or close to it. The interpreter I was looking for also had to be extremely discreet and to know the country and its mores well. Despite the fact that I had traveled extensively, I had never visited the Soviet Union. Finding such a person who was willing to undertake the assignment wasn't easy. Most interpreters with fluent Russian used the language professionally, and they were not prepared to risk their livelihood by being expelled or worse by the Soviet Union. In the end, I would have eight interpreters, from graduate students to academics, agree and then eventually back out because of fear. John, an environmentalist, the young man who finally came with me, was a last-minute discovery and a godsend. But it wasn't just the interpreters who had problems with the project; I had a few of my own. Having testified before Congress on human rights violations in Afghanistan when the hearings were covered by *Tass*, I had been told I would certainly be denied a Soviet visa; other journalists had been, after going into Afghanistan in a manner considered illegal by Moscow. One was threatened with arrest if he traveled to Russia. Once again, I chose to apply from England using my British passport, stating on my visa application with Intourist that I was a high school teacher, an innocuous characterization that I felt wouldn't raise any alarms in the Soviet Union. John was described as a graduate student at a London college.

The final nuts and bolts difficulties concerned the letters themselves. Many of the return addresses were not complete—vast apartment houses didn't have the actual apartment number, and one just can't wander freely around these mammoth buildings in search of a particular family as in the West without causing comment and probable intervention. Further research also showed that many of the letters came from cities that were simply off-limits to foreigners. Finally, we whittled it down to five addresses, one in Moscow; one in Zagorsk, the ancient seat of the Russian Orthodox Church, forty-four miles north of the capital and open to tourists; and three in Ashkhabad in Soviet Central Asia near the Iranian border. The last three came from Barkandai's diary, the second part of which he had used as an address book listing friends with whom he served. We also applied for visas to Tashkent, about five hundred miles directly north of Kabul, a major staging point for Soviet troops into Afghanistan, and the city where many of the Afghan children, including Naiem, were sent for Sovietization.

We were due to depart for Moscow in March 1986, but Intourist twice peremptorily postponed our departure at the last minute because they didn't want foreigners in the capital during the 27th Communist Party Congress. Finally, we were told we could leave for two weeks on April 22, Lenin's birthday. The Aeroflot Ilyushin jumbo-jet was three-quarters empty. The seventy or so Russian passengers toted without exception huge Toshiba radio/tapedecks purchased in London, which threatened to concuss seated passengers as the "boom-boxes" were swung down the aisles. No sooner had we taken off than the plane was filled with the pungency of the rough tobacco of Soviet cigarettes, a smell one soon learns to identify with Mother Russia, since the entire population appears to chainsmoke. During the three-and-a-half-hour flight, I read the English-language *Soviet Weekly* handed to me by the stewardess, an issue that contained a sixteen-page supplement on "Afghanistan Today," most of it devoted to "the signs of progressive change" and laying all modern ills in Afghanistan firmly at the door of the White House. My first week in the Soviet Union coincided with a "Week of Solidarity" with Afghanistan.

Three and a half hours after takeoff we landed at Moscow's Sheremetyevo airport, flying low over a vast sea of mud— Russia's oozing spring thaw had begun. The silver birches lining the airport brought to mind Chekhov and Tolstoy. Inside the dimly lit arrival terminal, I had my first experience with *"Skoro Budyet-ism,"* "It will be soon," the Soviet equivalent of a shrugged "Mañana." It took nearly three hours for the baggage to be unloaded from the plane and another thirty minutes to shuffle through customs. All the while, I became increasingly anxious about whether I would be able to smuggle in the letters and the xeroxed pages of the diary, or whether my trip would be aborted before I put a foot outside the airport. The papers, wrapped in thin foam rubber to cut down on the rustle, were secreted in the lining of my pocketbook, the same method I'd used going into Kabul. Instead of sewing up the seam again, I'd upgraded the system with a concealed velcro fastening, which would enable me to hide my notes throughout the trip. Although not perfect, I hoped the system would escape all but intense scrutiny. I needn't have worried. Our luggage was X-rayed, and suitcases were only spot-checked for seditious literature such as *Time* or *Newsweek*. Another concern disappeared when we reported to the Intourist desk. Because we were traveling individually, Intourist guides were optional unless we booked a sight-seeing tour; that meant we didn't have to shake their ubiquitous presence we had been told to expect. We had already decided to play tourists during the day and attempt to contact the families in the evening.

At the hotel we were consigned to, Intourist's choice, not ours, *Skoro Budyet-ism* struck again. In the Kosmos Hotel, the vast twenty-eight-story foreign tourist ghetto a lengthy Metro ride from the center of Moscow, we waited ninety minutes to check in, our ears bludgeoned the entire time by deafening piped music—a noise that assailed us so frequently in public buildings while in Russia that I began to wonder whether piped music had replaced religion as the opiate of the masses. There was no reprieve in my room, either: the radio built into the wall was minus its on-off switch, rendering it permanently on for the five days and nights I stayed there, room service and maintenance being unavailable at the Kosmos, and room changes seemingly just as impossible to effect. The Kosmos, while we were there, was mostly filled with hard-drinking East and West Germans who obviously did not feel that Gorbachev's new sobriety dictum applied to them. Fifteen Cuban Army officers were also in residence.

The following morning began with a fight to get breakfast. Three of the hotel's four large restaurants wanted only to serve groups and were blatantly hostile to individuals, an attitude we would run into repeatedly throughout the trip that left me wondering whether the hotels acquired it from the state or vice versa. The fourth restaurant closed in our faces. Outside, Moscow's climate was as chilly as the women guarding the entrances to the Kosmos dining rooms. A brisk wind blew off the river Moskva and across Red Square, where head-scarfed women painted viewing stands in preparation for the May Day festivities the following week. Costumed schoolchildren practiced their marching formations for the parade. And the ever-present line of tourists—at that time of year, mostly Russians—snaked around the square, inching sluggishly toward Lenin's tomb. Walking up Gorky Street, I was struck by the pallor of Muscovite faces, their complexions so sickly-looking they seemed tinged almost blue. Their faces brought a whiteness to Moscow's streets that the city had only just lost with the melting of the snow. Their wanness, I knew, was the result of a too long winter and a poor diet. While I was there, vegetables and fruit were impossible to find in government stores and difficult to afford in the farmers' markets, where a kilo of tomatoes was fetching 15 rubles (U.S. $23.00), and a cauliflower was two rubles ($3.00), and monthly salaries averaged 130 to 150 rubles. The nurturer in me longed to ship the entire population of Moscow off to some sunny beach and force-feed them vitamins.

Too numbed by the weather for sight-seeing to be pleasurable, we decided to contact Misha,* one of the city's better-known contemporary writers, for whom John was carrying some medica-

*His name and the names of other Soviets who granted me interviews in this chapter have been changed to protect their safety.

tion from a friend now living in the States. Misha's books and articles were "permitted" by the state, although when he was younger and perhaps more idealistic, they were banned. Having redeemed himself in the eyes of the authorities, but inwardly frustrated by his compromise, Misha still flirted with the dissident fringe. He was establishment enough, however, for us to decide not to take him into our confidence as to why we were in the country. After we called from a public telephone, less likely to be monitored than hotel phones, the writer and his wife, Galina, invited us over for tea. Seated in the cramped kitchen of their one-bedroom, ninth-floor apartment on tiny, rickety chairs I felt certain would collapse under us at any minute, we talked briefly about Misha's new book. But as soon as tea with red currant jam was served, the writer asked John why the United States had bombed Libya nine days before, a subject I was delighted he'd brought up as it led the conversation naturally into why the Soviet Union had invaded Afghanistan. The Soviet press had extensively reported on the Libya attack, replied Misha, but they hadn't, of course, admitted to invading Afghanistan. "For this reason, I believe the general Russian population, if you were to ask them, would be in favor of a Soviet presence in Afghanistan. The intelligentsia, and pacifists, like ourselves, are not. To be honest though, in this century our country has had so many problems, so many upheavals, beginning with the Japanese, the Chinese, then World War I, Stalin, World War II, now most people can't think of, don't want to think of, another war." Misha himself lost his father under Stalin and didn't get to know his mother until he was nine as she was imprisoned shortly after his birth in the purges. Added Galina, "Our young men don't want to go, except for the officers, and they are queuing up to go. Combat experience in Afghanistan gives them more money, quicker promotion, and more privileges on their return, such as the chance of a higher education. For them, there is definitely material benefit to this war."

Our conversation was interrupted by the couple's fifteen-year-old daughter, Alla, returning from school. A younger, trimmer version of her mother, except for her pixie haircut, Alla spoke English better than her parents. Hearing her mother's comment, she said. "In school today, we were talking about Afghanistan. One of my classmates just heard her cousin had been killed; he was only there three months. The letter came to his family yesterday. Now her seventeen-year-old brother wants to fight, to get revenge for his cousin."

"Many of our young men are dying in this war," added her mother. "We have relatives in a small town of forty thousand. Already there are seventy-five graves of soldiers killed in Afghanistan in the cemetery there. And I was visiting friends in a village in the Ukraine recently, when a funeral for a boy who served in Afghanistan was being held. Because of the new Gorbachev rules on sobriety, the father had been unable to buy alcohol and was serving the mourners moonshine, which is illegal. The police came and started arresting people. The father, already consumed with grief, went crazy and picked up a plank of wood. Before he could be stopped, he had clubbed one of the policemen to death. Of course, he was arrested and no one knows what happened to him after that." Galina broke off. "You know, we haven't discussed Afghanistan in front of Alla before, in case she offers up opinions in school that they wouldn't approve of."

"They tell us about Afghanistan in school," said Alla before disappearing to study; "they taught us that the Soviet Union is helping Afghanistan to defend itself against the undeclared war by America."

"Vietnam ended because of the pressure of the American people," said Misha. "That cannot happen here. The war machine is too powerful. Here if you take part in a demonstration, it's the quickest way to a prison camp. Most Russians only know what my daughter knows about this war, what the government tells them."

As we were leaving, Misha gave us the phone number of an elderly dissident friend of his who was also a close friend of Andrei Sakharov's. "Go and see him; you'll find him interesting to talk to."

It was 9:30 P.M. before we could contact Volodya. The phone call couldn't have been curter: "Come now, if you want to come." He hung up before we could ask travel directions. It took us an hour on the Metro to reach him. He lived in one of the enormous, austere buildings that stretch for blocks, dominating Moscow's architecture. By the time we arrived, the desk just inside the door was untended, a relief to both of us. In Moscow apartment buildings, it is assumed that the little old ladies who guard the entrances or operate the elevators are paid KGB informers whose job it is to report anything suspicious, particularly visits from foreigners. So concerned are the authorities about Russians having foreign visitors that a foreigner must register with the local police if he wants to stay in a Soviet citizen's apartment after 11:00 P.M.

Volodya lived on the eleventh floor, and despite the sprawling size of the apartment house, the elevator held two people comfortably and three very intimately, a typical feature in the Soviet Union, which necessitates that all furniture be carried up the stairs. Volodya was waiting for us as the elevator door clanged open. He was rawboned, and his steely gray hair was matched by a mouth full of metal teeth: Soviet dentists offer either gold or steel caps, never porcelain. Ushering us into a tiny but neat kitchen—his one other room was a bedroom-cum-study—he poured tea and served us sour milk pancakes with wild strawberry jam someone had obviously made for him. As he did, I noticed his work-worn hands that suggested a lifetime of physical labor rather than the successful career of a professor that I knew he had had. Despite the lateness of the hour, the radio in the room played loudly in the background throughout our visit—a common ploy by any Russian who has cause to believe his apartment may be bugged. Volodya, now seventy, looked frail and had dark shadows under his eyes. He told us he had cancer and that because of the shortage of certain medications in the Soviet Union, friends had tried to send him some from the West. "It didn't arrive; it was probably confiscated," he said matter-of-factly, in a manner so brisk it defied sympathy.

We made polite small talk, while both sides were aware that we were sizing each other up. Finally, the conversation turned to Afghanistan. "Sakharov was only exiled because he spoke out against Afghanistan," said Volodya. "Until he was forced to live in Gorky, we were very close friends." He slowly got to his feet and went into the other room. "I want to show you something," he said over his shoulder, returning a few minutes later with a photograph of the dissident. "This was taken last year, just after his hunger strike." He held out the snapshot to me. Sakharov, his head almost bald, was underweight and looked ill and considerably older than the sixty-four years he was then. "He lost twenty kilograms during that hunger strike," said Volodya. "He looks so bad in this picture, I didn't want to keep it when it was offered to me."

Volodya had been so disturbed by his friend's deteriorating physical condition that with little thought for his own safety, he wrote to Gorbachev, complaining about Sakharov's treatment. "I didn't think it would make any difference, but I felt I had to do it." Gorbachev didn't reply, but the KGB did. "I was warned that I was playing a dangerous game," said Volodya. "They told me that I needn't think my age and ill health would protect me from going to a prison camp. They said they had just sent a seventy-five-year-old to a prison camp, and they'd be happy to send me, too." Volodya shrugged. In a country where more than 2 million people are incarcerated in prison camps, and another 6 million are detained in special hostels, he wasn't surprised by the threat. I told Volodya he was a courageous man, but he didn't respond. He'd spent a lifetime defying his government and obviously didn't intend to let his age or infirmity change his convictions.

We left at 12:30 A.M., for the half-an-hour walk to the Metro station to catch the last train back to the hotel. Moving stiffly, Volodya accompanied us. "These days, walking helps me to sleep," he said. We said good-bye at the station and watched him begin to walk laboriously back along the deserted, badly lit street. He was obviously in pain, and I had only admiration for his quiet dignity and courage, and selfless concern for the suffering of others.

The following morning we took the Metro to Sverdlov Square to visit the Bolshoi Theater, a walk around it, sadly, the closest I would get because of the nature of my trip. The train into the city center was crowded, and I found myself straphanging next to five soldiers outfitted with full gear. Hanging off their duffles were their knee-high combat boots, and it was a shock to realize that the last time I had been that close to such boots was in Jalalabad, when they were strewn around in the gorge that was littered with the bones of Soviet soldiers eleven-year-old Noor Jhan had helped to kill.

Near the square, we stopped at one of the small newspaper billboards where copies of *Pravda* and *Izvestia* are posted daily for the public to read. On the front pages of both publications were large articles, complete with photographs, reporting on the "friendly" visit to the Soviet Union by Afghanistan's prime minister Sultan Ali Keshtmand, the man long touted to be Karmal's successor if the president ever fell from Moscow's grace. The articles made no mention of Babrak Karmal, which seemed portentous because the Afghan president was in the Soviet Union reportedly recovering from medical treatment. Neither article, however, threw any light on the Kremlin's current view of either man. "Russians read their newspapers by assessing what is left out, not by judging what is included in any story," said John. The day after we left Russia, Karmal was replaced by Moscow, not by Keshtmand as many expected, but by Major General Mohammed Najibullah, a thirty-nine-year-old lantern-jawed physician known for his ruthless and brutal efficiency in running KHAD, the feared Afghan secret police. Called "The Ox" by his countrymen, a nickname he acquired in college because of his preference for using brawn rather than brains to solve problems, Afghans say his methods of thuggery and intimidation have merely become more sophisticated over the years. Najibullah is considered a traitor by his own family, many of whom are *Mujahideen*—his uncle is a leading guerrilla commander in Gardez with the National Islamic Front of Afghanistan. But the freedom fighters have a begrudging respect for the new head of the Afghan regime's subversion tactics skills and his ability to infiltrate agents into Peshawar and Resistance groups.

Najibullah's appointment was such an unpopular choice that the ousted general secretary of the PDPA, who still retained his lesser post as president of the Revolutionary Council and his seat on the Politburo, discovered fans he may not have known he'd had. A group of young women staged pro-Karmal demonstrations and attacked the presidential palace with stones. Several died for their efforts. Eleven days after his appointment, Najibullah announced a collective leadership, a triumvirate that included himself; Babrak Karmal, who would be concerned with strengthening "state power organs"; and Prime Minister Keshtmand, who would be responsible for administration and economic policies. Six months after Najibullah's appointment, Karmal was forced to resign completely.

☐

After two days of playing tourist, we decided it was time to try to contact the first of our five families. The address we had was on Smirnovska Street near the Nikolsky Monastery, just inside the city limits. Because it was so far out, we took a taxi and gauged our arrival for 6:30 P.M., a time we guessed most workers would arrive home. It dropped us off at the end of Smirnovska, where a Kvass stand was doing a brisk business, and we walked along the tree-lined street with children playing in front of the five-story apartment houses. Numerous grandmotherly types sat on benches keeping a watch on their young charges, who were so well bundled up against the cold that they resembled little Sumo wrestlers. The women studied us closely as we walked past them trying to blend in with the scenery but aware that both of us stood out as foreigners in this blue-collar neighborhood. As they inspected us, we glanced surreptitiously at apartment house numbers. "There it is," I suddenly said to John, "that building over there, the yellow one with the six entrances."

Entering the five-floor walk-up, my nose wrinkled in distaste at the powerful stench of rotting garbage that filled the stairwell. The apartment we were seeking was on the second floor. Although we could hear voices in the apartments on each side, the doorbell, when we rang it, echoed hollowly, indicating the family wasn't home. We walked outside again, and the aged baby-sitters stopped their conversations to watch us leave. Knowing that Moscow has almost zero nightlife, we assumed we had merely beaten the boy's parents home from work. Since we were so close to the two-hundred-year-old onion-domed Nikolsky Monastery, we decided to pass the time there. A service was in progress when we arrived, and we sat down on a bench opposite the entrance until it was over. As the congregation began to file out, mostly elderly men and women dressed all in black, with a sprinkling of young people, it quickly became apparent that they were made very uncomfortable by our presence. In a country where religion is actively discouraged by the state and police have been known to beat up people attending services, strangers stationed outside a church were cause for alarm. When we started to enter the church, a man in his twenties stopped us. "No, no, it's closed; it's closed," he said nervously. We returned to the apartment; it was still empty. Finally, after three visits, each time receiving baleful glares from the women sitting outside, we decided it probably was not a very good idea, either for the family or ourselves, to hang around any longer. Reluctantly, we left. Searching for a bus that would take us back to the city, we discovered that the apartment house was 250 yards from a large police station.

The following morning, Saturday, we planned to visit Zagorsk, where the second family on my list lived. The spiritual center of Russian Orthodoxy, although open to tourists, required a visa. We hadn't applied for one because we knew that for any trip outside Moscow, an Intourist guide would be designated to take us and would be impossible to shake in such a small town. Instead, two "friends of friends," Andrei, a twenty-eight-year-old engineer, and Slava, a twenty-seven-year-old chemist, both of whom spoke excellent English, offered to drive us as Slava could borrow his parents' car. Slava's father, a colonel in the army and therefore one of the elite, was one of the fortunate 6 percent of Soviets able to purchase a car. As so often happens in the Soviet Union, confidences are rarely complete: we told the two men only that we wanted to visit a family in Zagorsk, and they didn't ask any questions. In Zagorsk, Slava asked directions from a local to the family's address. "It's in a very small village, just a few houses, twenty kilometers from here; it's not actually part of the town of Zagorsk," he said, looking concerned. "You can't go there. The moment you drive outside Zagorsk, people know foreigners aren't permitted. You'll get stopped immediately." Added Andrei, "It would be dangerous for your friends, too, if foreigners suddenly arrive in a small village; you'll stand out immediately." Slava made a suggestion: "Why don't I drive to the village and bring your friends back here? That would be the easiest solution, and they would probably feel more comfortable with that, too." I thanked him for his offer but knew I couldn't let him do it without telling him why I wanted to meet the family. He listened without interrupting as I explained the true nature of my visit. "I see," he said when I had finished. "In that case, I cannot participate. It would be far too dangerous for Andrei and me. And for the same reason, I am afraid I could not let you use this car." The second letter was obviously going to go undelivered. I was disappointed, but I understood their fear. We returned to Moscow. On the drive back, the conversation naturally centered on Afghanistan. "It was the first time I felt shame for my country," said Andrei. "My generation is too young to understand what happened with Czechoslovakia and Hungary, but the invasion of Afghanistan disgusted me. I read our newspaper articles about our

CAUGHT IN THE CROSSFIRE

friendship with the Afghans and looked at the photographs of Russian soldiers 'helping' those people. Then I listened to the BBC and Voice of America and learned what really happened. I felt sick. What we did in Afghanistan was like walking into somebody's house and saying, okay, this house is mine now; you have to leave. You can't do that." Shortly after Andrei was graduated from college in 1980, he received his conscription notice. "I realized there was a good chance I would be sent to Afghanistan, and I didn't want to go. A lot of my friends felt the same way. Some actually injured themselves so they wouldn't have to go. One spent two months in a mental hospital after pretending he was suicidal; that's almost as bad as spending two years in the army. I was luckier; several of my friends were medical students, through them I found a doctor who gave me a certificate saying I had kidney disease. I was exempted." Slava, too, managed to ensure he didn't get drafted. Through family contacts, he was able to "prove" he had an ulcer and was unfit to serve. "My country reveres war," said the young man who had grown up in a military family. "Russia lost 20 million people in World War II. Not only do they still talk about it in very romantic terms; they actually believe they won. It's strange, isn't it, when you consider the Germans only lost 8 million? I do not believe the Soviet Union will pull out of Afghanistan, not until the last Afghan who opposes them is dead."

The following day, John and I flew to Ashkhabad, the capital of the Turkmen Republic, and the southernmost republic and the hottest place in the Soviet Union. The town, a former oasis in the vast Kara Kum desert, was 90 percent destroyed by an earthquake in 1948 that lasted less than a minute but measured force 10 on the Richter scale. Virtually every family lost relatives. In the rebuilding of Ashkhabad, all of the Islamic architecture disappeared and so did the mosques. Ashkhabad today is a modern and utilitarian Soviet city, where war memorials are nearly as numerous as statues of Lenin. The city's only saving graces are the tree-lined streets and many parks provided to supply shade and respite from the region's 120 degree plus heat in the summer. Only the ankle-length, flowery dresses of the women, who still cover their hair with scarves in public, a modern version of the ancient veil, and the *tubeteykas*, embroidered caps worn by the

□ 320 □

men, are reminders of a colorful culture that has been since Sovietized.

Our first day in Ashkhabad, the streets were crowded with uniformed soldiers. Realizing there were far too many for a town of this size, we took a stroll to the railway station, a 10-minute walk from our hotel, the Ashkhabad. Our hunch proved correct; hundreds of fully equipped troops filled the station and the small park outside, many of them the elite Spetsnaz commando troops who had wreaked such havoc in Afghanistan. They were easily identifiable by their blue and white or turquoise and white striped sweaters, turquoise flashes on their uniforms, and matching berets worn at jaunty angles. The cut of their pants was different, too, from the baggy, ill-fitting ones issued to ordinary conscripts. Worn much tighter over the hips, they helped give the Spetsnaz a swaggering look. For the most part, the Russian commandoes were blond, blue-eyed young men sporting healthy-looking tans. It was hard to equate their athletic good looks with the silent killing techniques in which I knew they were skilled. Sitting in the large station waiting room, John eavesdropped on their conversations. It soon became apparent that the soldiers were part of a massive troop movement into Afghanistan via Tashkent. For many whose bags were decorated with Afghanistan stickers, it was obviously a second spell. A woman asked John what kind of soldiers the Spetsnaz were. He explained. "Ah, the *desant* [paratroopers]," she replied, "the ones they show on television all the time."

Throughout our stay in Ashkhabad, there were large numbers of troops at the station waiting for trains to Tashkent.

There was very little to do in Ashkhabad in the way of sightseeing even that first day, and the hours passed slowly. Finally, it was 6:30 P.M. and time to seek out one of the young men whose address had been in Barkandai's diary. Finding a cab in Ashkhabad wasn't easy, however, and eventually a private car stopped for us. As often happens in the Soviet Union, the driver picked up paying passengers to help defray the cost of gasoline, an illegal practice. He also chose to ignore the law that forbids anyone other than a taxi driver to give a foreigner a ride in his car. We·drove fifteen minutes in the direction of the racetrack on the eastern outskirts of the town and asked to be dropped off two streets past our destination. The area in which we found ourselves was an older part of town, very different from the main part of Ashkhabad with its Moscow-style apartment buildings. The roads were unpaved, and the small one-story homes were secreted behind high walls that encircled courtyards containing chickens, sheep, and the occasional cow, indicated by the sounds and smells emanating from behind them. Outside, many of the homes had grapevines growing over primitive, handmade arbors. Here and there, a few grimy children played in the dust. The scene was not very different from many in Afghanistan.

In my pocketbook were Marlboro cigarettes and chewing gum, gifts for the families we hoped to visit, which we had bought in the hard currency stores for foreigners. The supplies made me think of American GIs arriving in Europe during World War II who carried the same favors with them. We trudged for nearly thirty minutes along the dried mud road; the house we were heading for was at the far end. Suddenly, we were outside number 123, a low red brick house with a blue metal door set in the seven-foot-high wall. It was ajar and opened onto a short alley leading to a courtyard. Calling hello, we walked toward the sound of voices. Turning a corner, we came across a large Turkmen family in native dress, preparing their evening meal. Addressing a young man in his early twenties, we said we were looking for Geldi. There was a long minute of silence and then somebody replied he was dead. Now it was our turn to be nonplussed. Although we knew the letters we carried had been found on dead soldiers, I had assumed the men listed in the address book would still be alive. Before I could say anything, the young man we later learned was called Saliman, who was Geldi's older brother, said, "He died in Afghanistan, in 1983." By now, the family, which consisted of elderly parents, five adult daughters, Saliman and his wife, and their two toddlers, had stopped what they were doing and were gaping at us as if two Martians had landed in their yard. It was our turn for explanations. Fully aware that few Russian families would talk to American journalists, we told them we were from a religious organization in England that had acquired Barkandai's diary, and that we had been asked to write an article on Russian soldiers' dying in Afghanistan. They nodded their heads, so accustomed to never questioning authority it didn't occur to them to challenge our story or presence. We were invited inside the small living room carpeted with colorful rugs hand-woven from goats' wool. There was a small sofa in the room, but we joined the family sitting crosslegged on the floor, while the younger daughters bustled around bringing tea, bread, soup, and fried fish. Muslim hospitality was as strong here as it was in Afghanistan.

Almost as soon as I had sat down, Geldi's mother put a small cloth package in my lap. Unwrapping it, I found a metal and enamel five-pointed Red Star, her dead son's medal. She searched around in a closet and came back carrying a larger plastic-wrapped parcel, which she once again put in my lap. Inside were the family's snapshot collection of Geldi, put away for safekeeping. Nestling among the photographs was his green bordered death certificate, which said that he had been in the infantry and had died January 16, 1983. "He died with a bullet here," said the father, pointing to a spot immediately under his nose. "The bullet came out here," he added, gesturing to the back of his skull. "That's what they told us," and he demonstrated again the path of the bullet. Geldi's nineteen-year-old sister, who had been manning the teapot, looked as if she were about to cry. To break the mood, I began to look through the photographs. Most were amateur black and white snapshots, but there was an eight by ten hand-colored professional portrait of him. "We had that taken when he was conscripted," said the father, who was wearing one of the high karakul hats worn by many of the men in this region. The photograph showed a round-faced young man with the Mongolian eyes of the Turkmens, a slightly fleshy nose, and eyebrows that slanted up in the center, giving him a quizzical expression. There was a little fuzz over his mouth, a teenager's first attempt at growing a mustache, and his ears protruded in exactly the same angle from his head as his father's. Although not a handsome face, it was a friendly one.

Geldi's first year in the army had been served in East Germany; then he had been posted to Afghanistan. The photographs he had sent home from Afghanistan were very different from his conscription portrait, and until the family pointed him out I didn't recognize him. His body was considerably leaner, but it was his face that was the most changed: he looked ten years older than I knew him to be. "He had four months left to serve when he died," explained his father. "He was stationed in Jalalabad. They were ambushed by the *dushmans* [bandits]. Twenty men from his unit were sitting in a house when the counterrevolutionaries burst in and sprayed the room with machine gun fire. They all died. They sent his body back together with the body of another boy who had lived near here." The father sighed and then added wearily, "We know so many people who have lost sons. The government says there isn't a war in Afghanistan, but there is. And it's already seven years old.

"Geldi was a good son. He had completed eleven grades at school, when only ten are required. Before he went into the army, he was a truck driver, and every night he studied trucking regulations so he could get his license. He didn't know he was going to Afghanistan until he got there. He was only nineteen years old when he died." Added his wife, "Since that day, my husband has had pains in his heart, and his blood pressure is high."

I asked the family whether they knew why the war had begun. Geldi's oldest sister, twenty-one-year-old Fatima, a student at the local technical school, answered for them. "It was because America and Pakistan sent guns, and the fighting began. So we had to help the Afghan people. After all, Afghanistan has been part of the Soviet Union since our October Revolution." The rest of the family nodded in agreement. With years of disinformation like this, a two-hour visit was hardly time to disabuse them of such "facts." Added Saliman, "They showed us what is happening there on television. I didn't believe it in the beginning, but when I saw it on television I did."

When we left, the family presented us with two bunches of irises from their garden, and Fatima pressed a white plastic ballpoint into my hand. "White is for good luck," she said, inviting us back to celebrate May Day with them.

On the trip back to the hotel, I mulled over the conversation in my head. Once again, I was amazed at the control of information in a country with a population of 274 million. That control's efficacy was brilliantly demonstrated to me, however, during my second week in the Soviet Union. The day we traveled to Zagorsk was the same day that in Chernobyl near Kiev, the nuclear power plant accident had occurred, spewing a cloud of radiation across Europe. John and I would not learn about it until our plane landed at London airport the following week. As we deplaned, we were met by an announcement: "At the top of the ramp, you will find two gentleman from the National Radiological Protection Board who will check you for radiation. . . ."

Because our trip so far apparently had been surveillance-free, I had just tucked my notes on the first evening's interview into my pocketbook and had not bothered to hide them. I would regret that decision the following morning. It was Tuesday, a day when Ashkhabad's museums were closed, there was little else to do, and the town, like many in the Soviet Union, had few stores to browse through. A visit to the Communist Party Headquarters on Karl Marx Street, the first location mentioned in a Soviet-produced guidebook, didn't hold much promise, either. So we hailed a taxi and asked the driver to take us on a tour of the town; we had already had one on foot but thought perhaps he would be able to show us wonders in Ashkhabad that we hadn't discovered on our own. He crisscrossed back and forth through the streets, and I found myself becoming drowsy in the front seat as the temperature hit nearly ninety. I was lulled by the less than scintillating conversation going on between the driver and John. "Do elephants walk on the streets of London?" was one question John was asked. "No? Well, do Germans come from England?" I chuckled briefly over his exotic vision of England and then dozed off again. Sometime later I woke up with a start. The taxi had been flagged down by a policeman, who began to exchange angry words with the driver. "What's going on?" I asked John. "We're outside the city limits," he replied. I cursed. The first thing Intourist had informed us when we arrived at the hotel was that Ashkhabad was a border town, even though it was forty kilometers from Iran; therefore no foreigner was permitted to leave the town unless escorted by Intourist. We were about two kilometers outside Ashkhabad as far as I could assess, and of course, we were not in the company of any Intourist official. "Now what?" I asked. "With luck, the driver will bribe his way out of this; after all we've hardly left the city," said John, as he climbed out of the cab to join the two men. When he and the driver returned, John told me, "This one isn't the type you can buy off. He seems very officious." We sat sweltering in the taxi, staring at the policeman, as he stared back at us. Five minutes later, two unmarked cars containing eight plain-clothes gentlemen pulled up; one vehicle stopped in front of the taxi and one behind. They nodded brusquely at us and told the taxi driver, who was now looking very nervous, to drive us back to the hotel. The two vehicles provided a very close escort. It was then I remembered my interview notes. Although they were written half in scrawl and half in personal shorthand, the fact that I had notes at all could look strange under certain circumstances. I fumbled around in the front seat, trying to hide them in the lining of the purse without letting the taxi driver see what I was doing. Fortunately, his mind was on other matters.

In the hotel, we were led into a ground floor office by two of the men; the driver was taken to another room. We didn't see him again. What happened next was an hour-long interrogation led by the man who introduced himself as Mr. Berendka. Why had we left the city limits? What were we planning to do? Had we taken any photographs? Had we taken any notes? I tried to explain that we hadn't realized we had left Ashkhabad and said that if he came to London, he also would have difficulty identifying where the city borders were. But Mr. Berendka kept insisting we knew it was forbidden to leave the city; why had we broken the law? Berendka's insistence was more pedantic than threatening. As he asked the same questions, we gave him the same replies, and all the while I was furious at myself that we had been stopped for something so trivial. I also wondered how the policeman had been so sure we were foreigners from the glimpse he would have had of the taxi before he flagged us down. It occurred to me that we may have been under surveillance that day, but if we were, I thought it was merely a routine spot-checking. I was fairly certain that we hadn't been tailed the night before.

Eventually, both men seemed convinced that we hadn't been heading for the Iranian border to liaise with the Ayatollah or photograph whatever installations the Soviets may have had in the Kara Kum desert. Berendka painstakingly wrote out a four-foolscap-page report on our interview and asked us to sign it. Then he told John to remove the film from his camera and give it to him. I was relieved that John hadn't used his camera that day. We were warned that if we were caught repeating the same violation, we would "be in serious trouble." I wondered how Berendka would have responded had he known what we were doing in Ashkhabad in the first place. On leaving, I noticed for the first time that both men were dressed in gray with the same light blue shirts. Was this the KGB corporate look? I asked myself.

That evening I decided it would be wiser to pass up trying to find Afghan veterans. We went to the circus instead. The following day was our last in Ashkhabad, so this time we didn't have a choice. And because of the Tuesday incident, we had to check out two addresses in one evening. The first family we decided to look up lived close to the town's botanical gardens on Hippodrom Street. But when the taxi dropped us there we had difficulty locating the number. Because streets can veer into alleys in Ashkhabad and there were plenty of alleys in this neighborhood, we stopped a passerby to make sure we were still on Hippodrom. She said we were but told us the street was no longer called that; it had been changed to Khudaiberdiev Street. "Wow," said John when she had gone, leaving me in the dark as to what he was exclaiming about because the conversation had taken place in Russian. "It looks like the street has been renamed after the man we're looking for. After all, Khudaiberdiev is hardly a common name. They must have declared him a war hero." Streets in the Soviet Union are frequently renamed for political reasons. Every time a political figure falls from grace, dozens of streets named after that person in cities throughout the USSR have to be rechristened.

In this case, I felt the city fathers were unlikely to name a street after a war hero unless his family were solid party members, and I realized this was another interview it would be wise to forego.

Our fifth and final address seemed impossible to locate. Several drivers would not attempt to find it because they had never heard of it. Finally, a taxi driver said he lived in the same zip code and would take us to the post office there; maybe they could help us. We arrived after the post office had closed for the day. But this driver was a determined fellow and stopped a number of pedestrians until one finally was able to tell him. I wasn't surprised that the street was hard to find; it was only fifteen houses long. The single-story homes encircled by high walls were similar in style to the street Geldi lived on, except that they were somewhat more affluent. Once again, the metal door gave to our touch. We stepped inside and found ourselves in a spacious courtyard with a large vegetable garden in the middle and animal pens containing sheep around the edge. A slim young man in his midtwenties abruptly stopped talking to a woman who was obviously his mother.

"Yes?" he said in a less than friendly tone. We asked whether he was Mohammed B——. He squinted at us, and John repeated the Turkmen surname slowly in case he was mispronouncing it. "What do you want?" he asked without answering the question. John launched into our cover story. "Show me the diary," he demanded. We showed him the xerox pages and pointed out his address in the back. The young man riffled through the pages, and without looking at us told his mother to fetch his father. She hesitated. "Get him," he ordered sharply.

I didn't like the way things were developing. "Are we in trouble?" I asked John somewhat nervously, feeling handicapped because I needed to have everything translated and couldn't read the nuances. "I'm not sure," he replied, sounding as tense as I. "But I don't think he's very happy we're here." The boy said nothing further until his father, a tall, angular man with closely cropped gray hair, arrived; then he explained what had happened and gave him the diary. "Mohammed was my nephew," he said, looking at it. "He's dead; he was killed in the army in Afghanistan. My son, Abdullah, served in the navy; that's why he was confused." The father smiled at us, and a sense of relief went through me. "Why are you here?" We repeated our story. He invited us inside the house. Abdullah didn't join us. We were shown into a large carpeted room devoid of chairs but containing two closets stacked with colored quilts, a desk, and a television set. He gestured for us to sit on the carpet and, searching through the desk drawer, pulled out a letter. "This was Mohammed's last letter to us," he said, handing it to John. It was written from Jalalabad and reassured the family he was okay. "I only have two more months before I am demobilized," he had written. Barkandai's unit had obviously been decimated that day in Jalalabad. Mohammed's uncle, who introduced himself as Abdul, looked wistful as he started to talk about his nephew. "He was a wonderful boy, full of fire. He was the eldest of seven sons. Before he was drafted, he was a shepherd on a collective farm outside Ashkhabad. He was killed by bandits. Barkandai was a friend of his; I remember Mohammed talking about him."

"*Dushmans*, Basmachi, they killed Mohammed," added his wife, who had the strong features of an American Indian, as she came into the room to serve us tea, a thick *nan*-like bread, and honey from the bees they kept. "He was killed by Muslims," I said. "You are Muslim."

"Yes," replied Abdul. "Sometimes, Muslims can be bandits. But you're right: it is brother killing brother. I believe Afghans don't want democracy. The poor accepted the revolution; the rich didn't want it. It will be a long war until the borders are certain between the Soviet Union, Afghanistan, and Pakistan." Abdul sipped his tea thoughtfully and then shook his head and sighed. "I know what war is like from personal experience," he said. "In World War II, I was with our forces as they pushed from Byelorussia to Berlin in 1943. I was in the artillery and wounded twice with shrapnel in my back and arms. I stayed in Germany with the Occupying Forces two years after the war ended. The ordinary Germans were very nice to me. I didn't hate them. The people naturally don't want war; their governments do. It's the same with Afghanistan: we don't want it; the state does."

I asked Abdul whether he was aware that last year had seen the first antiwar demonstrations in the Soviet Union. "There has been nothing printed in our newspapers, or on television, but there have been rumors of demonstrations in Georgia and Armenia. I have also heard that Tadjik soldiers are deserting. There's been talk that some Turkmen forces have, as well."

"How do you feel about that?"

He paused again, before replying. "You know, those people might just be right," he said, his earlier party line suddenly forgotten. "If the United States were invading the Soviet Union, then it would be necessary to defend the country. But in Afghanistan, that's not the case. I listen to the Western broadcasts all the time; I'm aware of what is happening there." Abdul, a clerk in a government office, refilled our tea cups and urged us to help ourselves to more of his delicious honey. "I'll be honest; I don't want my youngest son to go. He's seventeen now and he's just received his conscription papers. He'll be enlisted next May, and already we are worrying about whether he'll be sent to Afghanistan."

"Could he opt to join the navy like Abdullah?" "No, we have no control over that. The government just sends you where they decide."

Abdul asked us why we thought a large state would want to invade a small state like Afghanistan. We explained the various theories put forward by Sovietologists. "All or most of the recent conflicts in the world, Iraq and Iran, Vietnam, Korea, all could have been settled by the UN," opined the Soviet, "but they don't want to look at what is going on. They're just not interested. Afghanistan could be settled, too, if the Soviet Union and the United States stopped trying to extend their influence over the country and just gave it economic aid. Look at Gorbachev and Reagan: they met at Geneva but they didn't agree on anything."

I asked Abdul if he was aware that nearly 2 million Afghans had died in the war so far, and that a third of their population were now living as refugees. "No, I didn't know it was that many," he replied. "I just know we've had a lot of coffins come home, too. When Mohammed and the other men in his unit died, they shipped all their coffins home. They were sealed and there was a fight over whether to open them." His voice trailed off, and the muscle in the side of his cheek begin to twitch. It had been three years since his nephew had died, but his sense of loss still seemed as fresh as if it had happened yesterday.

I glanced at my watch; we had been there three hours. It was getting late, and I felt it was time for us to leave. As we stood up, Abdul said. "When you write about Mohammed, write that he was a man who didn't know he was going to Afghanistan. Just say he didn't want to go. Write that the kids here don't want to go."